American and Muslim Worlds before 1900

Islam of the Global West

Series editors: Kambiz GhaneaBassiri and Frank Peter

Islam of the Global West is a pioneering series that examines Islamic beliefs, practices, discourses, communities, and institutions that have emerged from "the Global West." The geographical and intellectual framing of the Global West reflects both the role played by the interactions between people from diverse religions and cultures in the development of Western ideals and institutions in the modern era, and the globalization of these very ideals and institutions.

In creating an intellectual space where works of scholarship on European and North American Muslims enter into conversation with one another, the series promotes the publication of theoretically informed and empirically grounded research in these areas. By bringing the rapidly growing research on Muslims in European and North American societies, ranging from the United States and France to Portugal and Albania, into conversation with the conceptual framing of the Global West, this ambitious series aims to reimagine the modern world and develop new analytical categories and historical narratives that highlight the complex relationships and rivalries that have shaped the multicultural, poly-religious character of Europe and North America, as evidenced, by way of example, in such economically and culturally dynamic urban centers as Los Angeles, New York, Paris, Madrid, Toronto, Sarajevo, London, Berlin, and Amsterdam where there is a significant Muslim presence.

Amplifying Islam in the European Soundscape: Religious Pluralism and Secularism in the Netherlands, Pooyan Tamimi Arab
Islam and Nationhood in Bosnia-Herzegovina: Surviving Empires, Xavier Bougarel
Islam as Critique: Sayyid Ahmad Khan and the Challenge of Modernity, Khurram Hussain
Sacred Spaces and Transnational Networks in American Sufism, Merin Shobhana Xavier

American and Muslim Worlds before 1900

Edited by
John Ghazvinian and Arthur Mitchell Fraas

BLOOMSBURY ACADEMIC
LONDON • NEW YORK • OXFORD • NEW DELHI • SYDNEY

BLOOMSBURY ACADEMIC
Bloomsbury Publishing Plc
50 Bedford Square, London, WC1B 3DP, UK
1385 Broadway, New York, NY 10018, USA
29 Earlsfort Terrace, Dublin 2, Ireland

BLOOMSBURY, BLOOMSBURY ACADEMIC and the Diana logo
are trademarks of Bloomsbury Publishing Plc

First published in Great Britain 2020
Paperback first published 2021

Copyright © John Ghazvinian, Arthur Mitchell Fraas and Contributors, 2020

John Ghazvinian and Arthur Mitchell Fraas have asserted their right under the Copyright, Designs and Patents Act, 1988, to be identified as Editors of this work.

Series design by Dani Leigh
Cover image © Brian Stablyk / gettyimages.co.uk

All rights reserved. No part of this publication may be reproduced or transmitted in any form or by any means, electronic or mechanical, including photocopying, recording, or any information storage or retrieval system, without prior permission in writing from the publishers.

Bloomsbury Publishing Plc does not have any control over, or responsibility for, any third-party websites referred to or in this book. All internet addresses given in this book were correct at the time of going to press. The author and publisher regret any inconvenience caused if addresses have changed or sites have ceased to exist, but can accept no responsibility for any such changes.

A catalogue record for this book is available from the British Library.

Library of Congress Control Number: 2019949113

ISBN: HB: 978-1-3501-0951-3
PB: 978-1-3502-7786-1
ePDF: 978-1-3501-0952-0
eBook: 978-1-3501-0953-7

Series: Islam of the Global West

Typeset by Deanta Global Publishing Services, Chennai, India

To find out more about our authors and books visit
www.bloomsbury.com and sign up for our newsletters.

Contents

List of Figures	vii
Introduction *John Ghazvinian and Arthur Mitchell Fraas*	1

Part One Islam and the Making of the Early American Republic

1	Benjamin Franklin, Islam, and the Abolition of Slavery *Denise A. Spellberg*	9
2	The Greek War of Independence and the Ideological Manifestations of the Clash of Civilizations Theory in the United States, 1821–32 *Karine Walther*	18

Part Two The Muslim Experience in the Americas

3	Nicholas Said's America: Islam, the Civil War, and the Emergence of African American Narrative *Ira Dworkin*	33
4	An Islamic Surface Reading of African Muslim Slave Narratives *Zeinab Mcheimech*	45
5	Crossing Oceans, Transgressing Boundaries: Incorporating Muslims and Moriscos into Histories of Colonial Spanish America *Karoline P. Cook*	57

Part Three Muslim Worlds in the American Imaginary

6	"An Unwelcome Present": Simulation and Simulacra in the Unlikely Friendship of General Lew Wallace and Sultan Abdülhamit II *Bill Hunt*	71
7	The Lost Tribes of the Afghans: Religious Mobility and Entanglement in Narratives of Afghan Origins *William E. B. Sherman*	85
8	Imagining Empire: Islamic India in Nineteenth-Century US Print Culture *Susan Ryan*	98

Part Four Islam and American Empire: The Case of the Philippines

9	Subjugating the Sultan of Sulu: American Imperial Negotiations in the Muslim Philippines *Timothy Marr*	113
10	Native Americans, the Ottoman Empire, and Global Narratives of Islam in the US Colonial Philippines, 1900–14 *Joshua Gedacht*	128

11 An Ottoman Notable in America in 1915–16: Sayyid Wajih al-Kilani of
    Nazareth *William G. Clarence-Smith*   139
Epilogue: The Global History of American and Muslim Worlds before
    1900 *Heather J. Sharkey*   149

Notes   159
Bibliography   203
Notes on Contributors   219
Index   221

Figures

4.1	Bilali Muhammad, the *Ben Ali Diary* (MS 2807), 4–5. Courtesy of Hargrett Rare Book and Manuscript Library/University of Georgia Libraries	50
4.2	Bilali Muhammad, the *Ben Ali Diary* (MS 2807), 1. Courtesy of Hargrett Rare Book and Manuscript Library/University of Georgia Libraries	51
4.3	'Umar ibn Sayyid, Letter to John Owen (1819) Beinecke Library, Yale University, JWJ MSS 185	54
6.1	Lew Wallace, Untitled Portrait of Abdülhamit II, circa 1882, pencil sketch. Reproduced by permission from the collection of The Lew Wallace Study and Museum, Crawfordsville, IN. Photo by author	72
6.2	Lew Wallace, Untitled Portrait of Abdülhamit II, circa 1882, oil on canvas. Reproduced by permission from the collection of The Lew Wallace Study and Museum, Crawfordsville, IN. Photo by author	73
6.3	"The Turkish Princess," date unknown, oil on canvas. Reproduced by permission from the collection of The Lew Wallace Study and Museum, Crawfordsville, IN. Photo by author	74
9.1	"Sultan of Jolo & chiefs," Arthur Stanley Riggs Collection, Library of Congress, LC-USZ62-107904	117
9.2	Frank Moulan as Ki-Ram in George Ade's opera. Cincinnati; New York: Strobridge Litho. Co., 1902. Theatrical Poster Collection, Library of Congress, 2014636740	119
9.3	The Sultan of Sulu on board ship during his world circuit in 1910. Bain News Service, George Grantham Bain Collection (Library of Congress) LC-B2-1076-9 [P&P]	124

Introduction

John Ghazvinian and Arthur Mitchell Fraas

In the spring of 1782, a group of Philadelphia merchants, fed up with years of British assaults on their shipping and wanting to send a forceful message to the Royal Navy, fitted out an armed privateer, and charged it with the task of providing protection for their vessels. In a year that was full of such brazen acts of revolutionary zeal—in the midst of a long war whose consequences are well known to most Americans—the commissioning of yet another sloop to make yet another statement of indignation against British tyranny might not be of much interest to most historians. But what was striking about this particular act of revolutionary defiance in 1782 was the name the Philadelphians chose to give their vessel. Wanting to pay tribute to a man halfway round the world—a man whom they recognized as a like-minded freedom fighter and a fellow enemy of the British Empire—they named their ship the *Hyder Ally*. It was the name of the Muslim sultan of Mysore, in southern India.[1]

This act of naming—a symbolic linkage between the revolutionary ideals of American liberty and the rebelliousness of a Muslim potentate—might be remarkable enough. But some went even further. In April 1782, following a fierce fight in the Delaware Bay, the *Hyder Ally* defeated a British warship, and the news was met with great jubilation. And as the revolutionaries celebrated, they began to draw parallels between their own struggle and that of the real-life sultan, Haidar Ali—who for fifteen years had been leading the people of southern India in a series of campaigns against the British East India Company. It was as if this mysterious man himself—this unknown Muslim rebel—had somehow suffused the decks of the *Hyder Ally* with his anti-British spirit. Inspired by the victory, the New York poet Philip Freneau even composed a verse in praise of the sultan:

> ...an Eastern prince...
> Who, smit with freedom's sacred flame,
> Usurping Britons brought to shame,
> His country's wrongs avenging;[2]

Needless to say, today, we are faced with a very different American reality. On September 18, 2015, during a campaign rally in New Hampshire, Donald Trump, then a candidate for the presidency of the United States, was asked a question by a man in the audience, which began: "We have a problem in this country. It's called Muslims." Trump nodded in apparent agreement, as the man continued: "We know our current president is one. You know he's not even an American"—referring to then-president

Barack Obama. "We have training camps growing where they want to kill us. That's my question. When can we get rid of them?" After chuckling and interjecting that "we need this question," Trump responded simply: "You know, a lot of people are saying that . . . . We're going to be looking at that and plenty of other things."[3]

To set these two historical moments side by side is not, of course, to suggest that Americans were once possessed of an unqualified adoration for all things Muslim and that this golden age of toleration got lost somewhere along the way. Rather, it is to suggest that the relationship between "American" and "Muslim" worlds is much more complex than is often appreciated. Most educated readers, when pressed, might have some vague understanding that there was once a simpler era—before the days of televised images of bearded militants and training camps—when America's understanding of the "Muslim world" consisted mostly of orientalist fantasies drawn from the pages of the Arabian Nights—a cliché-ridden world of flying carpets, genies emerging from magic lanterns, and perfumed princes running their fingers through piles of jewels as they puffed unctuously from their hubble-bubble pipes. Some readers might even recall the early American republic's struggles with war and piracy along the "Barbary" coast in the early 1800s. But beyond this, most of us are stumped. When pressed, how much do we really know about the distant past of this particular relationship?

This volume aims to move us away from the contemporary perception of those like Trump who see "Muslims" as intrinsically at odds with all things "American"—to instead examine the long history of the intertwined Muslim and American worlds and bring back stories similar to those of the *Hyder Ally*. Even more than this, however, it seeks to raise a more basic question. What do the very words "Muslim" and "American" even mean when they are placed next to each other in juxtaposition (and even presumed opposition) like this? And what kind of service (or, potentially, disservice) are we doing when we continue to examine matters through this prism?

The basic problem will be familiar to anyone who has ever been asked to teach an undergraduate class with a name like "World History" or "Global History." There is a lingering tendency among global history textbooks to relegate all discussions of "Islam" to the earlier chapters that deal with the eastern hemisphere, and more or less forget about the existence of Muslims as history marches steadily and inexorably westward, culminating in the "American century." In the typical undergraduate history textbook, the "Muslim world" generally seems to disappear sometime after the Mongols and the Ottoman Empire, and does not make another appearance until the last few pages—where it rears its head again in the form of Osama bin Laden.

This clearly is ahistorical. Global history needs to be reenvisioned—and we believe the work we are presenting in these pages will go a long way toward making that change possible by reminding us all just how inextricably linked American and Muslim worlds really are, and always have been, and just how ahistorical it is to claim that they are forces that are alien and threatening to one another.[4]

In April 2017, hoping to bring about a change in this narrative, we convened a conference at the University of Pennsylvania, on the subject of "American and Muslim Worlds, circa 1500–1900." The first major conference of its kind to consider the multiplicity of American Muslim interactions before the twentieth century, the event brought together scholars from five continents, working on topics as diverse as slavery in the Americas, the Barbary wars, Muslims in colonial Brazil, and the US military administration of the Philippines. What follows in these pages, however, are not just "conference proceedings" in the traditional sense. Rather, it is a collection of chapters inspired by the conversations that took place during the several days that we spent with one another—including several written specially for this volume by those who helped put the conference together.

The first assertion we hope to make with this collection is that the long view matters. We believe the time has come to disrupt the prevailing assumption that when we talk about "American and Muslim worlds," we are talking about two entities that have come into conflict with each other in the later years of the twentieth century in the form of drone warfare, religious radicalism, terrorism, imperialism, or petro-politics.[5] Instead, we suggest, there is a long and deep seam of history here which can provide an important context for contemporary events—but which is also important in its own right. The chapters here move us away from the trap of "presentist" history, of arguing glibly that "we have to understand America's early relationship with Islam in order to understand present geo-politics." But neither do these chapters shy away from being relevant. Most scholarly collections dealing with Muslims and the Americas might include a chapter or two about the period before the twentieth century before moving on to more familiar territory.[6] This collection foregrounds the nineteenth and eighteenth centuries and helps challenge the framing of Muslim/American history.

This, by itself, is a point that urgently needs to be made. At a time when American politicians freely float the idea that Muslims can somehow be "banned" from the United States or hermetically sealed out of existence, there is something deeply important about scholarship that reminds us that some of the earliest American Muslims were the African slaves working the plantations of the Carolinas—and that some of these Americans even wrote memoirs in Arabic. At a time when an American president can be accused of being a secret Muslim by his enemies, Denise Spellberg's prior work demonstrating how Thomas Jefferson was frequently called an "infidel" with hidden Muslim sympathies by his opponents but yet remained blind to the presence of the many Muslim African Americans enslaved by his fellow citizens (and likely by him personally) is powerful and instructive. Likewise, her chapter in this volume takes up another founder, Benjamin Franklin, and his relationship with the peoples and ideas of Islam arguing for a much richer engagement than has been commonly known. For the nineteenth century, Zeinab Mcheimech provides a careful and creative reading of the surviving literary production of two enslaved American Muslims 'Umar ibn Sayyid and Bilali Muhammad. In examining their writing through a particular hermeneutical lens she shows how from the very beginning of the United States, enslaved Muslims were not simple receptors of foreign ideas but active participants in constructing American literary and intellectual frameworks of their own. Alongside these examinations of Muslims in America, Karine Walther encourages us to look to the Early Republic for the formation of a strong white American ideology of political and cultural difference between so-called Christian civilization and Islam in the form of the Ottoman Empire.

Our second argument is that it is time to move away from the tendency to assume that "America and the Muslim World" always means "the United States and the Middle East." We want to suggest instead that both "America" and "the Muslim World" are actually broad, global categories more than they are distinct political or geographic entities. Here, of course, we are standing on the shoulders of giants—namely, the legions of scholars who in recent years have begun to situate "American" history in the context of a broader "Atlantic world" and the scholars who have frequently reminded us that the "Muslim world" is not some monolithic force, but rather the collective experience of rituals, beliefs, cultural expressions, social and familial networks, political arrangements, and migration patterns undertaken by the world's billion or so Muslims (many of whom, not incidentally, happen to be "American" as well).[7] When we use these much broader definitions of "American" and "Muslim worlds" as our starting points, we believe, we inevitably arrive at a richer and more sophisticated understanding of the way the two have interacted throughout history. And this is especially true the further we go back in time.

In this volume, for example, Karoline Cook's work on Muslims and Moriscos in colonial Spanish America is bracing in its importance. It reminds us that the presence of Muslims in the early modern Americas is intimately tied to questions of empire and identity among those who have called themselves "American" for centuries. Similarly, Susan Ryan's expansive work here on Islamic India and the nineteenth-century United States reminds us of the importance of South Asian Islam in American conceptions of Muslims and their place in the world. Ryan deftly shows how Americans understood Indian Muslims as liminal British colonial subjects, complicated actors whose Muslim and colonial identities could be mixed, confused, and rejected. Likewise, in their work, Joshua Gedacht and Tim Marr provide an important reminder of the thousands of Muslim residents of the Philippines who came under the jurisdiction of the United States during its imperial involvement there beginning at the end of the nineteenth century. By showing how Americans and Muslims negotiated imperialism, religious identity, and political expediency together in the Philippines, both Gedacht and Marr make concrete the ways in which Southeast Asian Islam shaped American policy and discourse.

Our third argument is that it is no longer helpful, or even correct, to view "America" and the "Muslim world" as two separate, binary, and non-overlapping entities, with their own separate histories. We want to suggest instead that, really, there has never been a time when the histories of these two "worlds" have not been deeply and inextricably interwoven. Long before the age of twentieth-century geopolitics, the American and Muslim worlds informed, interacted, perplexed, inspired, confounded, and imagined each other in ways far more numerous than is frequently thought. Whether through the sale of American commodities in Central Asia, Ottoman consuls in Washington, orientalist themes in American fiction, the uprisings of enslaved Muslims in Brazil, or the travels of American missionaries in the Middle East, there was no shortage of opportunity for Muslims and inhabitants of the Americas to meet, interact, and shape one another from an early period. Ira Dworkin's work here examines the importance of Nicholas Said, raised as a literate elite Muslim in Bornu before being sold into slavery and traveling throughout the Middle East and Europe before arriving in Canada and the United States. Said's autobiographical narrative was read by thousands of Americans in the nineteenth century and Dworkin shows the ways in which Said was both American and African, Muslim and Christian, always deeply engaged in African

American exchanges around Islam and its place in America. Looking to Americans abroad, meanwhile, Bill Hunt challenges us in his chapter to think outside the usual bounds of nineteenth-century orientalism by examining the relationship between an American statesman and one of the most prominent Muslim leaders of the time and asking how the two understood their intertwined lives in Istanbul. In her epilogue to this volume, Heather Sharkey builds on this evidence to provide an incisive argument for why any "us-and-them" narrative of American and Muslim worlds is untenable.

Our fourth assertion is perhaps the most ambitious of all. When we first had the idea for the conference, our goal was to assemble in one room, for the first time, scholars working on such seemingly disparate topics as Barbary captivity narratives, Islam among enslaved Africans in the Americas, the US colonial administration of the Philippines, American missionaries, and orientalist themes in American literature, and ask if there is a larger synthesis that can emerge when we are all in dialogue with one another. The answer to this last question is, emphatically, "yes." We believe we have a new way of looking at the history of unstable categories like "American" and "Muslim" on our hands that allows us to show how they are globalizing—an exciting shifting of methodological and geographic boundaries that can begin, over time, to fundamentally reshape the field. That is, the chapters in this volume argue that we need to look to much broader geographical and temporal areas than even current transnational historical framings such as the "Atlantic World" allow.

That very Atlantic world story, in fact—for all the crucial service it has done in breaking Western historians out of their traditional national-history silos—is still far too often framed as a European, American, and African story, without much thought given to, say, the diversity of religious belief among those Europeans and Africans arriving in the new world, or the gaze cast back onto the "Muslim world" by non-Muslim settlers of the Americas. In this volume, by contrast, William Sherman masterfully tracks the engrossing and tangled story of a Persian apocalyptical/genealogical text and its interpretations both in Afghanistan and in the United States. Sherman's narrative connects two centuries, multiple continents, and several different religious and intellectual traditions, and places American evangelicals beside Sufi reformers in a way that challenges usual understandings of cultural exchange. Likewise, in his chapter, William Clarence-Smith examines one globally peripatetic Muslim to show the agency and importance of Muslims themselves in defining American political and religious visions of Islam. Clarence-Smith's main character, Sayyid Wajih al-Kilani, born in Palestine, and one-time mufti of the southern Philippines, died in the United States while promoting his vision of modern Islam alongside his own political future. This book highlights stories like al-Kilani's in order to demonstrate the ways Muslim and American worlds co-constituted each other and to complicate attempts at understanding these intertwined worlds through any easily available frames.

Despite making all of these arguments, this volume is not intended to be comprehensive, and there are many areas for future study and research. Astute readers will notice, for example, only one chapter engaging with the period before the eighteenth century. Likewise, the geographical scope of work on American and Muslim worlds needs to go far beyond the United States and North American dominated perspective that is presented here. We recognize this. And in our original call for papers, in 2016, we tried hard to encourage contributions from scholars of Latin America and the Caribbean. That we did not attract large numbers of such papers is testament to the many challenges that remain in getting scholars to think beyond the traditional subject boundaries that continue to separate us. We hope, therefore, that this collection of chapters can be the beginning of a conversation, rather than the final word on the subject of American and Muslim worlds before 1900.

One last point is in order here on the issue of chronology. Though the collection here includes chapters on the US colonial project in the Philippines which technically spill across the 1900 borderline in our title, we felt the importance of these Philippine examples made it important to provide a forum for this work. The messiness of history, which defies neat century breaks and frequently straddles artificial chronological divides, is a challenge that is familiar to nearly all historians. And we recognize that there is something necessarily arbitrary in our decision to include these chapters. Nevertheless, in this particular case, we believe there is an argument to be made that the US experience in the Philippines in the years around 1900 is a natural outgrowth and extension of the themes discussed in this volume. That is, the entanglement of imperialism, race, religion, and American identity played out in the Philippines serves as both a coda to an earlier period of American Muslim understandings and an entry point to the more frequently discussed twentieth-century US drama with Muslim worlds and as such a natural way to end this volume.

Whatever the limitations and inevitable lacunae accrued when one attempts to put together a collection of this kind, we believe it is a task worth undertaking. For far too long, academics have been content to study this subject in their own discrete and unconnected chambers. For years, scholars of international relations have happily studied US foreign policy in the Middle East, while historians have grappled with such issues as the Barbary wars or American missionaries. For years, art historians have examined images of the exotic in American painting, while scholars of slavery have looked for traces of Islamic ritual among the Africans brought forcibly to the Caribbean and to South and North America. Excellent work has been done in all of these areas but we believe the time has come to take a much broader approach. And we hope very much that publication of this book will go a long way toward making this possible.

Part One

Islam and the Making of the Early American Republic

1

Benjamin Franklin, Islam, and the Abolition of Slavery

Denise A. Spellberg

Islam and Muslims were not unknown to Americans during the founding era, and it should come as no surprise that Benjamin Franklin made several references to the faith and its adherents throughout his life. Although his views varied and were often contradictory, they provide a distinct parallel to the range of such ideas among his founding American contemporaries, including Thomas Jefferson. Unlike other Founders, such as Jefferson, Franklin did not own a Qur'an, but he did possess books about Islam.[1] Both men also owned slaves. But, unlike Jefferson, Franklin's views on the subject evolved by the end of his life. In Franklin's final published work, his plea for the abolition of slavery would be clothed in Islamic garb.

Franklin believed that Philadelphia should not only be a city in which all forms of Christianity were tolerated—he supported the practice of all faiths, including Islam. When, in 1739, the itinerant British evangelist George Whitefield, an Anglican cleric influenced by the founders of Methodism, could find no place to preach to enthralled crowds in Philadelphia, Franklin recorded in his *Autobiography* that Whitefield "was obliged to preach in the fields."[2] In order to remedy this situation, Franklin supported the construction of a new building he described as "expressly for the use of any preacher of any religious persuasion who might desire to say something to the people of Philadelphia."[3] Franklin insisted that "the design in building" not cater to any particular belief system.[4] Specifically referencing Islam, he asserted that "even if the Mufti of Constantinople were to send a missionary to preach Mahometanism to us, he would find a pulpit in his service."[5]

Franklin's view of Islam as a possible American religion was an unusual point of view for his day, but it was not unique. In 1776, Thomas Jefferson cited John Locke's 1689 essay on religious toleration, including the pivotal phrase: "Neither Pagan nor Mahometan nor Jew ought to be excluded from the civil rights of the commonwealth because of his religion."[6] Jefferson wrote in his own autobiography of 1821 that his beloved Virginia Statute for Religious Freedom, made law in 1786, was intended to be "universal," meaning that it was "meant to comprehend, within the mantle of its protection, the Jew and the Gentile, the Christian and Mahometan, the Hindoo, and Infidel of every denomination."[7] Two years before, in 1784, George Washington also included Muslims within his future worldview of American citizens. He wrote to a friend that religious beliefs for potential plantation employees mattered not at all: "If they be good workmen, they may be of Asia, Africa, or Europe. They may be Mahometans, Jews, or Christians of an[y] Sect, or they may be Atheists."[8] Universality in religious freedom for Franklin, Jefferson, and Washington included Islam.

Franklin's reference to the chief cleric, the mufti of the Ottoman Empire in Istanbul, indicated that he knew something of the importance of that Islamic power which had existed since the thirteenth century and threatened Europe until the end of the seventeenth century. Franklin's reference to "Mahometanism," reflected standard Anglo-American usage in an era when the word "Islam" was hardly ever used. At the time, Mahomet served as the standard English spelling of the Prophet's name, but the term "Mahometanism" implied a mistaken view of the faith, whose adherents worshipped God—not Muhammad, their human prophet.

Although Franklin's eighteenth-century ecumenical Philadelphia preaching house no longer stands, it is commemorated by a plaque at Fourth and Arch Streets, near Franklin's grave.[9] While Franklin wrote that he intended this new meeting house as a shared space for all, including Muslims, his views about Islam could also be condemnatory.

Franklin tossed off a derisive reference to Islam in the May 1741 edition of *Poor Richard*, the almanac which he first published in 1732.[10] As a genre, almanacs had existed in England since the seventeenth century and several pre-dated Franklin's in North America. *Poor Richard* succeeded famously, and according to Franklin biographer H. W. Brands, served as an outlet to "flaunt his wit, erudition, and general brilliance."[11] Readers clamored for copies of this notable fiscal success, and the author sold about 10,000 annually, not just in Philadelphia but from Boston, Massachusetts, to Charleston, South Carolina.[12]

In the May 1741 edition, Franklin wrote the following injunction and query:

Turn Turk, *Tim*, and renounce thy Faith in Words as well as
Actions: Is it worse to follow *Mahomet* than the Devil?[13]

"Turning Turk" referred to British and American captives converting to Islam when taken prisoner by North African Muslim corsairs. Seafaring Muslims in Tripoli, Tunis, Algiers, and Morocco, organized by their rulers, had raided English shipping since the sixteenth century. They directed their energies against the fledgling United States after 1783, when American vessels, without British naval protection in the eastern Atlantic and Mediterranean, became newly vulnerable. With the exception of Morocco, the rulers of these so-called Barbary States were Muslims of Turkish descent. Thus Britons and Americans collapsed the myriad ethnic identities of all Muslims into the single category: Turks. Of the hundreds of American sailors taken prisoner in North Africa, only a handful converted to Islam, a practice usually prompted by the hope of gaining one's freedom.[14] Four American sailors turned renegade and adopted Islam after the US frigate *Philadelphia* ran aground off Tripoli harbor in 1803. Although these converts gained their freedom in North Africa, their cooperation with the enemy prompted the enmity of their countrymen. The new American Muslim converts remained in North Africa when the rest of the American captives finally returned home.[15]

As historian Thomas Kidd observes, Franklin's query in the guise of *Poor Richard* provided a false choice between Muhammad and the Devil. Christian readers of Franklin's era would have answered that to follow one was to follow the other.[16] The majority of Protestant Christians in North America, no matter what their denomination was, would have condemned Islam as a false faith, founded by a false prophet's revelation. Such views crossed the Atlantic with the earliest English settlers to North America, supported by tracts lambasting the faith as antithetical to Christianity. In addition, the majority of American Christians viewed Islamic powers as political threats.[17]

There is, however, some irony in the possibility that the very word for Franklin's exceedingly popular almanac may have originated as an Arabic term "*al-manakh*" that spread into English from medieval Spain. Although this view is contested, the Arabic noun's meaning refers to a calendar. Yet another Arabic derivation may refer to "*al-munakh*," meaning the place where a camel kneels down at the end of a day's journey, a reference to both chronology and climate.[18] Franklin knew nothing of this possible Islamic linguistic connection. He instead proffered a pun that this genre was "an evident abbreviation of ALL MY KNACK, or ALL MAN's KNACK," as "the *ne plus ultra* of human genius."[19] Even when disparaged and unseen, connections between Islamic and American worlds existed.

Additional explicit references to Islam served other purposes. In contrast to his defamation of Muhammad in 1739, Franklin elevated the Prophet's exemplary battlefield conduct as he condemned the behavior of his fellow Christians in Pennsylvania. In 1764, he published *A Narrative of the Late Massacres, in Lancaster County*, a pamphlet decrying the murder of twenty peaceful Conestoga Native Americans by the Paxton Boys, Scots-Irish vigilantes, in December 1763.[20] These Pennsylvania frontiersmen acted in apparent revenge for different Native American raids hundreds of miles to the West during Pontiac's War.

Franklin defined this savage act against friendly Native Americans as a Christian atrocity, asserting that these murdered neighbors "would have been safer" among Muslims.[21] To prove this he cited an incident "recorded in the Life of Mahomet."[22] He detailed why the Prophet once rebuked his general, Khalid ibn al-Walid (d. 642), known as "the Sword of Allah," for putting to death bound prisoners who had already surrendered. The Prophet "applauded" those among Khalid's soldiers who refused to kill their captives at their general's command "for their humanity," but admonished their leader "with great indignation" as a "butcher."[23]

Franklin applied the Prophet's precedent to rail against violent fellow Pennsylvanians: "But our frontier people call themselves Christians!"[24] He argued that the murdered Native Americans "would have been safer, if they had submitted to the Turks; for ever since Mahomet's reproof to Khaled, even the cruel Turks, never kill prisoners in cold blood."[25] Franklin added that "the same laudable and generous custom still prevails among the Mahometans," according to a contemporary travel account.[26]

Although the list of Franklin's extant library books does not include a biography of the Prophet, his reference to this incident reflects a real event recorded in the earliest ninth-century biography of the Prophet, the *Sira*, of Ibn Hisham (d. 833). In that text, the Muslim general Khalid put to death bound prisoners of the defeated Banu Jadhima tribe near Mecca in 630. When news of this event reached the Prophet, "he raised his hands to heaven and said, 'O God, I am innocent before Thee of what Khalid has done.'"[27] In the original Arabic account, the Prophet declares this an additional three times.[28]

Franklin owned no text about the Prophet's life, but he did possess a three-volume Spanish-Latin-Arabic dictionary, printed in Madrid in 1787. It was a gift sent by a Spanish nobleman and Arabic linguist, Count de Capomanès.[29] Already famed in Europe for his discovery of electricity, Franklin's nine-year residence in Paris from 1776 to 1785 as minister plenipotentiary, or ambassador, to that nation brought him to the attention of other learned men, including two European scholars of Islamic language and law. Not only did their books end up in Franklin's library, but both men also wrote the Founder.

Sir William Jones, a British scholar and lawyer, sent Franklin a copy of his forty-eight-page book titled *The Mahomedan Law of Succession to the Property of Intestates*; it contained the original Arabic text by the twelfth-century author Muhammad ibn 'Ali al-Rahbi.[30] These complicated laws of inheritance were rendered in poetic *rajaz* verse, a notable Arabic meter. Kevin Hayes, an expert on Franklin's library, has suggested that the Founder might have used his Arabic dictionary to study this legal work in the original language.[31] Franklin, a linguistic autodidact, had already taught himself Latin, French, Italian, and German.[32] But there is no evidence that Franklin tackled the Arabic language.

The British scholar Jones, who had mastered twenty-eight languages by the time of his death, also wrote Franklin nine letters between 1779 and 1783.[33] By the time the author contacted Franklin, he had already gained renown as his generation's leading scholar of the Islamic world. More than erudition drew Jones to Franklin, for the British linguist's political views were decidedly pro-American. In a letter dated September 17, 1781, he complained of the "despotism" dominant in his own country.[34]

Franklin's third Islamic text was a gift from the French scholar Abraham Hyacinthe Anquetil-Duperron, author of *Législation orientale*, a treatise on government in the Ottoman Empire, Persia, and India. He sent Franklin the book with a note on March 14, 1779.[35] It addressed "the minister of the first free nation in America," and described his gift as a "useful text."[36] Anquetil-Duperron intended his comparative study of Islamic property law as a critique of the prevalent European presumption that Muslims were the abject subjects of oriental despotism. The French author demonstrated instead that Islamic legal codes prevailed in the practice of individual property inheritance and were not subject to the ruler's interference. We have no response from Franklin to this gift, but its author's name was already known to him. Six years before, while in London, Franklin had purchased Anquetil-Duperron's already famous 1771 translation of the Zoroastrian holy book, *The Zend-Avesta*, which would make its author renown as the father of Iranian studies.[37] Zoroastrianism was the official religion of Sasanian Iran before the rise of Islam, and its prophet Zarathustra, preached long before Christianity or Islam arose, sometime between 600 and 1500 BCE.

In Franklin's final published work, printed as a letter to the *Federal Gazette* on March 23, 1790, he provided an Islamic parody of congressional proslavery speeches.[38] This critique, written under the pseudonym "Historicus," represents the culmination of Franklin's evolution from slave owner to ardent supporter of abolition. His purchase of "several slaves" in 1748 reflected his economic success and new status in Philadelphia as a gentleman able, at the age of forty-two, to retire from the pursuits of commerce.[39] By contrast, two other historians claim that he began to own slaves earlier, a decade before, in the 1730s.[40]

Franklin's initial practice of chattel slavery linked him to two other notable Founders: the Virginian plantation owners Thomas Jefferson and George Washington. The comparison of Franklin to Jefferson and Washington on the subject of slavery illumines a common legacy treated differently by each man. As revolutionaries, each read about "slavery" in the works of British Whigs, for whom the term, according to renowned historian Bernard Bailyn, invoked "a central concept in eighteenth-century political discourse."[41] Each Founder opposed British tyranny, which reduced white American colonists to "slaves," a status that they understood politically as "the condition that followed the loss of freedom."[42]

The illustration of freedom and its opposite in *Cato's Letters*, a series of British political tracts popular among revolutionary American readers, focused frequently on despotism in the Ottoman Empire. This serial of political editorials cast the sultan's subjects as his "slaves"—and the ruler as the arch tyrant, supported by Islam: "Yes, Turkish slavery is confirmed, and Turkish tyranny defended, by religion!"[43] Franklin, as a teenager working at his brother's Boston newspaper, knew these tracts well. His first literary foray into print there "borrowed" from *Cato's Letters*, numbers 15 and 31, dating from February 1720 to late May 1721.[44] Depictions of North African Islamic dynasties also featured as sites of tyranny and slavery in these tracts.[45]

While Franklin, Jefferson, and Washington all fought for their individual freedom from the "slavery" imposed by the tyrannical British crown in the American Revolution, none could avoid knowing the "degradation of chattel slaves," which were "painfully visible" to each throughout his life.[46] As Bailyn observed of this revolutionary generation: "As Americans elaborated their love of liberty and their hatred of slavery, the problem posed by the bondage tolerated in their midst became more and more difficult to evade."[47]

Franklin, Jefferson, and Washington each responded differently to the unavoidable contradictions raised by their practice of slavery. Of course, Muslims may have been among their slaves. The possibility that each Founder owned Muslim slaves cannot be proven for either Franklin or Jefferson.[48] However, Washington did possess at least four slaves with likely Islamic monikers. These included a mother and daughter—"Fatimer" and "Little Fatimer," both named after the Prophet's daughter.[49] Whether Washington knew these two women or appreciated the direct connection on his plantation between Islam and slavery remains unknown.

Although Jefferson attacked slavery in his original draft of the Declaration of Independence, where he described the practice as "a cruel war against human nature itself," and as "violating its most sacred rights of life & liberty," the passage was excised after debate.[50] In later writings, his views about West African slaves were pointedly prejudiced. He wrote that blacks were "in reason much inferior" to whites.[51] Nor could he envisage a future in which freedom for slaves resulted in other than "convulsions, which will probably never end but in the extermination of the one or the other race."[52] Similarly, Franklin's views about blacks in 1770 were charged with prejudice. He wrote that while some slaves were "mild tempered, tractable," by contrast, "the majority are of a plotting disposition, dark, sullen, malicious, revengeful and cruel in the highest degree."[53] By contrast, according to historian Henry Wiencek, George Washington privately fretted about the practice of slavery, and "twice considered emancipation during his presidency," but found no political or familial "allies."[54]

On their deaths, Jefferson and Washington promoted different provisions for their slaves. The former, who owned hundreds of slaves, including the five surviving children born of his sexual relationship with Sally Hemings, freed only three during his lifetime and five at his death—all were his direct descendants.[55] By contrast, Washington's 1799 will insisted that all his slaves were to be emancipated on the death of his wife.[56] He chose this proviso in order to avoid the breakup of enslaved families.[57] Washington even directed that infirm and elderly slaves be clothed and fed.[58] More startlingly, in opposition to the slave owners' status quo staunchly prohibiting the spread of literacy among the unfree, he directed that orphaned child slaves be educated, taught "to read & write," along with "a useful occupation."[59]

Washington may have kept his desire for emancipation from his family and the American public at large, but one year after his death, all his slaves were freed.[60] Franklin, by contrast, in his 1757 last will and testament, had insured that two slaves, a husband and wife, be freed after his death.[61] However, Franklin's views of slavery and abolition remain the subject of historical debate. Historians disagree about the number of Franklin's slaves, how long he held them in bondage, and if he ever emancipated them all.[62]

These ambiguities about Franklin's relationship to slavery suggest to historian Emma J. Lapansky-Werner that in this regard he "remains something of an enigma," while another expert on this subject, David Waldstreicher, argues more bluntly that he was a "hypocrite."[63] The latter asserts this because Franklin never raised the question of abolition at the 1787 Constitutional Convention he attended in Philadelphia.[64]

Despite these criticisms, Franklin's final political act—his petition for the abolition of slavery—promoted a legal change that Jefferson had feared and Washington had failed to bring about as head of his new country's executive branch. Franklin's petition forced Congress to debate slavery and emancipation as critical issues for the new nation. The measure failed. The majority dismissed the petition a month after receiving it. Proslavery legislators claimed that as federal representatives they had "no authority to interfere in the regulations of particular states."[65]

Why did Franklin support abolition as his last political act? In part, because his early belief in inferior black temperament and in slavery as an economic necessity had changed.[66] Beginning in the early 1770s, he began to be influence by "his Quaker friend Alexander Benezet and the writings of British abolitionists."[67] While in Paris, Franklin absorbed additional antislavery sentiment from French intellectuals.[68] In 1787, Franklin became president of the Pennsylvania Society for the Abolition of Slavery, which had been founded by Quakers in 1775.[69] Although he did not raise the cause at the Constitutional Convention that same year, he proposed a plan for aiding free blacks two years later, in 1789, and the next year presented a petition for the abolition of slavery to the federal government.[70]

Franklin signed the pivotal 1790 "Petition from the Pennsylvania Society for the Abolition of Slavery," to Congress. It argued that "the blessings of liberty to 'People of the United States' ... ought rightfully to be administered, without distinction of colour, to all descriptions of people."[71] Franklin had not only identified the contradiction slavery posed to American ideals of individual liberty but also insisted on the necessity of "removing this inconsistency from the character of the American people" in order to "promote mercy and justice towards this distressed race."[72] Privately, Franklin's demand for legislators to abolish slavery elicited from President Washington a condemnation rather than an endorsement. In a letter to an in-law, the president described Franklin's initiative "an illjudged piece of business" and "a great waste of time."[73]

Unlike Jefferson and Washington, Franklin's plea that his new government abolish slavery served as an implicit directive to free slaves of all faiths, including Muslims. He did this, despite a reference in his abolitionist petition to "the Christian religion" as the religious source of this ideal for equality, which, he wrote, coexisted along with "the political creed of America."[74] Why, then, did Franklin opt for an Islamic parody as a vehicle with which to mock his government's rejection of their responsibility to end the perpetuation of slavery? The answer for Franklin fused the personal and the political.[75]

Franklin placed Georgia Congressman Jackson's defense of slavery into the mouth of a fictional Muslim named Sidi Mehmet Ibrahim. ("Sidi" is the Arabic contraction for *Sayyid*, an honorary title of esteem which also designates descent from the Prophet.) Jackson's speeches in Congress had directly impugned Franklin, the Quakers, and his petition. Personally, Franklin designed this satirical salvo as much in anger against Jackson, his congressional nemesis, as in support for abolition.[76] Franklin's Islamic device allowed this invented North African official to rail against a sect of his Muslim coreligionists, who in 1687 had sought "the abolition of piracy and slavery"—against Christians.[77] Franklin thus denigrated the defense of slavery by Christians in Congress by defaming them with the same arguments he placed in the mouth of a Muslim from Algiers.

Algiers represented a real foreign policy threat to American commerce in the eastern Atlantic and Mediterranean by this time. All Franklin's readers knew that in 1785, five years before the publication of this parody, Muslim corsairs based in Algiers had captured two American merchant vessels and imprisoned twenty-one American sailors.[78] Three years after Franklin's last publication, Algiers had seized eleven additional merchant ships and snatched over one hundred American prisoners.[79] The raids continued over the next two decades, and new American captives in Algiers were termed "slaves" by their countrymen. According to Islamic law, these Americans were not slaves but prisoners of war, which made them eligible for ransom and, eventually, freedom. Franklin's parody raised the question: Were American Christians the same as Muslims, or worse, with reference to slavery?

Franklin's invented Muslim character's pronouncements reflected the objections of southern slaveholders to any form of emancipation. He accurately described Sidi Mehmet Ibrahim as an ethnically Turkish military official (Mehmet is the Turkish version of Muhammad) who served as part of the ruling council, the "Divan of Algiers."[80] Both Jackson and Sidi Mehmet Ibrahim defend slavery for exactly the same reasons: abolition was a threat to their economic prosperity, and they could never recoup the financial losses of emancipating their slaves who, in any event, could never coexist as a free people. Freedom for slaves, according to Franklin's chief object of censure, Congressman Jackson, would result in "tumults, seditions, and insurrections."[81] Although Franklin's antislavery parody skewered both Muslim and Christian practices of slavery, he also unwittingly made the earliest case for the freedom of American slaves of Islamic ancestry, who then constituted as much as 20 percent of the total US slave population.[82]

The extent of Franklin's knowledge about Islam, though flawed, is also reflected in the text, which opens:

Allah Bismillah, &c.
God is great, and Mahomet is his Prophet.[83]

Since *bismillah* means "in the name of Allah," Franklin's first phrase was redundant, but he correctly placed this phrase centered above the commencement of the official directive, as most real Islamic documents would. His rendering of the *shahada*, the Muslim creedal statement, also contained an error. The first line should be "There is no god but Allah (God)," instead of "God is great," but his attestation about Muhammad as God's prophet was correct.

Franklin argued, through the invented Muslim Sidi Mehmet Ibrahim, that Christians in North Africa could also benefit from captivity in "a land where the sun of Islamism gives forth its light," as an opportunity for conversion to "the true doctrine."[84] This is one of the rare appearances in the eighteenth century of the word "Islam" instead of the problematic but predominant "Mahometanism." He correctly observed that the Qur'an permits slavery but also enjoins: "Masters, treat your slaves with kindness,"[85] which is indeed asserted in chapter 4, verse 36. Franklin's next attribution to the Muslim holy book—"Slaves, serve your masters with cheerfulness and fidelity"—is inaccurate, however.[86] There is no such injunction in the Qur'an; rather, this quotation echoes Eph. 6:5 in the Christian Bible: "Slaves, obey your earthly masters with respect and fear, and with sincerity of heart, just as you would obey Christ." Franklin, doubtless, inserted this verse deliberately, because his opponent, Congressman Jackson, also had invoked the Bible in his rejection of Franklin's petition for the emancipation of American slaves.[87]

In this supposedly Islamic argument against abolition, Franklin never mentions the numerous verses in the Qur'an that enjoin the manumission of slaves. Of course, this wouldn't have furthered his Islamic parody of southern proslavery arguments, but it would have been a more accurate representation of sacred Islamic precedents. Perhaps he never knew that in the Qur'an 2:177, "righteousness" is defined, in part, as "to set slaves free." As an act for the expiation of sin, the holy Muslim book also includes "the liberation of a slave," which is also commanded in verses 5:89, 4:92, and 58:3. Finally, Franklin never recognized that white American captives in North Africa did not suffer lifelong enslavement, as did black slaves of West African origin. As captives of war, white American prisoners may have languished for years, but most were ultimately ransomed and returned home.[88]

Franklin's invocations of Islam ran the gamut, reflecting a broad range of early American views of the faith. He first argued for the theoretical inclusion of Muslims as worshippers in 1739, then derided conversion to Islam as a false faith two years later. In 1764, he reversed position again, holding up the exemplary humanity of the Prophet Muhammad to upbraid violent fellow Christians in Pennsylvania. The diffusion of European knowledge about Islam impacted Franklin as an American intellectual. Spanish, British, and French scholars sent him books that featured the Arabic language and described Islamic legal practices. His final Islamic parody sought to denigrate the practitioners of slavery, whether Christian or Muslim, but ultimately never acknowledged the Qur'an's precedents for manumission.

Twenty-four days before his death, Franklin's final publication depicted Christians and Muslims both as capable of either opposition to or support for slavery. In this configuration, the minority of both religions demanded abolition and were each summarily defeated by the proponents of slavery. Franklin's linkage of the proslavery Congressman Jackson and the proslavery Sidi Mehmet Ibrahim proved that "men's interest and intellects operate and are operated on with surprising similarity in all countries and climates, when under similar circumstances."[89] Slave owners in the United States, Franklin analogized, were no more morally sound in their protestations than the most despised and threatening policies of enemy Muslim corsairs in Algiers. The comparison equated white American "slaves" detained in Algiers with black West African slaves held in the United States. For Franklin, finally, both were inimical to his concept of American ideals of individual freedom.

Franklin's varied observations about Islam demonstrate that early Americans viewed the religion and its practitioners with considerable curiosity and some real understanding. Even in the midst of actual conflict with Islamic powers, Franklin ranks among a distinguished minority of Founders who imagined Muslims as future citizens of their new country. Paradoxically, a slave owner and an abolitionist, Franklin alone surpassed both Jefferson and Washington in seeking to legally eradicate the glaring "inconsistency" that he identified at the heart of his country's founding "true principles of liberty": slavery.[90] In writing both as an American activist bent on ending slavery for a black population that included Muslims—and simultaneously as a fictional seventeenth-century Muslim ruler of Algiers determined to maintain the practice against white Christian Americans—Franklin's last publication provides a unique, enduring demonstration of the entanglement of American and Islamic worlds.

2

The Greek War of Independence and the Ideological Manifestations of the Clash of Civilizations Theory in the United States, 1821–32

Karine Walther

When political scientist Samuel Huntington published his article "The Clash of Civilizations?" in *Foreign Affairs* in 1993, he sparked heated debates across academic disciplines.[1] His argument, expanded into a full-length book in 1996 by the same title, asserted that religion was the "most important" of the "objective elements which define civilization," and he warned of an inevitable clash between Islam and "the West."[2] The impact of his theories would not abate in subsequent years. Indeed, to many policymakers, Huntington's theory appeared prophetic after the events of 9/11, an historical moment that led many to call for a paradigm shift in American foreign policy. Reaffirmations of Huntington's arguments became frequent throughout the media and policymaking circles as Americans grappled with the so-called Global War on Terror and the country's increasingly fraught policies toward Muslims both at home and abroad.[3]

Although Huntington's warnings may have caused an uncritical splash among Washington political elites, in academia, many scholars noted that his definition of "civilization" was in fact simply a repackaged version of largely discounted and outdated understandings about the world and its peoples, some dating back centuries.[4] But scholars have often ignored the existence of similar religio-civilizational thinking in the United States, dating back at least to the early nineteenth century. At key moments in American history, many Americans categorized "civilizations" along almost exclusively religious lines and asserted the existence of a "civilizational conflict" between Islam and the Christian West, ideas that mirrored Huntington's later theories. The most ardent advocates of this worldview interpreted these conflicts as part of an inevitable global war of "cross against crescent," a religio-civilizational zero-sum game in which only one side could win. Such rhetoric also drew upon and amplified existing undercurrents of American Christian nationalism, while simultaneously tightening American *global* affiliations with the so-called Christian Family of Nations.

This worldview emerged forcefully in the United States during the "Age of Revolution" that spread to the Ottoman Empire in the first decades of the nineteenth century as Americans witnessed what they understood as Ottoman Christian subjects rebelling against Ottoman Muslim rule. This chapter analyzes one specific moment to illustrate the existence of such religio-civilizational distinctions: the American response to the Greek War of Independence fought between 1821 and 1832. During the war, thousands of Americans maintained that the United States was a Christian nation, and as such, it had a duty to intervene in supporting the Greek cause because of the religio-civilizational ties that united them with Greeks. Although the actual origins of the Greek War of Independence were complex and the conflict drew on numerous political, economic, and ideological grievances, Americans interpreted the Greek struggle as part of a global religious and civilizational struggle between two opposing, monolithic, and incompatible civilizations.[5]

At this point, it is useful to cite Michael Hunt's work on the relationship between ideology and US foreign policy, in which he defines ideology as "an interrelated set of convictions or assumptions that reduces the complexities of a particular slice of reality to easily comprehensible terms and suggests appropriate ways of dealing with that reality."[6] Early American manifestations of the "clash of civilizations" theory, much like Huntington's more contemporary version, had little basis in the historical realities on the ground. In order to function, these ideological constructions overlooked the complexity of the Greek struggle, while also ignoring the centuries of deep and interwoven historical and societal ties between Ottoman Christians, Muslims, and Jews.

This ideological framing of the Greek War of Independence was not limited to a few policymaking elites; American activism on behalf of Greek Christians extended across the country and crossed class and denominational lines, bringing a broad swathe of the American public into a national conversation about American identity and foreign policy. Although American activists would not succeed in obtaining official US government intervention, they nonetheless offered their support in other important ways, including raising a significant amount of money for Greek revolutionaries, offering political and military advice, and sending arms, provisions, and even volunteers to fight alongside the Greek revolutionaries. The advancement of religio-civilizational rhetoric on behalf of the Greek cause thus had an important impact on the ground both for Americans and for the Greeks themselves.

American support for the Greeks drew upon deep undercurrents of Christian nationalism which was intricately tied to its political system. Although Americans often identified the United States as distinct from and superior to the political decadence of "old" Europe, many Americans nonetheless recognized themselves as the stepchildren of European Enlightenment thought.[7] But in contrast to Europe, where the rational secularism of Enlightenment theories conflicted with religious belief and the church, these political theories took a decidedly different turn in the United States, where American interpretations of Enlightenment thought merged more peacefully with American Christian beliefs.[8] For many Americans, the merging of Enlightenment theory with Christianity allowed religious nationalism to remain an important element in defining American national identity.

European religious and political thought contributed in shaping American beliefs in other ways. Enlightenment texts that vilified Islamic despotism contributed to other widely circulated Orientalist depictions of Islam that originated in both Europe and the United States, including travel narratives, biographies of the Prophet Muhammad that excoriated the Muslim faith, and theological literature.[9] These texts solidified long-standing conceptual boundaries distinguishing Muslims from the West in both Europe and the United States. As Mark Mazower notes, "In the writings of travelers, pundits and philosophers, powerful new polarities emerge—between civilized West and barbarous East, between freedom-loving Europe and despotic Orient."[10] As another historian notes, "This was not a simple opposition of Christianity to Islam, but of the whole culture, history, and sociopolitical structure of Europe-as-Christendom from an alien Empire based on incompatible principles of government, law and morality."[11]

Classifications merging religion with political and civilizational status were also intimately bound up with the influence of new theories of legal positivism that emerged in the late eighteenth century and were gradually replacing natural law as the legal basis for international law.[12] As opposed to theories of natural law, which were generally applied to all humans and nations regardless of religious identity, legal positivism increasingly defined all non-Christians, including the Ottoman Empire, as "uncivilized" and, therefore, outside the bounds of international law.[13] Meanwhile, because many Europeans and Anglo-American Christians understood the United States' religious and ethnic origins as stemming solely from Christian Europe, such theories reaffirmed the United States' inclusion alongside Europeans within the "civilized" realm of international law. No thinker better represented this view than the Russian legal theorist G. F. von Martens. As he noted in the introduction to his *Summary of the Law of Nations*, translated and republished in the United States in 1795,

> I thought it necessary to confine my title to the *nations of Europe*; although, *in* Europe, the Turks have, in many respects, rejected the positive law of nations of which I here treat; and though, *out* of Europe, the United States of America have uniformly adopted it. It is to be understood *a potiori*, and it appears preferable to that of, *law of civilized nations*, which is too vague.[14]

The advancement of legal distinctions between Christians and non-Christians emerged just as powerfully in the United States. In 1820, only one year before Greeks began fighting for their independence, the influential American international law theorist Henry Wheaton delivered a speech at the New-York Historical Society in which he presented his theories on international law.[15] The ideas Wheaton advanced that evening would later serve as the basis for his 1836 book, *Elements of International Law*, which would become one of the most influential nineteenth-century texts on the subject in both Europe and the United States. In his speech, Wheaton maintained that there existed no international or natural law which applied to "all mankind, in all ages and countries, ancient and modern, savage and civilized, Christian and Pagan." Instead, he argued, there existed only an "international law of Christendom," the origins of which could never have come from non-Christians but instead had emerged from "that class or family of nations over whom Christianity (in various forms, indeed, but in all with some good fruits) has exercised its greatest influence; I mean the civilized nations of Europe, and their colonies in the new world."[16] The United States, "though separated by a wide waste of waters from our European brethren," were "members of the same great family" for "we share the same literature, religion, and law of nations; [and] are united to them by a thousand tiers of affection and interest."[17]

While Americans were clearly part of this "great family," Wheaton explicitly noted that Muslims were outside of it. Wheaton's explanation for this exclusion was solely based on Muslims' religious beliefs, which was the determinant factor in their civilizational identity: "The Koran is their all-sufficient institute of ethical and political science; and their manners, government, and peculiar law of nations, still remain, for the most part, unchanged by the rapid improvements which have taken place in the Western world."[18]

Wheaton applied these legal theories directly to the Greek War of Independence. An ardent admirer of ancient Greece, Wheaton joined the Greek relief movement shortly after the outbreak of the war. His influence and dedication to the cause were so important that the New York Greek relief committee chose him in 1823 to petition Congress to recognize Greek independence.[19] His commitment to the cause did not end there. His widely influential study on international law, published in 1836—only four years after the end of the war—explicitly defended the legal rights of the "Christian Powers of Europe" to intervene on behalf of "civilized" Greeks and offered "a further illustration of the principles of international law authorizing such an interference . . . where the general interests of humanity are infringed by the excesses of a barbarous and despotic government."[20] Since Muslim countries were deemed outside the bounds of civilized nations, Wheaton argued, Christian powers had a right and duty to intervene on behalf of their religious brethren:

> If, as some writers have supposed, the Turks belong to a family or set of nations which is not bound by the general international law of Christendom, they have still no right to complain of the measures which the Christian powers thought proper to adopt for the protection of their religious brethren oppressed by the Mohammedan rule. . . . The rights of human nature, wantonly outraged by this cruel warfare, prosecuted for six years against a civilized and Christian people, to whose ancestors mankind are so largely indebted for the blessings of arts and of letters, were but tardily and imperfectly vindicated.[21]

Wheaton formulated his claims about the rights and duties of intervention in the Ottoman Empire not as an American, but as a member of the "civilized" Christian nations. Like most American philhellenes of his time, Wheaton had merged long-held American traditions of reverence for ancient Greece with political philhellenism and the desire for Greek independence from the Ottoman Empire.[22] The same period also saw a transition in European and American racial constructions of Greek whiteness, from what Athena Leoussi calls "Civic Hellenism" to "Racial Hellenism."[23] Europeans and Americans increasingly "built a sometimes tacit, sometimes explicit whiteness into this sense of shared identity between northern Europeans and their Hellenic 'ancestors.'"[24]

This merging of faith, foreign policy, and philhellenism also drew its strength from another important movement in the United States: the revival of religious enthusiasm of the Second Great Awakening that rose in the two decades preceding the Greek revolution. The populist religious movement built on existing revolutionary fervor and allowed Americans to question the authority of traditional elites, both religious and secular, while simultaneously calling for greater public participation in shaping the outcome of American society.[25] Another outcropping of this religious fervor was the birth of an important reform movement seeking to spread the morality and values of Protestant evangelical Christianity to American society and the world.

This spirit of moral Christian reform merged perfectly with the popular actions on behalf of the Greek cause as evangelical Christians sought to spread their political and religious values to the world and annihilate powerful non-Christian entities; destroying the "Islamic" power of the Ottoman Empire loomed large in these global plans. The anti-elitist tendencies of the Second Great Awakening also led Christian evangelicals to more publicly and aggressively question the government's traditional policies of nonintervention, particularly when it came to supporting Christians under Muslim rule. Christian evangelicals emerging from the Second Great Awakening thus fueled the flames of philhellenic sympathy for the Greek cause, as energized clergymen and their followers sought to support and free their Christian brethren abroad.[26] The participation of these evangelical Christians in philhellenic Greek relief efforts helped cement the ideological ties among the various intellectual, political, historical, and religious strands driving American sympathy for the Greek cause while uniting political elites with everyday Americans in an international effort.

Driven by these historical and far-reaching intellectual, legal, and religious trends in American society, Americans held an ingrained sympathy for the Greeks, paralleled with an antipathy for Muslims, that would shape their reaction to the Greek war. These sympathies were reinforced by the influence of American philhellenes on the press itself. Vocal public supporters of Greek independence included an impressive number of editors and journalists who decided what stories newspapers would cover and what their editorial interpretation of events would be. These included William Cullen Bryant, editor of the *New York Evening Post*; Edward Everett, editor of the *North American Review*; Colonel William L. Stone, editor of the *New-York Commercial Advertiser*; Charles King, editor of the *New York American*; Hezekiah Niles, editor of the *Niles Weekly Register*; and Thomas Ritchie of the *Richmond Enquirer*.[27] While serving as the editorial heads of these newspapers, these men contributed actively to committees dedicated to raising funds and lobbying the US government on behalf of the Greek cause. Furthermore, news about the war often came directly from European-educated Greek revolutionaries who had their own interests in mind when crafting their accounts.

Given the sources of information and the inherent bias of press editors, coverage that did not rehearse the dominant narrative of Greek Christian victimization at the hands of barbaric Muslim rule got little coverage in the American press. In a war of ongoing brutal civilian massacres perpetuated by both Ottomans and Greeks, press coverage focused overwhelmingly on Turkish abuses.[28] Greek revolutionaries' practices of torture and mass rape—and their massacre of more than ten thousand Muslim and Jewish civilians, including women and children—within the first few weeks of the rebellion were rarely covered by the American press.[29]

Ottoman government reprisals for the slaughter of Muslims escalated the violence, leading to the equally brutal rape and massacre of tens of thousands of Greek subjects and the public hanging of the Greek patriarch in Constantinople.[30] These demonstrations of violence were widely covered in the American press. In such accounts, Turkish rulers and soldiers became synonymous with "the followers of Mahomet," just as "Greek" and "Christian" became interchangeable terms. Turkish political despotism and violence were inextricably tied to Muslims' religious faith and were irrefutable evidence of religious fanaticism rather than the relatively typical, albeit unfortunate, physical repression of an imperial state maintaining order.

Given this philhellenic journalistic scope, within weeks of the breakout of the Greek revolution, American newspapers were already feeding the American public this one-sided narrative of the events that reaffirmed a "clash of civilizations" between Christians and Muslims. Soon after Alexander Ypsilanti, a leader of the struggle, issued a proclamation to the people of Moldavia on March 7, 1821, the proclamation quickly found its way to American readers via dozens of American newspapers in May and June 1821.[31] Americans who read his address were reminded that the "civilized people of Europe" (and by extension, the United States) were "full of gratitude for the benefits they received from our ancestors, [and] desire the liberty of Greece."[32] It was time to "deliver our country, to throw down the crescent from its height; to elevate the cross, the standard by which we may still conquer, and thus avenge our country and our holy religion, from the profanation and the mockery of barbarians."[33] Ypsilanti's address reaffirmed that Greeks were part of the civilized, Christian world and that this very affiliation morally legitimated war against Turkish Muslim rule.

Although the northern rebellion was ultimately unsuccessful, Greek revolutionaries had more success in Morea (the Peloponnese) and many of the larger islands. On March 23, 1821, only two weeks after the outbreak of hostilities, local revolutionary leaders addressed appeals to both European and Americans philhellenes.[34] American newspapers first gained access to the European appeal in July 1821, and reprinted it, often in its entirety.[35] The appeal once again pulled on religious and civilizational heartstrings to gain political sympathy. Greek revolutionaries invited "the united aid of all civilized nations to promote the attainment of our holy and legitimate purpose," as was their duty as the civilized offspring of ancient Greece.[36] Within a week of the appeal's publication, dozens of American newspapers republished a strongly worded pro-Greek editorial initially written for Philadelphia's *Democratic Press*, in which the author asserted "that *all* the civilized world" should sympathize with the Greek cause.[37] To lack such sympathy, by logical extension, cast the reader as uncivilized. The author left little doubt that Christianity was the key element defining modernity and civilization:

With *modern* Greece we have bands and ties and common principles which entwine it around our hearts and connect it with our dearest wishes, our holiest hopes. They adore the same God, they acknowledge the same Redeemer. They believe in a state of future rewards and punishments founded on the same promises and the same evidence as we do, in one word they are *Christians*. They are humble believers in that system of religion and morality which is believed in by all the portion of the world which do honor to Humanity.³⁸

Whereas Greeks were "modern" and "Christian"—terms the author himself emphasized in the text—their Islamic foes were "furious, bigoted, and persecuting enemies of Christianity." Religion, morality, and politics united these nations in a common struggle against Muslim enemies: "Our whole hearts, our principles, civil, religious and political, are with the Greeks and against the Turks."³⁹

The Greek revolutionaries' appeal specifically targeting the United States reached an American readership a few months later through Adamantios Korais, a Paris-based Greek scholar and revolutionary who had a network of influential American and European philhellenic contacts.⁴⁰ These included the classical scholar, clergyman, and one of the most important philhellenic leaders Edward Everett; Thomas Jefferson, American minister to France Albert Gallatin; and the American revolutionary hero and ardent French philhellene the Marquis de Lafayette (the latter subsequently lobbied his American philhellenic friends to send naval vessels to the area to aid the suffering Greeks).⁴¹ Greek revolutionary leaders had carefully chosen their messenger and tasked Korais with "enlisting the sympathies of Western Europe and America."⁴² Korais's contacts paid off; within weeks, dozens of newspapers across the United States had reprinted the story.

Once again, Greek revolutionaries meticulously crafted the proclamation, reminding their American audience of the religious, political, and historical ties that united the two countries:

> In taking the resolution to live and die for liberty, we feel ourselves drawn toward you by a natural sympathy. It is among you that liberty has found her abode, and she is worshipped by you as by our fathers. In invoking her name we invoke yours; feeling that in imitating you we imitate our own ancestors, and that we shall show ourselves worthy of them in proportion that we resemble you.⁴³

But Greeks also appealed to Americans because they saw the United States as the moral, political, and religious model leading the Christian Family of Nations: "Just, for you are free: Benevolent and generous, for your laws are the laws of the gospel." These qualities held the United States to a higher standard:

> Surely it is worthy of you to discharge the duty of all civilized nations, in expelling ignorance and barbarity from the native soil of the arts and of freedom. You will not imitate the culpable indifference, or rather the long continued ingratitude of some European nations. No, the country of Penn, of Franklin, and of Washington, cannot refuse her aid to the descendants of Phocion, Thrasybulus, Aratus, and Philopemen.⁴⁴

The publication of these Greek appeals throughout the American press helped launch a "Greek fever" in American society, as philhellenic activists began holding public meetings, and raising money for the Greek cause. Action extended to calls for the United States to take an official stand in support of the Greek cause, including recommendations that the United States send warships and an American military force to the area.[45]

Given this public and journalistic outcry, it did not take long for President James Monroe to respond.[46] Monroe shared the public's understanding of the Greek struggle as a civilizational and religious clash between Islam and Christianity. His first inclination was to engage the United States directly in the struggle. Strong pressure from Secretary of State John Quincy Adams, described by one contemporary as Monroe's "master spirit in foreign affairs," forced him to temper his public commitments.[47] In his annual message of December 3, 1822, Monroe nonetheless captured philhellenic sympathies while revealing the degree to which "Greek fever" had spread throughout American society:

> That such a country should have been overwhelmed and so long hidden, as it were, from the world under a gloomy despotism has been a cause of unceasing and deep regret to generous minds for ages past. It was natural, therefore, that the reappearance of those people in their original character, contending in favor of their liberties, should produce that great excitement and sympathy in their favor which have been so signally displayed throughout the United States. A strong hope is entertained that these people will recover their independence and resume their equal station among the nations of the earth.[48]

In August 1823, Monroe addressed the Greek cause during a cabinet meeting convened in part to discuss the administration's response to several domestic and international pleas for action.[49] Andreas Luriottis, the envoy of the provisional Greek government, had written Adams requesting official American diplomatic recognition of Greece and the right to call the United States an ally in its continued battle. Minister Albert Gallatin had also requested that the president send three navy ships to the area to help the Greeks in their battle against the Ottoman rulers.[50] The cabinet members also considered a proposal by Secretary of War John C. Calhoun to send an American secret agent to Greece to assess the political situation and offer the United States' private support.

Most of the cabinet members and Monroe himself supported more aggressive American action on behalf of the Greeks. Adams profoundly disagreed, maintaining that it would contravene the traditional American policy of nonentanglement and risked pitting the United States in a war against Turkey. By all accounts, Adams's primary goal was to maintain American neutrality vis-à-vis the Holy Alliance, the Ottoman Empire, and England.[51] Adams also disagreed with both the idea of sending a secret agent and Calhoun's choice of Edward Everett as the agent in question, noting Everett's clear bias in favor of the Greek cause.[52] In the end, Monroe's deference to Adams's foreign policy expertise convinced the president to keep the country above the European fray. Adams drafted a response to Luriotti expressing American sympathy but maintaining official American neutrality.[53]

Adams did not have the same influence with American philhellenes. Two months later, Everett, now the editor of the popular literary journal the *North American Review*, republished the entire original Greek appeal to the United States in an effort to reactivate the public call for US intervention in this war of "cross against crescent."[54] Stirring American Christian fervor for the Greek war would have powerful global consequences, Everett maintained, delivering another "country to the church of Christ; and do more to effect the banishment of the crescent to the deserts of Tartary, than all that has yet been achieved by the counsels of Christendom."[55] He called on the American government to send an investigative commission to Greece to ascertain how far the revolutionaries had come in shaping their new government. When this commission discovered what Everett already knew to be true, the United States would be forced to recognize Greece and send an American minister.[56] Everett also led the Boston Greek relief committee in issuing an appeal to the American people: "We call upon the friends of freedom and humanity to take an interest in the struggles of five millions of Christians." Everett invoked the efforts of his fellow clergymen "to take up a solemn testimony in the cause; to assert the rights of fellow men and of fellow Christians; to plead for the victims whose great crime is Christianity."[57] By the end of 1824, concerned citizens had raised more than $30,000 to aid the struggling nation.[58] At least a dozen American philhellenes also traveled to Greece to join the Greek revolutionary army. Among the best known was philhellene Samuel Gridley Howe, who left for Greece after finishing his medical degree to serve as chief surgeon in the Greek navy and set up hospitals for wounded soldiers.

Newspapers and journals continued to publish appeals and editorials in support of the Greeks. Undoubtedly prompted by this rising public clamor, President Monroe wrote a draft of a speech in November 1823, preparing to announce his famous doctrine as well as American recognition of Greek independence. His draft also requested funds from Congress to send an American minister to the area. The majority of his cabinet members once again endorsed the plan, but Adams repeated his warning to the president that his speech would be understood by Europeans as a "summons to arms," and urged Monroe to temper his commitment to the Greeks.[59] President Monroe again heeded Adams's warnings and delivered his now-infamous speech proclaiming the Monroe Doctrine (largely authored by Adams himself) along with a lukewarm statement expressing his hope that Greece would soon be independent.[60]

Adams's strong disagreement with advocates of intervention did not stem from his lack of sympathy for the Greek cause. Indeed, Adams joined many philhellenes in conceptualizing the world in terms of civilized Christian powers opposed to barbaric Islamic despotism. As his later writings would reveal, he was deeply antagonistic to the Ottoman Empire and felt that only by eradicating Muslim rule would peace come to the world. Much like Calhoun, Adams vehemently blamed the Holy Alliance for supporting authoritarian rule in its own political systems while propping up Ottoman imperial rule. But Adams disagreed with interventionists in his understanding of the role of American foreign policy in eliminating this political corruption. Whereas many philhellenes and proponents of American intervention believed that more aggressive foreign policies would spread American liberal political values abroad, Adams maintained that it would only embroil the country in the very political corruption it was trying to avoid. As he had argued in a well-known 1821 speech forecasting his later development of the Monroe Doctrine, the United States did not go "abroad in search of monsters to destroy." Instead, the nation led by example in providing the world with the true model of government and affirming the rights of mankind.[61] Although Adams's stance may have starkly contradicted the more aggressive aims of interventionists, at their core, both foreign policy visions revealed a fundamental belief that the United States was a benevolent force for political freedom and liberty in the world. The disagreement was not over American political and moral superiority, but how to maintain it and spread it to the world.

Much to Adams's chagrin, Monroe's speech did not signify the end of the story. Only six days later, Massachusetts representative Daniel Webster responded to Monroe's lukewarm support for the Greek cause by proposing a congressional resolution asking the United States to send an agent to Greece. In January 1824, he presented these arguments during a week-long congressional debate, which included heartfelt speeches by numerous members in support of recognition, including powerful Speaker of the House Henry Clay.[62] They delivered their speeches to a packed house, attended by virtually all of the representatives.[63] As the Philadelphia *National Gazette* noted, Webster's proposal had gained the "profound attention by the whole House," and "every auditor seemed to be penetrated with the justice and holiness of the cause of a people contending at once for Liberty and Christianity."[64]

During his speech, Webster rehashed the civilizational and religious distinctions between Greek Christians and Ottoman Muslims: the Ottoman Empire was a state powered by the "ignorant and furious faith" of Islam, a religion whose level of fanaticism was matched only by its incapacity for change.[65] Webster was particularly appalled by the inversion of civilizational hierarchies in the Ottoman Empire. In Greece, "millions of Christian men, not without knowledge, not without refinement, not without a strong thirst for all the pleasures of civilized life, [are] trampled into the very earth, century after century, by a pillaging, savage, relentless soldier."[66] No other case merited a greater call for Christian action; the Greeks "stretch out their arms to the Christian communities of the world, beseeching them, by a generous recollection of their ancestors ... by the common faith, and in the name, which unites all Christians."[67]

Although Webster was initially confident that his resolution would pass, Adams once again stepped in to thwart any possibility of action. The secretary of state reached out to Representative Joel Poinsett, who had initially expressed support for Webster's resolution, and convinced the congressman to represent the administration and speak against the resolution during the debate.[68] Poinsett's speech, broadly understood as conveying the administration's strong stance against the resolution, doomed Webster's attempts.[69]

Such debates, which were widely covered by the American press, revealed the powerful interplay between government actions and public opinion and the impact of civilizational discourse on American foreign policy. Vocal public demands could shape the ideological framing of American foreign policy debates, despite their inability, in this case, to garner presidential or congressional support for official action. Many Americans believed that the US policy of nonintervention had a moral and spiritual limit; spreading political liberty and protecting Christian brethren made sense to a nation that saw itself as divinely ordained to lead the world in its path to progress.

And yet, the same men who asserted the need to defend political liberty and Christianity abroad and lamented the tragic state of Greeks "enslaved" by Turkish Muslim rule were incapable of turning their critical lens inward—in part because of the blinding power of the myth of American benevolence. American global classifications of civilized and uncivilized peoples merged with similar domestic beliefs in a mutually reinforcing process. Both visions relied on the same fundamental logic of civilizational difference. Americans did not recognize the irony of placing appeals for the Greeks side by side with notices for runaway slaves or advertisements announcing the sale of "a great variety of household and kitchen furniture" that included in its list "Four Negroes, accustomed to house work."[70] Indeed, who would pity the oppression of slaves who have no more humanity than furniture? Nor did philhellenes perceive hypocrisy in appeals denouncing the condition of Greeks made "slaves to the most cruel and remorseless tyranny" while expressing "gratitude to the Almighty for our own national blessings" of liberty.[71] Indeed, arguments about the enslavement of Greeks versus African Americans demonstrated the complex ways in which ideas about "civilization" functioned both in the domestic and international spheres.

One of the rare occasions on which Americans explicitly compared the situation of black slaves to that of Greeks was when the French chamber passed a law in 1826 criminalizing the African slave trade. American editorials denounced the law for failing to include white slaves. Though his goal was not to defend the African slave trade, one editorialist maintained that there were some benefits to the Africans in question: "When they tear a negro from his forests, he is transported to a civilized country; he finds chains there it is true; but religion, which can do nothing for his liberty in this world . . . at least consoles the poor negro, and assures him of that deliverance in another life." In contrast, the enslavement of Greeks went against all conceivable laws of nature and humanity and, by extension, the established racial hierarchies of man: "This race [of Greeks] is civilized and christian [sic]—To whom are they sold? To Barbary, and to Mahometanism. Here the religious crime is united to the civil and political crime, and the individual who commits it is guilty in the tribunal of the God of Christians, as well as the tribunal of civilized nations."[72] In denouncing this "crime," the author reaffirmed distinctions in international law between the rights of civilized versus uncivilized peoples and domestic distinctions between blacks and whites.

But the culminating expression of philhellenic racism came from the father of American philhellenism himself, Edward Everett. Having been elected to Congress in 1824, the ardent supporter of political liberty for Greeks defended the enslavement of African Americans at home, maintaining that should there be a slave revolt in the South, he would be the first to get his musket and volunteer to put down such a rebellion, for he would rather see the United States "sunk in the bottom of the ocean" than turned into a place like Haiti, where slaves had successfully thrown off white rule.[73]

Over the next few years, the rhetoric of clashing civilizations that came to so often define American perceptions of the Greek struggle continued to energize American society as new reports from American volunteers fighting for the Greek cause made their way to American shores.[74] Between 1827 and 1828, American Greek relief organizations raised more than $138,000, which they invested in relief aid that filled six cargo ships.[75] During this time, American philhellenes also continued to coordinate with European philhellenes, perhaps constituting one of the first cases in which transatlantic nonstate actors organized to push for humanitarian government intervention in another country.

Although American aid helped clothe, feed, and—to a certain extent—arm the Greek revolutionaries, European military intervention ended the struggle. This initiative by the British, French, and Russians began in 1826 and led to the infamous Battle of Navarino in 1827 and the destruction of both the Ottoman and the Egyptian navies. Negotiations between the great powers and the Ottoman Empire finally led to the official declaration of Greek independence in 1832. Although the war was waged in part as a battle for political liberty, the Greeks soon found themselves at the political mercy of the European powers who, after excluding Greek revolutionaries from negotiations, imposed a foreign prince to lead the country.

Despite the disappointment of many Greeks in the face of peace concessions, Americans celebrated their independence and saw in the Greek war a victory in the larger global civilizational struggle between Islam and Christianity. As Howe noted in his memoirs, "The Independence of Greece is not to release her children alone from the thralldom of the Turks, but it will open the door for the advance of liberty, of civilization, and of Christianity in the East."[76] In 1831, on the eve of Greek independence, support for this belief emerged from an unlikely source: John Quincy Adams. Although Adams had adamantly maintained the US policy of non-intervention during the war, his virulent antipathy to Islam and the Ottoman Empire transcended that of even his most ardent philhellenic opponents. Adams articulated these views in an essay he wrote for the *American Annual Register* while he was serving as a Massachusetts Representative to Congress—which is perhaps why he chose to keep his essay anonymous. The essay's acerbic assault on Islam, rehashing virtually all existing anti-Muslim tropes of the period, warrants citing at length.

Ostensibly focused on the history and politics of Russia, Adams's essay began instead with a history of Islam and the Prophet Mohammed, who had through "the preternatural energy of a fanatic, and the fraudulent spirit of an imposter . . . spread desolation and delusion over an extensive portion of the earth."[77] Speaking on behalf of his faith, the Prophet Mohammed had further declared "undistinguishing and exterminating war . . . against all of mankind."[78] Using all capital letters to emphasize his point, he virulently denounced the Prophet Mohammed and the Islamic faith: "THE ESSENCE OF HIS DOCTRINE WAS VIOLENCE AND LUST: TO EXALT THE BRUTAL OVER THE SPIRITUAL PART OF HUMAN NATURE."[79] According to Adams, a global war between Muslims and Christians would continue as long as the "merciless and dissolute dogmas of the false prophet shall furnish motives to human action."[80]

Still, Adams offered some hope for eventual success, promoting the duty of Christians to dominate the rest of the world for "his superior acquirements have vested him with the privilege, and imposed upon him the obligation of becoming the teacher of his less enlightened fellow creatures."[81] Although Adams maintained that Christianity was defined by the "doctrines of the meek and peaceful and benevolent Jesus" the only option for Christians was to battle Islam through violence: "As the essential principle of his faith is the subjugation of others by the sword; it is only by force, that his false doctrines can be dispelled, and his power annihilated."[82] Although Adams's actions had been the most important factor in keeping the United States from helping the Greeks, he lay all of the blame on European corruption:

> If ever insurrection was holy in the eyes of God, such was that of the Greeks against their Mahometan oppressors. Yet for six long years, they were suffered to be overwhelmed by the whole mass of the Ottoman power; cheered only by the sympathies of the civilized world, but without a finger raised to sustain or relieve them by the Christian governments of Europe; while the sword of extermination, instinct with the spirit of the Koran, was passing merciless horror over the classical regions of Greece, the birth-place of philosophy, of poetry, of eloquence, of all the arts that embellish, and all the sciences that dignify the human character.[83]

Despite his strong stance on American neutrality, Adams nonetheless agreed with many Americans in maintaining that Islam was a global problem that needed to be eradicated to secure world peace. This goal, Adams hoped, would be among the future endeavors to which the newly freed Greeks would contribute.[84]

Although Adams's fear of corrupting the purity of the American political project prevented him from supporting formal intervention on behalf of the Greeks, his vision of the profound civilizational differences between the Muslim world and the Christian Euro-American Family of Nations aligned him with philhellenes in shaping a powerful alternative to American national identity. The Monroe Doctrine may have been an essential national policy in maintaining the American national project, but it could not erase the civilizational and religious affiliations that united Americans and European Christendom. Adams's vision of American global identity reaffirmed another component that connected him to the philhellenes: a strong belief in American benevolence.

The Greek War of Independence would not be the last time that ideas about civilization, religious difference, and American munificence shaped American interactions abroad. As the fallout from the Eastern Question continued, Americans would side again and again with Christian Ottoman subjects in their revolts against Ottoman rulers. By 1916, as Europe was in the midst of the First World War, the American Christian missionary Samuel Zwemer would argue that the struggle between the cross and the crescent in "Western Asia" represented the "greatest battlefield" in the world for the "clash of modern civilization against the teaching of Islam is evident on every hand."[85]

Over the next two hundred years, simplistic understandings of the Islamic world would reemerge repeatedly when Americans witnessed conflicts that happened to pit Christians against Muslims. It would be a mistake to trace an unbroken trajectory from the nineteenth century to the post–Cold War period and, more importantly, to the post-9/11 era. Yet it would be equally erroneous to discount the ways in which American discourses about Islam have persisted in the recent relations of the United States with the Muslim world, albeit in varied forms. Huntington's theory resonated with Americans after 9/11, not because it was accurate but because religio-civilizational discourse has a long history of shaping how some Americans have identified with the world.

Part Two

The Muslim Experience in the Americas

3

Nicholas Said's America: Islam, the Civil War, and the Emergence of African American Narrative

Ira Dworkin

Among nineteenth-century African American autobiographies, Nicholas Said's "A Native of Bornoo" occupies a unique place as perhaps the most widely read narrative by an African Muslim in the United States. Said's account was written in English and published in the *Atlantic Monthly* in 1867, one of the most important white literary publications of the era which, Susan Goodman declares, "reflects the story of a nation and its aspirations."[1] The editorial introduction to "A Native of Bornoo" states that Nicholas Said, born "Mohammed-Ali-Ben-Said," was known as a storyteller during the Civil War when he enlisted in the 55th Massachusetts Regiment "because," according to a June 1863 interview in a Connecticut newspaper, "all his folks seemed to be doing so."[2] While in the military, "attention was first directed to his case by the tattooing on his face, and by the entry in the company descriptive book, which gave 'Africa' as his birthplace."[3] Likely one of his officers, "probably Norwood P. Hallowell, a commanding officer who also spoke about Said elsewhere," according to Allan Austin, "had the autobiography published in the most prestigious journal of the day."[4] Said gained access to the *Atlantic* as a result of his military service, which provides an important national context for "A Native of Bornoo"—the subject of this chapter. (Said published *The Autobiography of Nicholas Said, a Native of Bornou, Eastern Soudan, Central Africa*, in Memphis in 1873.[5]) This personal history marks him as a distinctive subject immersed in and representative of a community he sought to serve militarily. In this venue, his stories of his African Muslim heritage became part of the culture of African Americans both fighting for freedom from slavery and confronting the forms of discrimination within the US military that would characterize the country's Jim Crow regime for the next century.

The very circumstances of the narrative's publication as a result of his national military service immediately render Said's autobiographical account "American." Its focus on his experiences of slavery implicitly places it in dialogue with the "slave narrative" tradition—a category which has come to subsume a diverse corpus of presumptively Christian nineteenth-century African American writing. Said's autobiographical accounts are admittedly ill fits for many of that tradition's conventions; however, their tenuous relationship with established genres provides valuable insight for rethinking the entire narrative tradition on whose margins it sits as an autobiography that is deeply invested in its author's African history and Muslim faith. Said's *Atlantic Monthly* text is making its way into the canon: it is included in its entirety in the third edition (2014) of the *Norton Anthology of African American Literature*.[6] Part of my aim is to further place "A Native of Bornoo" in dialogue with foundational works of African American literature, especially Frederick Douglass's prototypical writings, in order to reevaluate some of the conventions of early African American narrative, particularly around questions of nation, ethnicity, and religion, by taking up Frances Smith Foster's call "to complement, complicate, and challenge popular concepts about the ways in which African-American literary production began and developed by highlighting roles of language, religion, and organization in defining and developing an African-American press."[7] While the white-edited *Atlantic Monthly* had an ambivalent relationship with its few black contributors during the 1860s, Said's writings can usefully be appreciated as part of the trajectory that Foster delineates.

Reading Nicholas Said, Rereading Frederick Douglass

Said's writings are part of a larger culture of African American letters, whose founding arguably occurs in an Afro-Arabic tradition of what Ronald A. T. Judy calls "New World Arabic slave narratives."[8] When Ayyub ibn Suleiman Diallo (anglicized as Job Ben Solomon) wrote a letter in Arabic in 1731 requesting that his father purchase his freedom, James Oglethorpe, one of the founders of the Georgia colony, was moved to arrange for the purchase of Ayyub's freedom, an exchange which, for Henry Louis Gates, Jr., symbolizes "the relationship between freedom and literacy dramatically."[9] That relationship is articulated perhaps most prominently in *Narrative of the Life of Frederick Douglass, an American Slave* (1845), which over the past several decades has emerged as one of the founding texts of African American literary studies, and has been generally recognized as one of the most canonical works of nineteenth-century English-language literature. The rapid literary appreciation of this work within a range of national spaces has overshadowed the way that the *Narrative*, along with Douglass's other diverse writings, is part of a much more heterogeneous literary tradition.

The canonical reading of Douglass holds that the ability to read and write is an instrument of emancipation. Starting from its prefaces by William Lloyd Garrison and Wendell Phillips, prominent white abolitionists, the *Narrative* persistently evokes images of Douglass writing and reflecting on his life in slavery. Garrison's preface cites a speech given by Irish abolitionist Daniel O'Connell:

> "An American sailor, who was cast away on the shore of Africa, where he was kept in slavery for three years, was at the expiration of that period, found to be imbruted and stultified—he had lost all reasoning power; and having forgotten his native language, could only utter some savage gibberish between Arabic and English, which nobody could understand, and which even he himself found difficulty in pronouncing. So much for the humanizing influence of THE DOMESTIC

INSTITUTION!" Admitting this to have been an extraordinary case of mental deterioration, it proves at least that the white slave can sink as low in the scale of humanity as the black one.[10]

Via O'Connell, Garrison here marks English as the signifier of American civilization in contrast to the "savage gibberish" that seems tainted by its encounter with Arabic. Yet the English that Douglass studied was itself infused with engagements with the Muslim world. In his *Narrative*, he details the definitive rhetorical influence of Caleb Bingham's popular *The Columbian Orator* (1797), whose contents include both a speech by O'Connell and David Everett's play "Slaves in Barbary, A Drama in Two Acts," an exemplar of the popular genre of North African captivity tales that O'Connell and Garrison allude to.[11] In these ways, Douglass's own literacy is likewise bound up with "barbary" discourse around questions of language, race, religion, and nation.

While Douglass's 1845 *Narrative* carefully details his efforts to read as a humanistic pursuit within a European tradition, he reveals additional details in his second autobiography, *My Bondage and My Freedom*, published in 1855. Here, for instance, Douglass mentions that, in his youth, he was aware of the influence of African languages on the Lloyd plantation in Maryland:

> There is not, probably, in the whole south, a plantation where the English language is more imperfectly spoken than on Col. Lloyd's. It is a mixture of Guinea and everything else you please. At the time of which I am now writing, there were slaves there who had been brought from the coast of Africa. They never used the "s" in indication of the possessive case. "Cap'n Ant'ney Tom," "Lloyd Bill," "Aunt Rose Harry," means "Captain Anthony's Tom," "Lloyd's Bill," &c. "*Oo you dem long to?*" means, "Whom do you belong to?" "*Oo dem got any peachy?*" means, "Have you got any peaches?" I could scarcely understand them when I first went among them, so broken was their speech; and I am persuaded that I could not have been dropped anywhere on the globe, where I could reap less, in the way of knowledge, from my immediate associates, than on this plantation.[12]

Douglass is not particularly celebratory of African languages or of African American intellectual life on the plantation, but he does demonstrate an analytical understanding of some of its linguistic influence, and by presenting himself as both foreigner and translator he makes an argument that language is not racially delimited. These founding moments of literacy point us toward a wider linguistic world, which, as Foster suggests, can be a foundation for rethinking the parameters of early African American literature based on recognition of multilingual literacies within communities of enslaved people.[13]

Also in *My Bondage and My Freedom*, Douglass writes that after the death of his mother Harriet Bailey, he learned that not only was she literate but "that she was the *only* one of all the slaves and colored people in Tuckahoe who enjoyed that advantage."[14] Furthermore, Douglass was likely aware of the steadily growing free African American community in Maryland, which, as historian Barbara J. Fields details, by 1850 had literacy rates exceeding 50 percent and who "imparted to the slaves—often in secret and at grave risk to themselves—what learning they possessed."[15] It is odd that the earlier *Narrative*, which documents its author's literacy in such detail, makes no mention of his early exposure to African languages, his mother's ability to read, or wider African American literacy. Although, according to his 1845 *Narrative*, he "never saw" his mother "to know her as such, more than four or five times in my life," a decade later, by the time of *My Bondage and My Freedom*, his mother's visage comes into clearer focus: he recalls her features well enough to notice a striking resemblance in a picture of Egyptian king Ramses he finds in James Cowles Pritchard's *The Natural History of Man* (1843).[16]

Douglass biographer William S. McFeely posits his own theory of Harriet Bailey's genealogy, speculating that her surname "Bailey," which has no clear origins among whites in Talbot County, Maryland, could be a variant of "Belali," a common name among West African Muslims and one not unknown in the antebellum United States.[17] In Islamic history, Bilal al-Habashi (Bilal the Abyssinian) is an enslaved Ethiopian who is emancipated due to his adoption of Islam and becomes the first muezzin. He is a crucial figure in antislavery and anti-racist interpretations of Islam. McFeely's conjecture, though unsubstantiated, further enables readers to frame Douglass within African American traditions of literature and literacy that have Arabic and Islamic linguistic roots that predate the Middle Passage of transatlantic slave ships. There is some compelling speculation, for example, that poet Phillis Wheatley may have been literate in Arabic, a possibility which provides new ways of reading her work and the tradition of which it is a cornerstone.[18]

Here I want to propose something similar to what Ala Alryyes has argued in the introduction to his translation of the autobiography of Omar ibn Said, a West African man enslaved in North Carolina. Omar ibn Said incorporates the qur'anic chapter *al-Mulk* in his 1831 narrative, arguing that God is the only owner (*mulk* comes *malaka*, which means "own" and "have dominion"), which is an effective anti-slavery argument. It is also, Alryyes asserts, very similar to the argument that David Walker makes in his 1829 *Appeal in Four Articles; Together with a Preamble, to the Coloured Citizens of the World*, which insists that "God Almighty is the sole proprietor or master of the WHOLE human family."[19] There are multiple possible explanations for this confluence—perhaps Omar ibn Said was familiar with Walker's *Appeal* (although he could not read English) and selected this particular verse on that basis. Alternately, Alryyes asks, "What if a particular Muslim argument against slavery, which finds its expression in *Surat al-Mulk*, has spread orally and was incorporated by Walker in his *Appeal*?" which is conceivable given Walker's acquaintance with prominent Muslim writer Abdul Rahman.[20] Alryyes's immediate question begs a larger one: Are there Islamic allusions within African American literature that remain unexplored as a result of the failures of modern readers to recognize them?

Alryyes notes that Omar ibn Said explains his literacy as both individual and collective; his literacy is intertwined with his faith. He contrasts this with Douglass's *Narrative* which frames literacy as "a gift of his mistress," Sophia Auld, who began to teach Douglass to read.[21] However, in *My Bondage and My Freedom*, Douglass describes being roused to literacy by hearing her read the Bible aloud, which suggests an experience similar to Omar's.[22] Its reference to the Bible hints at a context and community that was not visible ten years earlier, and renders Auld's kind instruction as something other than an individualized gesture native to the South. *My Bondage and My Freedom* presents a less individualistic and more complicated genealogy of Douglass's education. Its attention to African languages, his mother's literateness, and his own tutoring contribute to a narrative that demonstrates itself to be cognizant of literacy outside of the white/Christian/European/American world.

Such a shift would, I believe, be consistent with Douglass's increasing transnational engagements. In the decade between the publications of *Narrative* and *My Bondage and My Freedom*, 1845 to 1855, Douglass spent two years in exile in England, Scotland, and Ireland, and otherwise developed an analysis of slavery as part of a global system of economic exploitation that was no longer geographically bound. In his July 5, 1852, oration "What to the Slave is the Fourth of July?" he explains:

> The arm of commerce has borne away the gates of the strong city. Intelligence is penetrating the darkest corners of the globe. It makes its pathway over and under the sea, as well as on the earth. Wind, steam, and lightning are its chartered agents. Oceans no longer divide, but link nations together. From Boston to London is now a holiday excursion. Space is comparatively annihilated.[23]

Douglass's cosmopolitan theorization is consistent with Karl Marx's *Grundrisse*, written a few years later in the late 1850s (though not published until the late 1930s) in similar language that describes capital accumulation as the "annihilation of space by time."[24] This expanding appreciation of globalization is consistent with Douglass's engagement with Islam, Africa, and the Arab world, and as such provides a context for thinking about a writer like Said as integral to the literary tradition rather than as an exception to it.

These engagements shaped how Douglass saw his family, himself, and his community. More than thirty years later in 1887, after Douglass traveled to Egypt, he told the *Washington Post* that "I must say I returned from my trip with the conviction that the negro [sic] could not be connected with these people. The Egyptians proper are a people by themselves. They are not Caucasians, but they are not negroes [sic]."[25] Yet he continued to publicly reflect on the connection. In the second edition of his third autobiography, *Life and Times of Frederick Douglass* (1892), he describes seeing "a small army of Arabs" loading the steamship in Port Said: "As I looked at them and listened to their fun and frolic while bearing their heavy burdens, I said to myself: 'You fellows are, at least in your disposition, half brothers to the negro [sic].'"[26] This moment of identification is reinforced by an encounter with a white American family at the Giza pyramids who initially presumes Douglass to be "an Arab," until being corrected by their own recognition of Douglass's celebrity.[27] Douglass embraced his misidentification as an Arab as part of "a day to be remembered," his visit to the Great Pyramids.[28] Despite his public declarations of ambivalence, in his diary, he privately expressed a fondness for Islam:

> I do not know of what color and features the ancient Egyptians were, but the great mass of the people I have yet seen would in America be classed with Mulattoes

and Negroes. . . . I can easily see why the Mohomitan [sic] religion commends itself to these people, for it does not make color the criterion of fellowship, as some of our so called Christian Nations do? All colors are welcomed to the faith of the Prophet.²⁹

This worldly sensibility was characteristic of Douglass's late career, when he received a series of high-profile political appointments including, in 1889, as US consul at Port-au-Prince, Haiti. Although the federal government, which once considered him a criminal, chose Douglass to represent US interests abroad, it soon regretted the decision. Douglass was considered overly sympathetic to Haiti and an impediment to US efforts to establish a naval base at Môle Saint-Nicolas. Secretary of State James G. Blaine effectively demoted Douglass by appointing a naval officer to handle the negotiations, which ultimately failed as Haiti valiantly refused to cede any of its hard-earned territorial sovereignty.³⁰ (A few years later, the US navy established a base directly across the sea from Môle Saint-Nicolas at Guantanamo Bay, Cuba, whose US occupation remains ongoing.) A reconsideration of Douglass—from his youthful reading of Everett's play to his late accounts of his time in Egypt—might reframe those traditions of which he has become a representative figure, and allows for new possibilities of reading Douglass's increasing awareness of his own subjectivity shaped by African languages, Arab ancestry, and forces of globalization.

Through these years, Douglass develops a critical perspective on globalization, and over time develops a pointed appreciation of his own relationship to a network of transnational processes that demand our continued attention. Douglass's ambivalence about his identity as an American is coupled with his identification with Egyptians and appreciation for Islam. My analysis of Douglass, in the context of a study of Said, is intended to open up space for a consideration of Said's autobiographies not as eccentric idiosyncrasies, but rather as texts that, as Safet Dabovic argues, "attempted to open new conceptual spaces for thinking about black transnationality in the Americas."³¹ Jason Frydman similarly proposes rethinking the African Diasporic tradition in a manner "that displaces Protestant spiritual autobiography and the Spanish picaresque novel as privileged origin, while asserting greater centrality to the Caribbean basin and the Senegambia region as formal and philosophical engines of the African diasporic literary tradition."³² While Said was not Senegambian, he can usefully be situated as a product of what Ousmane Oumar Kane terms "West African cosmopolitanism," which provides new ways for thinking historically about the origins of African American writing.³³ Such expanded definitions of African American narrative, which includes African and Muslim worlds, enable readers to rethink the contours of national identifications in African American literature and culture.

Nicholas Said and the Black Literary Subject

"A Native of Bornoo" consciously stands at the margins of several prominent literary genres. It is a postbellum slave narrative, written in the United States by a person of African descent who was never enslaved in the United States. In the opening paragraph,

Said begins with a gesture that demonstrates him to be familiar and adept with the established conventions of African American narrative. He opens with the kind of apologia that is pro forma of the autobiographical tradition: "Reader, you must excuse me for the mistakes." However, within this very first sentence, he pivots by explaining that English is not his "mother tongue" and that he never studied it in school. In the next sentence he explains, "The only way I learned what little of the [English] language I know was through French books."[34] In this opening paragraph, Said decenters the English language in ways that implicitly challenge Garrison's assertion regarding English in the preface to Douglass's *Narrative*. Said clearly asserts his multilingual heritage as a way to account for any perceived deficiencies in his account. His humblebrag skillfully engages West African traditions of life writing that foreground educational narratives, which is compatible with those versions of nineteenth-century African American literary history that foreground the trope of literacy.[35]

Said follows the sentence about reading French with the standard opening phrase of American autobiography, "I was born," which is so famously and profoundly inscribed by Douglass at the start of his *Narrative*.[36] And in this sentence, after noting his fluency in French, he reports on the provincialism of Western readers: "I was born in the kingdom of Bornoo, in Soodan, in the problematic central part of Africa, so imperfectly known to the civilized nations of Europe and America."[37] Said uses this conventional moment to criticize European ignorance which contrasts with how Douglass uses this device to reflect on his own ignorance and that of other enslaved people regarding their birthday, parentage, and other details of ancestry. Then, instead of immediately providing the autobiography that his invocation of "I was born" suggests, Said instead takes a deep dive into the political and military history of Borno, describing his parents' lineage before reasserting his birth two pages later: "I was born in Kooka, a few years after the Waday war of 1831."[38] His repetition of the singular "I was born" posits a multivalent personal genealogy of a subject whose multiple births defy the narrative convention of autobiography. Then, after accounting for his siblings, he returns to the question of literacy, noting that his eleven brothers were taught both Arabic and Turkish. Said himself received formal instruction in Arabic and Kanuri, his mother tongue. After three years, he passed an exam in Kanuri, and after another year and a half he graduated in Arabic, which, he previously noted, "is very much in use among the higher class of people, as the Latin is used by the Catholic priests."[39] Said's literacy, however, does not protect him or otherwise provide a path to freedom as popular readings of writers like Douglass suggest.

Said's experiences are characterized by relative privilege—aristocratic lineage, formal education, proximity to wealth and power, and international mobility. Add to this a comparatively benign description of his experiences of the physical depredations of slavery which for American readers provides an implicit contrast to chattel slavery in the United States. This kind of comparison might be explained by reading the narrative as a postbellum autobiography, one in which the shifting meaning and signification of slavery and freedom are shaped by its particular engagements with Islam. By the time Said published "A Native of Bornoo," the abolitionist imperative that saturates so much antebellum African American writing was being transformed in ways that necessarily change the kinds of literature that gets written and the ways it is read.

A number of scholars have, for good reason, noted the relative absence of Said's "religious beliefs" from his autobiography.[40] However, though subtle in certain respects, Said's ongoing literary engagements with Islam comprise several of the most significant moments in the narrative, which he wrote a decade after his deeply ambivalent supposed conversion to Christianity. If we read "A Native of Bornoo" as a slave narrative, even though its atypical narrator is born free (and here we can still see parallels to Douglass who, though he was enslaved upon his birth, consciously details his descent into the hell of slavery), the moment of his capture marks his passage into slavery. This scene begins with him organizing a group of forty friends to take an excursion into the woods during Ramadan. There, they cook a feast of chicken, eggs, and fruit, while engaging in boisterous shenanigans, which results in the capture of eighteen boys from their party. Their capture and enslavement during the holy month of Ramadan could hardly be interpreted as coincidental as Said not only ignores his mother's warnings, as he frequently did, but also violates Islam and more gravely encourages others to do so. Their captors, also violators of Islamic law, got drunk and high, which some of Said's companions exploit in order to escape: "We succeeded in breaking the chains, and four of the oldest boys took their captors' arms, cut their throats, jumped on their horses, and succeeded in making their escape."[41] For his part, Said did not successfully escape. He was recaptured and beaten.

After his capture, Said explains, "My lot was that of an Arab slave, for I was bought by a man named Abd-el-Kader, a merchant of Tripoli and Fezzan. He was not an Arabian, however, but a brown-skinned man, and undoubtedly had African blood in his veins."[42] In setting up this difference by seeming to upend the racial dynamics of slavery, Said simultaneously affirms the fundamental way the institution of slavery creates racial categories whereby one can be an "Arab slave" when neither the enslaver nor the enslaved is "Arabian." He also marks his position as an outsider to the racial institution of US chattel slavery.

In Tripoli, Said is sold to Hadji Daoud, whom he then accompanies to Mecca. Here Said expresses his profound regret that "I had not come of my own free will and for the express purpose of a pilgrimage, and therefore was not permitted to go with Daoud to the grave of the Prophet, and was obliged to content myself without the title of Hadji, which is one much respected among the Mohammedans."[43] For Said, his enslavement is not marked solely by the physical brutality which he experiences after his capture and which has justly come to define accounts of slavery in the United States. This moment reveals that, for Said, manumission from slavery must include the freedom to make the Hajj in accordance with Islamic law. The prohibition against Said making religious pilgrimage reveals a profound injustice that, despite appearances otherwise, exposes the limits of his mobility. Notwithstanding his cosmopolitan itinerary, this refusal of the title of "Hadji" must be understood as marking his experience of the violence of slavery and the denial of his freedom.

"A Native of Bornoo" is ostensibly the autobiography of a convert from Islam to Christianity, whose religion may be marked by its publication under the name Nicholas Said (not his birth name "Mohammed-Ali-Ben-Said"). Said the author is always already nominally Christian even if Said the subject is a Muslim for most of the course of the narrative. When previously recounting the history of Borno and its heroic leader, Mohammed al-Kanemi (d. 1837), Said unconditionally writes of "Allah, who protects the innocent and punishes the guilty, was smiling over him."[44] This invocation, which references the divine protections in the present tense, does not sound like the commentary of a former Muslim. After his denial at Mecca, Said provides one of his text's most direct articulations of religious identity:

> While in this service [as an enslaved valet to Prince Nicholas of Russia], I was baptized in St. Petersburg, November 12, 1855, into the Greek Church, my name being changed from Mohammed-Ali-Ben-Said to Nicholas Said. Prince Nicholas was my godfather. I shall always feel grateful, so long as I live, for Prince Nicholas's kindness to me; but I cannot help thinking that the way I was baptized was not right, for I think that I ought to have known perfectly well the nature of the thing beforehand.[45]

Said's supposed conversion to Christianity, occurring after his attempted pilgrimage, is described with profound ambivalence. Said softens his critique of the hoodwink baptism with articulations of gratitude for the well-meaning kindness of his namesake. In what becomes a trademark device, he tempers his religious commentary and borderline heresy in a way that both eases its publication and maintains the integrity of his opinions. From the vantage point of the conventions of the slave narrative genre, in which Christian conversion was a common trope, Said skillfully handles the subject of Christianity with delicacy. In being duped into conversion, a significant denial of agency to a person whose assertions of autonomy are so thoroughgoing, he remains unwilling to embrace Christianity if it requires, or is otherwise built upon, his ignorance.

Beyond religion and the name change, many of Said's experiences—including racial harassment at the hands of white children in Dresden—are familiar tropes within African American literature, including Ayyub ibn Suleiman Diallo's account of having dirt thrown at him while at prayer in Maryland.[46] His annotated autobiographical account of his African ancestry resembles Olaudah Equiano's *Interesting Narrative* and his travels in Europe, including his observations of the Crimean War, place him in dialogue with Mary Seacole's *Wonderful Adventures*. Ultimately, an unrepaid loan to his white employer forces Said to remain in North America unwillingly, not unlike the experience of an earlier native of Borno, James Albert Ukawsaw Gronniosaw.[47] This is the exact moment where "A Native of Bornoo" ends. Said does not incorporate the story of his Civil War service into his autobiography. His fate in this narrative is the result of his failure to fast during Ramadan and being blocked from his pilgrimage, two of the pillars of Islam. His Civil War service cannot be integrated or assimilated for the purpose of redemption because he rejects the possibility of such a redemption. It is his continued economic vulnerability to white patrons that provides the most appropriate ending to "A Native of Bornoo."

Nicholas Said and the Perils of American Exceptionalism

Grounded in an expansive and inclusive African American literary tradition in the ways I have outlined, readers should resist any facile presumptions about what that literary identity meant to Said. While justly celebrated, Said's history in the 55th Massachusetts Regiment remains "imperfectly known" even while it provides the foundational backstory for the publication of "A Native of Bornoo." How can readers assess the tension within a narrative whose production is entirely American, but which resists those claims in other, arguably more significant, ways? Ultimately Said's omissions allow space for others to tell the story of his military career through official government records and various forms of interpretation and speculation (including my own). Readers need to explore the pronounced lacuna and national ambivalence that shape his autobiographies.

Among the ways that Said's narrative is American is his framing of his story and through a series of direct allusions to the United States that are far more academic than autobiographical. Mohammed al-Kanemi is described as "the Washington of Bornoo, ... the man who undertook to liberate his country and restore her former prestige."[48] The intent of this comparison is clear. Not only is Borno a "civilized" nation, but moreover its history compares favorably to that of the United States. Said's comparison may be more subtle than it appears. Al-Kanemi, like Washington, refused an offer of the crown. Al-Kanemi's desire to serve the people was never self-interested or for the purpose of acquiring a title. His initial unwillingness is considered noble: "Like all great men, he refused the sceptre."[49] When al-Kanemi does become potentate, he does so on terms described as almost accidental as he "now found himself the absolute ruler of Bornoo, nor had that kingdom ever any greater ruler."[50] His political success stands in contrast to his personal aspirations.

Said's uses for the United States remain precise and strategic. During his European travels and hobnobbing with the wealthy and powerful, Said experiences an epiphany:

> About this time I began to think of the condition of Africa, my native country, how European encroachments might be stopped, and her nationalities united. I thought how powerful the United States has become since 1776, and I wondered if I were capable of persuading the kings of Soodan to send several hundred boys to learn the arts and sciences existing in civilized countries.[51]

In this remarkable passage, Said expresses his opposition to European imperialism and his admiration for the United States. He would like for the youth of his nation to be educated "in civilized countries" like the United States so that they can become better "warriors" with the resources to "contend against superior weapons and tactics" of colonial forces.[52] Here the United States is not desirable as a permanent destination, but rather as a source of technical assistance which he would like to use for military purposes. For Said, military service, including his own record in the 55th Massachusetts, is more a part of an anti-imperialist training initiative than an American nationalist enterprise.

While Said was immersed in an African American community during his service, his experiences as an African-born Muslim were unusual but not unique. At least one other member of the 55th Massachusetts lists Africa as his birthplace, and there were other African-born soldiers fighting on behalf of the Union during the Civil War, which points to the presence of Africans and Muslims in these well-educated African

American communities.⁵³ The distinguished roster of fellow volunteers includes Joshua Dunbar (father of poet Paul Laurence Dunbar) and James Monroe Trotter (father of journalist and activist William Monroe Trotter), among others. Said's stories of Africa and Islam became part of the culture of African Americans fighting both for freedom from slavery and against discrimination in the military.

After rising to the rank of sergeant, Said requested a demotion to corporal so that he could serve as a hospital medic. He changed his rank on September 1, 1864, shortly after and perhaps in response to the June 15, 1864, Army Appropriations Act, which publicly acknowledged the inferior medical treatment received by African American troops.⁵⁴ Said's decision to serve in a hospital unit represents a form of political protest and a rejection of military conventions of advancement and promotion at a time when there were ongoing protests by soldiers over a range of issues, most prominently unequal pay. As Christian G. Samito points out, "Not only did the unequal pay issue foster protest in itself, but it generated skepticism among black soldiers that they would receive justice on other issues. The ensuing level of distrust between black soldiers and white officers devastated morale and made outbreaks more prevalent even once the pay issue was resolved."⁵⁵ Military clampdown on African American protests led to the June 18, 1864, execution of Wallace Baker, a member of the 55th Massachusetts who served with Said in Company I, for refusing the orders of and fighting with a white commanding officer.⁵⁶ But the soldiers in the 55th Massachusetts were undeterred in their protests as seventy-four members of Company D directly appealed to President Lincoln, less than a month later, on July 16, 1864.⁵⁷ Said continued his activism after his demotion and was listed as an officer (specifically "Ex-Sergt.") for an October 10, 1964, celebration that took place when African American soldiers finally received their back pay.⁵⁸ The fact, if not the details, of Said's military service seemingly fits with the long-standing belief that military service can serve as a pathway to full citizenship for African American communities.⁵⁹

The broader claims regarding the Americanness of Islam remain important and compelling. In June 2009, newly elected US president Barack Obama visited Egypt to deliver a major address on the relationship of the United States to Muslim people around the world. Before addressing pressing matters of foreign policy, he deconstructed the opposition of the United States and Islam, the shibboleth that was used against him by Islamophobic opponents. After opening with "a greeting of peace from Muslim communities in my country," Obama makes it clear that "America and Islam are not exclusive" and that "Islam has always been a part of America's story," providing a remarkable series of examples from the Treaty of Tripoli in 1796 to boxer Muhammad Ali representing the nation by lighting the Olympic torch at the 1996 Atlanta games.⁶⁰ Obama's assertions that neither Islam nor Muslims are foreign to the United States remain widely misunderstood within popular political discourse at a time when Muslims (and people perceived to be Muslim) are increasingly the victims of travel prohibitions, hate crimes, incarceration, and other forms of US state violence. Such assertions serve a crucial polemical purpose in a time of grave crisis; however, it is important to reflect critically on the implications of such claims, and in the case of Said, as with any individual subject, to determine how the subject saw himself.

Said would fit nicely into Obama's narrative even if, as Hussein Rashid and Precious Rasheeda Muhammad argue, his 1873 *Autobiography* "does not deliver that 'Muslim hero' fiction."[61] The appeal of his biography is extraordinary, and his American story undermines a great deal of pernicious popular, albeit thoroughly debunked, rhetoric regarding the permanent foreignness of Muslims.[62] While the long-standing history of Islam and Muslims in the United States is widely acknowledged in many venues thanks to the work of historians such as Edward Curtis IV, Sylviane Diouf, Kambiz GhaneaBassiri, Michael Gomez, Denise Spellberg, and many others cited here, I would like to make a corollary point about the ways that Said reveals how Islam is central to African American literature. The tension between a kind of inclusive United States, which is how his narrative is often deployed, and a possibly more radical rejection of Americanness, which we can see in his military demotion, his decision to self-publish after appearing in the *Atlantic*, and his apparent decision not to write about his experience in the United States, might be seen to approximate a sort of hybridized cosmopolitanism. However, what happens if we find ways to read Said less as an invitation to a more inclusive definition of what it means to be American (and American literature) than as someone whose narrative recommits itself to inscribing an African Muslim historical identity in the wake of the Civil War by affirming the impossibility of his inclusion and assimilation in the United States, a union whose preservation he defended militarily and where he remained until his death several decades later?[63]

While the basis for the circulation of Said's autobiography is his service in the Civil War, his writings themselves seem to implicitly reject this part of his identity opting to reinscribe Africa and Islam in substantial ways. The question I am left with is how to reconcile the popular appeal of Said's Americanness—the part of his story that facilitated the publication of "A Native of Bornoo"—and the actual subject of the autobiographical text which has little to say about his Civil War service. It is reasonable to read Said's circumspection regarding the Civil War as strategic given the potential risks in disclosing his military service, especially in Memphis in the early 1870s; however, his autobiographies effectively negotiate a range of social constraints so that we can locate multiple layers of narrative agency in this elision without ignoring his profound vulnerability. In this conjunction, it is tempting to claim Said's Americanness via his military service; however, I would like to argue that this represents a misreading of his actual autobiography which much more pointedly uses an American narrative form to reject American exceptionalism and to create space to reinscribe African history—particularly the modern history of the Borno Empire—and his Islamic identity. A careful reading of those inscriptions creates new ways for reading American literary history, through Said's contribution to the *Atlantic Monthly*, as a richly contested site of engagement with new ways of appreciating the writings of a figure like Frederick Douglass and the tradition he represents, rather than the unified "story of a nation" that Goodman evokes.

4

An Islamic Surface Reading of African Muslim Slave Narratives

Zeinab Mcheimech

In the early to mid-nineteenth century, Ralph Waldo Emerson, a key figure of the American Transcendentalist movement, turned his gaze toward the East, perusing Islam along the way. In developing his Transcendentalist thought, Emerson took inspiration from Islamic philosophy and history, reading translations of Ibn-Ḥauqal's *The Oriental Geography of Ebn Haukal: An Arabian Traveller of the Tenth Century* (حوقل ابن تصنيف ممالك و مسالك كتاب) and Fakir Jany Muhammad Asaad's *Practical Philosophy of the Muhammadan People*.[1] However, Emerson's interest in Islam remained an interest in a *distant* Islam—a mystical Islam of the East. Absent from his gaze was the local Islam being practiced in the United States by enslaved African Muslims, who played a small but intriguing part in nineteenth-century American culture. While Emerson turned his gaze eastward, a few enslaved African Muslims in the United States were composing their own manuscripts on Islam.[2] Among the most enigmatic records left behind is a diary penned by Bilali Muhammad, which has come to be known as the *Ben Ali Diary*, and a letter written by ʿUmar ibn Sayyid in 1819 addressed to Major John Owen.[3] In this chapter, I emphasize the major difference in how these writers and Emerson approach Islam.[4] Instead of attending to the ways Islam engenders mystical understandings and earthly transcendence (Emerson's focus), ʿUmar and Bilali emphasize the centrality of the ritual practices of daily life, particularly prayer, in Islam. Even the nineteenth-century scholar and theologian Tayler Lewis recognized the significance of prayer for Muslims, commenting that "Mohammedanism is eminently a religion of prayer."[5] Because the interweaving of prayer with daily life is central to understanding Islam, I suggest that the focus on daily, integrated *rituals* calls for interpretative practices that differ from the sublime mysticism and universalist ethos undergirding Transcendentalist hermeneutics and the hermeneutics of suspicion—the latter a common approach to literary analysis adopted by literary critics. A divergent interpretive approach, then, will not search for esoteric, mysterious, or subversive meanings buried in the moments of illegibility in Bilali's and ʿUmar's manuscripts. Instead, Bilali's document, a manual on ritual prayer, and ʿUmar's document, a supplication, are plentiful of meaning on the surface and not an obscure or exotic mystery to be plumbed.

Although this chapter focuses on 'Umar's and Bilali's manuscripts, I bring up Emerson because he is representative of a practice of interpreting Islam from a Western perspective during the nineteenth century. As such, my treatment of Emerson in this chapter will be superficial precisely because he received Islam *superficially* and missed the Islam being practiced in the United States. In contrast to the Emersonian style of distancing and exoticization, and to more accurately define the challenges of reading these African Arabic manuscripts, I first retrieve a model for an Islamic reading practice from one of the foundational moments in Islam: Prophet Muhammad's first divine revelation of the Qur'ān. I contend that this scene, in which the Prophet is commanded by the angel Gabriel to read the illegible, is the starting point for developing an Islamic reading practice of literature at the present moment in academia. In turning to one, out of several, Islamic traditions of textual analysis, I also find an *exoteric* (as opposed to an esoteric) model of Islamic hermeneutics, known as *zāhir* (literal meanings) and *sharh* (gloss). In contrast to *tā'wil*,[6] or spiritual hermeneutics, which aims to find the esoteric or inner meaning (*bātin*) of a sacred text, the Zāhirite school of interpretation recognizes meaning at the surface of a text. This reading model takes the surface as a significant source of meaning; in so doing, this mode of interpretation makes available a set of literary-historical readings that restore to us the meanings that would have been simultaneously obvious and spiritually essential to Muslim writers and readers such as 'Umar and Bilali.

Intriguingly, this twelfth-century school of interpretation, Zāhirism, finds echoes in recent trends in Anglo-American literary studies. Indeed, scholars like Rita Felski, Heather Love, Sharon Marcus, and Stephen Best have called for alternative approaches to literary criticism that extend beyond a hermeneutics of suspicion, which produces readings committed to unearthing the underlying or repressed meaning of a text.[7] According to the hermeneutics of suspicion, the incomprehension and illegibility that characterize 'Umar's and Bilali's Islamic documents are axiomatically mysterious and opaque and demand uncovering; in this sense, the hermeneutics of suspicion can lead too easily to the rehearsal of Orientalist tropes. However, there is a difference between the value assigned to incomprehension and illegibility in an Orientalist reading that exoticizes illegibility, and the experience of incomprehension and illegibility that characterizes Prophet Muhammad's initial experience of Qur'ānic revelation. I deploy what Marcus and Best call surface reading, where the surface denotes "what is evident, perceptible, apprehensible in texts; what is neither hidden nor hiding."[8] Bringing together insights from recent developments in Anglo-American literary criticism and compatible elements from Islam, I build a reading practice that expands the field of American literary criticism and nuances readings of Islam in America. This kind of exoteric, surface reading not only unsettles nineteenth-century Orientalist assumptions about Islam evident in readers such as Emerson but also, and more particularly, offers new ways to accurately explain and understand the role of incomprehension and illegibility in the texts written by the enslaved African Muslims practicing Islam in the United States.

Reading for the zāhir or literal is one possibility among several Islamic reading practices developed by Muslims (*tafsir, ta'wiil, tafhīm*).[9] Nonetheless, it is significant that I draw on the zāhirī tradition for two reasons: (1) The treatment and experiences of Muslims in the United States, which are not hidden nor unknown, call for critics to engage with Islam at the surface. In other words, rather than rely on the hermeneutics of suspicion to read Islam, I'm calling for a reading strategy that does not treat Islam as something that requires unearthing or excavating. (2) In addition, as I mentioned earlier, literary critics like Heather Love, Rita Felski, Sharon Marcus, and Stephen Best, among others, have called for new reading practices, and have suggested surface reading or flat reading as an alternative to the hermeneutics of suspicion. Because an Islamic interpretive practice already exists that espouses some of the same concerns as surface reading, this chapter foregrounds this particular reading tradition in Islam. My aim is to offer a reading strategy that will extend and expand our understanding of Islam in the United States. Ultimately, my hope is that literary critics and general readers would approach Islam, not with suspicion or a desire to uncover some hidden meaning but with the assumption that what is at the surface is just as meaningful.

Islam and Surface Reading

Prophet Muhammad's first Qur'ānic revelation (*al-wahy*) provides an epistemological frame that circumvents the logical or rational without losing access to meaning, and offers a powerful analytical resource for interpreting the idiosyncratic mode of writing of Bilali's *Diary* and 'Umar's 1819 letter. The texts of Bilali and 'Umar initially appear incomprehensible due to the distorted condition of the manuscripts, especially Bilali's, which renders aspects of it indecipherable or unreadable. This illegible condition gives rise to problems of incomprehensibility, a failure of cognition.

To advance an approach for interpreting incomprehensibility via a reading practice inspired by Islam, I turn to the first revelation received by Prophet Muhammad. While meditating in a cave in Mount Hira near Mecca, Prophet Muhammad received his first revelation in the form of a book, from which he was asked to "read" (اقْرَأْ). According to Abu Muhammad ibn Hisham, Prophet Muhammad's biographer, the Prophet is recorded as saying: "Whilst I was asleep, with a coverlet of silk brocade whereon was some writing, the angel Gabriel appeared to me and said, 'Read!' I said, 'I do not read.'"[10] The injunction, here, is to read the unreadable. In this decisive moment of Islam's beginnings, the unfamiliarity of the writing and the strangeness of the voice so unsettled the Prophet that he fled the cave and returned to his wife Khadija bint Khuwaylid. Khadija, in turn, interpreted the Prophet's experience with the unreadable as a sign of his prophecy. As the literary critic Abdelkebir Khatibi puts it, Khadija "deciphered certain signs of prophecy . . . on that of her husband. She read, in a way, on the imaginary body of Islam where, illegible to Mohammad himself, the prophetic message becomes apprehensible by the feminine body."[11] Khatibi's reading elevates the place of the female reader in the Islamic tradition, even when this reader has gone unnoticed by some scholars. Indeed, Khadija's reading dramatizes the Islamic reader par excellence: she looks for signs of revelation on the surface of her husband's body, which would include his countenance and demeanor in his response to the unreadable. Significantly, while Khadija makes sense of the incomprehensible, she does not make it legible. That is, Khadija cannot and does not translate the content of this revelatory moment, but still finds value in Muhammad's encounter with the incomprehensible. In her interpretation, then, she finds profound significance—signs of prophecy—in that which cannot be read. Prophet Muhammad's experience of Qur'ānic revelation, which is revealed as an unknown and temporarily unreadable book, offers a model of interpretation that simultaneously maintains a grip on the value of incomprehensibility and that also recognizes the essential role of the reader. Notably, Prophet Muhammad must first return home to Khadija to begin understanding his experience of divine revelation.

Ultimately, Prophet Muhammad's experience offers an interpretive approach in which revelation or divine knowledge occurs outside intelligible language; in fact, this moment suggests that illegibility and unreadability are necessary features of a text that produces knowledge for and with its readers. In this context, the illegible text enables a state of *hayrah* (الحيرة) in the reader, a term denoting puzzlement or perplexity, which engenders humility and initiates learning. This humbled opening to the unknown, underscored in many religious traditions' understanding of mystical experiences, including Judaism, Christianity, and Buddhism, captures the epistemic value of the incomprehensible and unknowable through a scene of reading.[12] Indeed, Prophet Muhammad's state of *hayrah* is prompted by the imperative to read, *iqra*. In this tradition and particularly through its first revelation, meaning can be communicated without the receiver fully comprehending it. Simply put, incomprehension can be meaningful. I take incomprehension, then, as neither simply a side effect of confusion that requires resolution nor merely a symptom of the text's resistance to the reader. Rather, incomprehension serves as a confession of sacred knowledge that is consonant with faith in Islam.

Nonetheless, one person's surface reading is another person's suspicious depth model reading. The difference is the readers' respective reading competencies. Departing from deep or symptomatic readings, I analyze Bilali's and 'Umar's respective African Arabic manuscripts by first accounting for the surfaces of each document, which are suffused with Islamic signs. These manuscripts are difficult to read due to their unique orthography, which means some of the words do not correspond to standard Arabic; for example, in some instances Bilali substitutes the letter *lam* (ل) for *waw* (و), *tha* (ث) for *ta* (ت), and so on, whereas 'Umar confuses the *hamza* (ء) and *'ayn* (ع) and *seen* (س) with *sheen* (ش), among other letters. The quality of the manuscripts has also deteriorated over time.[13]

Another approach to grasping the illegible can be found in the very concept that both manuscripts meditate upon: revelation. More specifically, I examine Bilali's use of the concept of *katam* (concealment/preservation) and his rumination on revelation and 'Umar's Qur'ānic citation from *Surat Al-Baqarah* (*The Cow*), verses 285 and 286, which focus on the Prophet and revelation—that foregrounds the role of illegibility and incomprehensibility in the Islamic intellectual tradition. Drawing on Khatibi's observation that "as soon as there was writing [in Islam], there was the illegible,"[14] I would like to suggest that incomprehension can be regarded as the basis for knowledge and, in particular, as a basis for faith. While I use Bilali's and 'Umar's documents as case studies for a *zāhir* or surface reading, this reading is preserved for readers familiar with Islamic discourse and knowledge.

Emerson's Islam

Numerous critics, such as Suzan Jameel Fakahani and Jeffrey Einboden, have examined the role of Islamic sources and Islamic prophecy on Emerson's philosophical thinking, noting Emerson's use of Islamic expressions, sources, and histories in his work. Emerson was clearly influenced by Sufi mysticism, often citing the Persian poets, Muḥammad Shamsuddīn Ḥāfiẓ and Saadi Shirazi. Indeed, Einboden discovers an openness and appeal to Islamic sources in Emerson's early private writings, appeals that would inform Emerson's "poetic identity."[15] Even as early as 1819, Emerson cited the following Qur'ānic verse in his journal:
"In aforetime I created Jan from out of a scorching fire.
Alcoran."[16]
For Einboden, this citation encapsulates Emerson's synthesis of the spiritual and material, which would become a central principle of the American literary and philosophical movement Transcendentalism. The citation also illuminates the "persistent hiddenness that attends [Emerson's] Islamic interests."[17] Yet Emerson's interest in Islam was private or hidden in another sense: he was fascinated by the spiritual and intellectual ethos of Islam and overlooked or perhaps dismissed its ritualistic aspects, specifically the embodied prayer and Qur'ānic recitations that are central tenets of Islamic belief. In many ways, Emerson himself performed a symptomatic reading of Islam with the aim to unravel what he deemed as "the mysterious East" that inspired in him, as Einboden noted, "a spiritual rise from physical fire."[18] Ultimately, by orienting himself to the hidden and mystical in Islam, Emerson embraced an Islamic ethos distinct from that of the enslaved African Muslims in America.

Islam beyond the East

While Emerson was preoccupied with "the mysterious East," Bilali Muhammad and 'Umar ibn Sayyid were practicing Islam in the United States, an Islam derived from West African Muslim societies. Born in Timbo, Guinea, Bilali Muhammad was captured at the age of fourteen and taken to Nassau, Bahamas, to work as a slave at the Middle Caicos plantation. Ten years later, he was sold to Thomas Spalding of Sapelo Island, Georgia, where he became head driver on the Spalding plantation. Although the date of the manuscript is uncertain, we know that Bilali, shortly before his death in 1859, gifted his manuscript to the Southern writer and Presbyterian minister, Francis Goulding. Goulding shared the document, which became known as the *Ben Ali Diary*, with his friend, Joel Chandler Harris, a nineteenth-century writer famed for his notoriously offensive folksy dialect.[19] The manuscript found a readership beyond Harris once Francis Goulding's son, Benjamin Goulding, gave the manuscript to the Georgia State Library in 1931.[20] Soon after, the manuscript began to attract numerous scholars and critics who would begin the long process of decipherment, most notably the American linguist Joseph H. Greenberg.[21] The *Diary* has since confounded generations of scholars for numerous reasons. To begin with, the poor physical condition of the manuscript rendered aspects of it illegible, not least because the script was faint and, in sections, not even visible (see Figures 4.1 and 4.2).

Beyond its deteriorated state, Bilali's manuscript was generally unreadable due to its unique orthography. Arabic script is used to transliterate Fula words (Fulfulde, Pulaar), requiring the reader to be proficient in both Arabic and Fula. Finally, its nineteenth-century categorization as a diary is confusing because the manuscript does not record Bilali's life, as one might expect, but rather Islamic ritual,[22] with a focus on prayer.

While Bilali's manuscript found an audience in Harris, who could not have comprehended the document since he did not read nor understand Arabic, 'Umar's literacy was embraced by the American Colonization Society, a society founded in 1816 that encouraged manumitted slaves to emigrate to Liberia.[23] In 1807, 'Umar was captured from his hometown in Futa Toro (present-day Senegal). At the age of thirty-seven, 'Umar found himself in South Carolina degraded to the status of slave. In 1810, 'Umar eventually escaped from his second owner, and was bought by General James Owen of Fayetteville, North Carolina.[24] 'Umar's 1819 manuscript, his earliest extant manuscript, was housed at the Andover Theological Seminary in Newton, Massachusetts, until it was recently damaged. 'Umar's letter was initially given to John Louis Taylor, vice president of the American Colonization Society (ACS) in North

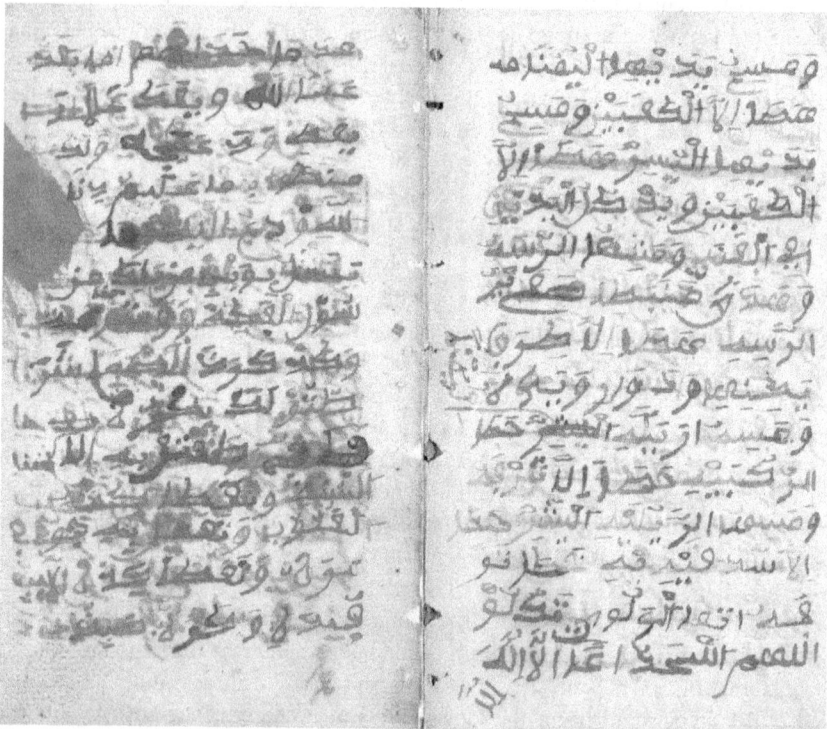

Figure 4.1 Bilali Muhammad, the *Ben Ali Diary* (MS 2807), 4–5. Courtesy of Hargrett Rare Book and Manuscript Library/University of Georgia Libraries.

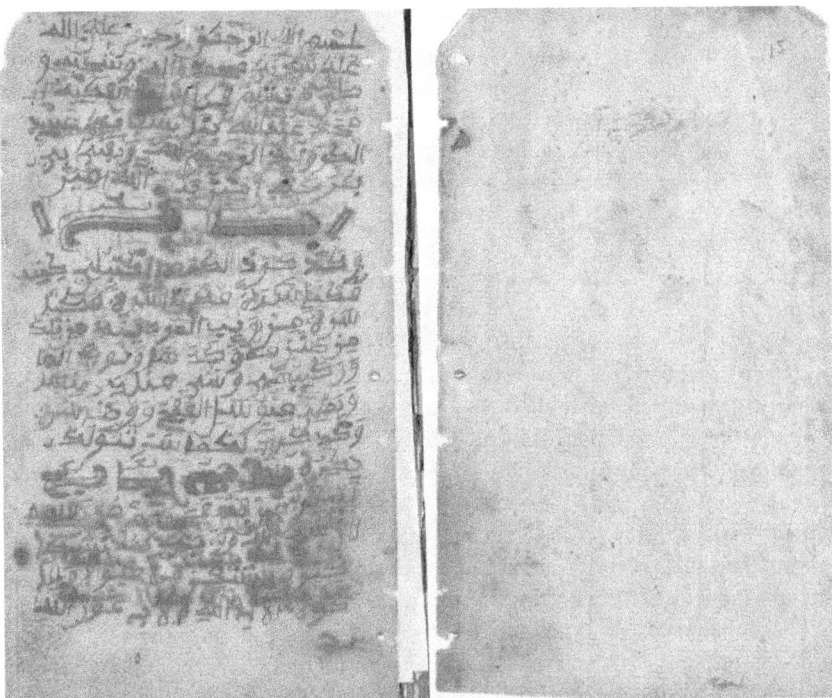

Figure 4.2 Bilali Muhammad, the *Ben Ali Diary* (MS 2807), 1. Courtesy of Hargrett Rare Book and Manuscript Library/University of Georgia Libraries.

Carolina, who then sent it to Francis Scott Key, author of "The Star-Spangled Banner." Yet those involved in the circulation of the manuscripts, such as members of the ACS, were invested in the potential to harness the slave's Arabic literacy to convert African Muslims to Christianity, as scholars like Ala. A. Alrryes and Allan D. Austin have pointed out,[25] rather than engage with the patently Islamic elements of the documents.

Reading Islam at the Surface

Reading Islam at the surface means moving beyond interpreting African Arabic manuscripts as narratives of resistance. Critics who have attempted to grapple with the illegibility of Bilali's manuscript have either dismissed the manuscript as gibberish (Nicholas N. Martinovich),[26] or attempted to decipher its illegibility (Joseph Greenberg), or suggested that the text is subversive because it evades meaning (Safet Dabovic and Ronald Judy).[27] Although these scholars have offered important and persuasive claims about the document's possible meanings, they all approach the unreadability of the *Diary* in a similar way: illegibility is either a challenge to be overcome by rendering a text legible or "a defiance of signification itself."[28]

Instead of changing the manuscript's condition or arguing that its indeterminacy is a form of resistance, I examine the quality of material illegibility on its own terms and the condition of incomprehension that arises from its complex writing, with the aim of determining the extent to which the text offers an approach to reading, through its invocation of figures of concealment, obfuscation, and revelation. One sense of incomprehension emerges from the different possible translations of Bilali's words, specifically one word (see Figure 4.2, the third word from the right in line one under the heading باب).

This specific word has been translated by Ronald Judy as story ("القصة") rather than concealment/*katam* ("الكتم"). Judy translates the line as follows, "Write me books that are a brief exposition" ("وقد قاد القصة اكتب لى كتب مختصرة").[29] I suggest, however, that this phrase could be read as "concealment has led me to write brief books" ("مختصرة كتب لي اكتب الكتم قاد وقد"). Tellingly, the term "*katam*" ("الكتم"), or "concealment," carries two ideas: writing under constraint and preservation. Essentially, Bilali makes his concealment manifest and thereby simultaneously locates and deflates the impulse to "unveil" or engage in close reading. Significantly, *katam* also refers to a plant used to make dye and ink, usually of a reddish-blackish tinge, which resembles the color of the ink Bilali uses. *Katam*, then, refers to the writing of the manuscript: a reference that points inwardly only to reveal the surface—the color of the ink—that is visible to the naked eye.

Bilali's injunction to write evokes the Qur'ānic call to recite or read. Just as importantly, this injunction signals the critical role of writing for the enslaved African Muslim. This writing in the language of the slave's religion (Arabic) signals more than just the enslaved subject's faith. As Judy observes, Bilali writes in an African Arabic script known as *al-khaṭṭ at-takrurī*.[30] But the etymology of *al-khaṭṭ*, as Judy points out, is also multifaceted and assumes a concern with space, property, and storytelling: "From the *khaṭṭ* derives *khuṭṭa*, which is a piece of real estate, a space mapped out according to a plan, a line of action. By this same lexicographic token, the *khaṭṭa* is a state of affairs, a story (*qiṣa*), and playfulness among the bedouin (*al-a'arāb*)."[31] This mode of writing, which maintains the sense of private property, and while seemingly irreducible in its playfulness, presents a strategy of preservation or *katam* via amorphous writing. Bilali commences his concern with writing by playing with the notion of brevity. While he acknowledges that his condition requires that he write "brief" books, he uses the space of the paper to repeat "brief" three times. The extension of brevity through repetition provides readers a temporary reprieve, a brief regulation of breath, from the strain required to read the rest of the manuscript.

Bilali's reflections on reading and writing, underscored in his Qur'ānic citations on books, invite readers to consider multiple approaches to reading. As Yusuf Progler shows, Bilali's concern with reading is evident in his citations of the Qur'ānic chapters "The Reality" (*al-haqq*) and "The Sundering" (*al-'inshiqāq*), where he amalgamates verses from these chapters to express that "for he who is given his book in his right hand [Q 69:19 and 84:7], he shall be reckoned with by an easy reckoning [Q 84:8]. And as for he who is given his book in his left hand [Q 69:25] and behind his back [Q 84:10], he shall be committed to the flaming fire [Q 84:12]."[32] Ostensibly a means of validating Bilali's adherence to Islam, the verses also point to the key role of positionality, for both reader and writer, in interpreting the text. That is, Bilali's concern with reading exceeds the book of deeds and the kind of reading that takes place in the hereafter or in a purely mystical realm. At the same time that the verses provide insight into Bilali's preoccupation with his own spiritual record, they shed light on his anticipation of the narrative's circulation since the subsequent movement of the manuscript between hands made its survival possible. This preoccupation with reading returns us to Islam's primal moment, specifically to the moment of unreadability and revelation.

The manuscript anticipates the convergence of knowledge and incomprehension with the arrival of dawn. After a section of vanishing lucidity, Bilali introduces the phrase: "until the emergence of dawn," or "الفجر مطلع حتى," a verse found in the Qur'ānic chapter al-Qadr, "The Power" or "The Night of Decree" (11:1; 13:9). This line, extracted from a chapter on the first revelation of the Qur'ān sent to Prophet Muhammad in the cave of Hira, gestures to the interplay between revelation and incomprehension, since a discussion of revelation is deeply connected to an encounter with illegibility as evident in Prophet Muhammad's first revelation. This interplay between revelation and illegibility in Bilali's manuscript is not merely thematic, however. Bilali follows this verse with five lines that appear indecipherable (see Figure 4.1). These lines seem to flow under the emergence of dawn without meaning or clear direction. This gesture draws our attention, albeit in an elliptical manner, to the significance of the incomprehensible. That is, in glossing the unreadable, these lines seem to operate as internal acknowledgments of indecipherability. Perhaps in this state of incomprehension, the reader prepares herself to receive knowledge or revelation. As it turns out, Bilali prepares his readers for prayer, the ultimate ritual of submission, as the indecipherable lines are followed by the Islamic call to prayer. Although discussions of incomprehensibility in the Islamic tradition revolve around the inimitability (i'jaz) of the Qur'ān (since the Qur'ān is considered to comprise God's speech) and the incomprehensible nature of God (since believers do not know the innerworkings of Allah), Bilali's manuscript enables us to consider illegibility in the context of prayer. The indecipherable lines lead readers to contemplate the everyday lived practice of daily ritual.

Indeed, the phrase "until the emergence of dawn" refers to the time of the first prayer. The reference to dawn or *fajr* also serves to intensify the reading process since, as Michael Sells contends, *fajr* also carries the idea "of a violent transformation."[33] As such, this revelatory verse gives the term "concealment" or *katam* a secondary meaning: transformation. This transformation happens beyond or outside language. The transformed reader, the manuscript suggests, would take up the call to prayer. With the reference to the emerging dawn, the seepage of Bilali's reddish brown ink from the previous page resembles a faint shadow, as if the sun has risen and cast its light on the sleeping Muslim. But more than conjuring an image of repose, this phrase is rooted in discourse around Muhammad's first revelation and his submission to Islam with the help of Khadija's critical interpretation. The manuscript's illegible condition, which opens it to new interpretations, and its reference to revelation, preserves an Islamic perspective that is perceptible to a Muslim reader.

'Umar's Manifest Plea

So far, I have been suggesting that Bilali's focus on the doctrinal through his emphasis on ritual and prayer enables us to derive a reading practice that differs from a deep and or subversive reading practice; in this section, I will offer a reading of 'Umar's 1819 manuscript that also departs from a suspicious interpretation. Reading 'Umar's document at the surface or zāhir means that instead of seeking and finding agency and resistance in a document penned by a slave, I read the document as an account of 'Umar's faith and experiences of slavery.[34] To engage in this zāhirī reading of 'Umar's document, I will first discuss a few parallels between Emerson and 'Umar to underscore their distinct approaches to Islam.

In the same year that Emerson jotted the Qur'ānic verse on jinn or "Jan" in his journal, 'Umar composed a letter that mainly comprised Qur'ānic verses. Lying dormant in 'Umar's 1819 manuscript is an illustration of a Seal of Solomon that would occupy Emerson's dreams. A few years after his Qur'ānic citation, Emerson contemplated the Seal of Solomon in a letter he penned to his aunt Mary Moody Emerson in 1822: "When I lie dreaming on the possible contents of pages, as dark to me as the characters on the Seal of Solomon, I console myself with calling it learning's El Dorado."[35] It might be tempting, then, to perceive the illustration of the pentacle in 'Umar's manuscript as a sign of hiddenness or secrecy that would reveal profound truth once decoded. Indeed, 'Umar's letter is peppered with symbols, including the Seal of Solomon, and the following markers that appear as Arabic vowels: *sukun*, *kasratein*, or *fathatein*—and geometric patterns with barely readable words inscribed within (Figure 4.3). These markers seem to point to an encoded and opaque document, tempting the critic to decode or elucidate the manuscript. These markers are in fact symbols of faith, which are neither silent nor repressed but visible and manifest. These symbols are a confession of knowledge that is consonant with faith in Islam. Rather than implying a resistive tactic, 'Umar's rectilinear geometric figure, beautifully illustrated (Figure 4.3), testifies to his faith as it is a characteristic feature of Qur'ānic aesthetics.

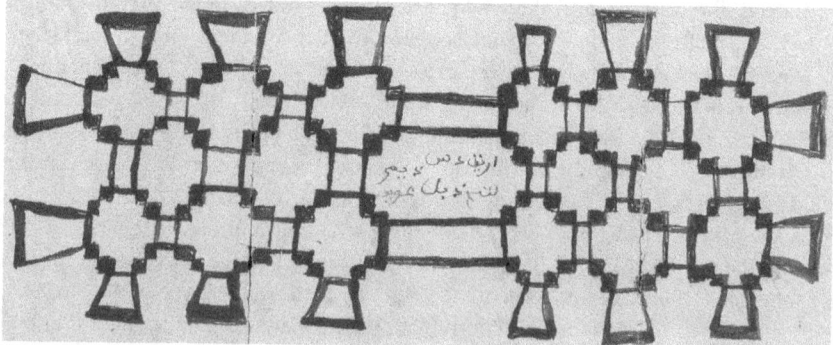

Figure 4.3 'Umar ibn Sayyid, Letter to John Owen (1819) Beinecke Library, Yale University, JWJ MSS 185.

Although 'Umar's letter, or supplication, seems to have all the trappings of an esoteric text ripe for paranoid reading, it also makes an explicit and direct request: a request or desire to return home. By reading the manuscript at the surface, readers can gloss 'Umar's poignant statement translated by John Hunwick as follows: "I wish to be seen in our land called Āfrikā in a place of the sea/river (al-ba–hr) called K-bā (or K-bya)."³⁶ Hunwick's translation captures the spirit of the original sentence—and editorializes it. 'Umar's statement is both evocative and moving, not only because 'Umar desires his homeland but also because he imagines his freedom in terms of being seen by others, and not a solitary return. At the zahir or literal level, the longing for home and intimacy is manifest rather than hidden. Although I recognize the value in approaching the text as an enigmatic document full of underlying meanings, I would also like to consider what critics might miss when they are preoccupied with unearthing deep messages or perceiving it "as something of a talisman."³⁷

Here, I consider a different translation of 'Umar's line, one that refrains from editorializing the original text.

Umar's statement can be roughly transcribed as

"كبى يسمى البحر مكلى في أجركم على يسمى بلدنا من يتراءى أن أراك اني"

An unedited literal translation would read as follows: "I see to appear/envision [although this word is not entirely clear] from our country named on [illegible words] in the sea called Kaba" (1.11). What would it mean to read this statement at the literal level or to read for its explicit meaning? The more conventional approach to translation may at times tame a text by filling in the missing gaps. It may be just as significant to contemplate the inscrutability of the text as it is to read the text at a semantic level.

In my translation, 'Umar's wish is not fully legible. While it is possible to make out some of the key words in this sentence, such as "our land," "name," "sea," and even the prepositions "from" and "in," the rest of the sentence seems to comprise a collection of random letters.

In seeking deep meaning that underlies 'Umar's letter, critics have privileged 'Umar's request over the rest of the document's content. In addition to this plea, 'Umar's document contains verses from the Qur'ān and lines from an Arabic grammar book by the twelfth-century writer Abu Muhammad al-Hariri of Basra.³⁸ Hunwick's authoritative article on 'Umar's 1819 manuscript argues that "the rest of the document is . . . padding for ['Umar's] expressed wish [to be home], which is buried deep among Qur'ānic and other quotations."³⁹ Yet in using the term "padding," Hunwick ascribes depth to 'Umar's wish, while conceiving of the citations, the rest of 'Umar's letter, as superfluous in comparison. By reading the citations as vehicles for 'Umar's wish, Hunwick places more value in 'Umar's original pronouncements than in his borrowings. That is, Hunwick elevates the role of originality and imagination by subordinating 'Umar's borrowed citations. Because this subordination assumes a hierarchical relationship between mimesis and individual creativity, it risks reducing the manuscript to a single line.

Instead of searching for hidden clues that might unravel aspects of 'Umar's strategies of resistance, accounting for what is present or manifest in the document, we can attend to 'Umar's confusion, insecurity, vulnerability, and uncertainty in the face of slavery's horrors. Indeed, the very haphazardness of the words, the move between comprehension and incomprehension, certainty and uncertainty, more closely reflect 'Umar's position as a man condemned to slavery. Whereas 'Umar's "I" is clear, what he sees—for the emphasis appears to be on seeing and on being seen—can only be murky and inaccessible to readers. Rather than perceive a subversive voice buried below the mysterious text waiting for critics to uncover repressed meaning,[40] readers perceive that the moments of unintelligible writing convey as much about the slave's condition and vulnerability as do the other instances that editors have translated in the clear, polished prose that erases the uncertainty and messy qualities that characterize 'Umar's writing.

Conclusion

In the nineteenth century, key American writers, like Ralph Waldo Emerson, Edgar Allan Poe, Lydia Marie Child, and Herman Melville, turned to Islamic ideas, themes, and terms for inspiration. Yet for all the range of Muslim types and Islamic ideas, these writers neglected or missed the African Muslims practicing Islam in the United States, who were next door all along. 'Umar and Bilali's respective documents provide important information for interpreting Islam in the United States. In their writings, they empty Orientalist codes and instead convey their attachment to their faith and the lived practice of daily ritual, in which prayer becomes the most important and the simplest thing *because* it is done every day and is easily accessible, a regular part of life, abundant in meaning on the surface. In this chapter, I have suggested that this obvious attachment to Islam calls for new interpretive practices for reading Islam in the United States that are distinct from the hermeneutics of suspicion. Using a methodological approach inspired by Islamic traditions (Prophet Muhammad's first revelation and Zāhirism) and "post-critique" scholarship (surface reading) to interpret Bilali's manuscript and 'Umar's document, I have shown that the manifest and literal elements of the text, here incomprehensibility and disjointedness, direct us to their meaning: Bilali's manuscript offers a method to read the purportedly inscrutable Islam by foregrounding the everyday practice of ritual prayer and 'Umar's document offers a direct proclamation of faith and an account of an identity severed by the conditions of slavery. Ultimately, opening up modes of interpretation to include the manifest or zāhir broadens literary critics' engagement with representations of Islam by moving beyond suspicious readings.

5

Crossing Oceans, Transgressing Boundaries: Incorporating Muslims and Moriscos into Histories of Colonial Spanish America

Karoline P. Cook

In 1583, Licenciate Cristóbal de Ovalle began making provisions for his household to accompany him from Spain to the island of Hispaniola so that he could assume his post as captain general and president of the Royal Court (*Audiencia*) of Santo Domingo. As one of the most powerful governing officials on the island, Ovalle nonetheless needed to secure royal permission to bring his wife Beatriz de Argote's thirteen-year-old slave to the Indies. The girl whose name was not mentioned in the document was described as a Morisca in the petition—a term that referred to both her Muslim ancestry and her status as a convert from Islam to Christianity. She had entered Beatriz de Argote's service at the age of nine. Ovalle attested in his petition to the Council of the Indies that the enslaved Morisca "is a very good Christian and she takes communion every fifteen days."[1] Furthermore, they would all reside together in the city of Santo Domingo where Ovalle alleged that "there are no Indians, and therefore the inconveniences cease."[2] Ovalle requested a royal license allowing the Morisca to cross the Atlantic to remain in his wife's service for a restricted period of time, promising to cover the expense of her voyage back to Spain "when his majesty wishes it."[3]

Why was someone so young perceived as a threat to the Crown by her mere presence in the Americas? Laws spelled out the conditions under which individual Moriscos could travel, usually as slaves or servants accompanying an elite household, with strict limits on their mobility and severe consequences if these were breached. Even once officials secured licenses for Moriscos in their household to travel, their stay was generally limited to a period of three or four years. Financial penalties for officials not complying with the terms of the license and failing to return enslaved Moriscos to Spain could be high. Ovalle therefore had to emphasize, in his petition, the Morisca's Christian piety in addition to the lack of opportunities she might have to interact with indigenous peoples. Despite Ovalle's statement to the contrary, a small indigenous population struggled to survive on the island of Santo Domingo, and other indigenous women and men were transported to the island as slaves.[4] Ovalle's assertions engaged directly with the Spanish Crown's anxieties regarding Muslim presence in the Americas. The Crown's attempts to define and maintain the boundaries of its empire as Catholic and its vigilance regarding the presence of Muslims in the New World reflected both the religious anxieties of the Reformation era and related discourses about Moriscos as potentially disloyal subjects due to developing racialized arguments that associated their Muslim ancestry with their character and propensity for rebellion. Religious restrictions on emigration also reflected how the Spanish Crown was justifying its title to the Americas using papal support for its role in spreading Christianity globally. Nonetheless, despite prohibitions on their emigration, both enslaved and free Muslims and Moriscos crossed the Atlantic and contributed to the formation of colonial society.

Focusing on Iberian Muslims as well as on converts to Christianity from Islam in the Spanish empire, this chapter will evaluate the importance of including Muslims and Moriscos in histories of the early modern Americas. To better understand how the Spanish empire functioned, as well as early constructions of "race" and the fluid formation of identities, it is crucial to analyze the political and social implications of imperial authorities' anxieties concerning Islam. Such a focus traces the long history of Muslims in the Americas to the late fifteenth and early sixteenth centuries and highlights the complex ways individuals negotiated their status and relationships in colonial society.

The Context

In contrast to the Portuguese and English examples, the Spanish Crown repeatedly prohibited Muslims and Moriscos from crossing the Atlantic and settling in the territories it claimed in the Americas. During the sixteenth century, Spanish monarchs remained intent on restricting emigration to individuals who could prove both their "old Christian" ancestry and their exemplary Christian conduct. Royal and ecclesiastical authorities feared that the presence of Muslims and Moriscos in the "New World" would interfere with missionary campaigns to convert indigenous peoples to Catholicism, one of the Spanish Crown's main justifications for its claims in the Western Hemisphere, and they invoked Pope Alexander VI's bull *Inter Caetera* for support.[5] Issued in 1493, this bull granted jurisdiction over lands "discovered" in the Western Hemisphere to the Crown of Castile, and charged Ferdinand of Aragon and Isabel of Castile, as the "Catholic monarchs," with the duty of promoting the global expansion of Christianity.[6] The prohibitions on Muslim and Morisco presence in Spanish America resulted in a silence in the historiography regarding their significance for studies of colonial society. The presence of Muslims and Moriscos in Spanish America influenced discourses about citizenship and belonging as well as the construction of ethnic and juridical categories related to emerging notions of *casta* and *raza*.

Royal policies targeting Muslims in the Americas reflected contemporaneous shifts in attitudes toward the Morisco population in Spain during the sixteenth century. They also responded to actions taken by the enslaved, as was the case following a major slave uprising on the Caribbean island of Hispaniola in 1521 whose participants were predominantly Muslims from the Jolof Empire in the Senegambian region of West Africa.[7] Following their rebellion, the Crown issued decrees in 1532 and 1534 prohibiting the passage of "negros gelofes" to the Spanish Caribbean.[8]

Beginning with the conquest of the Nasrid Emirate of Granada in 1492, royal policies toward Muslim minority communities on the Peninsula became increasingly repressive, presenting a departure from previous centuries. Ferdinand and Isabel initially negotiated a treaty with the Granadan Muslim (*mudéjar*) population that followed earlier models allowing conquered peoples to maintain their religious practices and institutions in exchange for paying a tax to the ruler.[9] However, arrangements broke down quickly and the *mudéjares* faced growing pressures to abandon Islam. Cardinal Francisco Jiménez de Cisneros staged mass baptisms and mounted campaigns to convert the Granadan Muslims to Catholicism, thereby violating the terms of the surrender treaty. Furthermore, the *mudéjares* were prohibited from purchasing land and bearing arms, markers of high status. Pressures placed on the Granadan Muslim population reflected broader changes at the national level, and the centralizing interests of the Spanish monarchs. The establishment of the Spanish Inquisition in 1483 and the expulsion of the Jews from the Peninsula by edict in 1492 signaled a shift in policy aimed to define Spain as a Catholic nation. Because such political and religious changes coincided with missionary anticipation about evangelizing in the Americas as knowledge about a "New World" reached Europe, definitions of belonging to a Spanish nation and empire, and concurrent debates over just and effective governance (*buen gobierno*) engaged with the status of its peoples as Christian subjects and vassals.

By 1499, Granada's Muslim population rose up in rebellion, frustrated by the violations of the surrender treaty. When royal forces suppressed this first uprising in the Alpujarras mountains near Granada, the *mudéjares* were given the impossible choice to either accept baptism or suffer exile. Most chose baptism, not wishing to be forced from their homes. From that moment the new converts acquired a new legal status as baptized Christians, and were labeled "Moriscos." They faced a period of religious instruction as neophytes, people who were new to the faith and should be treated with leniency by ecclesiastical authorities. But by the mid-sixteenth century the Moriscos faced growing surveillance from church authorities who suspected that many families continued to practice Islam in the privacy of their homes. Indeed, many Granadan Moriscos secretly maintained their faith in Islam, given the coerced nature of the baptisms, and justified by the concept of *taqiyya*.[10] According to this principle expressed in a *fatwa* that the Mufti of Oran Ahmad ben Yumaʿa issued in 1504 to the Granadan Moriscos, if they remained true to Islam in their hearts, because they were living under duress, they were permitted to show the outward signs of being Catholics: attending Mass, confessing their sins to a priest, and taking communion. Because of their status as baptized Christians, Moriscos became subject to the Inquisition and faced pressures to stop speaking in Arabic and to renounce their local styles of dress and lifeways. They became subject to the Catholic sacraments of baptism, confirmation, the Eucharist, penance, marriage, and last rites. While many Granadan Moriscos continued to practice Islam, it is also important to remember that some who were born by the mid-sixteenth century may have identified as Christians, and Moriscos in other regions across Spain converted under a diverse set of circumstances that reflected each community's local history. After several generations passed many Moriscos considered themselves "good and faithful Christians."[11] Yet because discourses about Moriscos, fueled by anxieties about their potential to ally with the Ottomans and French as a "fifth column," represented them as apostates and rebels, and asserted they would never assimilate and become loyal subjects due to their Muslim ancestry, arguments made by some commentators to expel them from the Peninsula found support at court. In 1609–14, Philip III issued the decrees of expulsion, forcing thousands of Moriscos across the Peninsula into exile.

Coercive measures and suspicion of the Granadan Moriscos coincided with renewed preoccupation over purity of blood (*limpieza de sangre*) across the Iberian world. The purity of blood statutes barred anyone possessing Muslim or Jewish ancestry from attending universities, holding prestigious posts, practicing a range of professions, or emigrating to the Americas. They resulted in waves of denunciations before inquisitorial and ecclesiastical tribunals that rival families lacked the requisite "old Christian" ancestry. Individuals accused of having tainted lineages could have their property confiscated and a sentence of heresy could undermine their social position and that of their family for generations. The language used to exclude descendants of Muslims and Jews incorporated medical terminology about bodies and inheritance, operating under the assumption that the blood of non-Christian ancestors transmitted characteristics such as lack of trustworthiness and loyalty. Moriscos were thus perceived as rebellious and disloyal. Widespread social anxieties about purity of blood combined with the tense political context that Moriscos faced during the sixteenth century.

Not surprisingly, fears regarding Muslim and Morisco presence in the Americas grew during the second half of the sixteenth century in ways that reflected the changing political relationships between Muslims and Christians on the Peninsula and in the Mediterranean. Beginning with the 1501 instructions issued by King Ferdinand and Queen Isabel to Hispaniola's first governor Nicolás de Ovando, royal decrees (*cédulas*) prohibited Muslims, Jews, converts from Judaism and Islam, and their descendants from traveling to the Americas.[12] Charles V and Philip II continued to issue such *cédulas*, citing concerns about the passage of non-Christians and new Christians to the viceroyalties of New Spain and Peru. In a royal decree that he issued first in 1543 and reissued in 1550, Charles V ordered, "We are informed that there have passed and pass daily to these parts some enslaved North African men and women (*berberiscos*) and other free persons newly converted from Islam, and their children, although it is prohibited by us. They should in no way pass because of the many inconveniences that have followed."[13] Charles V's decrees attest to the presence in the Americas of Muslims from Tunis, Algiers, the kingdom of Morocco, and other parts of the Maghreb, who were enslaved during the Spanish and Portuguese campaigns to conquer cities on the North African coast.

The Crown and the Council of the Indies issued instructions to royal officials residing in the viceroyalties of New Spain and Peru that reiterated the religious imperatives behind the restrictions on travel and settlement. In 1580, the Count of Coruña Lorenzo Suárez de Mendoza traveled to Mexico City to assume his post as viceroy. He was given the royal instructions that stressed:

> Because in the year 1543 we [the Crown] issued a royal provision sealed with our seal, by which we ordered to cast out from all our Indies all Moriscos both free and enslaved who were in them, and because it is expedient to the service of Our Lord

and our [service] and the Christianity of the Indians that the said provision be carried out due to the great harm they [Moriscos] could cause the Indians because they are so tender in the faith.[14]

Such laws targeted both converts from Islam and their descendants, resulting in a policy based on the notion of descent that was further aligned with anxieties about purity of blood. For example, royal instructions issued in 1550 to Mexican Viceroy Luis de Velasco included a provision that "they expel from the Indies the *berberisco* slaves and other converted Muslims (*moros*), and their children."[15] Such concerns that Muslims and Moriscos would upset evangelization programs intensified with the religious turmoil during the Reformation and the Habsburg monarchy's concomitant rivalry with the Ottoman sultan.

Vigilance over Muslim and Morisco presence in the Americas intensified during Philip II's reign (1556-98) which coincided with Spain's victory over the Ottoman navy at Lepanto, and increasing scrutiny of the Granadan Morisco population after their uprising in 1568-71. The decrees issued by Philip II used vehement language to characterize the Moriscos that invoked medical imagery, revealing how attitudes toward Moriscos at court and on the Peninsula were changing. The establishment of inquisitorial tribunals in Mexico City and Lima by 1570 aimed to tighten religious surveillance across the viceroyalties. Indigenous peoples were not subject to the Inquisition which was reserved for individuals with European and African ancestry, including converts from Judaism and Islam.[16] In 1570, Philip II issued a provision to the royal courts of law (*audiencias*) in the Americas requesting that their judges and officials aid inquisitors while the Inquisition tribunals were being established. The king's provision stressed the duty that local officials had to stem heresy, by preventing the settlement of new Christians within their jurisdictions: "By divine clemency and grace our Kingdoms and lands have been cleansed of all error, and this pestilence and contagion has been avoided. It is hoped that by divine mercy [our lands] will be preserved from now on to avoid and remedy that so great an offense to the Faith and Christian religion does not pass to these parts."[17] References to Moriscos as a "pestilence and contagion" had been invoked by commentators in Spain such as Pedro Aznar Cardona who proposed arguments in favor of their expulsion. Notions of citizenship increasingly incorporated only people without Muslim or Jewish ancestry into definitions of who belonged in the Spanish nation. Despite heightened scrutiny from the center, the extent to which such laws restricting emigration were enforced in practice depended on local circumstances and the interests of colonial officials. Recent research on the Spanish empire has demonstrated a degree of fluidity and unevenness in the ways laws were enforced in practice.[18] Beyond simply ignoring the royal decrees, petitioning and litigation presented ways individuals could pursue their interests and negotiate their status in the courtroom. Rulings and legal decisions following the petitioning or litigation process could then have implications for future legal decisions in other parts of the empire.

In this context of defining and regulating the boundaries of a Catholic empire, the term "Muslim" or *moro* was becoming a racialized denunciation leading to the prosecution of individuals for not only practicing Islam but also having Muslim ancestry. Contemporaries applied the label "Morisco" to a range of people, from individuals who were forcibly baptized in Granada and who struggled to maintain their religious beliefs and practices in secret to voluntary converts in Castile who found themselves conflated with the Granadan Moriscos as potentially disloyal subjects. The term "Morisco" acquired racialized connotations during the early modern period, as it became associated first with religious ancestry, and increasingly with the mixed-race descendants of Africans and Europeans, specifically the child of a Spaniard and a *mulata*, as a *casta* category in the fluid racial hierarchies of early colonial society.[19]

Enslaved Muslims and Moriscos

Often members of the elite petitioned the Crown for permission to bring their Morisco slaves to the Americas. While labeled "Moriscos" in the documents, as mentioned earlier, this term encompassed a wide range of individuals, meaning in its broadest sense a convert from Islam to Christianity. Not only individuals forcibly baptized in Granada at the turn of the sixteenth century but also converts from Islam born in Algiers, the kingdom of Morocco, sub-Saharan Africa, or the Philippines were subject to being labeled Moriscos. The term *berberisco* was also used to refer to some of the enslaved North Africans, but as Aurelia Martín Casares has noted in the context of Granada, it did not always refer to someone born in the Maghreb but could also be applied to their children born on the Iberian Peninsula, suggesting contemporary Iberian notions of descent that extended beyond membership in a religious community.[20]

The enslaved Morisca in Beatriz de Argote and Cristóbal de Ovalle's household in Santo Domingo was not alone. Spanish officials traveling to the Americas to assume their posts petitioned the Crown on a not insignificant basis to take one or two enslaved Moriscos or *berberiscos* with them to work in their households. A substantial number of the enslaved were women. To what extent can we learn about their lives from the available sources, given how little information each petition contains? Some patterns emerge. Many of the petitions for licenses to bring enslaved Moriscas to the Americas were submitted during the years following the second uprising of the Granadan Moriscos in 1569–71. Facing increasing inquisitorial surveillance and pressure to renounce both Islam and their regional practices and identities, many Granadan Moriscos rose up in protest. They moved into the mountainous Alpujarras region surrounding the city, resisting until their efforts were suppressed by royal forces. Many Moriscos faced enslavement as punishment for their participation in or support for the uprising. Aurelia Martín Casares estimates that as many as 10,000 Moriscos were enslaved during this Alpujarras uprising, and of these a substantial proportion were women.[21] The petitions that Spanish officials submitted to the Council of the Indies reveal that these Granadan women were among the enslaved Moriscos brought to the Americas. Members of the royal forces who suppressed the Alpujarras uprising had careers that spanned the Iberian world, and some acquired posts in the Americas. In the service reports (*relaciones de méritos y servicios*) that they submitted in support of their applications for powerful positions, these men highlighted their exploits during the "War of Granada" as proof of their loyal service to the Crown. For example, Alonso

Bazo de Andrada, who was purveyor and commissary general in the Alpujarras, entrusted his relative Pedro Fernández de Andrada to take the family's Morisca slave Luisa to join them in Mexico City.²² In 1573, Bazo de Andrada had been appointed to administer the estate (*hacienda*) of the Marqués del Valle, Martín Cortés.²³ Two years later in 1575 the king granted Luisa permission to travel to Mexico because "her masters had sent for her." Her license noted that she could remain there until Bazo de Andrada and his wife returned to Spain, with no time limits placed upon her stay. The *cédula* nonetheless emphasized that Luisa could not remain in Mexico unsupervised or of her own accord.²⁴

In 1576, Doctor Martín de Aliaga, newly appointed judge of the *audiencia* on the island of Hispaniola, obtained a royal license for "a Morisca for his service." She would join two other slaves who would accompany his household. Aliaga was required to pay a hefty deposit to guarantee she did not leave the island "for any other part of the Indies."²⁵ That same year the king also granted a license to Ruy Díaz de Mendoza to bring with him to Mexico two enslaved Moriscas, described only as "unmarried." Díaz de Mendoza's imminent departure from the Andalusian port of Sanlúcar de Barrameda to assume his post as treasurer for the viceroyalty of New Spain enabled him to request the king to allow him to pay the deposit of 2,000 ducats directly to Viceroy Martín Enríquez upon his arrival in Mexico City rather than to the officials at the House of Trade in Seville before his departure.²⁶ Philip II instructed the viceroy in a second *cédula* that an account be drafted recording Díaz de Mendoza's payment to ensure that the two women "be returned to these kingdoms within four years' time from the day they embark [at Sanlúcar]."²⁷ Two years later in 1578, Philip II confirmed in a third *cédula* that the deposit had been paid. The king ordered officials at the House of Trade to save the deposit until the four years passed and the Moriscas were returned to Spain. Should Díaz de Mendoza not comply, the Seville officials were to deduct the appropriate penalties from the deposit "because it is important to our service that they [the Moriscas] not remain in those parts."²⁸

Evidence shows that some colonial officials complied given the financial penalties involved, while others ignored the orders. For example, in October 1579, officials at the House of Trade opened an inquiry into the number of Moriscas returning to Spain on that year's armada. The officials in Seville were following orders that instructed all shipmasters of the fleet to "declare which Moriscas of the Kingdom of Granada were brought [to Spain] in the said ships from New Spain and to whom the said Moriscas belong."²⁹ After carrying out the investigation, the Seville officials recorded that the shipmasters "all declare that they did not bring any Moriscas, except Gerónimo de Ojeda who declared that he brought one belonging to the Licentiate Obregón, corregidor of Mexico City, and he presented her before the judges and officials in the inspection which they carried out."³⁰ Evidence clearly indicates that officials in the years immediately following the Granada uprising were focused specifically on Morisco women who were taken to the Americas as slaves, indicating a sizeable enough number to warrant an inspection of returning fleets.

Morisco women were also sold at auction in slave markets in the viceroyalties of Peru and New Spain. In April 1582, the Viceroy of New Spain the Conde de Coruña submitted his petition to the Council of the Indies in which he stated that "he purchased a Morisca slave in Mexico City who is a very good cook and a preserve maker, and because she is necessary for his service, he asks to be granted license to have her in his service despite any order to the contrary."[31] The Council's initial negative decision prompted him to submit a second petition. The Conde de Coruña elaborated on his previous petition, emphasizing that he "had purchased her out of necessity due to his advanced age."[32] The Council relented and in June 1582 authorized the Conde de Coruña to retain his Morisca slave "despite what is ordered that people of the said nation cannot be in those parts."[33] The Morisca cook could only remain in his household in Mexico City for a period of three years. The king ordered the viceroy to "keep track of her. You must provide an account of her whenever you are asked and likewise of her children if she has any."[34] After the three years ended the viceroy was required to send her back to Spain. He died one year later in 1583, raising the question of what happened to the Morisca cook? Surveillance not only over members of the "Morisco nation" but also over their children in the Spanish viceroyalties reflects heightened Crown anxieties about policing the boundaries of empire, defining citizenship and belonging according to religious ancestry so as to not undermine definitions of the empire as a guardian of Catholicism during a period of global religious reform. The women, men, and children ensnared by such policies faced the consequences of barriers to social mobility, the policing of their whereabouts, enslavement, and deportation. A few rose to challenge these conditions.

Evidence from the petitioning process indicates that some individuals found ways to escape their enslavement. In 1549, Francisco Mexia who was "involved in fiscal matters in the House of Trade" in Seville complained to the king how ten years previously his Morisca slave Ana de Chaves had escaped captivity in Guatemala. It had come to his attention that she had settled in the Andean highland province of Arequipa.[35] Mexia noted that "in addition to being his slave and having left and absented herself, because she is a Morisca she should not be in the Indies."[36] The *cédula* issued in February 1549 ordered that information be gathered about Ana de Chaves and "if you determine she is a Morisca, send her to these Kingdoms along with any goods that she has, directly to the officials of the House of Trade."[37] No further information about Ana de Chaves survives from this petition, although other cases raise suggestive questions. Given the political upheaval in the Viceroyalty of Peru with the revolt of the *encomenderos* and its aftermath, the years between 1549 and 1554 were a time when people could manage to remake themselves.[38]

As a point of comparison, research on West African Muslims enslaved in Spanish America indicates that their presence from the early sixteenth century onwards was met with similar restrictions. Following the abovementioned slave rebellion on Hispaniola in 1521, the Jolof were targeted in the royal decrees in order to limit their influence on the plantations. A royal decree issued to officials of the House of Trade in 1532 betrays some of the assumptions about the "gelofes" ten years after their coordinated act of resistance:

> I have been informed that all the harm that occurred on the island of San Juan and other islands during the uprising of the black people, and the deaths of the Christians that occurred, were caused by the blacks from Jolof who are on [the

islands], being, as it is said, proud and disobedient and rebellious and incorrigible. Few of them receive punishment.[39]

The decree goes on to note that the Jolof influenced "those who are peaceful, from other lands and of good customs," because they "attract them in this way to their bad lifestyle, by which Our Lord is not served and our profit is harmed."[40] The economic impact of the rebellion, and the networks formed and strategies used by the enslaved as suggested by this *cédula*, led the Council of the Indies to rule that in order to "pacify" the Caribbean islands and to stop the upheaval the Jolof caused "during the uprising and also in other matters," they should not be taken to the Americas "without our express license."[41] Instructions issued by the Crown in 1532 to the officials of San Juan de Puerto Rico present additional stereotypes of the Jolof that echoed contemporary representations of Muslims and Moriscos, citing an earlier report sent by the Lieutenant Governor of San Juan to the Council of the Indies. The Lieutenant Governor argued that the Jolof should not be allowed on the island of San Juan "because they are a bellicose people. . . . If any uprising among the blacks were to occur, the people of this nation would be its instigators."[42] As was the case with enslaved Moriscos and *berberiscos*, it is unlikely the restrictions were closely observed, given the presence of enslaved Jolof men and women in the Spanish viceroyalties throughout the sixteenth century.[43] While excellent studies have focused on enslaved African Muslims in the Portuguese and British Atlantic, more research on Spanish America remains to be done.[44]

Voluntary Emigration

In addition to people who were enslaved, free Muslims and Moriscos also crossed the Atlantic and settled in Spanish America. Because they had to emigrate clandestinely, individuals sought strategies to circumvent the controls enforced by officials at the House of Trade in Seville. Moriscos could purchase falsified licenses and pay witnesses to testify that they were "old Christians" whose piety was "public and notorious" in their home communities. Witnesses emphasized an applicant's regular attendance during Mass and observance of Catholic feast days. They also noted how regularly they took communion and confessed their sins to the priest. If an applicant's family became suspect, their surnames could be altered to distance themselves from a relative whose *sanbenito* (penitential garment) was displayed publicly in their parish church, indicating they had incurred the condemnation of the Inquisition.[45]

Beyond obtaining a falsified license to emigrate, individuals could enlist as soldiers or as sailors on fleets crossing the Atlantic and, once they reached a port in the Americas, abandon the ship. Royal decrees complained about this practice. Other *cédulas* highlighted the strategy of traveling on ships departing ports in Lisbon and the Canary Islands that had fewer controls than Seville.

Evidence from legal disputes brought before the *audiencias* in Spanish America suggests that some Moriscos joined the early expeditions to conquer indigenous lands. Diego Romero's participation in the invasion of New Granada is a case in point. Having joined Gonzalo Jiménez de Quesada's first expedition in 1537, Romero acquired wealth through his involvement in the "conquest" and subsequently made claims to noble status—a practice not uncommon among those seeking rewards for serving the Crown in early campaigns. In 1554, Romero's rival Cristóbal de Monroy brought a suit against him before the Audiencia of Santa Fe in order to seize Romero's encomienda or grant of indigenous tributaries granted by the Crown to the first conquerors of a region. Monroy claimed Romero was a Muslim and a runaway North African slave and summoned witnesses in the Spanish city of Alcalá de Henares who agreed to testify to Romero's Muslim ancestry. He also requested that doctors inspect Romero for evidence of circumcision. Because of Romero's high status and connections in colonial society, he was able to marshal witnesses who testified that he was a good Christian and his noble status should exempt him from being examined by the doctors as this would shame him. Romero argued that regardless of whether he was a Morisco, his loyal service to the Crown and honorable qualities should exonerate him. Romero ultimately won his case, demonstrating how reputation could be invoked and fashioned in colonial society, at times proving more important that ancestry or religious identity.[46]

In addition to facing trial in the secular courts, many individuals found themselves vulnerable to prosecution before the inquisitorial and ecclesiastical tribunals. The accusations leveled against suspected Moriscos highlighted practices that the broader Christian population associated with the secret observance of Islam. Influenced by the edicts of faith that representatives of the Inquisition read aloud in public settings to identify actions and statements that undermined Catholic teachings, local residents scrutinized each other for practices they associated with Islam, Judaism, Protestantism, witchcraft, sodomy, bigamy, heretical propositions, and a range of other religious "crimes." Suspected Moriscos could be accused of praying in Arabic and invoking the Prophet Muhammad, refusing to eat pork, and slaughtering animals in the halal manner. They likewise faced denunciations more broadly leveled during the Reformation, that included mocking the Eucharist, desecrating Catholic images, questioning the Trinity, or denying the divinity of Christ and the virginity of Mary.[47]

Suspected Muslims and Moriscos found themselves in a precarious position as a direct result of the colonial policies that labeled them potentially disloyal subjects. The language used by some Spanish jurists and theologians to describe Moriscos on the eve of their expulsion from Spain drew on medical imagery that cast the Moriscos as a threat to the body politic. The assumptions underlying descriptions of Muslims and Moriscos in this context, characterizing them as a "contagion" suggestive of the spread of heresy as disease is echoed in the racist discourses of later centuries. Such descriptions were also apparent in the wording of the legislation restricting their emigration, and this had very real implications for Moriscos' lived experiences. Anyone accused of being a Muslim or Morisco faced deportation to Spain and prosecution by the court at the House of Trade in Seville. They stood to lose their property and status in colonial society, and if they had been enslaved and gained their freedom, they could be re-enslaved and sold at public auction. Facing destitution, suspected Moriscos brought their cases to court, litigating for their survival in colonial society.

Conclusion

Examining the presence of Muslims and Moriscos in Spanish America during the sixteenth and seventeenth centuries, and across the Americas more broadly, is crucial. Despite prohibitions on their passage, Muslims and Moriscos crossed the Atlantic and formed part of colonial society from the time of the first Spanish settlements in the Caribbean. Research on the actions and presence of Moriscos in the Americas sheds light on their role in both actively shaping local societies as litigants, interpreters, artisans, *encomenderos*, or healers, as well as how discourses surrounding their presence continued to influence broader debates about status across the Iberian world. Their influence can be traced through the stories of individuals who found themselves bound up in viceregal institutions as petitioners, litigants, or defendants, and who possessed a wide range of interests and expectations. Although the numbers of Moriscos appearing in the documentation do not reach the thousands, smaller numbers still generated intense anxieties among the functionaries of the Council of the Indies, the royal *audiencias*, and the ecclesiastical and inquisitorial tribunals, raising questions for Spanish officials about how to define the boundaries of the empire and how to establish citizenship.[48]

An analysis of the attitudes projected onto Moriscos embedded in the sources can reveal how a population that was in the process of defining itself as "Spanish" (*español*) during the sixteenth and seventeenth centuries understood how the empire functioned and envisioned their place within it. Spaniards brought with them to the Americas definitions and practices of conquest and settlement that were influenced by their experiences with Muslims on the Peninsula and in the Mediterranean. The position of Muslims and Moriscos within debates over how to insert oneself in the category "español" is a crucial question for understanding the shape colonial society assumed by the eighteenth century.

Beatriz de Argote's desire to bring her thirteen-year-old Morisca slave with the household to Santo Domingo is illustrative of just one of the multiple ways in which Muslims and Moriscos crossed the Atlantic even at the height of Spanish church and state efforts to prohibit their passage. The chaos ensuing from Sir Francis Drake's capture of Santo Domingo just three years after their arrival, in 1586, and reports of the English freeing slaves and holding Captain General Cristóbal de Ovalle's household hostage raise questions about what might have happened to the enslaved Morisca had she survived the sack of the city.[49] The volume, the patterns of ebb and flow of Muslims and Moriscos in the Americas, may never be fully known given the often clandestine journeys they undertook, yet their influence was perceived and acknowledged by contemporaries. The assiduous work of current investigators is uncovering in various archives more and more data that are beginning to shed new light on the subject and open up new avenues for research. In order to understand how the institutions of the Spanish empire functioned at the local level, as well as to understand how juridical and ethnic identities were being constructed actively through litigation, it is also important to analyze the social and political consequences of the anxieties that ecclesiastical and civil authorities held regarding Islam. It was not a unidirectional process through which Spaniards brought their institutions and experiences forged during the so-called Reconquest with them to the Americas where they were adapted to local circumstances, but rather that the histories of interactions between Muslims and Christians continued to evolve simultaneously on both sides of the Atlantic. These new approaches explore the complex ways that individuals accused of being Moriscos negotiated their status and relationships in colonial society.

Part Three

Muslim Worlds in the American Imaginary

6

"An Unwelcome Present": Simulation and Simulacra in the Unlikely Friendship of General Lew Wallace and Sultan Abdülhamit II

Bill Hunt

> *I have always loved Art, and been thankful for the gift to discern the cunning next to the divine in the most commonplace contrivances. . . . That is to say, to me there is Art in everything we construct.*
> —Lew Wallace, Introduction to *Famous Paintings of the World* (1894)

> *General Lew Wallace says he thinks the Sultan of Turkey is an honest man. Did the Sultan of Turkey ever owe General Wallace any money?*
> —*The Kansas Semi-Weekly Capital*, May 4, 1900

It is an underreported nuance of history that the author of the best-selling American novel of the nineteenth century would strike up a burgeoning friendship with the last autonomous sultan of the Ottoman Empire, caliph of Islam, and *amir al-mu'minin*, Abdülhamit II—the Grand Seigneur himself, that perennial bogeyman of the Western world.[1] General Lew Wallace, better known at the time for his military blunders than for creating *Ben-Hur: A Tale of the Christ* (1880), was appointed America's chief diplomat to the Sublime Porte in 1881.[2] Cables from Istanbul disclosing that Wallace had come to know the sultan on "intimate terms"[3] quickly became the stuff of national obsession in the United States. In July 1882, *The Cincinnati Commercial Tribune* captures the singularity of the moment and the cause for excitement: "There is no record of equal familiarity between the head of the Mohamedan world and the representative of a so-called Christian Government, and the Powers of Europe may well look upon it with mistrust, particularly as General Wallace has had military experience, and is able to give advice of great value to the Sultan."[4] The bonds and amity forged between these two principals of the United States and the Muslim world, it seemed, had the power to disrupt or even challenge European global hegemony. Newspapers from this period giddily report the latest incidents in the relationship, always offering some intimation of the dividends it might pay out for America's emerging geopolitical interests abroad.

Perhaps the best surviving evidence of a genuine rapport shared between the two men are the *objets d'art* produced and exchanged during the course of Wallace's embassy. Fearing that his portraits might violate Islamic conventions against figural representation, Wallace secretly sketched two profiles of the infamously camera-shy Abdülhamit from memory (Figure 6.1, Figure 6.2).[5] Conversely, a life-size oil painting, gifted by the sultan, still hangs in Wallace's Crawfordsville, Indiana, studio (Figure 6.3). Apocryphally titled "The Turkish Princess," the work depicts a preadolescent subject reclining on a leopard-skin rug. She is posed suggestively and in a manner that clashes with her apparent age. Her enigmatic, anything-but-placid gaze back at the viewer is reiterated by the stuffed head of the big cat immediately beside her. The aggression communicated by the leopard's bared fangs belies and complicates the princess's Mona Lisa smirk. Dulled over by time and the elements, "The Turkish Princess" has been deprived of its original luster, so museum docents sometimes permit visitors to activate the flash on their cameras for photographs of the painting. The burst of light revivifies subdued pigments, producing an image that recuperates the portrait's lost colors. In other words, the artifact is now best seen through the production of its simulation. Postcards of the princess are also available for purchase at the museum gift shop.

In the early 1880s, news of the sultan's generosities scandalized the American reading public (even as it titillated), piquing anxieties of how transcultural affiliations abroad might jeopardize the project of national rapprochement and rebuilding at home. As soon as intelligence regarding "The Turkish Princess" made landfall in the United States, the painting began to take on a life of its own: a progression catalyzed by the domestic reproduction and circulation of its narrative in newsprint. Over the span

Figure 6.1 Lew Wallace, Untitled Portrait of Abdülhamit II, circa 1882, pencil sketch. Reproduced by permission from the collection of The Lew Wallace Study and Museum, Crawfordsville, IN. Photo by author.

"An Unwelcome Present" 73

Figure 6.2 Lew Wallace, Untitled Portrait of Abdülhamit II, circa 1882, oil on canvas. Reproduced by permission from the collection of The Lew Wallace Study and Museum, Crawfordsville, IN. Photo by author.

of one summer, the princess would metamorphose from an inanimate "counterfeit on canvas,"[6] as one newspaper terms it, into a corporeal person, intended by the sultan to serve as Wallace's personal sex slave.

Bogged down in the minutiae of his wartime exploits, Lew Wallace died in 1905 before completing the second half of his autobiography.[7] He never produced a comprehensive account of his friendship with Abdülhamit or wholly addressed controversy surrounding "The Turkish Princess." The recuperative description that follows here constitutes a neglected, yet essential episode in the long record of engagement between peoples of the American and Islamic worlds. It draws from scores of contemporary accounts published in American newspapers, both ephemeral and long-form, to salvage this forgotten history. What ultimately emerges from this archive suggests that professional encounters between elites of the Ottoman Empire and the United States occasionally transcended the set protocols and the polite, diffident etiquette dictated by "soulless diplomacy."[8] Journalists routinely described relations between the sultan and the general through a discourse of sympathy, intimacy, and "reciprocal affection."[9] This chapter asks, in part, how the transcultural intimacies and personal bonds reportedly enjoined between Sultan Abdülhamit and General Wallace might help to reframe scholarly and popular perceptions of the history of exchange

Figure 6.3 "The Turkish Princess," date unknown, oil on canvas. Reproduced by permission from the collection of The Lew Wallace Study and Museum, Crawfordsville, IN. Photo by author.

between the United States and the Muslim world in modernity. It also asks how a seemingly endless sequence of political hostility and military intervention across hemispheres, so often rationalized and abetted on the grounds of cultural difference and miscommunication, could be well understood as a modern phenomenon.

Not by chance, the media frenzy engendered by "The Turkish Princess" coincides with the initial phase of teleconnection between the Americas and the Muslim world. Circuiting together continents, the Atlantic Telegraph Cable had become reliably operational only as recently as the second half of the 1860s.[10] Its use dramatically altered the speed at which information was circulated and the modalities through which it was communicated. Dispatches that would have previously taken weeks or months to traverse the ocean were now spirited across in a matter of hours, creating an up-to-the-day news cycle for international affairs.[11] Because of the Atlantic Telegraph, transmissions hailing from Istanbul would have been imbued with an immediacy and freshness that enabled readers to become intimately connected to the running narrative of the friendship. Given the usual content broadcast via the transatlantic cable—information regarding the daily transactions of foreign financial markets or far-off political developments—news of the ongoing bonhomie between the sultan and the general would have borne a uniquely personal, human dimension, which existed in complement to its obvious geostrategic significance. The scopic privileges afforded by transoceanic telegraphy thereby fashioned American news creators and consumers into virtual participants, attuned to the most recent, serialized updates from Turkey.

With an arresting simultaneity, it was discovered that this new technology was ripe for exploitation. Because of the exponentially larger, timelier yield of information produced through teleconnection with the Old World, counterfeiters in the United States could easily produce and circulate their own telegraphed international news. Fabricated, simulacral narratives could be introduced amid the breadth of simulational information received and then be passed off as the genuine article. Manipulated to conform to cliché or personal vendetta, these simulacral accounts of Turkey reinforced and concretized a set of racist assumptions and Orientalist ideologies, rather than countering or neutralizing them.

Concerning how reproductions invariably represent the corruption of a primary trace, the terminology of Jean Baudrillard's *Simulacra and Simulation* (1981) proves invaluable in this context. Baudrillard forges a distinction between the *simulation*, a reproduction that diminishes a still-extant, originary artifact, and *simulacrum*, a reproduction of an alleged original, which no longer exists or never existed.[12] A source of Baudrillard's inspiration might be linked back to Walter Benjamin's "The Work of Art in the Age of Mechanical Reproduction" (1936), for its examination of how extrinsic political significations are interposed onto a primary artifact during the process of its mass reproduction.[13] While remaining mindful of such contributions, it should be noted that Susan Elston Wallace, the spouse of Lew Wallace who accompanied her husband on his deployment to the Ottoman Empire, entertained her own suspicions regarding the dubious affinities between an original and its subsequent imitations.

Enjoying a formidable literary career in her own right, Susan Wallace published a cycle of travelogues based on time spent in the eastern Mediterranean.[14] Of these, *Along the Bosphorus* (1898) addresses the thorny problematics surrounding representation and re-creation—processes so often forbidden among various denominations of the Abrahamic faiths. Replicating a scene from Harriet Beecher Stowe's *Sunny Memories of Foreign Lands* (1854), *Along the Bosphorus* presents the tableau of an artist in a Dresden gallery, struggling mightily to paint a faithful pastiche of Raphael's *Sistine Madonna*.[15] The copyist's impending failure gives the narrator pause to reflect upon the "immeasurable distance which may lie between an original and a copy; a portrait and the object reproduced, —the distance between a dead statue and a spiritualized something that suggested or sat for it."[16] As Susan Wallace anticipates Baudrillard's interest in iconographic simulations of the divine,[17] the correspondence between trace and simulation is, at best, always imprecise and, at worst, highly doubtful. This insight likely represented a hard-won, personal lesson for Susan and Lew Wallace. While they resided in Turkey, their own fictive, simulacral *doppelgängers*—caricaturized distortions of themselves—ran amok and created pandemonium in American newspapers.

An exploration of the publicity generated by Lew Wallace's presence in the Ottoman Empire requires some examination of the circumstances leading to his ambassadorial appointment. Wallace's diplomatic tenure abroad was as much a product of his literary reputation as it was a consequence of his public disgrace and the threats posed to his personal safety in the United States. Initially overlooked by critics and consumers after its 1880 publication, *Ben-Hur* did catch the attention of President James Garfield in the spring of 1881.[18] Exposure to the region's antiquities and life in Turkey, Garfield hoped, would give Wallace material to begin a follow-up novel.[19] A foreign posting had the added benefit of getting Wallace out of the country and away from the domestic hostilities that lingered stateside. Even as late as 1881, popular sentiment held Wallace largely responsible for the Union debacle at the April 1862 Battle of Shiloh.[20] Specifically, Wallace was faulted for the delays of the Third Division, under his command, in reinforcing a flank of the Union army during combat.[21] Shiloh was, at the time of its occurrence, the deadliest battle in United States history.

Summarily fired by Grant and demoted to the rank of colonel, Wallace went on to command a force defending Washington, DC, from a last-ditch Confederate assault in the 1864 Battle of Monocacy.[22] He sat on the military tribunals presiding over the prosecutions of Lincoln's assassins and the commandant of Andersonville Prison; he was tasked with pacifying hostile remnants of the Confederacy in Texas.[23] Despite these contributions toward seeing the war to its conclusion, Wallace expended no small amount of effort or ink in postwar life defending his tactical decisions at Shiloh.[24] In a letter of gratitude, Garfield, a fellow Shiloh veteran, alludes to the battle's strain upon Wallace's reputation. The president thanks the author for the pleasure of reading *Ben-Hur*, which has "lightened the burden of my daily life and renewed our acquaintance which began at Shiloh."[25] Informally, via his appointment, Wallace joined a minor postbellum exodus of stigmatized former generals, publicly impugned either for botched campaigns during the war or for unpopular postwar political leanings. Ambrose Bierce recognizes this trend in an installment of *The Devil's Dictionary* first published in late August 1881: "CONSUL, n. In American politics, a person who having failed to secure an office from the people is given one by the Administration on condition that he leave the country."[26]

James Longstreet, formerly a general of the Confederacy, immediately preceded Wallace as American ambassador to the Ottoman Empire.[27] Longstreet had provoked Southern ire during the Reconstruction Era by publicly advocating national reconciliation and political realism. In open letters, he informed fellow Southern whites that "we are a conquered people" and pleaded for their "moderation, forebearance, and submission."[28] Longstreet additionally led a racially mixed security force in the suppression of insurgent New Orleans whites during the 1874 Battle of Liberty Place, cementing his status as a target of Lost Cause animus for the remainder of his life and thereafter.[29] He remained at the posting in Istanbul for approximately four months.[30]

Later dubbed "The American Dreyfus," General Charles Pomeroy Stone was imprisoned without cause or trial for a period of six months, following a Federal calamity at the 1861 Battle of Ball's Bluff.[31] By 1870, a still-anathematized Stone was commissioned by the armed forces of Egypt to serve as aide-de-camp to Khedive Isma'il Pasha.[32] In this role, Stone joined a cohort of nearly fifty former Union and demobilized Confederate officers then active in the Egyptian military.[33] Serving from 1870 to 1883, he was eventually promoted by Isma'il to the rank of *ferik pasha*, the equivalent of lieutenant general, and placed in command of some 40,000 soldiers.[34] Stone acted as connector and interlocutor between heads of state during former President Ulysses S. Grant's 1877 tour of Egypt. Through a translator, Grant commended Stone to the khedive, attempting to convey that he was innocent of any wrongdoing or negligence during the war.³⁵

Stone's and Wallace's paths would cross during their sojourns abroad, revealing how the wounds of war and its public humiliations were still poignantly felt almost two decades after the cessation of combat. Wallace, describing an encounter one "melancholy night" at Shepheard Hotel in Cairo, remembers Stone, "his eyes moist with tears," still haunted by "his tribulations in America."³⁶ With uncannily similar circumstances underlying their emigration, the meeting between the two uprooted former generals was a moment of mutual recognition, commiseration, and catharsis. In aggregate, the examples of Wallace, Stone, and Longstreet suggest an unofficial policy of expatriating public figures who might have otherwise fallen victim to the still-palpable domestic tensions of the postbellum. Their parallel lives represent a forgotten epilogue to the American Civil War: the nations of the Muslim world offered safety and anonymity to a coterie of war refugees, both Union scapegoats and reconstructed Confederates, whose lives were otherwise imperiled in their country of origin.³⁷

After Wallace's arrival in Istanbul during the summer of 1881, early reportage concerning his first audience with Abdülhamit captures how transoceanic telegraphy had already altered the omnipresence and transactional flows of information around the planet. Not only were American newspapers able to produce an account of this meeting on a timescale of days, they incorporate the detail that the sultan inquired "with solicitude concerning the president of the United States. He asked that his assurances of sympathy be communicated to the President."³⁸ Garfield, still clinging to life, had been mortally wounded in early July but would not succumb until late September. The chain of communication manifest in this exchange—news of the attack on Garfield reaching Turkey and, afterward, reports of the sultan's condolences in American print media—would previously have taken weeks or months to circulate between continents. The Atlantic Telegraph compressed the lag time for this chain of communications down to an interval of days, supercharging the exchange rates of both diplomatic dialogue and media exposure.

Accounts that follow relate Wallace's being summoned back to court to confer with Abdülhamit on the merits of American governmental organization. In March 1882, *The Boston Herald* recounts that the two men "spent several hours" in conversation and that "the Sultan sought much information concerning America, especially in regards to the judicial system in the United States and the mode of collecting taxes."³⁹ By September of the same year, *The Herald* again records in a news brief that "Gen Wallace, the United States minister, dined with the Sultan last evening,"⁴⁰ offering no additional, related information, by way of content or paratext. In a similar fashion, the October 1882 *Denver Republican* informs readers, via a gloss, that "General Wallace was entertained by the Sultan at his palace at Constantinople,"⁴¹ supplying no further detail. The quanta of information related in such "Telegraphic Brevities"⁴² abandon the exposition of long-form narrative journalism and instead serialize the latest, most concise happenings in the friendship. The transatlantic cable could add day-to-day amendments to the running storyline and, in turn, reconfigure the structure and sequence through which the narrative was related. The account, told in piecemeal, thereby acquires its own laconic, telegraphic idiom and syntax.⁴³

Beyond the insights that the new ambassador could impart concerning American bureaucratic innovations, the ulterior motivations behind Abdülhamit's personal interest in Wallace were evident to at least one observer. In August 1883, a writer for the *New York Herald* supplies a telling rationale concerning why the sultan now "poured out his troubles to General Wallace."[44]

> Abdul Hamid is really very kind hearted and of a most affectionate disposition. He has always longed to have an intimate friend among the European representatives at the Porte—one whom he could fully trust, and who might at a pinch prove an able advocate in representing the Turkish side of any question before the world. His Majesty does not need a counsellor so much as a confidant who will listen to him and accept his views; and for the personal interest of such a friend he would do anything. No gift would be too costly, no honor too high for the Sultan to bestow upon his friend could they only be accepted.[45]

The strategic perspectives of a comparatively disinterested foreigner, who did not represent a sovereignty with imminent territorial ambitions upon Ottoman domains, would have been indispensable to the sultan. Abdülhamit might have also seen in Wallace a potential future advocate and mouthpiece, who might one day help to cultivate popular perceptions of Islam, the Ottoman, and the sultan himself in the West. These incentives nevertheless remain ancillary, in the editorialist's judgment, to a besieged ruler who is isolated and badly in need of a sympathetic friend.

Beyond such sentimental, political considerations, the sultan might also have been eager to initiate an acquaintance with a published novelist and amateur painter like Wallace. In keeping with a precedent of connoisseurship of European fine arts among Ottoman royalty, Abdülhamit accompanied his uncle and the ruling sultan, Abdülaziz—a self-taught history painter—to Paris for the 1867 Exposition Universelle.[46] Eschewing his uncle's love of pictorial art, Abdülhamit was an aficionado of opera during his reign: translating, composing, and staging operatic arrangements within the confines of Yıldız Palace.[47] Whatever forces underlay the increasing familiarity between the two men, American readers learned by 1883 that Wallace's sway with the sultan had allegedly created competitive resentment in corridors of Ottoman power.[48]

A key token of the sultan's affection and largesse, "The Turkish Princess" would come into Wallace's possession in 1882, less than a year after his first encounter with Abdülhamit. A correspondence published in *The Indianapolis Sentinel* specifies that the sultan noticed Wallace admiring the portrait and loaned it to the US legation in Istanbul as a means of bypassing protocols against the receipt of presents by American diplomats.[49] It then offers eyewitness ekphrasis of the painting.

> Her face at once enchants you. The great languid eyes, the soft curve of the cheek, the full red of the lip, instantly storm the most rugged heart with a perfect childish beauty. Yet there is something in the swell of the nostrils, something in the curl of the mouth, that makes you feel your sudden sympathetic smile to be unappreciated. The girl looks you squarely in the face, without for a moment condescending to forget that she is a child of the house of Osman, and that 400 years of conquest

have fortified her baby throne of luxury against all disturbance. The child sits there upon a tiger skin among the velvet cushions every inch a princess.... It is the life-size portrait of a Princess, but a Princess of barbaric splendors."[50]

Contrary to the provenance suggested in this passage, the signature, color palate, and aesthetic of "The Turkish Princess" implicate Paris-based painter Charles Louis Lucien Müller, whose established opus includes a number of Orientalist paintings of female subjects.[51] The contours of a calligraphic inscription, adorning the painting's fabric backdrop, resemble the Ottoman sultanic *tuğrâ*, a royal seal, signaling that the painting may have been commissioned by Abdülaziz or by an Ottoman intermediary in France.[52]

Leaked, cable-bound news of "The Turkish Princess" initially reached the United States in the summer of 1882. As the painting began to attract the attention of media outlets, the interest and disdain occasioned were not primarily centered around the dubious legality of the sultan's gift-giving.[53] Rather, they were a product of the animacy and corporeality that "The Turkish Princess" would acquire through her ongoing articulation and rearticulation in print. A first round of objections, raised by *The Boston Daily Advertiser* on July 7, censures none other than Abdülhamit and does so on unexpected terms. By owning a work of figural art, it complains, the sultan has disobeyed the Islamic prohibition against representational simulations. *The Advertiser*, misattributing this convention as a qur'anic injunction, chastises: "The caliph violates the Koran, which prohibits all pictures of living creatures."[54] In spite of these concerns, the commentator still trusts that the painting represents something durable and of substance in the realm of the political. "It is to be hoped that his [Abdülhamit's] intimacy with Mr. Wallace is not a mere form, but a happy essence and sound on the extending influence of this country."[55] Deploying language that marks the distinction between the authentic and the illusory, *The Advertiser* understands the painting as convincing evidence that Wallace's geniality is functioning in support of American interests overseas. Furthermore, this criticism, levied against the sultan by a Boston newspaper, urges some association of the kindred apprehensions surrounding iconography in the Islamic world and among the New England Puritans, which share, as a common point of origin, the Second Commandment of the Decalogue.

Three days later, a *Cleveland Herald* article, entitled "General Wallace and the Turkish Girl," bemoans the painting's mere simulation of a Turkish princess, in preference to an actual odalisque. "Under the old dispensation, before the Commander of the Faithful took to wearing London cut trousers and Paris patent leather boots, the present would have been a real flesh and blood houri with ravishing form and dreamy eyes, instead of painted counterfeit on canvas."[56] The gift's lifelessness represents an unfortunate byproduct of reform and Westernization in the Ottoman Empire. Had "The Turkish Princess" been exchanged in an earlier age, to the article's lecherous disappointment, she would have been a factual, bona fide concubine.

By July 25, *The San Francisco Bulletin* becomes even more demonstrative and trenchant, rescripting reports from Turkey to conform with the representational presumptions of an Orientalist imaginary. It insists that Lew Wallace was, in fact, bequeathed a corporeal person and revels in the impending controversy that his return to the United States will create. "Newspapers are pretending that this was only a painting of a Turkish girl. But the old practice of Sultans is to give and take presents of real girls, of which they have more than paintings."⁵⁷ A protest is issued: "What will Lew Wallace do with his Turkish girl? The laws of this country will not stand it. Let him sell her to Barnum for his caravan."⁵⁸ This proffered solution falls somewhere short of parody. In 1856, P. T. Barnum sent a representative to Istanbul, in earnest, to procure a "Circassian Beauty," who was to be forcibly employed in Barnum's circus.⁵⁹ Wallace's imagined assumption of the role of slaveholder here threatens an insupportable legal impasse in the postbellum United States, destabilizing the recently reasserted distinction between Western freedom and Eastern bondage. Resolving this dilemma by putting Wallace's personal harem slave on public display, the article recourses to tactics of common use and mass consumption as offsets to the general's attempted monopolization of "his Turkish girl."

The imagined crisis reaches a boiling point in the September 24, 1882, edition of *The Indianapolis Sentinel*, the Wallace's hometown newspaper. As indicated by its headline, "An Unwelcome Visitor: How Mrs. Gen. Lew Wallace Received the Sultan's Gift of a Circassian Beauty," the piece focuses heavily on the words and actions of Missus Wallace. It reports that an entourage of palace eunuchs deposited "upon the inside door mat" of the Wallace's Istanbul residence "a big eyed, beautiful Circassian girl, whose lustrous orbs and sparkling jewels were but little obscured by the filmy gauze veiling that covered her from head to foot."⁶⁰ Mrs. Wallace (here named "Maria") gawks at the odalisque and enlists a domestic helper to explain the visitation. An embarrassed house dragoman relates the intentions behind the sultan's "magnificent present," explaining that "His Highness has smiled upon my master and sent him his choicest slave." The Circassian Beauty "will bring my master's coffee to him when he awakens in the morning and affectionately superintend his mornings' ablutions."⁶¹

A stock vaudevillian scenario of rolling-pin-wielding housewife pitted against would-be home wrecker ensues—only the rolling pin, like the scene, has been Orientalized. During household deliberations, Mrs. Wallace "stealthily fingered a bric-a-brac cimetar [sic] and glared at the offending present."⁶² Too sheltered to perceive danger, the bemused "present" is rousted violently by Maria Wallace, who "flew at the present, grabbed it by the shoulder, and was hustling it downstairs." Despite this confrontation, it is made painfully clear that any diplomatic misstep on Lew Wallace's part has the potential to escalate into international conflict. "Stroking the Present's brow in a gentle and fatherly way," the simulacral General Wallace plays the ham-fisted, aspiring polygamist, who outlines the grave ramifications of declining the sultan's offering. Rejection would be "enough to declare war on the United States right off and massacre us all." Ignoring her husband's attempts at parley, Maria Wallace issues an ultimatum: "Fraid of international complications are you, you salacious old wretch.... I'll show you what kind of a Bulgarian atrocity you're married to," likening herself to the Ottoman Empire's violent crackdown on Bulgarian nationalist insurgents following the 1876 April Uprising. Having learned his lesson, General Wallace ultimately relents and concludes that "sooner than go through the like again he would see the whole [North American] continent bathed in blood, and the American eagle bombarded until it hadn't a pin feather to its name."⁶³ As the cultural pressures and sexual temptations of the Orient threaten the fragile domestic order of a monogamous American household abroad, the ensuing melee nearly spirals into an existential, genocidal crisis for the United States.

Tracing the provenance of "An Unwelcome Visitor" and the routes of its transmission in print media helps to contextualize the narrative and reveal an underlying agenda. *The Sentinel* attributes the piece to *The Omaha Daily Bee*, where it appeared as "An Unwelcome Present" on August 25, 1882.[64] The version published in *The Bee*, in turn, identifies *The San Francisco Wasp* as the source of the story and pauses to marvel at its own redactions. "This is all that the modest telegraph consented to say about the occurrence, though the San Francisco Wasp found ever so much more to be told."[65] The details suitable for publication in bohemian San Francisco have been bowdlerized during the text's telegraphic transmission to the more-conservative Midwest. The commentary here offers tantalization via absence, through the spectral eroticism of its own self-attributed expunctions.

The Bee omits in its variorum that, as the source of the material, *The Wasp* is a periodical dedicated to satire. Moreover, the acting editor-in-chief of *The Wasp*, Ambrose Bierce, had intimate motive for exacting a literary vendetta on Lew Wallace. Bierce was a veteran of Shiloh and had serialized the seminal short story "What I Saw of Shiloh" in *The Wasp* during the previous winter.[66] The prime suspect as ghostwriter, Bierce was no stranger to the distortional and displacing effects of contemporary print culture. He had complained, as early as 1870, of how East Coast and European media outlets pirated his original writings with impunity.[67] First published in *The Wasp* on August 5, 1882, the fictional vignette regarding the Wallaces would resurface in newspapers as far away as New Zealand.[68]

As widely as this narrative was circulated, it is difficult to assess how skeptically it was received during each link of its mass reproduction and dissemination—either as a lurid bit of actual news or, more plainly, as Biercian character assassination and comedy. Still, the corpus of simulacral narratives that surround "The Turkish Princess" substantiate long-standing Western discourse regarding Eastern degeneracy and the dangerous attractions of *going native* in a foreign milieu. In "An Unwelcome Present," the enthusiasm and haste with which the simulacral Lew Wallace recourses to bigamy insinuate that he is more than willing to *turn Turk* and, in so doing, abandon the onus of American republican virtue and national identity. The caricatured Wallace's impulsive transition to *renegado*, lured to adopt another culture because of its sensuality and political appeals, forebodes a larger trend of postbellum brain drain, in which the permanent absences of disillusioned expatriates might endanger the ongoing work of national reconciliation. Printed rumors attesting that Wallace had been offered a leadership role in the Ottoman government or military, not limited to the "Commander-in-Chief of the Turkish armies,"[69] exacerbated broader concerns about the cultural continuity of a nation still foundering in the aftermath of secession and civil war. A perceived threat of cultural divestment manifests itself in Bierce's satire, typifying isolationist reaction to the transcultural intimacies ascribed to Wallace and Abdülhamit so frequently during the previous year.

The allegations narrated into being through simulacra of "The Turkish Princess" proved to be enduring. Accounts of the sultan's benefaction of an actual slave dogged the Wallaces well after the turn of the century.[70] As such, "The Turkish Princess" provides an object lesson on the means through which the immeasurable distance, embedded in all processes of reproduction, can be used to manipulate specious artifacts into a condition of virtual authenticity. The work of narrative simulation, especially between continents, created fissures for the deceptive insertion of textual forgeries.[71] Through the mass circulation of its narrative and the resignifications then incited, the gifted painting transitioned, Pygmalion-like, from an inorganic representation into an embodied person. Protestations of the princess's corporeality are then narrated by Bierce into a scene of violence that is equally familial, international, and apocalyptic in scope. As "An Unwelcome Present" comes home to roost in Indiana, the narrative becomes increasingly malicious through its de-contextualization from satire into newsprint. Rather than shedding aural authenticity and valence energy through its mass reproduction, a denaturing process imagined by Benjamin,[72] the painting becomes more embodied and more authentic through the amendment of each new layer of detail and storyline, augmenting a swelling narrative cloud. Baudrillard might understand this as an instance of the *hyperreal*, simulacra deployed to authenticate the existence of a fictitious primary trace, in support of any number of cultural, political, and psychological certainties.[73]

Through their mass retelling, simulacral narratives were circulated into authenticity, and, in this process, they exposed a critical weakness. The accumulation and re-dissemination of countless reports, collected from the far-flung reaches of the globe via transoceanic telegraphy, made information that had previously remained remote and inscrutable now appear to be superabundant and hyper-accessible. Up-to-the-day intercontinental news, which had not yet had the time to become antiquated, acquired a vitality and agency of its own. The newly actualized organicity of telegraphed international news generated, in turn, a susceptibility and euphoria among news producers and consumers, intoxicated by the recent geometrical enlargements of the global media apparatus and the attractions of unfettered, panoptical planetary surveillance.

Such a euphoria proved hospitable to the simulacral forces of dissonance and distortion that drove the transubstantiation of "The Turkish Princess"—and to the charlatanisms of fake narrative, fabricated substance, and the personal agendas accompanying them. Given the gleeful vulnerabilities of the period and a popular tendency toward confirmation bias in an age of media revolution, hard-earned qualities of hesitation, skepticism, and hostility toward potential misinformation had to be developed over time by cooler heads. Within the fog and instability of a freshly teleconnected media ecosystem with a novel planet-wide reach, the skeptical callouses that should have backstopped news of "The Turkish Princess" were found to be anything but reflexive and automatic. The higher output of international news resulted in a deficiency, in which false positives could be deployed to overwhelm and alter narratives in a way that supported, rather than mitigated, a pervading Orientalism.

Lew Wallace was recalled in 1885 and departed Turkey wondering if the sultan's niceties were authentic or merely artifice, undertaken for the purposes of statecraft.[74] Yet, as the years wore on, his loyalty to Abdülhamit proved unwavering. In the wake of the so-named Hamidian Massacres (1894–96), Wallace would even become the sultan's chief American defender against accusations of genocide. As reports of the mass extermination of the Ottoman Empire's Armenian citizenry reached the international community, suspicions regarding Abdülhamit's role in instigating or abetting the killings abounded—allegations that Wallace ultimately attempted to repudiate. On the Chicago leg of an 1895 lecture tour entitled "Turkey and the Turks, With Glimpses of the Harem," Wallace was "openly hissed" by a contingent of Armenians, "who expressed their feelings without restraint," for his failure to condemn the sultan.[75] Facing mounting outcry from his audience, Wallace categorically denied that Abdülhamit could have facilitated or condoned the attacks on Armenians. Preaching restraint, he instead characterized Abdülhamit as a capable ruler who was "misunderstood and misrepresented."[76] Media depictions of Abdülhamit as a calculated, ruthless tyrant were, Wallace repeatedly argued thereafter, distortions of the man in actuality; they should always be received with some measure of doubt. The emerging figure of "the Red Sultan, Abdul the Damned, or the Ogre of Yıldız Kiosk,"[77] as the sultan later came to be known in the West, in no way represented the actual individual with whom Wallace had become personally acquainted during the previous decade. The persistence of Wallace's negation begs the question of how his own caricature and mass simulacralization in American media during the 1880s informed his subsequent defense of Abdülhamit.

The interconnected lives of Sultan Abdülhamit and Lew Wallace represent a unique moment of parity, in which interactions between representatives of Islamic and American worlds seem to have been anything but distant, remote, or lost in translation. Because of the history that followed, the friendship also constitutes something of a tragicomic historical irony. The embattled creator of Ben-Hur, the archetypal figure of Muscular Christianity in American cinema, found a kindred spirit in Sultan Abdülhamit, one of the last remaining barriers to the colonial partition of the Ottoman Empire and the creation of the modern Middle East. With a striking zeal and regularity in intervening years, American cultural representations have deployed more-muscular facsimiles of Ben-Hur to quell chaos and restore order in former Ottoman domains. An allegory of national disenfranchisement and recuperation, Ben-Hur's violent reclamation of his reputation and cultural identity is a key feature in the novel's filmic adaptations during various postwar periods, in 1907, 1925, 1959, and 2016.[78]

At the moment that Lew Wallace and Abdülhamit befriended one another, the United States and the Ottoman Empire both stood on the brink of similar national-imperial crises—of secession in the former and partition in the latter. Both predicaments were brought about and intensified by the eruption of ideologies of race nationalism, which imperfectly attempted to draw national borderlines encircling a single people with a single shared language, culture, and history. Such re-entrenchments could, it was imagined, reduce the threat of territorial loss or cultural-racial decline. The demands of sustaining the nation and empire in a newly teleconnected world provoked redoubled efforts aimed at the exclusion, expulsion, and de-legitimation of the bodies which did not belong, to predictably disastrous effect.

The glitches in teleconnectivity that plagued media reports of the friendship between the sultan and the general did not bode well for future teleconnected engagements between the United States and the Muslim world. The relationship instead provided ample opportunity for the reactionary insertion of simulacral falsifications in print, which grew more sensational as they were reproduced and retransmitted. Because of the ways it threatened cultural identity, reportage of the intimacy between the sultan and the general was distorted, by use of simulacra, to the point of absurdity, in order to reassert the sanctity and coherence of a raced American nationhood. At that embryonic moment of teleconnection and now, dissimulational narratives, recirculated until they are rendered authentic, have been pressed into the service of symbiotic nationalist-Orientalist ideologies, personal vendetta, war making, and mercantile gain. Rather than familiarizing the world to itself, the first age of teleconnection was preempted by strategic distraction and chatter. In 1882, the newly wired global communications network was manipulated to reinscribe the nation within and the Orient without.

Acknowledgment

The author would like to wholeheartedly thank the staff of The Lew Wallace Study and Museum and his father, James Hunt, for the research assistance offered in preparation of this piece.

7

The Lost Tribes of the Afghans: Religious Mobility and Entanglement in Narratives of Afghan Origins

William E. B. Sherman

Grand Contested Election for the Presidency of the United States.
Whaling Voyage by One Ishmael.
Bloody Battle in Affghanistan[1]

In the early seventeenth century, Afghans within the Mughal Empire began to inscribe and circulate genealogies that narrated Afghan descent from ʿAbd al-Rashid Qays Pathan—a hero in the time of Muhammad and a descendant of Afghana, son of King Saul.[2] The Afghans were, in short, Israelites. Moreover, they were *lost* Israelites. As the Israelites faced the judgment of God acting through Nebuchadnezzar, these Afghans wandered in exile to the Sulaiman Mountains—the border regions between present-day Afghanistan and Pakistan. While European and American Christian missionaries and colonists have sought the "Lost Tribes of Israel" across the globe, here we find an *"Afghan* Lost Tribes" narrative that awaited the first missionaries as they arrived in nineteenth-century Peshawar. Unlike other reports of Lost Tribes, the narrative of the "Afghan Lost Tribes" does not begin in the biblical imagination of Christian missionaries. Rather, the older roots of this narrative permitted cross-confessional routes that enfolded Christian interpretations of the Lost Tribes into a longer history that cannot be fully claimed as Christian or Muslim, American or Afghan. Christian exegetes cross-referenced Afghan genealogies with the book of Revelation in order to find clues to an apocalyptic future, while the founder of the Ahmadiyya Movement, Mirza Ghulam Ahmad (1835–1908), and Ahmadi Muslims turned to Anglo-American reports on the "Afghan Lost Tribes" to bolster Ghulam Ahmad's bid for universal messianic authority. The story of the Afghan Lost Tribes was a wandering one, and its nomadism entangled communities, historical imaginations, and identity formations along the Afghan frontier.

This chapter analyzes three moments in the process of this entanglement. We begin with brief consideration of the context from which Afghan genealogies first emerged in order to justify the Afghan presence in the multiethnic Mughal court. We then move to an analysis of Anglo-American Christian missionary sources in which the "Afghan Lost Tribes" narrative influenced the practice of the Peshawar missionary and became an indication of the eschatological role to be played by the apocalyptic Afghan "kings of the east."[3] Next, we consider the Ahmadi interpretation of the "Afghan Lost Tribes" narrative—filtered through English-language sources—as the theological grounds upon which Ghulam Ahmad claimed his role as *mahdi* (guided one) and *masih* (messiah). Finally, in the conclusion, this chapter offers a brief analysis of how the history of this entanglement runs against contemporary imaginations of Afghanistan as isolated and timeless.

The idea of the Lost Tribes has enchanted audiences for centuries, offering coherence to sacred history and colonial geographies. There is indeed something alluring and exotic about these materials: legendary genealogies, murdered missionaries, a romance novel penned by a priest, accounts of Jesus's death in India, and "proofs" that the Afghans had walked straight from the pages of the Hebrew Bible. The enchantment of these stories has repeatedly drawn Anglo-American audiences to imagine Afghanistan as a place that has slipped from time, an inverted and violent Shangri-La in which both the blessedness and the brutality of "biblical" life continues. With greater irony than most, Herman Melville's Ishmael seeks to comprehend his own fate by anchoring his whaling journey to the steady patterns of history: a "*Grand Contested Election*" and a "BLOODY BATTLE IN AFFGHANISTAN." Afghanistan still appears in American accounts as the "graveyard of empires," and *biblical* joins *medieval* as a common descriptor of Afghan life.[4] In tracing the peripatetic narrative of the "Afghan Lost Tribes," this chapter offers a counterpoint to the Anglo-American imagination of Afghanistan as timeless and isolated; the story offered in this chapter is one of mobility, entanglement, and change. As Muslims and Christians read and retold the histories and legends of others, American Christian, Afghan Muslim, and Ahmadi identities—"Islamic" and "Western" histories—emerged co-constitutively in response, contest, and dialogue.

Certainly, the *idea* of an Israelitic Afghan community contributed to a larger project of conscripting "Orientalist" images into "globaliz[ing] the authority of the cultural power of the United States."[5] Attempting to move beyond the discussion of American Orientalisms, however, I argue that it is historiographical error to assume Anglo-American agency and Muslim passivity along the frontier. This chapter deliberately brackets the Christian missionary reports between two other moments in the life of the Afghan Lost Tribes narrative. My entry into this literature is as a scholar of Islamic texts and their reception—texts that include genealogies that braid a people's origins with the cosmic history of God and God's prophets. This particular Islamic discourse of blessed Afghan history weaves from "Asian Muslim" worlds into "Anglo-American Christian" worlds and back again. The history that I tell of American Orientalism—of missionaries fashioning a sense of American culture and identity through narratives of the "Orient"—is but a chapter in a larger history in which Muslims of South Asia have appealed to the narrative of the Afghan Lost Tribes to make meaning of the spectacular religious diversity (and consequent anxiety of alienation) that characterizes South Asia. It is thus possible to enfold American interpretative acts of "Orientalism" and self-fashioning into an "Islamic history" of prophets and *mahdis*.

The Afghan Sons of Saul in Mughal India

The prevalence of genealogical texts among Afghan communities in the nineteenth and twentieth centuries has tended to confirm the preconceptions of Anglo-American commentators on Afghanistan: this is a land of insularity, tribalism, and parochialism. The genealogy, in this imagining, functions as a literary equivalent to endogamy; it is a technology for maintaining an inherent separation from other groups. Contrary to this interpretation, I show that these texts emerged in cosmopolitan and competitive Mughal courts as a bid for Afghan blessedness in prophetic history. In this section, I examine how Afghans in the early seventeenth century wrote genealogies that describe the Afghans as the descendants of Israelites. This narrative—which I am calling the "Afghan Lost Tribes narrative"—addressed the specific concerns of Afghan nobles in the diverse courts of the ruling Mughal Empire in South Asia. The genealogical literature of the Afghans, therefore, has a genealogy all its own that invites a different history than one of Afghan isolation and parochialism.

From the perspective of Mughal authorities in the sixteenth century, the Afghan place in the empire was a troubling one.[6] Though the meaning of the Persian term *afghan* was fluid, many of the early rivals and threats to the emergent Mughal Empire were identified as Afghan, and the consolidation of Mughal power involved their violent defeat, dislocation, and incorporation. Accompanying the construction of Mughal towers of stone and skull, chroniclers in Mughal courts tended to denigrate the Afghans as a pestilent people whose rare military victories over Mughal armies were the product of their swarming, locust-like brutishness.[7] While the perceived Afghan "threat" to the Mughals had been substantively defeated by the beginning of Jahangir's reign in 1605 CE, there were many Afghan nobles and generals who were active in Mughal courts but occupied a suspect space, derided as a barbarous and unlettered people. Genealogies offered a potential remedy.

We can turn to one of the earliest and most widely circulating genealogies in order to understand the effect of the Afghan Lost Tribes narrative: Niʿmat Allah Harawi's *Tarikh-i Khan Jahani va Makhzan-i Afghani* (hereafter, *Afghan Treasure Chest*) written circa 1612 CE.[8] Following the arguments of Nile Green and Robert Nichols, I suggest that Harawi's text—and the subsequent proliferation of Afghan genealogies in the seventeenth century—responded to the anxious place of Afghans in multiethnic, multireligious Mughal courts.[9]

Harawi's *Afghan Treasure Chest* begins the history of the Afghan people by describing the pre-corporeal prophetic light of Muhammad as it alighted upon the body of Adam.[10] From Adam's loins, the light of prophecy passed to his sons and descendants, eventually reaching Abraham, Isaac, Jacob, and then Judah.[11] Among Judah's descendants, we find Saul—known as *malik talut* or "the tall king" of the Qur'an.[12] Just before Saul's death, he impregnated two wives who would bear children named Asif and Afghana. Harawi tells us that Asif and Afghana became the most celebrated courtiers and generals of King Solomon's court. Due to Afghana's service in advising the construction of Solomon's Temple (*bayt al-maqdis*), God blessed Afghana with many sons and descendants known as the Afghans.[13]

As for the generations that followed, Harawi relates that the Israelites' devotion to God waned, and Nebuchadnezzar's armies delivered God's punishment upon the Israelites.[14] Though steadfastly pious, the Afghans were scattered along with the other Israelites. Some wandered south to the Ka'ba built by Abraham in Mecca; most Afghans fled east to the Sulaiman Mountains (*koh-i sulayman*) to raise the banner of monotheism in a distant land. During the life of the prophet Muhammad, these Afghans temporarily returned to Arabia to aid God's messenger. The leader of the Afghans was a champion named Qays, and Qays's heroic deeds earned him blessed titles from Muhammad.[15]

First, Qays received the name *'Abd al-Rashid*. Then:

> The angel Gabriel revealed [to Muhammad] that the attachment of the descendants of Qays to the faith would be so strong that it would be like the wood upon which [ship-builders] lay the keel when constructing a ship—a wood that sailors call *Pathan*. . . . Muhammad conferred the title of *Pathan* upon 'Abd al-Rashid Qays. Amongst [his descendants] arose dervishes, devotees, and saints who excelled in deed and speech.[16]

This revelation serves an etiological purpose for a Mughal audience, for it roots the common term in India for Afghans—*Pathan*—in an act of angelic philology. Harawi's narrative presents the anointed 'Abd al-Rashid Qays Pathan as the heroic forefather of the Afghan nobles of Harawi's Mughal setting. The remainder of *Afghan Treasure Chest* clarifies the lines of descent from the four sons of Qays to the various Afghan tribal networks of Mughal India.

What do we make of this effort by Harawi to find an exalted Afghan past in the narrative crevices of prophetic history? *Afghan Treasure Chest* was among the earliest of such accounts, but Afghan genealogy proliferated as a genre throughout the subsequent centuries.[17] There has been a tendency to treat such genealogies as literary technologies of insularity and parochialism—they are merely the means by which Afghans locate themselves in complicated networks of tribe and clan. And, indeed, these genealogies have been central to tribal negotiations of inheritance and land rights since the era of British colonial governance in the North West Frontier, if not earlier.[18]

By demarcating these genealogies as *Afghan texts* addressing an Afghan tribal audience, however, we ignore the extensive narrative in *Afghan Treasure Chest* that precedes the lines of descent from the sons of Qays. This story of Saul and Qays does not attest to the stability of Afghan identity within webs of lineage; quite to the contrary, the invocation of Israelitic history represents an effort to reconfigure—perhaps create— Afghan Muslim identity in a Mughal courtly context marked by cosmopolitanism and competition. Far from the bastard descendants of a demon and his captives—as one rival narrative suggested—*Afghan Treasure Chest* seeks to identify the Afghans as the inheritors of prophets and kings.[19]

To be Afghan was to be of the "Lost Tribes." By emphasizing displacement and absence, the Afghan Lost Tribes narrative opens the possibility of fluid sacred geographies—of a blessed people migrating from Jerusalem to Afghanistan. The Lost Tribes narrative does not merely address questions of place; it is also a matter of time. There is not a simple movement of righteousness from Adam to Muhammad and onward to the Afghans. Rather, Harawi's story attests to multiple timelines. It is polychronic, unfolding both as linear progression and as blessed repetition. To be Afghan was to be an inheritor of those who built the Temple in Jerusalem, prayed at the Ka'ba following Nebuchadnezzar's displacement, and defended the faith in India. The status of the Afghans was changed not by the revelation of the Qur'an but by the revelation of their name: *Pathan*.

Afghan Treasure Chest cast history as the stuff of Afghan belonging in an era of Mughal cosmopolitanism, but the life of this genealogy was an unpredictable one. Harawi's narrative of the Afghan Lost Tribes would wander beyond the imperial court to become the raw discursive material out of which Christian missionaries constructed their own notions of history, belonging, and apocalypse.

The Kings of Revelation at the Peshawar Mission

The bullet that killed the Presbyterian missionary Isidor Loewenthal as he wandered his courtyard in April 1864 ended the American Christian mission to the Afghans for the rest of the century.[20] As Loewenthal sought to relieve his frequent headaches in the late-night air, the *chowkidar* (watchman) guarding his residence mistook Loewenthal as a midnight thief.[21] The death of Loewenthal, however, did not untangle imaginations of American Christian identity from the Afghan Muslims of Peshawar. After all, the Afghans were members of the Lost Tribes who had been found again, and Loewenthal's reports on the matter and those of his English successors continued to braid American and Muslim worlds together long after the acquittal of Loewenthal's *chowkidar*. This section begins by considering the emergence of the Afghan Lost Tribes narrative in English-language discourses before assessing the ways in which the narrative shaped both the Peshawar mission and American imaginings of the apocalypse.

The 1867 edition of *The Missionary Magazine* included an excited description of the Afghans that emphasizes their status as lost Israelites.[22] Published by the American Baptist Missionary Union, this anonymous article offers a litany of proofs that the Afghans were lost Israelites—and these proofs held promises of the future.[23] Aside from Afghan self-representation as descendants of Saul, Christian missionaries perceived physical and social indications of the Afghans' biblical past. In physiognomy, the Afghans resembled the patriarchs of the Hebrew Bible. They practiced the ritual of the "scapegoat." The Afghan social norms of retribution and "eye-for-an-eye" punishments were identical to the *lex talionis* of the Israelites. The names of the Afghans—such as *Yusufzai*, "son of Joseph"—were shot through with biblical referents, and the place names of the frontier resonated with a biblical geography. As the report in *The Missionary Magazine* concludes, these Afghans were the key to the awaited Christian future.[24] As swarthy mountain warriors who possessed a spark of biblical blessedness, the Afghans could be the ultimate evangelists in Central Asia, Iran, eastern Russia, and other places beyond the reach of Protestant missions. And according to a more apocalyptic chronology, these found-again Israelite Afghans might very well be the "kings of the east" prophesied to cross a desiccated Euphrates in Rev. 16:12 upon the opening of the sixth vial.[25]

The report of *The Missionary Magazine* condensed for an American audience what had been a sprawling discourse on the Lost Tribes of Israel and their potential location in Afghanistan. In the seventeenth and eighteenth centuries, British Christians adapted the narrative of the Lost Tribes as a means of interpreting the expansive British colonial project.[26] To establish the empire was to make whole the fractured peoples of God and to potentially bring the "semi-civilized" lost Israelites to their own fulfillment under colonial rule.[27] The growth of British imperialism accompanied the emergence of an eschatology of Judeocentrism, as Richard Cogley has described.[28] This was a vision of the End with geographic specificity—a vision in which the locations of the Holy Land and the Jewish diaspora would stage an imminent apocalypse. Reflecting a world that had become increasingly connected, knowable, and conquerable, English and American Christians braided together biblical hermeneutics and a careful perusal of ethnographic and historical knowledge flowing from the colonial frontiers to the theological centers of Protestant Christianity in Boston, New York, Manchester, and London. In short, to identify the Lost Tribes throughout Anglo-American colonial expansion was not simply an act of historical curiosity. Nor was it merely a process of imperial epistemology in which the unknown became categorized and knowable through a biblical framework. Finding the Lost Tribes served as an opportunity—or a proof, perhaps—of the millenarian unveiling of a triumphant Christian civilization.[29]

As *The Missionary Magazine* article offered its readers "proofs" of the Afghan Lost Tribes—physiognomy, naming, custom, sartorial habit, and so on—these forms of evidence would have been legible to an American audience that had encountered similar claims elsewhere. Across the globe in the eighteenth and nineteenth centuries, Anglo-American missionaries and adventurers "found" the Lost Tribes in Japan, among the Karen people of Burma, in various parts of Africa, among the Tatars, amid various Native American populations, on and on.[30] But for some Christian interpreters, it was the Afghans' own narratives of Israelitic origin that distinguished their bid as members of the Lost Tribes—a recognition that "every Afghan from the Amir on the throne of Kabul to the poorest tiller of the soil believes himself borne of the *Bani-Israil*, or Children of Israel."[31] The first claims made in Anglo-American networks of information regarding the Afghan Lost Tribes began precisely with Afghan narratives of their origins such as *Afghan Treasure Chest*—and not with a missionary's speculation.

In 1790, William Jones of Fort William College investigated a report that the Afghans were Israelites.[32] Jones confirmed this identification by pointing both to Persian histories of Afghan Israelitic origins and to the similarities between Chaldean and Pashto. Jones's reputation as a brilliant Orientalist pushed the Afghan Lost Tribes narrative into wide circulation to be repeated by some of the most prominent European and American experts of Afghanistan. Thus, in the mid-nineteenth century, Alexander Burnes, James Fraser, H. G. Raverty, J. P. Ferrier, George Moore, Joseph Wolff, and other travelers and scholar-administrators working in Central and South Asia extended and confirmed the inquiry of Jones.[33] Through their memoirs and diaries, these authors contributed vignettes of "biblical law," catalogues of "Jewish names" among the Afghans, sketches of Israelitic physiognomy, and so on that would eventually inform the report in *The Missionary Magazine*.[34]

Unlike other instances of Lost Tribes found again, Anglo-American Christians did not control nor initiate this narrative act of identification. Indeed, the peculiar polyvocality of this Lost Tribes encounter both shaped the evangelizing practices of the Peshawar Christian mission and entangled Anglo-American Christian imaginations with a discursive tradition that was not fully contained by Anglo-American writing. For the remainder of this section, we will examine the role of the Afghan Lost Tribes narrative in shaping the missionary practice at Peshawar before concluding by considering its apocalyptic interpretation in the United States.

In 1855, the American Presbyterian Isidor Loewenthal arrived in Peshawar to work at the Church Missionary Society.[35] At the time, the senior CMS evangelist was Carl G. Pfander. Best known as the author of *The Balance of Truth*, Pfander was a dogged polemicist who aggressively confronted the non-Christians of India with the wickedness of their beliefs. Pfander's polemics set the tone of the recently established Peshawar mission: fiery speeches delivered in Hindustani in the bazaar.[36] Pfander's approach was not unique, and the CMS publications of the 1850s suggest that CMS missionaries in South Asia had often performed their duties in racialized and agonistic ways. An editorial in an 1852 issue of *The Church Missionary Intelligencer*, for example, emphasized that "Mahommedanism" could only rise where Christianity failed, but a renewed Christianity could accomplish "the full humiliation of the Mahommedan powers."[37]

Loewenthal broke from these habits of the CMS. He quickly learned Pashto, and he preferred quiet, sympathetic conversation to brash polemic. To the consternation of British officials, Loewenthal frequently left Peshawar to visit nearby villages.[38] Loewenthal's loudest confrontations were saved for his British colleagues as he bluntly critiqued esteemed officials such as Raverty for their incomprehension of Pashto language and Afghan culture.[39] In explaining his departures from CMS practice—in justifying his eagerness to adopt local dress, food, and language—Loewenthal invoked the special status of Afghans: their vigor, their connection to sacred history, and their "half-civilized nature" as members of the Lost Tribes of Israel.[40]

But Loewenthal's career in Peshawar was a short one, abruptly concluded by a bullet from his *chowkidar*'s rifle. Despite the antipathy British officials held for the method of Loewenthal's evangelism, he had shifted the course of the Peshawar mission. A few months after Loewenthal's death, the Anglican priest Thomas Patrick Hughes arrived in Peshawar and remained for over twenty years. Peculiarly unbeholden to CMS convention, Hughes's own missionary practice echoed Loewenthal's concern for sympathetic engagement and liminal spaces.[41]

Like his American predecessor, Hughes devoted himself to study and learned Pashto, Persian, Arabic, and Hindustani. He adopted local dress, and he ventured beyond Peshawar for extended stays in small Afghan communities. In one report, Hughes explains that he had success in reading texts with local women as they had patience for concentrated textual study.[42] This is a remarkable departure from the typical British representation of the frontier as a place of illiteracy, violence, and insurmountable gender separation.

Hughes was a prolific author, and he submitted dozens of articles, reports, and histories to *The Church Missionary Intelligencer*, *The Indian Evangelical Review*, *The Missionary Gleaner*, and other global Christian periodicals.[43] Frequently, Hughes noted the Israelitic origins of the Afghans. The narrative of the Afghan Lost Tribes was useful for Hughes in convincing his superiors, colleagues, and readers of the necessity of his evangelism in Peshawar. As Hughes explained, not only were the Afghans admirable for their vigor and their loyalty during the "mutiny" of 1857, but they were lost Israelites whose history must be "bound up with the religious history of the world."[44]

Over the course of two decades, Hughes pushed the CMS in Peshawar toward a mission marked by sympathetic encounter. Hughes's commitment to evangelizing among Afghans "as one fallen sinner should speak to another" received architectural form in the construction of the All Saints' Memorial Church.[45] Completed in 1883, the church is a manifestation of the liminality that characterized the Peshawar mission under Hughes's leadership. Fashioned like a Mughal mosque with domes and minaret-esque towers, the interior of the church featured calligraphic inscriptions of the Bible in Persian translation while the worship space included wooden screens to allow for residents of Peshawar to maintain a practice of *purdah* (gender separation). Robert Clark, a senior CMS missionary, described the building upon his visit as "a beautiful, and perhaps almost unique, Christian church in the midst of this great city of the Afghans. . . . [The church] is a successful adaptation of mosque architecture to the purposes of Christian worship."[46]

We should not lose sight of the triumphalist, racialized, and imperialist ideologies that mark Hughes's dispatches from Peshawar. Hughes valued the Afghans for their hardiness and the passion of their commitments, and in this way Hughes reiterated a contrast made by British commentators between the strong Afghans and the "weaker" peoples in other parts of India.[47] The British Empire represented a providential unfolding of God's empire, and the Afghans—as *future* Christians—would be the vigorous vanguard of Christian rule in the darkness that lay beyond the Khyber Pass.[48] The narrative of the Afghan Lost Tribes became useful for Hughes because it allowed a careful balance of Hughes's presumption of a racialized, Christian triumphalism and Hughes's habit of cultivating liminal spaces for evangelical encounter.

Nor should we overstate the influence of the narrative of the Afghan Lost Tribes on the practices of Loewenthal and Hughes. Both published their skepticism on the matter, and Hughes quite carefully rejected the litany of "proofs" that we find in *The Missionary Magazine*. According to Hughes, the "physiognomical resemblance" between Afghans and Jews is negligible; the retributive practice of *lex talionis* characterizes all variety of "tribal" peoples; the connection between Pashto and Chaldean is unverifiable; and Hughes had never witnessed or heard of a "scapegoat" ritual among the Afghans he visited.[49]

Whatever Hughes's personal evaluation, he was willing to propagate the narrative for his Anglo-American audiences. When publishing dispatches from the frontier, Hughes repeatedly insisted that the Afghans were "bound up with the religious history of the world" by mentioning their Israelitic origins.[50] Under the pseudonym Evan Stanton, Hughes wrote a novel titled *Ruhainah* that received multiple publications in the United States.[51] In *Ruhainah*, a gallant British captain falls desperately in love with the daughter of an Afghan chief. Hughes scattered mentions of the Afghans' Israelitic origins throughout his novel. After twenty years on the Afghan frontier, Hughes retired from his post in Peshawar and settled in New York City to work as a rector of the Church of the Holy Sepulchre.[52] He continued to speak about the Afghan frontier, and he delivered a public lecture at Bleecker Hall on March 17, 1887, during which Hughes described the narrative of the Afghan Lost Tribes for his American audience.[53]

From these reports and dispatches of Hughes and Loewenthal—and from the publications of Jones, Burnes, Wolff, and others—the narrative of the Afghan Lost Tribes wandered from the networks of Orientalists and missionaries in Asia, and it entered the churn of a vivid American apocalyptic imagination. In Harawi's *Afghan Treasure Chest*, we find that Afghans refer to any leader—whether a local elder or a powerful governor—as *malik* or "king" in recognition of their descent from Saul.[54] The Afghans are thus a people of "kings." In the Lost Tribes logic of sources such as Joseph Towers's *Illustration of Prophecy* and *The Missionary Magazine*'s 1867 report, the coincidence of Afghan Israelitic origins and the presence of multiple "kings" suggests that the Afghans are the "kings of the east" mentioned in Rev. 16:12: "And the sixth angel poured out his vial upon the great river Euphrates; and the water thereof was dried up, that the way of the *kings of the east* might be prepared."[55]

Biblical concordia and apocalyptic treatises of the nineteenth century reiterated this identification of the Afghans as the prophesized kings of the east. Consulting *The Bible Cyclopedia*, for instance, we find under "Rev. 16:12" an unquestioned identification of the "kings of the east" as the Afghans.[56] The Lost Tribes of the Afghans thus gained an apocalyptic future to accompany their biblical past, a point well made by a mid-nineteenth-century American depiction of the End Times.[57] As discussed by Timothy Marr, the image includes a complex diagram of the seven vials of Revelation, and accompanying this diagram is a reproduction of a sketch featured in Mountstuart Elphinstone's report on his 1808 mission to Peshawar.[58] The message is clear: this sketched Afghan is a glimpse of what will pour out from the vials of the end times.

In these various ways, the narrative of the Afghan Lost Tribes facilitated the entanglement of Afghan pasts and Christian futures. The Afghans were not simply a people to be brought into the Christian fold. They were well-attested Israelites, and they were actors of the apocalypse. Afghan genealogical texts, Afghan oral histories, and Afghan practices thus became the means by which Anglo-American Christians understood Christian purpose, Christian identity, and the possible forms of Christian evangelization. This chapter, however, is not solely concerned with the Orientalism of Christian understandings of Afghans. Just as Harawi's *Afghan Treasure Chest* slipped from an Afghan-Mughal discursive context to become a text of *Christian* self-fashioning, so too did these dispatches and travelogues describing the Afghan Lost Tribes migrate from an Anglo-American Christian discourse and wander into the literature of Ahmadi Muslim reformers in the Punjab.

The Ahmadi Unveiling of Jesus among His Afghan Flock

South of the Peshawar CMS mission, in the cities of Lahore and Qadian, Mirza Ghulam Ahmad began to reveal the word of God. In Ghulam Ahmad's own way, he was joining a generation of Muslim intellectuals addressing the crisis of religious authority confronting the Muslims of South Asia in the wake of the tumultuous conflicts of 1857.[59] As Adil Hussain Khan has argued, Ghulam Ahmad developed a reformist message and critique of traditional institutions of Islamic learning that located the truth of this modern, reformist Islam in the figure of Mirza Ghulam Ahmad himself, the messiah and *mahdi* embodying the word of God.[60] This section describes how Ghulam Ahmad grounded his messianic claim in the narrative of the Afghan Lost Tribes—a narrative which Ghulam Ahmad understood by engaging both Persian- *and* English-language sources on the Afghan Lost Tribes. We learn, therefore, something of the eclectic nature of Ghulam Ahmad's reasoning, but, moreover, we see how a figure such as Ghulam Ahmad enfolded the Anglo-American Christian discourse on the Afghan Lost Tribes into a broader history of Islamic unveiling as imagined by Ghulam Ahmad and his followers known as the Ahmadiyya.

In the 1890s, Ghulam Ahmad began composing a work that would be published in 1908 in Urdu as *'Isa hindustan mein*—and officially translated by members of the Ahmadiyya community as *Jesus in India* in 1944. *Jesus in India* is but one of many voluminous works attributed to Ghulam Ahmad, but it effectively evinces the tenor of Ghulam Ahmad's religious message and the centrality of the Afghan Lost Tribes in Ahmadi Muslim theology. The book begins by making explicit the bold eschatology of Ghulam Ahmad: "God has revealed to me that the real Promised Messiah who is also the *Mahdi*, tidings of whose appearance are to be found in the Bible and the Holy Qur'an and whose coming is also promised in the *ahadith* is none other than myself."[61] If we look past the bid for personal embodied authority in this statement, we see that Ghulam Ahmad is offering a radical reinterpretation of eschatological events. The *mahdi* (guided one) is identical to the *masih* (messiah). In most Sunni Muslim accounts, the *mahdi* appears just before the Day of Resurrection to guide the Muslim community, and the *mahdi's* appearance coincides with second coming of the *masih*, Jesus. According to Ghulam Ahmad, however, God has revealed that Ghulam Ahmad occupies the position of both the *mahdi* and the *masih*—the guided one and the messiah.

But why collapse these distinct roles for the two principle protagonists of Islamic eschatology? Among the reasons for this messianic creativity, the teachings of Ghulam Ahmad reflect the poly-religious colonial environment of British India from which they emerged. Having witnessed the success of British armies and the techniques of British missionaries, Ghulam Ahmad and the Ahmadiyya set out to deliver his reformation in "modern" ways: magazines, pamphlets, "scientific reasoning," and a commitment to robust evangelism.[62] Assessing the religious landscapes and technologies of British India, Ghulam Ahmad attempted to reach the multitude of diverse religious communities. And thus, he competed not only with the Sufi families of Lahore or the jurists of Lucknow but also with the Christian missionaries sent from Boston or Manchester. In claiming both the title of *mahdi* and *masih*, he was bidding for the responsibility of both roles and correcting the claims of both Christians and other Muslims. As he writes, "In this age the greatest sympathy one can show to the Christians is to draw their attention to the True God who transcends the traumas of birth, death, pain and suffering. . . . The one good service one could perform for the Muslims would be to reform their moral condition."[63]

Claiming to be the *mahdi* is a controversial if comprehensible claim to make in Islamic religious contexts—a claim made by many Muslims before Ghulam Ahmad such as Ibn Tumart (d. 1130 CE) of the Almohad Caliphate, Sayyid Muhammad Jawnpuri (d. ca. 1505 CE) of the Mahdawiyya movement in India, and Muhammad Ahmad (1884–85) in Sudan. Claiming to be the messiah, however, requires revision to Islamic and Christian histories alike. For Ghulam Ahmad's Christian audiences and interlocutors, Jesus was the messiah, having been raised from the dead after his crucifixion. In prevalent Islamic traditions, God had lifted Jesus from the cross before his death, preserving him in heaven until the appearance of the *mahdi*. In order to perform this bit of theoretical maneuvering—in order to be both the messiah and the *mahdi* for the diversity of his imagined constituents—Mirza Ghulam Ahmad needed an alternative account of Jesus.

The Afghan Lost Tribes narrative contributed to such an alternative history of Jesus's life for it provided the necessary proof that Jesus's career was unfinished at the time of his crucifixion. In *Jesus in India*, Jesus's earthly presence did not end in Palestine, and, according to Ghulam Ahmad, nor do key passages in the gospels suggest such an ending. Ghulam Ahmad places immense weight on Jn 10:16: "And other sheep I have which are not of this fold; I must also bring them, and they will hear My voice; and there will be one flock and one shepherd."[64] As Ghulam Ahmad interprets the verse, "Jesus had to make this journey for the divine object underlying his mission was to meet the lost tribes of Israel who had settled in different parts of India."[65] After decades of teaching in the Afghan highlands and Kashmir, Jesus died naturally and was buried in Srinagar at the Roza Bal shrine—a shrine that, according to the Ahmadiyya, has been misidentified as the resting grounds for a Sufi saint named Yuza Asaf.[66]

The narrative of the Afghan Lost Tribes thus serves a crucial role in Ghulam Ahmad's messianism, providing the historical justification for the continuation of Jesus's career beyond Palestine. Most compelling, however, is the epistemological entanglement that *Jesus in India* makes visible. While Ghulam Ahmad provides scriptural evidence that Jesus did not die on the cross, he links Jesus to India through a wide-ranging and eclectic set of sources: Persian genealogies of the Afghans, premodern Indian medical texts, French travelogues, and the array of Anglo-American accounts of the Afghan Lost Tribes that we considered above. Ghulam Ahmad approvingly discusses Harawi's *Afghan Treasure Chest*, but his consideration of Persian and Pashto histories is brief.[67] More extensively, Mirza Ghulam attends to the arguments of Jones, Moore, Ferrier, and Burnes. Jones's philological assessment of Pashto language's Chaldean roots holds particular prominence in the logic of *Jesus in India*.

In Ghulam Ahmad's own reconstruction of the Afghan Lost Tribes narrative, it becomes clear that he privileges the English-language accounts over Harawi's version. When the Anglo-American accounts differ from *Afghan Treasure Chest* in narrative details, Ghulam Ahmad opts for the more recent Anglo-American version. In short, Ghulam Ahmad is not guided by a preference for those sources that are internal to the religious tradition with which we usually identify him.

In the eclecticism of *Jesus in India*'s bibliography, we glimpse the texture of entwined religious histories. For Ghulam Ahmad, there was no way or reason to distinguish the religious narratives of recently arrived evangelicals from those of Sunni ʿ*alims* and Sufi *pirs* who had inhabited the Punjab for generations. The world was an entangled one that demanded a renewed and clearer explication of the true story of Jesus's life. This was a story based in Kashmir and Afghanistan, and a story that reconfirms that the kings and prophets of the Bible and the Qur'an are neither locked in an inaccessible past nor bound to the environs of Jerusalem and Mecca. By reiterating the narrative of the Afghan Lost Tribes through mention of both Harawi's *Afghan Treasure Chest* and the Anglo-American discourse on Afghan identity, Ghulam Ahmad enfolded Christian and Muslim histories alike into his own eschatological imagination. For the Ahmadiyya, the Afghan Lost Tribes narrative was just such a story that could rupture barriers between Islamic and Christian worlds, allowing Ghulam Ahmad to present himself as the savior-reformer to multiple religious communities at the turn of the century. In its nomadic entrance into Ahmadi theology, the narrative of the Afghan Lost Tribes bolstered Ghulam Ahmad's efforts to read a "Christian discourse" as constitutive of Ahmadi Islamic messianism.[68]

Conclusion

The US American invasion of Afghanistan in October 2001 was, for most media outlets, an introduction to a region that had received sparse coverage in previous years. Attempting to explain the context for this latest military action, news correspondents and US military officials drew upon familiar and unexamined tropes. Reiterating the conclusions of previous agents of empire, Americans emphasized the importance of tribe and lineage, the significance of *pashtunwali* as an inviolable code of conduct among the Pashtuns, the tragedy of repressive gender norms, and the "medieval" and even "biblical" nature of Afghan social and legal practices.[69] The majority of Americans describing Afghanistan conjured a haunting timelessness for a region that they believed had slipped from history.

In most cases, the appeal to the "biblical" nature of the Afghans was simply a melodramatic means to describe a society that Americans struggled to understand. Others, however, intended something quite different in their description of Afghan society as "biblical." The focus cast upon Afghanistan by Western media revealed a startling revelation: here were stories identifying the Afghans as members of the Lost Tribes. The media outlets that covered this story did so with considerable irony and self-assured superiority. The retrogressive Taliban—so stuck in their ostensible "fundamentalism" and hostility to religious difference—were perhaps the not-so-distant cousins of Jewish communities in Israel.

The claim that the Afghans are the Lost Tribes of Israel continues to be repeated, quite frequently, until today.[70] In addition to media outlets' ironic invocation of the narrative, some American Christians use blog posts and Facebook comments to reiterate that the Afghans are the "kings of the east" who will return to Israel in time for the dawn of Armageddon. Elsewhere in the realm of YouTube videos and Twitter, certain Pashtun commentators continue to repeat this claim as a way of valorizing a community that has witnessed intense violence over the past forty years and whose rights have been severely restricted by the Pakistani government.

It means something quite different to describe the Afghans as "biblical" today than it meant for much of the past 400 years. The prophetic nature of the Afghans' past had been a marker of their centrality and participation in the unfolding of God's plan for humanity. Predominantly, the description has now become a sign of atemporality and isolation—and an excuse, moreover, to explain the US government's inability to accomplish security goals abroad. It has become an act of self-amnesia that masks our role in the current violence in the region by shifting the cause of turmoil onto an unchanging and isolated cultural landscape.[71]

These genealogies of the Afghan Lost Tribes are more profoundly unpredictable than we have assumed.[72] They do not fix and determine the past. Rather, they pass between communities of interpretation and speak to contingent anxieties and present concerns: be that Afghan belonging in Mughal courts, the success of Christian missionaries in Asia, or the messianic reconfiguration of Islam in India. In the hands of some interpreters, the blessed genealogy may offer some glimpse of the future, for the genealogy provides semiotic material to be made sensible according to apocalyptic frames. These nomadic texts are polychronic—the result of external "contextual" and internal "textual" trajectories intersecting in order to speak to various pasts, divergent presents, and possible futures.[73]

The narrative of the Lost Tribes of the Afghans is one that invites us to reflect upon our disciplinary boundaries and habits for representing religious traditions. The history of the Lost Tribes narrative reveals the unpredictable mobility of texts and genres. Ghulam Ahmad pushes the boundaries of Islamic history by reading Anglo-American sources—sources that themselves attempted to reconcile the ideals of Christian missionary work and the visions of a millenarian nationalism with the reality of struggle, encounter, and failure in the Islamic world. These "Christian" sources, moreover, made their claims by interpreting and translating Afghan genealogies written in Persian and Pashto. These Afghan genealogies, in turn, were efforts to create a space of belonging for the Afghan community in the cosmopolitan Islamic court of the Mughals by developing qur'anic, extra-qur'anic, and biblical stories of King Saul.

It is the mobility of this narrative across the division of Christian and Islamic histories that is particularly compelling. There is no single original context that satisfactorily explains the genre of the Afghan blessed genealogy, for this story about the Afghan past became one useful to the performance of Afghan and American identity, Christian and Muslim sanctity. The history of Islam exists in its iteration and retelling—so, too, the history of Christianity. And, as this narrative of the Afghan Lost Tribes has suggested, such retellings are intimately bound up with the tellings of others.

8

Imagining Empire: Islamic India in Nineteenth-Century US Print Culture

Susan Ryan

When nineteenth-century Americans thought about Muslims—whose adherents worldwide, as Karine Walther has argued, were homogenized and stereotyped as a monolithic and in some sense racialized Other—those living in India did not figure as prominently as did their counterparts in North Africa, the Ottoman Empire, the eastern Mediterranean, or, by the end of the century, the Philippines.[1] The United States, after all, was not engaged in armed conflict with Indian Muslims, as had been the case with North Africans in the Barbary Wars of the early nineteenth century; nor did it stage a military occupation of India, as it would in the Philippines at the turn of the twentieth century. Unlike "Western Asia," as American missionaries dubbed Palestine and other near eastern locales, India did not figure into the Christian eschatology to which many early Americans subscribed, nor was the subcontinent featured as prolifically in American travel narratives as were Egypt and other Mediterranean destinations.[2] And India's Muslims, unlike those in the Ottoman Empire, represented no threat to European sites, most notably Greece, with which many Americans felt a strong cultural and intellectual affinity.

Despite this relative marginalization within nineteenth-century US discourses on Islam, India—more generally conceived—attracted a great deal of attention among the era's authors, editors, and readers, as evidenced by the myriad poems, stories, missionary reports, and periodical pieces that addressed the region and its inhabitants.[3] A matrix of missionizing efforts and economic interests, in addition to a vexed triangulation with Great Britain—whose colonial domination of the subcontinent peppered conversations about US slavery and racial injustice—shaped Americans' responses to India, framing it, paradoxically, as a land of heathen abominations and hierarchical abuses, on the one hand, and of exotic luxury or spiritual enlightenment, on the other. Within this larger conversation, Islam (or, in the lexicon of the era, "Mohammedanism") emerged as a crucial if sometimes occluded element. When Americans talked about India—an entity on which they, like their British counterparts, imposed a unity and coherence that underestimated the region's enormous linguistic, ethnic, and geographical diversity—they typically referred to indigenous populations that adhered to various forms of Hinduism (an emphasis made clear in the region's variant name: Hindoostan).⁴ But if we delve into specific discussions of social, cultural, and political practices on the subcontinent, an intriguing engagement with Islam becomes evident.

Given the lack of direct military conflict, we might expect Americans' perceptions of Islamic India to be less hostile than what we see in reference to North Africans or "Turks." Indeed, in some accounts Islam, as an Abrahamic religion, emerges as a relatively salutary force in representations of the subcontinent, insofar as its monotheism contrasted starkly with Hinduism's baffling (to westerners) array of gods. Further, Indian Muslims were sometimes identified as protesting against what British and American missionaries saw as Hinduism's abominations. These representations within mid-nineteenth-century news reports, missionary accounts, and travel narratives—however scattered and occasional—complicate some widely held assumptions: that Americans saw native South Asians as an undifferentiated mass of "heathens"; that Americans represented Islam as taking precisely the same form in all parts of the globe; and that American readers were exposed only to accounts of Islam that placed it entirely in opposition to Christian values or perspectives.

Such representations are nevertheless at odds with the most sustained accounts of Islamic India that appeared in mid-nineteenth-century American print culture: those that emerged in the months following the 1857 Sepoy Rebellion (sometimes called India's First War of Independence).⁵ Here US commentators—and the British authors whom American editors chose to publish or reprint—addressed the religion's adherents in terms that aligned with the era's most belligerent stereotypes and that prefigured much of twenty-first-century American Islamophobia. Such renderings, at their most extreme, figured Muslims as an irredeemably violent people at war with the West, whose faith only fueled and facilitated their aggression. These American musings (and, by extension, my analysis of them) have less to do with the complex realities of Muslim-Hindu-British encounters in South Asia than with the meanings that US readers derived from the highly mediated accounts they consumed—meanings made all the more pressing in light of Americans' fraught identification with and attempts at self-differentiation from Britain at midcentury.⁶ As Americans considered and debated what roles they might assume in the wider world and how they might resolve contentious matters at home, the mix of identities and conflicts at play in British India served as a crucial site of inquiry.

The first part of this chapter examines US commentary on Islamic India apart from the Sepoy Rebellion, while the second focuses specifically on responses to the violence of 1857. The hostile cast of the latter notwithstanding, an array of tensions and contradictions pervades both discourses, suggesting that Islamic India elicited a range of affects among American observers—fear, certainly, but also a grudging admiration, as a desire to keep the eastern Other at a safe distance mixed with the notion that Muslims' supposed single-mindedness and certitude lent them a geopolitical advantage that invited careful consideration. Despite the discourse's frequent derogation of Islam, then, these accounts emerge as a kind of militancy primer for American readers—one made especially pertinent by the fact that the United States at midcentury was increasingly invested in its own expansionist potential, already realized to a degree through the Louisiana Purchase (1803) and the Treaty of Guadalupe Hidalgo (1848), and imagined via persistent fantasies of annexing Cuba, Canada, and other sites in the Americas.[7] The notion of Islamic ascendancy, in other words, emerged as an element to be both defeated and emulated, as the very ideologies that rendered Islam objectionable to American observers were also identified as the sources of its power. As I will argue, a kind of subterranean mirroring—persistent but unacknowledged—structured the discourse, bringing Americans and the Indian Muslims they imagined into an illuminating if uncomfortable proximity.

Islamic India

In nineteenth-century US print media, references to India and to Islam abound, but texts addressing the two in conjunction are far less numerous. Because of the scattered nature of my sources, I have organized my discussion topically, pulling from various articles and commentaries in order to sketch out some of the key ideas around which Americans' perceptions of Islamic India coalesced. The result is less a comprehensive overview of American attitudes than an account of how their impressions might be understood in reference to broader domestic and transnational touchstones.

Given how much time, money, and ink American reformers and religious authorities invested in the temperance movement, Muslims' well-known abstention from alcohol constituted just such a node.[8] One would expect Muslim sobriety to elicit widespread admiration—especially in relation to India, insofar as intoxication was said to play a key role in the coercion of Hindu widows facing suttee—a topic that attracted much attention among American editors and readers.[9] Along those lines, a piece aimed at children named temperance as one of Muslims' admirable traits (alongside an "abhor[rence] of theft" and a "scrupulous" attention to "worship"), while an article pitched to adult readers noted that "drunkenness cease[s]" when the Muslim faith gains prominence in a given area of the globe.[10] But other authors pointed to Muslim temperance as a fault or weakness, a short-sighted restriction that ushered in more pernicious vices. An anti-temperance-law article that appeared in the June 1852 issue of the New York-based *Democrat's Review*, for instance, argued that "the general proneness to indulgence does indeed lead those who are stinted in one appetite, to resort to the over-exercise of another . . . Thus the Mohammedan, deprived of wine, solaces himself with opium, with coffee, frequent and strong, with hot bathing and extra wives."[11] If human beings habitually gravitated toward "indulgence," any heavy-handed prohibition on alcohol, the author implied, might lead to the Islamicization of Americans—and, by extension, to risky experimentation with mind- or mood-altering substances and corporeal luxuries. The *New York Evangelist*, too, linked abstinence from alcohol to the perils of opium use: "The religion of Mohammed forbids the use of intoxicating drinks, and the followers of the prophet resort to [opium] as a substitute." Such habits, the author intoned, ought to be "left to Turks and Hindoos, to Asiatics and Africans, while civilized Europeans and Americans seek a more intellectual life—a life of duty and affection, which will include, from its beginning to its close, far more serene and perfect happiness than can be snatched from the spells of intoxication."[12] Though this author registers a preference for sobriety's "dut[ies] and affection[s]" over any kind of "intoxication," the specter of foreign indulgence (as opposed to a regrettable but altogether familiar alcohol use) looms.

These comments align with a broader American xenophobia in which opium figured into a range of anti-immigrant and Asia-phobic discourses, but they also signal Islam's availability within US print culture as a reservoir of spiritual, political, and behavioral risk.[13] In that regard, Islam mirrors a homegrown religious movement—Mormonism—that elicited a great deal of Protestant panic at midcentury and that, intriguingly, shared with Islam a rejection of alcohol consumption and an acceptance of polygamy. Brigham Young's many wives, after all, were sometimes referred to in orientalist terms as his "harem." The comparison went well beyond wine and wives, however; as Timothy Marr has noted, Americans hostile to Mormonism framed the religion's founders as "deceivers, despots, and debauchers in the islamicist mold of Muhammad," even as this strategy worked to "contain" Islam by comparing it to "the fringe phenomenon of the Latter-day Saints."[14]

The link to Mormonism highlighted for American readers Islam's tolerance of polygamy—a practice that, as we might expect, was often cited as evidence of the latter's mistreatment of women (though Christian missionaries also criticized Hindu men for having multiple wives).[15] But commentators struck other, more complimentary notes regarding India's Muslim women as well. One of the most open-minded, albeit condescending, pieces I have encountered praised their literary accomplishments: "It will be surprising to many in the civilized nations of the Western world to learn that there have been, and there are at the present day, female poets in India, not only among the Hindoos, but among the Mussulmans." The author continues: "In modern times it is rather the Mussulman women who cultivate Indian poetry: the idea is erroneous that they seek to please their husbands by mere physical beauty." The article also claims that women in India have more opportunities to acquire knowledge than do other women in the East, noting the availability of translations of various works and the prevalence of newspapers. "The Mohammedan women of India can read the Koran," the author notes approvingly, "for it is translated into the common language."[16] These remarks counter Western stereotypes regarding the oppression of Muslim women (that they are kept ignorant, that they are expected to be no more than pretty ornaments, that they have no independent engagement with the writings of their faith). Like so many midcentury magazine pieces, this one is anonymous, so the author's broader investments (in India, in Islam, in women's rights) remain unclear, but the emphasis here on learned, non-Christian women is atypical of the era.

Other commentary was considerably more critical, as authors expressed the notion, widely held in the West, that only Christians truly respected women. "Save where Christianity has recognized her true character and relation," noted a piece in the Boston-based missionary paper the *Heathen Woman's Friend*, "[woman] is ignorant, degraded, enslaved, and debarred from many of the privileges and enjoyments of life."[17] An article titled "Condition of Women in Heathen Countries" asserted that Muslims commonly believe that women have no souls, though the author conceded that this teaching is not actually to be found in the Koran.[18] In the Indian context, though, US commentary on the abuse of women focused primarily on Hindu communities, with suttee as the main target of protest. Occasionally Muslims are described as working to prevent suttee. A long article on widow burning, from the May 1869 issue of the Cincinnati-based *Ladies' Repository*, lamented that India's erstwhile Muslim emperors had tried but failed to eradicate the practice.[19] In other accounts, a kind of exotic, unassimilable violence shapes the scene, differentiating the interventions of Muslims from the restrained and rational actions of Christian missionaries. An article that appeared in the *Religious Intelligencer* (New Haven, CT), for example, featured a Muslim man who, upon witnessing a Hindu widow's immolation-in-process, "approached near enough to reach her with his sword, and cutting her through the head, she fell back and was rescued from further suffering by death."[20] The unnamed observer, whose account was published in a British parliamentary report and reprinted in at least two US papers, seems impressed by the man's resolve but shocked by his method.

As this anecdote suggests, Islam figured into missionaries' accounts of their efforts to convert India to Christianity, though commentary on Hinduism was far more abundant.[21] Commentators expressed particular discomfort with Hinduism's multiple gods, which they found not just contrary to Christian teachings but confusing and in some cases sinister. The Hindu penchant for elaborate visual and material representations of deities irked those who were invested in Protestantism's austerity and its elevation of word over image. In that regard, Hinduism struck many as an eastern analogue of Roman Catholicism, whose rituals, supposed worship of saints, and ornate pictorial representations troubled its Protestant critics.[22] Islam's aversion to such images and its monotheism, meanwhile, represented a possible point of connection for Protestant missionaries and other Anglo-American commentators. Granted, the vast majority of nineteenth-century accounts of the faith were relentlessly derogatory (e.g., the *Methodist Magazine* [New York] referred to Muslims as the "deluded sons of Mohammed," while a later piece called both Hinduism and Islam "fatalist and dreamy creeds," noting the rarity with which "the ideas and enlightened thought of England penetrate the darkness of the mind trained in the religion of Brahmah, or Mohammed").[23] But other observers represented the faith in a more positive light. Bayard Taylor's 1853 account of his travels in India, for example, includes the following description of a mosque: "It is a sanctuary so pure and stainless, revealing so exalted a spirit of worship that I felt humbled, as a Christian, to think that our nobler religion has so rarely inspired its architects to surpass this temple to God and Mohammed."[24] Others framed Islam as closer to Christianity than were the subcontinent's other religious traditions (especially Hinduism). "The better class of Mahommedans have some knowledge of the God of Abraham," remarked an observer in the February 16, 1822, issue of the Boston-based *Christian Watchman*, suggesting that this familiarity might provide an opening for conversion to Christianity.[25] Another early piece (from 1825) notes that "the Muselmans are already a sort of heterodox Christians," subscribing to certain Christian tenets, but not to others (most notably the belief in Christ's divinity). Similarities between the Koran and the Christian Bible drew notice as well. As the same commentator writes, "The Koran shines, indeed, with a borrowed light, since most of its beauties are taken from our scriptures: but it has great beauties." Unsurprisingly, a critique of Muslim arrogance intrudes, as the author notes that "the Muselmans will not be convinced that [those beauties] were borrowed."[26]

This perception of similarities between the two religious traditions could take on disparate connotations, however. On the one hand, familiarity with Christianity and some common textual investments were taken as evidence, in some quarters, that Muslims would embrace Christianity more readily than would their Hindu coresidents—and thus might be integral to a strategy of missionizing the entire region. On the other hand, the notion that Muslims had some awareness of Christianity and yet persisted in rejecting it suggested that their conversion might prove more challenging—and might, too, be used as evidence of stubbornness and fanaticism (both commonly appearing threads in the conversation) among Islam's adherents. The reverend John C. Lowrie, a Presbyterian missionary to India, reinforced these last points, noting that "there is less prospect of [Muslim] conversion than of any class"—a fact made more worrisome by his observation that "the proportion of those who embrace the religion of Mohammed is much larger than I had supposed, and composed of better classes of the people."[27] For Lowrie, India's Muslims are numerous, socially prominent, and unreachable—a bad combination in terms of his missionizing project.

While some accounts represented Hindus and Muslims as equally resistant to conversion and a few noted Muslims' comparative receptiveness (the Boston-based *Missionary Herald*, for example, asserted in 1846 that "the crescent of Mohammed has already turned pale" in the face of Christian persuasion), the more commonly expressed position was that the latter were extraordinarily difficult to Christianize.[28] As a commentator remarked in the *Biblical Repertory* (New York), the "acute and wily disciples of Mohammed" were especially adept at defending their beliefs.[29] And the *Missionary Herald* opined in 1850 that "we are well aware that Mohammedans, wherever found, constitute a difficult, and, hitherto a comparatively unfruitful field. They are every-where noted for intolerance, self-righteousness, and blind, unreasoning confidence in their own system. They regard themselves as God's peculiar people, and look with feelings of hatred and contempt upon all opposing religions." And yet, the same piece noted, western India might be the most "favorable" site for their conversion—Muslims in India, the author claimed, are "destitute of power. They are a conquered people; their pride has been humbled; their spirit of intolerance has been in a measure subdued."[30] Missionaries would be safer doing their work in west India, the author adds, than in majority Muslim countries whose residents might prove even more hostile to their efforts.[31]

Muslims figured into these writings as missionizers as well. A number of British and American commentators, in fact, noted anxiously that Islam was spreading more readily in India than was Christianity. Hindus, as Americans understood them, conceived of religious identity as a matter of heredity, and so were uninterested in converting others to their faith. Muslims, meanwhile, were perceived to be aggressive proselytizers, willing to use threats if gentler forms of persuasion failed. In an intriguing counterpoint to this explanation, the Unitarian minister and progressive reformer Thomas Wentworth Higginson wrote in 1871 that Islam's relative advantage in India owed not to the use of force but to the fact that the religion entailed "no spirit of caste, while Christians have a caste of their own, and will not put converts on an equality."[32] Whatever the origins of Muslims' missionizing successes, this sense (or fear) of losing out in a competition for native Indians' souls resonated with colonial North American tropes of competitive religious dominion, as Protestants and Catholics vied for native converts. And in most iterations, the notion of Islam's competitive advantage in South Asia aligned with a larger discourse of Muslim aggressiveness—a matter about which American observers were profoundly ambivalent.

Much Anglo-American commentary represented the practitioners of Hinduism as gentle to a fault—a mild, slender, effeminate, even feeble population whose strict standards regarding conduct toward animals seemed to westerners impossibly exacting. For some, Hindus represented a quintessential victimhood, their passivity setting them up for repeated, bloody invasions and campaigns of conquest. They "consider themselves as subjects by nature and born to obedience," as one American missionary noted, quoting a British official in Punjab.[33] These perceptions abounded, despite the fact that they clashed with outraged western representations of violent Hindu customs—not just suttee but a range of bodily trials and mortifications advanced under the aegis of religious devotion. Against this contradictory backdrop, India's Muslims emerged as a force to be reckoned with, "self-asserting, turbulent, and fanatical," as one commentator put it, in contrast with the "mild, submissive-looking Hindoo."[34] As a piece in the *Missionary Herald* noted, Muslims are "a spirited, energetic people" who have "much more courage than the Hindoos" and "are much less mild and gentle."[35] Indeed, many western commentators framed Muslims' supposed boldness and propensity for violence as axiomatic, a kind of cultural-religious hallmark. Even when ostensibly doing good—for example, halting the suffering of a burning widow, as noted earlier—the Anglo-American's imagined Muslim is brandishing a sword.

A pervasive notion in these documents holds that Muslims seek out violence in part because of the intensity and character of their religious convictions. The "typical" Muslim in Anglo-American discourses on India believes in his heart that infidels deserve death, sooner rather than later. For instance, a "Letter from India" that appeared in the New York-based *Independent* (1858) asserts that "the slaying of 'infidels'" is, for the "followers of the false Prophet," a "mere pastime."[36] Islam and violence are inextricable for these commentators—so much so that the alignment takes on the status of common sense, as when a contributor to the *Ladies' Repository* in 1871 imagined a Muslim invasion of India: "Eight hundred years ago, the conquering hordes of the Moslem came pouring through the Hindoo Koosh, with the sword in one hand and the Koran in the other."[37] In an intriguing reversal, the author refers to Muslims' militant missionizing on the subcontinent as a "crusade."

For many commentators, this supposed propensity for violence among Muslims owed to a pervasive fatalism (though fatalism was elsewhere aligned with passivity in US conversations on Islam). That is, Muslim combatants fought with unusual intensity, various authors claimed, because they believed the time and place of their death to be foreordained. A soldier might take ridiculous risks in combat, believing fervently that, if it were not his time to die, he would not. But conversely, if it were his appointed time, cowardice would not save him and thus was not worth the reputational risk. Further, British and American authors insisted, the notion that paradise awaited worthy martyrs reinforced a sense of invincibility. That is, righteous violence would always yield rewards, if not through victory then through the delights of the hereafter. A sense emerges here that Muslims' ideology, however wrongheaded from an Anglo-American

Protestant point of view, lent them an unfair and perhaps unanswerable advantage over both Hindus and Christians. For Western commentators, this was a deeply misguided population whose delusions somehow served the interests of their increasingly global dominance. And so the missionary imperative (i.e., to Christianize India's "heathen") was more than usually implicated in geopolitical power gambits, even as, I would argue, tropes of Muslim aggression fed an under-acknowledged fantasy of emulation, of a Christianity (and a US territorial expansion) more militant than otherwise. As one commentator noted in the context of the Sepoy Rebellion, "Christ said he did not come to send peace, but a sword."[38]

Muslims and the Sepoy Rebellion

The 1857–58 Sepoy Rebellion, during which native soldiers launched a large-scale revolt against British rule, shocked both British and American observers, not just in terms of the scale of the violence on both sides, which was staggering, but also insofar as supposed inferiors had managed to carry out an elaborate and, at least for a time, successful conspiracy against the British, one sufficiently destructive that it called into question the viability of the empire itself.[39] For many commentators, India's Muslims—numerous among the sepoys (a term that referred to indigenous soldiers serving under British command)—were the rebellion's chief fomenters and villains. As evidence of this pattern of blame, a piece in the *Albion*, a New York-based weekly, intoned that Hinduism, in advance of the violence, "needed the hot breath of Muhammadan fanaticism to give it life and energy."[40]

As Nikhil Bilwakesh has shown, American responses to the rebellion varied widely. Many saw in it the specter of slave uprisings at home, with dark-skinned native Indians standing in for the South's enslaved population, while others, including Irish immigrants who had ample reason to mistrust the British, considered the travails of the latter in India to be a just comeuppance for their mistreatment of native Asian populations, not to mention of other colonial subjects.[41] Americans' disposition toward slavery also informed their attitudes toward the embattled British. Proslavery partisans so resented British abolitionist agitation that they took a certain satisfaction in the latter's troubles, although fears of a domestic race war tended to overwhelm their schadenfreude. Abolitionists, meanwhile, generally took Great Britain's side, insisting that colonial rule differed markedly from chattel slavery as practiced in the American South and emphasizing the degree to which the British might enlighten and improve the Indian subcontinent.[42] Soon enough, as Bilwakesh notes, the term "sepoy" took on a life of its own; for instance, it was used to refer to both Confederate and Union forces during the Civil War, signaling brutality from any quarter rather than the armed rebellion of a subjugated population.[43]

If the rebellion focalized American attitudes toward and anxieties regarding slavery, racial difference, and violence at home, not to mention toward British colonialism, it also provided an occasion for thinking and writing about the Islamic presence in India and what it might mean for Western/Christian/imperial intervention, both there and elsewhere. Long before 1857, British and American observers had often characterized

India's Muslims as deceitful and mercenary, representing them as opportunistic outsiders regardless of how long their families had been in residence. One piece, published in 1844, went so far as to suggest that Russia was using Indian Muslims as spies in its designs on the region.[44] The rebellion only amplified this ambient mistrust. The *Biblical Repertory*, for instance, which devoted more than 130 pages of its July 1858 issue to the conflict, declared that "the Mussulmans were the originators and plotters [of the rebellion], [while] the Hindus were the dupes"; along similar lines, a British officer whose account was reprinted in the United States described the Hindus as "befooled" into joining the conspiracy.[45] Again, we see in these renderings an energetic and agentive—if also destructive—Muslim population, acting on the passivity and naivete of Hindus with the ultimate goal, as one American missionary put it, of establishing "a Mohammedan despotism" in India once the British were driven out.[46] Muslim temperance takes on a sinister tone here as well; supposedly a key element of the sepoys' early success was their ability to remain sober while taking advantage of the habitual inebriation of the British, thus weaponizing an ostensible virtue.

The specific forms of this alleged Muslim deceit varied from one account to another—and sometimes within a single published piece. Some charged that Muslim sepoys had spread rumors among their Hindu counterparts that the army's recently introduced Enfield rifles took cartridges that had been greased in cow's fat, contact with which would cause devout Hindus to lose caste.[47] (Contamination via animal fat was a prominent element in accounts of the rebellion's origins—some attributed the ferment to an analogous rumor that Enfield cartridges had been laced with pig's fat, to the outrage of Muslim soldiers.[48]) Another supposed Muslim ruse was an unsuccessful attempt to dupe the British into destroying a Hindu holy site, so that the latter would believe that the former were out to destroy their religion.[49] In various accounts to which American readers were exposed, Hindus came to regret their participation in the rebellion and their alliance with Muslims, longing instead for a return to their former circumstances under British rule, a representation that aligned Muslims with the meddling northern abolitionists who populated US proslavery fiction at midcentury.

That Muslims and Hindus were able to form an alliance at all surprised some observers. As one piece noted, "Mohammedans and Hindus, who have nothing in common, except a hatred of the truth, joined in a crusade against Christians"—despite the fact that, according to this account, the Muslims despise "idol-worship" and the "Brahman is, perhaps, the subtlest and at the same time the grossest idol-worshipper that can be found."[50] This unlikely cooperation elsewhere acquired a scientific spin:

> All that was necessary to produce an outbreak of the hostile elements which everywhere existed in abundance, was combination. . . . India has long been like a vast galvanic battery, pregnant with latent fires. It was only necessary to bring the poles together to produce an explosion. The moment the Mussulman and the Hindoo joined hands the circuit was completed, and the whole fabric of British power trembled at the shock.[51]

Interfaith alliance, this author insists, could be downright explosive.

The accounts of the Sepoy Rebellion that appeared in US print media included, as we might expect, graphic descriptions of atrocities committed against British men, women, and children. I will not belabor those here—the details presented in some sources are beyond disturbing—except to note that Muslim cruelty is not only emphasized but also tied explicitly to Islam as a religion. To a Muslim, as one commentator wrote, "all infidels are dogs, whom it is an act of piety to destroy"; "the Mohammedan," the same piece asserted (without irony), "is a ferocious animal, made so by his creed, which inspires him with a blind, vindictive exclusiveness, that makes him a true demon as soon as the restraint of fear is taken off."[52] Accounts of Muslim sexual aggression toward British women pervade these texts as well, in keeping with the era's broader attributions of lasciviousness to male practitioners of Islam.[53] Although, as Jenny Sharpe has noted, no evidence has emerged to substantiate the charge that British women were subjected to widespread and systematic rape during the rebellion, such claims appeared often in commentators' descriptions.[54] While some framed the rape of British women as a kind of essentialized Muslim behavior—a reference to "the lustful Mohammedan rabble" is but one example—others suggested that these acts were fueled by resentment of British women's relative freedom and outspokenness.[55] If Western stereotypes regarding Hindu effeminacy and timidity worked to diminish their representation here, opposite impressions of Muslim power and aggression fueled these accounts of "licentious" violence.

While most discussions of the rebellion that appeared in US newspapers and magazines dwelled on violence against British victims, the aggressive actions of the British were occasionally detailed. One such article (originally published in *Blackwood's* and reprinted in New York City's long-running *Eclectic Magazine*) featured a bracing eyewitness account of the execution of sepoy rebels, penned by a British official stationed in northwestern India.[56] The piece recounts a particularly gruesome execution method, by which the accused—ten at a time—were tied to large cannons ("9-pounders") that were then fired:

> It was a horrid sight that then met the eye: a regular shower of human fragments of heads, of arms, of legs appeared in the air through the smoke and when that cleared away, these fragments lying on the ground—fragments of Hindoos, and fragments of Mussulmans all mixed together, were all that remained of those ten mutineers. Three times more was this scene repeated; but so great is the disgust we all feel for the atrocities committed by the rebels, that we had no room in our hearts for any feeling of pity; perfect callousness was depicted on every European's face; a look of grim satisfaction could even be seen in the countenances of the gunners serving the guns. But far different was the effect on the native portion of the spectators; their black faces grew ghastly pale as they gazed breathlessly at the awful spectacle.[57]

The account mixes horror and self-justification. After elaborating on a markedly disgusting scene, the author reverses his terms, projecting matters back onto the rebels themselves whose "atrocities" have left the English with no room for "pity." A "perfect callousness" describes the British onlookers here, whose capacity for affect—indeed, whose very humanity, this account suggests—has been driven out by the events of the rebellion. And yet, the scene seems calculated to produce an emotional response in the reader, who is invited to absorb the bystander's repressed or evacuated horror and perhaps to extend a moment of sympathy to those "ghastly pale" native observers, momentarily whitened by what they have seen.

If the eyewitness-author of this piece disavows all capacity for sympathy, he nevertheless admires the Indians' "pluck" and stoicism. "Nothing in their lives," he writes, "became them like the leaving of them. Of the whole forty, only two showed any signs of fear, and they were bitterly reproached by the others. . . . They certainly died like men."[58] This fortitude he attributes to the sepoys' faith, though here there's no differentiation between Muslims and Hindus: "Their religion, bad as it may be and is, in all other points, at least befriends them well at the hour of death."[59] But if the rebels' religious faith enabled them to face such a violent death with equanimity, it also made this execution method especially fearsome insofar as it rendered a proper funeral ritual—in either the Muslim or the Hindu tradition—impossible. The individual tied to the cannon, the author notes,

> knows that his body will be blown into a thousand pieces, and that it will be altogether impossible for his relatives, however devoted to him, to be sure of picking up all the fragments of his own particular body; and the thought that perhaps a limb of some one of a different religion to himself might possibly be burned or buried with the reminder of his own body, is agony to him.[60]

The conspiratorial mixing of Hindus and Muslims—in another author's rendering, the "galvanic battery" whose explosion shook British India—gives way to a literal mixing of blood, bones, and flesh designed to obliterate sepoy resistance and restore European authority. Though the author and original publishing venue here are British, the fact that the *Eclectic*'s editor chose this piece for reprinting from among a vast range of options suggests that its insights were perceived to be relevant to an American readership. American responses, however, were not uniformly sympathetic to the British: the Boston-based *Ballou's Pictorial*, for instance, called the sepoys' "atrocities . . . revolting," but added that the retaliatory measures the British chose—the aforementioned execution method in particular—"savor of ferocity" and seem "impolitic as well as terrible."[61] The *New York Observer*, meanwhile, endorsed the view that the East India Company's "misgovernment" had caused the rebellion and criticized the bloodthirsty tone of British press coverage.[62]

The execution-by-cannon that the *Blackwood's/Eclectic Magazine* piece relates appears to have been chosen precisely because it violated both Hindu and Muslim religious injunctions regarding proper treatment of the dead; the British in this instance were quite consciously out to demoralize the rebels by undermining their religious practices. They were, in other words, engaging in a holy war—just as British and American observers accused the sepoys of doing: "There would have been no revolt, or it would have assumed an entirely different character," one US commentator intoned, "were it not for the deadly hostility of the [Indian] people to Christianity."[63] But if both sides were in some sense pursuing a holy war—in conventional Western terms, a conflict between light and darkness, between Christianity and heathenism—any number of commentators excoriated the British for their prior attempts at religious neutrality with regard to India. That is, the British East India Company had long held that excessive interference in native Indians' religious practices would lead to civil unrest and possibly violent resistance; as a result, its officials were for a long while reluctant to crack down on practices like suttee and were unsupportive of Christian missionary efforts in company-controlled areas. Peace and profit mattered more to the company, its critics alleged, than faith.

According to the *Biblical Repertory*, the Sepoy Rebellion proved that the British East India Company's strategic religious pluralism had backfired: "They went about India, as men entering a cavern filled with bats and unclean birds, with dark lanterns, for fear of disturbing the inhabitants. Enough of light, however, gleamed through [in the form of missionary activity] to arouse and terrify the spirits of darkness. Had they allowed the light to shine freely, those spirits would have fled or quailed."[64] Christian dominion, in other words, represented the only path to peace and enlightenment in India. In most accounts, this ascendancy was to be achieved through the conversion of both Hindus and Muslims to Christianity, however challenging that project might be. But in some quarters we see a fantasy of displacement or destruction rather than absorption. The British official who related the obliteration of sepoy corpses in such detail offered a version that merits our attention. In response to the July 1857 Cawnpore massacre, in which rebelling Indians killed scores of British women and children, he imagines a wholesale reinvention of Delhi, a city that had long been a site of Muslim power and influence. Once the city's native inhabitants are "exterminate[ed]"—"we have no wish to embarrass ourselves with prisoners," he writes—an entirely new space can be created: "Not one stone should be left on another to tell posterity that this was Delhi; but in its room should be built a new city with a new name—a city, not full of Hindoo temples, and Mohammedan mosques, but beautiful with Christian churches, chapels, and schools." He calls it "fit retribution" that Delhi "should be utterly destroyed; and that on its site should be built another city, to be the center from which victorious Christianity should radiate."[65] This fantasy of remaking India—from its architecture to its faith—begins, crucially, not with conversion but with annihilation.

* * *

As the foregoing analyses suggest, Americans' impressions of Islamic India were contradictory, even chaotic. If some authors asserted a degree of alignment between Christian and Muslim beliefs and sacred texts, Islam emerged elsewhere as a pernicious and unholy force—a threat to peace, order, and Christian progress in South Asia and beyond. As I have argued, that critique is itself contradictory, betraying a lurking Western impulse toward emulation amid more overt articulations of fear and disgust. Timothy Marr's work on American Islamicism identifies a shift among mid-nineteenth-century artists, authors, and cosmopolitans toward a "romance with oriental masculinity" that dwelled less on "the darkness of despotic antichristianity" and more on Islam's "outlandish models of male liberty and power."[66] In the context of India, however—perhaps because of the Sepoy Rebellion's astonishing brutality—

the American attraction to Islam, though still heavily gendered, is less aesthetic than militaristic. When an American missionary counseled Christians to embrace the sword in their engagement with India or a British official imagined—indeed, pined for—wholesale slaughter in Delhi, each was in some sense appropriating the extremity that the West attributed to Muslim men. At a moment when Americans were imagining and beginning to enact their own ascendancy, first in North America and soon enough around the globe through a range of military, missionary, and economic ventures, they found the versions of Islam then entering the national discourse to be both repellant and curiously compelling.

Part Four

Islam and American Empire: The Case of the Philippines

9

Subjugating the Sultan of Sulu: American Imperial Negotiations in the Muslim Philippines

Timothy Marr

Why did you come here? For land? You have plenty at home. For money? You are rich, I am poor. Why are you here?
—Jamalul Kiram II, the Sultan of Sulu. To Captain Pratt, the American commander of the 23rd Infantry who relieved the Spanish in Jolo on May 20, 1899[1]

When the United States wrested the Philippines from Spain in 1898, it also assumed control over southern islands that were the homelands of thirteen different Muslim groups who now comprise *bangsamoro*, or the Moro nation. For the previous three hundred years, the East Asians the Spanish called "Moors" (from the Greek work Μαύρος "black") had successfully resisted their attempts to integrate them into their Philippine empire. The southern Philippine islands of Mindanao and the Sulu Archipelago comprised a dynamic global contact zone where expanding transoceanic cultures collided and embraced. The Islamic diaspora had spread furthest eastward from Arabia across the Indian ocean into these islands off the coast of Asia. They also represented a transpacific "frontier" of American national territory at its furthest and most tropical southwest. Focusing on the American colonization of the Moros in the "wildest west" of Southeast Asia reveals more planetary latitudes to American engagements with the world's Muslim peoples too often confined by the distorted centrality of the Arab Middle East. Though the "East Indies" were an important locus of intercultural encounters since the American pepper trade between Salem and Sumatra in the late eighteenth century, Americanist scholarship has not adequately focused on problematic imperialism in Muslim Maritime Southeast Asia, in particular the colonization of Moro peoples as national subjects and the paternalistic attempts to prepare them for a democracy to which they did not consent.

The 1898 war between the United States and Spain ended with negotiations for a Peace Protocol in Paris in September. President McKinley and his diplomats pressured Spain to cede the whole of the Philippines for a payment of $20 million so that none of its territory could be transferred to another European power. In an attempt to solicit more concessions from the Americans, Spanish diplomat Eugenio Montero Ríos argued that "the Islands of Mindanao and Sulu . . . have never formed a part of the Philippine Archipelago proper."[2] British Philippine "expert" John Foreman related that these southern Philippine Islands comprised a "hornet's nest" of "turbulent Mussulmans who virtually refuse to recognize other rights than those of their sultans," who might regard American government as "a brand-new conquest."[3] William Day, president of the Peace Commission, resisted their annexation citing "so many acres of Mohammedans" who "were believed to be depraved, intractable, and piratical" and would only be "a source of trouble and expense."[4] Nevertheless, the final treaty of transfer included the Moro homelands and went into effect on April 11, 1899. The American decision to assume possession over Mindanao and Sulu was ultimately an expression of national desire to perform its newly regnant power in the eyes of European nations who themselves had interests in Southeast Asia and the Pacific Islands. The Moros would indeed remain a "problem" during the half-century when the Islands were politically under some form of control by the United States. The Americans did not adequately understand the political situation into which they had stepped, the nature of the lands they had "annexed," and the cultures of Malay Muslims whom they claimed as national subjects.

Jamalul Kiram II saw the departure of the Spanish, who had occupied a walled city in Jolo since 1876, as a prime opportunity to resume his sovereign authority over his islands under local Islamic customary law which placed the Sultan as the representative of the Prophet Muhammad. Amirul Kiram had been fourteen years old when his half-brother Badarruddin died of cholera in 1884 launching a long succession struggle that affected his influence even after he finally became the Sultan of Sulu ten years later. As Sultan he traveled under his own flag to Mecca for *hajj* during which he hired a police guard of twenty Punjabis and other bodyguards and ordered a large amount of ammunition.[5] The departing Spanish general in Sulu transported the Sultan, his household, and his police to the southern island of Siassi which he saw as a base from which to reinforce his prestige by outmaneuvering contending *datus* (local leaders) on the main island of Jolo, as well as to raise revenue through duties, taxation, tributes, and the granting of fishing and shelling licenses to supplement the income he received by leasing North Borneo to the British.[6] The Americans were afraid that the Sultan would also assume control over Jolo, and even more that Moro warriors—known for their militant resistance—might open up another theater of the Filipino insurrection by joining the rebellion. Commanding Major General Elwell Otis's capacity to send troops to replace the Spanish military in the southern islands was limited by his growing campaigns against Filipinos fighting for independence in the north.[7] The Sultan was surprised when the American Army occupied Jolo in May 1899 relieving the Spanish garrison with their own force of 755 men from the 23rd Infantry. This inaugurated the Moros' "American Problem": how to deal with the arrogant intrusion of alien colonizers whose ways they could not comprehend and with whose values they were forced to contend.

The dynamics of this intercultural encounter are illustrated by examining the negotiations of a series of later treaties and agreements, beginning with the Bates Agreement of 1899, through which the United States sought to impose its sovereignty over the Sultan of Sulu. The abrogation of the so-called Bates Treaty in 1904 eventually led to the Carpenter-Kiram Memorandum in 1915 in which the Sultan of Sulu renounced all claims to any sovereignty other than those which he possessed as the head of an Islamic religious community under United States law. A study of American treaty discourse with the Sultan of Sulu—revealed through translations that have left and enduring record of attitudes and strategies of the parties involved—illuminates the insular hypocrisies of national "benevolence" when Americans confronted Muslim peoples whose differences often confounded them. This imperial paradox featured the imposition of American sovereignty over Sulu in the name of progress at the same time that the Sultan was promised that his traditional and inherent rights would be fully recognized. The United States sought to civilize the Moros by imposing cultural power and exercising military violence in ways that were fundamentally autocratic in character. The supersession of the Sultan's hereditary authority through diplomatic coercion was supplemented by a condescending paternalism at odds with the American promise to bring the benefits of democracy to the islands.

In July 1899, Military Governor Otis instructed Brigadier General John C. Bates to "formulate an agreement" with the Sultan of Sulu to maintain peace and solicit his allegiance to the United States.[8] The fact that the military viewed it as necessary to sign a supplement to the Treaty of Paris revealed the uncertainty of American claims to these islands. Their lack of intercultural intelligence led to apprehension about the legendary power of Sulu's resistance in ways that exalted the political status of the Sultan into an orientalist potentate exercising full control not only over his own Tausug *datus* in the Sulu Archipelago but even over other Moro groups on the island of Mindanao. American negotiators planned to duplicate the terms of a Spanish Treaty of 1878 but soon discovered that Spain never had "a definite fixed policy of control over the archipelago" and "never attempted to deprive the Sultan of the administration of the island."[9] What the United States did have in its favor was an 1885 protocol in which Great Britain and Germany had recognized Spanish sovereignty over the Archipelago. The final articles of what came to be called the Bates Treaty acknowledged the "Government of the Sultan" and "the rights and dignities of His Highness the Sultan and his datos" and asserted that "all their religious customs shall be respected" and that the Sultan would be responsible for "crimes and offenses . . . committed by Moros against Moros."[10] However, these concessions did not replace the bottom line of the American mission: to get the Sultan to accept the "right of absolute sovereignty on the part of the United States," or as General Bates baldly expressed it during the negotiations: "We can occupy any point in the archipelago where we may wish to go."[11]

The transcripts of these conferences reveal the righteousness with which Americans asserted authority through "promised assurances" that they sought the improvement, advancement, and welfare of the Moros through commerce, agriculture, and education. The Sultan deployed deferring tactics to resist a reckoning with American power by sending his brother and his principal advisor, Hadji Butu, to try to understand American intentions. These negotiations faced many challenges that emerged out of linguistic misunderstandings and cultural incommensurabilities. Bates admitted that "it is very difficult to get along when we do not understand each other's ways," and Hadji Butu acknowledged that "it is like both parties sitting over a hanging sword, not knowing where they were."[12] Bates used the Sultan's delay to travel though the islands and impress the major *datus* with American power by liberally distributing bags of pesos, US flags, and letters acknowledging them as "good friends" of the US government. Several Moros attested to the Sultan's youth and immaturity and that he gave in too readily to the counsel of his advisors and was not acquainted with the "white race."[13] Even before he met the Sultan, Bates had come to regard him as "a good deal of a nonentity" and was convinced of his inability to "rally the datos to his aid in any effort to antagonize the United States."[14]

Bates ended the Sultan's evasiveness by traveling to his Jolo home in Maimbun on August 14, almost a month after his arrival in the islands. The issue of sovereignty most contentiously negotiated to the very end was whether the Sultan would be allowed to fly his own flag among the islands of his Sultanate in Sulu and North Borneo. The Americans were unyielding that the stars and stripes "must be higher—must be supreme."[15] This international authority became the symbolic issue that Bates pushed to press the Sultan and his advisors with the reality of his subjection. "The Sultan's flag is not recognized by the nations of the world," Bates asserted, and only the American flag would offer him military protection as an "American citizen." "Otherwise," Bates warned, "no one would know who he was."[16] The Sultan felt that he was being "made to lose his own flag" in a manner that "made him look awfully small."[17] This drama was actually enacted in November 1901 when the American Captain on Bongao, an island near Siassi, viewed the flying of the Sultan's flags over the vintas carrying his family as "open defiance of my authority," and forced him under threat of arms to surrender them.[18] The Sultan complained that such an action "lessens my own personality before my subjects" and thus did not carry out the American promise of "uphold[ing] the dignity of my person"[19] (Figure 9.1).

During the second day of negotiations in Maimbun, Bates invited the Sultan and his advisors to a visit aboard the USS *Charleston*. This naval ship had been selected for the journey to impress the Sultan and *datus* with the technological prowess of the United States. Reports of the negotiations in the American press emphasized the astonishment of the Moros as they encountered the marvels of modern machinery: the buzzers, fans, lights, ice machines, bicycles, megaphone, and phonograph that one journalist equated with "the power of civilization."[20] Once on board the officers summoned subordinates by pressing a button; others toyed with the Moros by letting them think that only Americans could breathe on an incandescent bulb and cause it to light up. When the Moros claimed it was Christian magic, the Americans turned on another bulb in response to the blowing of Moros and called it a "Mohammedan" light.[21] After the Sultan was given a megaphone to call one of his followers down from the mast, he reportedly took its measurements and said he would make one himself.[22] After trying "all kinds of schemes" to get the Sultan to sign the Treaty, Bates's *aide-de-camp* reported that a phonograph was the instrument that fully convinced the Sultan of American power.[23] Minstrel Recordings of "ragtime ditties" such as "All Coons Look Alike to Me" were reportedly played which so frightened the members of his party that, in their consternation, they bowed down onto the deck in prayer. The Sultan was astonished when his own voice was reportedly recorded, and he dictated orders to his followers.[24] The American administrators reportedly played these recorded voices to

Figure 9.1 "Sultan of Jolo & chiefs," Arthur Stanley Riggs Collection, Library of Congress, LC-USZ62-107904.

the different *datus* they later visited in the Archipelago to cower them "into a state of terror."[25] The last negotiation during the Treaty signing involved Bates acceding to the Sultan's request to send a phonograph to his mother who later thanked him for the "voice engine."[26]

Nevertheless, it was military technology that was most fully brought to bear to impress the Sultan of American might. The *Charleston* weighed 3,730 tons and was the most powerful ship ever to have anchored off Jolo—its visible presence by day and searchlight at night dismayed the Moros on the shores. Captain George Pigman invited the Sultan to "see what kind of protection we have got to offer him if time should come when it would be necessary."[27] When the Sultan pulled the trigger of the Colt rapid fire gun, he was said to have been so frightened that he could not loosen his hold and an officer had to cut the ammunition tape.[28] The Sultan watched the firing of a shell from the eight-inch gun land on his island two miles away—right where the commander said it would, and thanked the Captain for showing "him the big gun, as he had never seen one before." In a masterstroke of the political theater of gunboat diplomacy, Captain Pigman indicated that the guns could be used to stop any war on his island and then told the Sultan that since he recognized American sovereignty over this province, "I am going to fire a salute, so that when he pulls off he will know that this salute is fired for him personally."[29] (He received a seventeen-gun salute; twenty-one-guns would have been fired for a head of state.) Bates had ominously announced that "we can not [*sic*] see a war going on among them without doing something."[30] Suitably awed, the Sultan agreed to the Treaty, which included annual subsidies for him and his inner circle, and traveled to Jolo city five days later for the signing ceremony.[31] After the first two years of occupation, American's military might would consistently be deployed by the Army and Navy, and after the First World War by its leadership of the Philippine Constabulary and Scouts, to subdue Moros who resisted American authority, often in a manner that that spawned more rebellion. (See Joshua Gedacht's chapter in this volume.)

The intercultural struggle between the American Army and the Sultan stemmed partly from the fact that words like sovereignty and slavery had differing interpretations within their respective societies.[32] In fact, the word sovereignty was never translated into Tausug versions of the Bates Treaty. The Tausug word *baugbog* used instead of sovereignty really meant protection or defense.[33] Slavery was the subject of the tenth article of the Bates Agreement: "Any slave in the Archipelago of Sulu shall have the right to purchase freedom by paying to the master the usual market price."[34] Anti-imperialists and many Democrats argued that this contravened the Thirteenth Amendment's prohibition of slavery "within the United States, or any place subject to their jurisdiction" and for this reason the Senate never officially ratified the Agreement. The fact that the United States had formally agreed to pay a form of tribute to a little-known Muslim Sultan with slaves and concubines opened up vituperous criticisms in Congress and in the domestic press. The agreement with the Sultan was caricatured as a perverse Republican resurrection of the same "twin relics of barbarism" that the nation had spent a violent half-century trying to extirpate from the American continent. One congressman joked that he would value the judgment of Brigham H. Roberts of Utah, whom Congress had refused to seat because he was a polygamist.[35] A bigamist even used the Sultan's example to claim immunity from punishment.[36] The *Washington Post* editorialized that "the inclusion of this picturesque barbarian, with his harem, slaves, and despotic rule, under the 'banner of freedom' makes the utmost limit of the incongruous in our expansion of the 'home of the free.'"[37] William Dean Howells wrote that the Spanish, 20 million richer for dispensing with the Islands, "must have been convulsed with laughter to see us re-establishing slavery within our limits and draping a Mahometan prince in the tatters of our constitution."[38] Mark Twain satirized the "SULTAN OF SULU, wrapped in the Star Spangled Banner. Attended by 2000 slaves and 800 concubines," depicting him "light[ing] his pipe with a copy of the Fourteenth Amendment."[39]

Such burlesque was most fully popularized by the smashing success of George Ade's comic opera, *The Sultan of Sulu: An Original Satire in Two Acts*, which debuted in Chicago in March 1902 and sold out 192 performances on Broadway in New York before touring for five more years around the nation. Playwright Ade gained his material when visiting his journalist friend John McCutcheon in the Philippines who had been present for the negotiations of the Bates Treaty and had reported that the Tausugs were "a splendid spectacle" in which "all the colors of the rainbow... make up their glorious apparel."[40] In the opera, a Sultan "Ki-ram" is portrayed as an extravagant polygamist in ludicrous costume. The Sultan can't manage his eight wives and they divorce him, suing for alimony that collectively threatens him with bankruptcy. Ki-ram is a madcap Mikado who accedes to American civilization through the ironic agency of the cocktail. "The target of satire proves to be not the actual figure of the sultan, polygamy, the Moros, or the Philippines," writes Victor Roman Mendoza about the "racial-sexual excess" of the opera. "Rather it is the panicked, Orientalist discourse around these tropes itself"[41] (Figure 9.2).

Reports by the press and by travelers and officers frequently magnified Moro exoticism through descriptions of their colorful clothing and barbaric bearing in ways that ultimately accentuated their disappointment with stature of the real Sultan of Sulu. For example, when Helen Taft, the wife of William Howard Taft who headed the second Philippine Commission, toured the southern islands, she called them "the realm of the comic opera sultan." She was very impressed by the Joloaño *datus* who came on board the *Sumner* with exquisite knives stuffed into their sashes, and who "were by far the most picturesque figures we had seen ... of a different build, lithe, active and graceful, with a free and defiant gaze which offered a strong contrast to the soft-eyed modesty of the Christian tribes." She expected the Sultan "to be accoutered in three times as much

Figure 9.2 Frank Moulan as Ki-Ram in George Ade's opera. Cincinnati; New York: Strobridge Litho. Co., 1902 Theatrical Poster Collection, Library of Congress, 2014636740.

barbaric splendor" but was disenchanted when he arrived, welcomed by his seventeen cannon salute.[42]

Americans had assumed that Jamalul Kiram II's exalted position as Sultan endowed him with the authority to maintain order in the Sulu Archipelago. When the Sultan of Sulu's appearance, personality, and power matched neither stereotypes of despotic authority nor those of violent savagery, his reputation was supplanted by satirical parody that deflated his authority. Cultural performances of ethnic ridicule emasculated, infantilized, and racialized the Sultan in ways that subjugated him into figurehead acceding to but incommensurate with American ideals of leadership and governance. The rendering of Moro difference into comic caricature heightened the indignities of imperial annexation experienced by the very peoples they had taken on the trust to "civilize." The American authorities took away the Sultan's power, assaulted his dignity, and then hypocritically held him accountable for not effectively exerting his authority.

The real Sultan's qualms about signing the Bates Treaty were revealed by his concerns that he would be held responsible if any Tausug acted violently against white men intruding on their lands, an eventuality over which he had little control. He reportedly warned his leaders before Bates had arrived "not to molest them [the Americans], because they are like a box of matches—you strike one and they all go off."[43] Bates assured him that he would only have to "look up the culprits and turn them over for punishment," and that "he will find that we treat him with justice and will not take any advantage of him."[44]

The sparse number of Americans who settled in the Archipelago for any extended time left traditional culture to thrive amid the colonial regime. Since morality was understood locally in a Moro context, the attempts of American forces to maintain order through arrest and incarceration were themselves sometimes viewed as arbitrary if not alien or infidel forms of justice. Cesar Suva has suggested that the American occupation was a "skeletal" form of "colonial demi-rule" that he calls "the form of a security apparatus." It left the native Tausugs to share "in essence a para-state in an *informal* and almost unseen capacity" that was performed "through pre-existing Tausug political and social practices."[45] Moro customary law was at odds with American principles of justice—it allowed a murderer to pay a fine and imprisonment was considered a fate only worthy of a slave, so that it was a constant challenge for the Sultan to deliver up Tausugs who had flouted American orders. This was most dramatic in the cases of slaves who were granted emancipation papers by the American military who came to represent a source of power that conflicting *datus* could enlist to advance their interests and punish their enemies. Regional rivalries resulted in retaliatory episodes involving cattle and horse stealing, slave raiding, arms smuggling, and the burning and looting of houses. The ongoing unrest included violent deaths and eventually Moro *juramentados* who sacrificed their lives in suicidal attacks with bladed weapons in a jihad against American intruders that pushed the US Army to exert even more coercive control.

In contrast with the American belittling of the Sultan, the foremost Joloaño historian of the Tausugs, Samuel Tan, argued that Jamalul Kiram II should be considered an "unsung hero" because of his consistent "peaceful resistance" to "preserve and protect the freedom and dignity he and his people had enjoyed since ancient time."[46] Though the Sultan's power to resist was circumscribed by the asymmetry of American military might, his efforts to maintain the prestige of his office reveal steady effort to hold the Americans accountable to the promises they had made and to the values they claimed to uphold, as well as to ensure the financial benefits that accrued to him as ancestral leader. While the Sultan accentuated his dependence on American generosity, supplicating them as a "son" who desired to do the bidding of his "father," at the same he consistently reminded Americans of his authority over his own people as Muslim Sultan. To cite but one example of this tenuous strategy, the Sultan petitioned the American governor-general of the Philippine Islands in November 1900 for refund of the duties he was forced to pay on furniture, a mirror, and soap that he had purchased in Singapore. By limiting his duty-free purchases to goods acquired only in the Philippines, the Bates Treaty had cut off traditional free trade routes and revenue collection between Sulu and other ports in Muslim Maritime Southeast Asia.[47] Sulu Governor Major O. J. Sweet tried to explain that removing import duties "would make the American people believe you did not want to advance in civilization and raise your own necessities of life."[48] The Sultan expressed insight into American cultural expectations by arguing that a furnished home and washed clothes—"goods necessary to civilize the Moro people"—would help him set an example to his people.[49] This very attempt to adapt to American practices led some of his *datus* to resist him. The "stumbling blocks to civilization," the Sultan complained, "tell the people that I have adopted the customs of the white people and am not following up the laws and customs of our forefathers."[50]

In extant letters to the American administrators, the Sultan acknowledged that he must follow the American's command "in accordance to whatever customs and law, with reasonable cause or not." He appealed that his loss of wealth was a result of "you my elders of the American race who had exercised the authority of the Eagle placing me as it were in fact in a cage." Nevertheless, the Sultan rattled this cage and cried out that his "right to be cared for" included any "support which befits my position vis-à-vis the other potentates under the government of Whitemen." He insinuated that his leadership of Islam in the Sulu Archipelago endowed him with an exalted prestige compared to which even the American governor-general is but "the choice of the electorate" and "one authorized by the President," who themselves were all under almighty Allah.[51] The extant letters from the Sultan to American officials reveal his unsuccessful demands that he be allowed to engage in the pearl fishery and opium trade, to have the slaves who left his home returned, and that he be provided with arms (and permitted to import the ammunition he had ordered on *hajj* that had arrived in Singapore from England) so that he could "punish the bad men in my country ... to be able to keep the country quiet."[52]

In 1901, Jamalul Kiram II shared a remarkable document, the translation of which stipulated nine "rules and regulations the Sultan is guided by" and which served to justify that the obstinacy of his subjects was not a reflection of the local authority with which he was endowed. Commenting on local interpretations of Islam, he announced that he represented the Prophet Muhammad as "absolute monarch" who is "all-powerful within the limits of his territory." As "father to all his subjects" he held responsibility to administer justice and judge leniently on his own authority, bestow positions of power, to urge his people to be good, and to promote Islam.[53] (To understand Turkish attempts to instruct Moros in more orthodox forms of Sunni Islam, see the contribution by William Gervase Clarence-Smith in this volume.) In contrast to the Sultan's claims, George W. Davis, who rose from leading American troops in Mindanao and Sulu to commanding the Army in the Philippines, argued that the Bates Treaty "should never have been made" and complained of the "sultan nuisance," arguing that if he "is to be retained as a puppet kingling, he should be stripped of all real power through measures has have been so successfully employed in other oriental lands."[54] "Very soon the Sultan of Sulu will be only a character in history and no one will regret his exit," later claimed the general, "not even his own people and race."[55]

It was the Sultan's inability to control the actions of his own people that was cited as the prime justification for the abrogation of the Bates Treaty four years later. Seeking direct control over the Muslims in the southern Philippines, the United States established the Moro Province in 1903, whose authority would remain under the control of the US Army for ten years. Its first governor was Leonard Wood who acted precipitously to establish his own authority by attempting to remove any Moro opposition. In December 1903, Wood charged that the Sultan was both powerless and unwilling to prevent ongoing anti-American resistance or to uphold American laws including those against slavery and theft. To Woods the Bates Treaty wrongly "recognizes the authority of a class of men whom we have found to be corrupt, licentious, and cruel" and he found the Muslim Tausugs to be "nothing more or less than an unimportant collection of pirates and highwaymen, living under laws which are intolerable."[56] Woods called Jamalul Kiram II the so-called Sultan in his report, degrading him as "a gambler and an intriguer, with not a spark of courage or patriotic and paternal interest in his people," and wrote in a private letter to Governor Taft that the Sultan was "degenerate, dishonest, tricky, dissipated, and absolutely devoid of principle."[57] Wood worked successfully to unilaterally abrogate the Bates Agreement on March 4, 1904.[58] "As residents of the Moro Province," Woods ordered the Tausug residents of the Sulu Archipelago to be "subject to . . . the sovereignty of the United States."[59]

This development caught Sultan Kiram by surprise and he registered his alarm to Governor-General Luke Wright by asserting that he accepted "the President for my father" and "has always abided by the articles" of the Treaty. Ending the arrangement had the effect of taking "our living," which he found the same "as if you take away our souls." "I and all my subjects," wrote Kiram, "beg of our father the President thousand times: 1st we ask not to put yokes on our necks that we cannot bear, and don't make us do what is against our religion, and don't ask us to pay poll tax forever and ever as long as there is sun and moon, and don't ask taxes for land which are our rights of the Moro people." In arguing "from a white heart and clear without a stain" for his "rights at religious head of the Moros," the Sultan asserted that "I will go and see law and justice, as long as there are people in the world who keep law and justice."[60]

The full bore of Wood's paternalism remains on display in the transcripts of the shipboard conversations he had with the Sultan and Hadji Butu on June 30, 1904, where Wood attempted to bribe them to travel to Manila to seal symbolically their full concession to American sovereignty. After affirming his conviction that the United

States would be "here forever, unless some greater country comes and drives us away," Wood cut the Sultan down to size by refusing to recognize his rights. Since "under our law and the constitution of our republican government there is no such thing as a Sultan," he ruled that therefore "your rights as *a nation* are nothing" (emphasis in original). But he also attempted to pander to him by assuring him that, since the Americans were friendly and fair, the Commission would consider awarding him "reasonable and moderate" sum because "we want him to continue in a position of dignity among his people." He lectured the Sultan: "We don't come to him as a cow to be milked, but rather as one comes to a man in distress to give him assistance." Wood shared the adage that "he that expects little will not be disappointed" and even urged the Sultan to live "a simple and unostentatious life . . . like the founder of your own religion" (the Prophet Muhammad).[61]

The Sultan visited Manila for the first time in October 1904 where he attempted to negotiate an annual pension larger than the British paid to the sultan of Johor in Malaya, arguing that as "the United States is a wealthier country than England, I think its liberality should be much larger."[62] On November 12, 1904, the Philippine Commission passed Act 1259 providing a smaller annual payment for the Sultan and his advisors and clearly asserted that this was not a right but rather an expression of generosity that, unlike the Bates Agreement, was premised on the Sultan's ongoing cooperation.

The Sultan of Sulu was intended to be the most glamorous visitor from the Philippine Islands to the largest World's Fair yet to be organized, the Louisiana Purchase Exposition of 1904 in St. Louis. Officers in charge of the Exposition's Ethnological Exhibits saw the real Sultan as a "good advertising card" and the *Los Angeles Times* asserted that "in pomp and panoply of retinue [he] is likely to overshadow all foreign potentates visiting the fair."[63] However, the testy relations leading to the abrogation of the Bates Treaty led to the cancellation of the invitation to the Sultan and the Tausug Moros from Sulu and the visitation instead of two villages of Samal and Maranao Moros from Mindanao where lesser *datus* were made to fit the bill.

It was not until 1909–10 that the Sultan of Sulu journeyed to see the country that had subjugated his islands. He was prevailed upon to make a trip around the world by Charles J. Werble, a German Jewish immigrant who, as a former infantry soldier, had risen from teaching school in the Sultan's village to become his advisor and who traveled with him throughout the journey as his agent and interpreter.[64] It was the first time that a Sultan of Sulu had traveled further west than Mecca, much less traveled to the Americas. He was pitched in the press in his role as a picturesque oriental potentate who was the only sitting monarch in American territory. Despite the Sultan's dignified mien and affable smile and the fact that he and his suite of six were dressed in dapper (and tight-fitting) black suits purchased in Paris, the appearance of the five-and-a-half-foot Sultan disappointed expectations. One cartoon depicted Uncle Sam greeting him with a "Howdy Sult!" and the *New York Tribune* called him a "Jolly Little Sultan." "A comic opera king is in town," it began, before pointing out his short stature and that his long name was the only thing exotic about him.[65] Though he was rumored to have hundreds of thousands of dollars of pearls with him, the fact that he sold them in Europe to raise needed funds and to avoid American customs duties took the sheen off his opulence. While in Italy the Sultan traded in his blackened teeth for gold crowns. The hereditary rank Americans valued appeared but nominal and titular, shorn of real power, and he was forced to travel as a private citizen at his own expense. One newspaper explained that "to keep him out of mischief, Kiram has been permitted to continue believing himself immensely powerful."[66] The "picturesque" yet "pathetic" spectacle of a dusky Muslim despot reduced to a pensioner of the United States could never live up to his burlesque reputation as the comic opera king once regnant in American popular culture[67] (Figure 9.3).

The Sultan's journey to the United States was designed, however, to protect the dignity of the Sultan and also to have important political effects. The sultan's circulations as a man of manners who had adopted Western accoutrements symbolized the effectiveness of American tutelage in civilizing the Moros away from their practices of polygamy, slavery, and martial revenge. Werble had hoped that the Sultan's travel would encourage him to "become a reformer in the interest of progress and civilization when he returns" and explained to reporters that the sales of the Sultan's pearls were to raise funds to hire American schoolteachers so that his people might learn English.[68] The tour also presented to the Sultan and his party the superior technological prowess of the civilization that had colonized his islands. Soon after his arrival in New York City, the Sultan asked to be taken to the top of the Times Building, a picture of which he had been given and kept with him at home, announcing that the view from above was "greater a million times than I ever dreamed it was" and "nearer heaven on earth than I was ever before."[69] Former Sulu Governor Hugh Lenox Scott, a man the Sultan called "father," had just stepped down as the superintendent of West Point and was asked to welcome the Sultan, and he advised him that he "must tell all the Moros how strong and powerful America is."[70]

Figure 9.3 The Sultan of Sulu on board ship during his world circuit in 1910. Bain News Service, George Grantham Bain Collection (Library of Congress) LC-B2-1076-9 [P&P].

In Washington, Jamalul Kiram toured the Capitol and met with President Taft in the White House, complaining of his loss of revenue, but his presence was overshadowed by the visit of a Chinese prince who, unlike the Sultan, had an official escort of American cavalry.[71] Some editorials argued that the Sultan should be entitled to an official reception to honor his hereditary royalty and "make him feel that the Western World is not altogether the abode of cold, heartless people," and that "it is not his fault that we took his country" and "stripped him of practically every particle of power he had."[72]

The Sultan's stay in the States was intended to be longer, but Werble, trying to fend off Americans desirous to capitalize on him in ways that were disrespectful, including trying to put the Sultan on the stage, whisked him across the country. He only stayed a day in Chicago where one newspaper recounted that he was mistaken for a porter by another traveler.[73] While he was in Hawaii for the final leg of his return home, reports related that his journey "has been an eye opener and he has marveled at the bigness of the world, the grandeur of nations, the wealth he has seen in many industrial enterprises"[74] which made him realize "how puny his own place is."[75] When he met Philippine governor-general Cameron Forbes, Ralph Waldo Emerson's grandson, on November 2, 1910, after he landed in Manila, the Sultan told him in English he was "a changed man" with plans "to buy modern furniture, use ice, and live like a white man" as well as to "build a new, magnificent, and modern house" for his palace in Jolo.[76]

After the election of Woodrow Wilson in 1912 placed the Democrats in control of the government for the first time since annexation, the United States instituted a process of "Filipinization" to turn over important operations to the control of natives of the Islands. As part of this process the Moro Province was ended and governance changed from military to civilian control. When Frank Carpenter was appointed the civilian American governor of the new Department of Mindanao and Sulu, he sought to extinguish any further claims to sovereignty by the Sultan by another series of diplomatic negotiations. Carpenter had served in 1899 as General Bates's private secretary and his indispensability as executive secretary under Forbes led some to believe that he had been in line to become the next republican governor-general of the Islands. One of Governor Carpenter's primary accomplishments in Mindanao and Sulu was the "Memorandum" he negotiated with the Sultan over ten days of sequestered conferences in 1915. In the Carpenter-Kiram Agreement the Sultan agreed to relinquish any claims to temporal sovereignty over Sulu including rights to tax collection and arbitration in exchange for an annual stipend, a grant of land, and recognition of his authority as the leader of Islam in the archipelago.

This memorandum directly acknowledged that prior to the "American occupation" the Sultanate had been a de facto "independent sovereignty" with claims over the "internal affairs of government of the Sulu Archipelago," that had never been "lost or relinquished" by the abrogation of the Bates Treaty, because the Sultan himself had never taken up arms against the United States nor expressed any complete submission in writing.[77] An article in the Philippine periodical *Graphic* later assigned diplomatic success to the Department's Filipino Secretary, Isidro Vamenta, who convinced the Sultan that he was a Christian "brother" who would protect him and assured him that signing the memorandum was in his best interest and "that it will not make [him] a sort of non-existing personality among my people."[78]

The Carpenter-Kiram Agreement, "relinquishing all existing and future claims" against the Government of the Philippines, limited the Sultanate to "ecclesiastical prelacy or authority only." Carpenter argued that it had "transcendent political importance" because it constituted "not only the renunciation by him of his prerogatives as Sultan, but his full acknowledgement of the sovereignty of the Government" in a way that advanced "the policy of amalgamation" leading to the "complete triumph" of the American political ideals of integrating the Islands.[79] When Carpenter later appealed to Congress for a pension for his twenty-two years of civilian service in the Philippines, letters on his behalf argued that the Agreement had saved the United States millions of dollars in indemnity, enabled the keeping of order in the Philippines during the First World War (when Ottoman Turkey was an enemy) with a minimum number of Constabulary garrisons, and removed a thorny obstacle to eventual independence.[80]

Throughout the remainder of the reign of Sultan Jamalul Kiram there were few important departures from the general relations between the Sultanate of Sulu and the Philippine Government established under the Carpenter-Kiram Agreement. However, the Sultan consistently sought to define the boundary line between "ecclesiastical" and "temporal" rights and privileges to the advantage of his income and prestige. A week after the signing the Memorandum with Carpenter, the Sultan sent out a cyclical letter to his followers enumerating his "rights and privileges" broadly in term of "*suku*": the rites of Islam from which he claimed customary authority to collect revenue through marriage and divorce fees, alms, charity, booty, and taxes (*zakat*).[81] The Sultan continued to contend that his rights as the head of the "Mohammedan Church" authorized that all cases involving Moro "domestic relations" be tried in the *agama* or Islamic courts. He created thirty local "agama" courts, appointed judges and deputies, with whom he shared some of the fees and penalties, only a small portion going to the plaintiffs. This created a "racket" in the late 1920s and early 1930s as many Tausugs took crimes which should have been tried in the provincial courts into this parallel system of justice as a result of the Sultan's customary authority.[82] In this way the "abdication" engineered by Carpenter rather than curtailing his power contributed, according to an American former Secretary-Treasurer of Sulu, to "adding considerably to the royal income," making him "a far more important figure that he was in the days when he was merely a figurehead."[83]

In 1931, Governor-General Dwight Davis appointed Jamalul Kiram to replace Hadji Butu as a senator of the 12th District—the only one in all the Islands not filled through democratic election—to symbolize his incorporation within the emergent Filipino state. The Sultan was described entering the Senate chamber wearing a "fez of navy blue striped with brilliant yellow" and carrying "an ivory cane of gleaming white headed with carved gold."[84] The *Philippine Free Press* rehashed his reputation from Ade's opera as a profligate polygamist and joked about his 1904 journey to Manila when he was granted pesos, purportedly to "buy such presents for the ladies of their households as will keep them in good humor."[85] Samuel Tan argued that the Sultan's refusal to participate fully as senator, partly because he "neither participated actively in word or deed," was a continuing attempt to maintain his own culture in the demands of outsiders that he change his allegiance.[86]

The Sultan's home in Jolo was destroyed by a typhoon in 1932, and he was not reappointed as senator in 1934. That year, the provincial governor limited the prerogatives of his power by expressly preventing his courts from ruling on criminal cases and imposing correctional punishment, emphasizing that all cases and contributions should be voluntary and recorded and penalties should be given to the offending parties.[87] Jamalul Kiram II died on June 7, 1936, six months after the inauguration of the Philippine Commonwealth as the stage before independence. His obituary in the *New York Times* recounted the legend of a man who fell from a pinnacle of glory when "he had a retinue of chiefs, clothes of brilliant velvets and silks, a golden scepter and finger rings set with pearls as large as grains of corn."[88] Philippine president Manuel Quezon acted quickly to remove "the impression that there is a dual government for the Moros." He revoked any special laws, preferential treatment, and concessions the Americans had afforded the Moros, including any official status given to any citizens with the title of Sultan or *datu*.[89] Since Jamalul Kiram II had no children, his death—and the suspicious death of his brother six months later—set off struggles of succession that have not been conclusively resolved, even though Fernando Marcos made a ruling during his presidency. Many Moros, often in the name of changing understandings of Islam, continued to resist attempts by the United States—and later the Japanese, and, after 1946, the Philippine state—to deprive them of political power, economic resources, and the cultural and religious customs of their ancestral domains, and a new autonomous region of Bangsamoro is in the process of being established in the Philippines in attempts to end the violence that continues in Jolo and other Moro homelands.

10

Native Americans, the Ottoman Empire, and Global Narratives of Islam in the US Colonial Philippines, 1900–14

Joshua Gedacht

After a swift triumph in the Spanish-American War in December 1898, the United States negotiated the purchase of Spain's largest Asian colony, the Philippine Islands, and quickly moved to establish its control over the archipelago.[1] However, local Filipino revolutionaries had been waging resistance against Spain long before US soldiers arrived in Manila Bay.[2] Instead of recognizing American authority, these anti-colonial rebels moved to declare an independent Philippine Republic on January 23, 1899. Within a month, Filipino resistance broke against the United States, consuming much of the predominantly Catholic regions of Luzon and the Visayas, or two-thirds of the Philippines land mass.[3] The conflict soon devolved into a three-year war of pacification in which approximately 250,000 Filipinos lost their lives.[4]

Against this backdrop, the US military decision to send two battalions of the 23rd Infantry to a distant, predominantly Muslim area of the southern Philippines garnered scant attention.[5] Although Mindanao and Sulu comprised one-third of the territory of the Philippines, it only had a sparse population of 300,000 Muslims and even fewer animists.[6] No rebellion immediately erupted in this region. The leader of one local kingdom, Sultan Jamalul Kiram II of Sulu, entered into an 1899 agreement with the United States known as the Bates Treaty, which stipulated that in return for a recognition of American sovereignty, Muslim Filipinos' "religious customs shall be respected."[7] In contrast to the rest of the Philippines, relatively quiet conditions prevailed in Mindanao and Sulu.[8]

Yet, despite this comparatively subdued entrance, American involvement in Muslim regions of the Philippines gradually descended into violent conflict. After 1903, when the United States established a separate military administration known as the "Moro Province" for the local Muslim "Moro" inhabitants, a decade-long war of rebellion ensued.[9] In one battle alone, the "massacre" atop Sulu Island's Bud Dajo volcano, between 600 and 1,000 local Muslims perished.[10] Some estimates place the death toll for the wider pacification of Mindanao and Sulu at 10,000.[11] Moreover, the initial blandishments of religious noninterference gave way to assertions of Muslim depravity and savagery.

This chapter will examine how fluid discourses on race, religion, and progress intersected in Mindanao and Sulu to drive both spectacular episodes of violence and colonial experiments in religious engagement.[12] As Karine Walther argues in *Sacred Interests*, a strain of civilizational thinking that pitted Christians against the barbarous blasphemies of Islam in a global clash had long been engrained in American history, dating back to the Revolution and even the initial Jamestown settlement.[13] US military officers serving in Mindanao exhibited this enduring mistrust of Muslims, a contributing factor in colonial violence.

However, as the introduction of this volume notes, such religious antagonism comprised an important, but hardly singular, determinant in American views of Islam. In 1782, revolutionary American colonists expressed their admiration for a Muslim sultan from Mysore in southern India who had resisted the incursions of their common enemy, the British, even going so far as to name an armed privateering vessel, the *Hyder Ally*, after a fellow "freedom-fighter."[14] Similarly, the chapters in this volume explore a wide variety of historical encounters with Muslims ranging from military clashes in the Mediterranean to African Muslim slaves living on American plantations to missionary involvement in the Middle East.[15] In these diverse encounters, Muslims might sometimes materialize in American consciousness as enemies or fanatics or racial inferiors; at other times, however, they might be allies or even peers.

Echoing the arguments of this volume that "America" and the "Muslim World" comprise "broad, global categories," this chapter will move beyond a narrow, dyadic conception of US-Middle East or US-Philippine relations.[16] Instead, it will explore the far-flung circulation of narratives of race, religion, and progress across disparate locations and contexts, as ideas about indigenous Native Americans, Ottoman Muslims, and "progressive" governance traveled from South Dakota to the southern Philippines in Southeast Asia, from Washington to Palestine and Istanbul and back again. This chapter will argue that while these contingent discourses sometimes aligned in broadly Islamophobic configurations that produced brutal violence against Muslim Filipinos, at other times they supported colonial experimentation in promoting Islamic religious practice as a means to civilize local inhabitants.

"A Cruel and Heartless Crusade": Conquest from South Dakota to the Southern Philippines

In spite of the heavy cost visited on residents of Mindanao and Sulu, violence was not preordained, and US rule in the region started with less overt warfare, at least by comparison to the "Indian Wars" in the American West or the large-scale campaign of pacification unfolding in the rest of the Philippines.[17] The Bates Treaty of 1899 enshrined a modicum of noninterference in Moro religious practice.[18] This decision to recognize Moro religious practice, however transitory, represented a startling contrast from past American experiences of pacification against non-Christians. What made this moment ripe for such a departure?

Over the long history of conquest that marked the expansion of the United States across the interior of the North American continent, soldiers, settlers, and missionaries often invoked religion as pretext for various acts of dispossession committed against indigenous Native Americans.[19] For example, the infamous 1890 Battle of Wounded Knee in South Dakota, which killed 150 to 300 Lakota Sioux on the South Dakota plains, hinged on discourses of Christianity, heathenism, and savagery.[20] By the late 1880s, anxiety spiked over the "frenzy and fanaticism" of the "heathen" practitioners of the Ghost Dance, a ritual in which Lakota Sioux propitiated the return of the vanished Buffalo. Newspapers and politicians worried that Lakota stirred by "false prophets" would shortly make a "crusade upon whites," contributing to the charged atmosphere that produced bloodshed at Wounded Knee.[21]

The experience of conquering Native Americans at places like Wounded Knee provided a powerful precedent for US military personnel in the Philippines. Long before US armies invaded Asian archipelagos, Americans had a history of drawing analogies between the indigenous peoples they encountered and the specter of distant nonwhite peoples. For example, the very first settlers at Jamestown in the 1600s interpreted local indigenous peoples through the lens of Ottoman Turks, as implacable heathens and religious enemies. Likewise, when private American sailors started to push across the Pacific in the early 1800s, they deployed deep-seated ideas about Native Americans to make sense of indigenous peoples in places like Hawaii, Fiji, and Kiribati, often leading to outbursts of violence.[22] Several historians of the southern Philippines have similarly observed that US soldiers drew immediate comparisons between their new "heathenistic" Muslim charges in the Philippines and Native Americans.[23] Such analogies both reflected and reinforced the sense among troops that conflict with local Muslims was inevitable.

However, these narratives risk overlooking how experiences with non-Christian Native Americans did not exclusively produce uncompromising belligerents but also furnished a cautionary tale about the dangers of religious interference. The initial hesitance to tamper with Muslim practice manifest in the Bates Treaty derived as much from expediency and the deployment of American troops outside Mindanao during the Philippine-American War as it did from concern for Moro freedom of religion.[24] Yet, even as counterinsurgency demands subsided after 1902 and US officers devoted more attention to the southern Philippines, shame over past episodes with Native Americans persisted. Although steeped in discourses of racial and civilizational superiority, some military officers hoped to avoid past mistakes.

One chastened veteran was Brigadier General George W. Davis, commander of the Mindanao and Sulu division in 1901–02.[25] A veteran of various "Indian Wars," Davis offered an improbable avatar of humanitarian sentiment, as he compared the "North American Indians" to the Moros by arguing that Muslim Filipinos constituted the "peer of any savage . . . in cruelty and brutality."[26] Reflecting ideologies of civilizational hierarchy, Davis noted that like Native Americans, the Moros "hold human life no more sacred than an animal," and should thus remain under "a government by the military."[27] Shared savagery thus justified indefinite military rule.

However, even as General Davis expressed predictable views about race and American empire, he also articulated remorse for previous mistakes. In a passage from a 1902 report, Davis lamented the United States' record with Native Americans as a poor template for Moroland:

> Those of us who have . . . [observed] the failure of the Americans to civilize and make American self-governing citizens of "our Indian Wards" not unnaturally have the feeling that the failure is due to a mistaken policy . . . for a century the Indians died off or were slaughtered. The result has been disastrous to the aborigines. . . . Cities have been rebuilt over the ashes of burned tepees. . . . There can scarcely be found an intelligent . . . human being . . . who will not acknowledge that the crusade has been as cruel and heartless as any recorded in human history.[28]

Thus, while General Davis unflinchingly supported American rule and the abrogation of the Bates Treaty, he thought a replay of the "cruel" Indian policies would bring "dishonor." The "ashes of burned tepees" provided a haunting specter.

Davis's critique of American frontier policies partially emanated from "noble-savage" type romanticism. The officer's predecessor in Mindanao, General William Kobbe, judged that "the Moros are like the best of the North American Indians . . . in love of independence, dignity, and pride."[29] Admiration for the "noble savage" did not translate into genuine respect; Davis still deplored Mindanao as a "beehive of Mohammedan savages."[30] However, Davis also believed that "we cannot eradicate the deep-seated [Moro] religious conviction . . . our duty [is] to respect this . . . deeply rooted prejudice and to utilize it."[31] Could this desire to avoid past atrocities and "utilize" religion promote restraint, or would underlying intolerance, inevitably, beget violence?

Leonard Wood, Progressivism, and Religious Intolerance

The first real test for the sustainability of peace came in 1902, when the Philippine-American War wound down, freeing more troops for deployment to Mindanao and Sulu. Military officers who had bristled at the strictures of the Bates Treaty now saw an opportunity to exert greater control, and Brigadier General George Davis released a report that would provide the foundation for the "Moro Province" government launched in 1903, including direct military governance through a governor-general and the establishment of a legislative council.[32]

Meanwhile, political infighting back at home led to the appointment of a new, self-described "Progressive" governor in Mindanao and Sulu: Brigadier General Leonard Wood. Erstwhile pro-consul of Cuba and a celebrity from the Battle of San Juan Hill, partisan rivalries nonetheless stalled his ascent to the upper echelons of US government, prompting President Theodore Roosevelt to send his confidant to a remote post in the southern Philippines.[33] While this assignment represented a professional setback, Wood nonetheless told President Roosevelt upon his arrival in Zamboanga "that there is most important work to be done" here, hoping to demonstrate how an "armed progressive" with a military zeal for good government could secure modern development even in the "Moro" hinterlands.[34]

Once in the Philippines, the new governor-general's interventionist agenda typical of the American "progressive" movement did not bode well for harmonious American relations with Muslim Moros. As Timothy Marr describes in this volume, Wood exhibited scant patience for the rights of the Sultan of Sulu or local Moro culture, instead moving unilaterally to abrogate the Bates Treaty.[35] The governor-general signaled a shift away from "respect" for "Moro customs" toward a more negative conception not just of indigenous practices but also of Islam specifically. Wood declared that "these Mohammedan communities have no legal organization or fixed form of government," and he also invoked the possibility of "holy war," or *juramentado*, a widely feared type of attack in which a man went "through a form of religious preparation" and took an "oath to die killing Christians."[36] Writing to the governor-general of the Philippine Islands and future president William Howard Taft Wood warned that the Muslim faith of the Moros "teaches them that it is no sin to kill Christians."[37] As a result, "our Mohammedan friends," according to Wood, "have to be thumped a little now and then."[38] Such a narrative underpinned Wood's violent military offensives that resulted in 250 Moro deaths in one battle alone.

Colonial Massacres and Islam

This latent threat to Wood's progressive vision appeared to materialize in May 1905, when a group of Muslim Filipinos took refuge from American authority by settling on the top of an extinct volcano named Bud Dajo, an encampment that would become the site for one of the worst atrocities in the history of American empire.[39] Initially, the gathering aroused little concern. Sulu district governor major Hugh Scott, a noted ethnologist who had defused tensions in Oklahoma over various Ghost Dance practices, perceived little threat to American "good government" at Bud Dajo.[40] However, a sudden influx swelled the encampment size by November 1905, engendering deep anxiety.[41] In January 1906, with Scott on home leave, the acting district governor of Sulu, James Reeves, reported on intelligence that these people on Bud Dajo "were going to fight" against the Americans and "were ready to die."[42] Furthermore, these anxieties began to merge with long-standing religious prejudices. Military concerns over "fanatical Mohammedans" spurred the acting US governor of Sulu district to declare that "almost any happening would throw the interest and active participation of the great majority of Moro people with the crowd of Bud Dajo."[43] Thus, when a Muslim informant reported on Bud Dajo, it was news of "250 persons praying" on Hari Raya (*'Id-al-Fitr*) that raised alarm.[44] After Leonard Wood decided to eliminate the encampment in February 1906, he sent 300 US troops to destroy this encampment.[45] The ensuing bombardment of the mountaintop encampment, according to Colonel John Duncan, resulted in "no living Moro" being found.[46] Approximately 600 to 1,000 Muslim Filipinos were killed here.

Islam, in turn, emerged as one of the principal justifications to suppress the outcry that ensued after Bud Dajo. *The New York Times*, the Anti-Imperialist League, and others inveighed against the lopsided slaughter at Bud Dajo, with no less a luminary than Mark Twain decrying American soldiers as "Christian butchers."[47] Yet, Wood's defenders hewed to the discourse of Muslim savagery, and the American-owned *Mindanao Herald* newspaper depicted Bud Dajo as an inevitable consequence of religion:

> General Wood . . . [and his forces] have no excuses to make or pardons to beg for their work at Bud Dajo. . . . Neither did [Moro] husband and wife care to have their children survive them. . . . No blame attaches to our forces. They did their duty . . . regretfully. . . . Mohammedan religion and custom made it necessary to fire in the direction of women and children.[48]

While General Wood expressed some regret at these actions, he still picked up on this putative Islamic indifference to women and children, writing to President Theodore Roosevelt that "one and all were fighting not as enemies but as religious fanatics, believing Paradise to be their immediate reward if killed."[49]

This trope of fanatical Islam thus played a critical role in stifling the outcry over Bud Dajo. Despite the short-lived controversy, General Wood obtained the position of Philippine commander in 1907, served as US Army chief of staff in 1910, and vied for the Republican presidential nomination in 1912.[50] In later years, *The New York Times* ran headlines about Muslim Filipinos as "relentless in their Fanatical Attack on Western Civilization," while the subsequent American Moro Province governor-general John J. Pershing invoked the prospect of "holy war" to justify the destruction of "between three and four hundred hopeless fanatics" in 1913.[51] Such military "triumphs" played a role in propelling Pershing to the position of commander of the Allied Expedition Forces in the First World War. The specter of Islam helped to facilitate impunity for imperial massacres.

Modern Mohammedanism and the Ottoman Empire

While the brutality of Bud Dajo underscores the dominance of a religious interpretive framework for making sense of Muslim Filipinos, regrets about past atrocities against Native Americans sometimes materialized as did concerns about interfering too hastily in local customs. However, for most US officers, the appearance of peaceful conditions or cooperation belied religious resistance: Islam and progress seemed irreducibly incompatible. Nevertheless, despite those dominant frameworks of civilizational and religious conflict, the dissonant views and contradictory impulses driving professions of "respect" found in the Bates Treaty did not vanish. Not all US military officers perceived religion as an obstacle to the progress in Mindanao and Sulu. To the contrary, one American district governor in Mindanao who subscribed to Wood's "armed progressivism" also believed Islam could be the vehicle for "modern Mohammedanism" and the end of resistance. For this officer, Islam could redeem the Moros.

Captain John Park Finley arrived in the Moroland colonial capital of Zamboanga in 1903. Finley first enlisted in the military with US Army Signal Service, receiving instruction in meteorology, and he then served in the American Great Plains, where his work on tornadoes earned him a reputation as the "First Severe Storms Forecaster."[52] In the Philippines, Finley's scientific background captured the attention of Leonard Wood, himself an erstwhile army doctor. The Moro Province governor-general mentored Finley and appointed him to a position as District Governor of Zamboanga.[53] Moreover, Finley's commitment to science, "progressivism," and racial hierarchy prompted him to undertake a thorough ethnological survey of Mindanao's peoples. Reflecting his background as a veteran of the Great Plains, with its extensive Native American population, Finley initially focused his attention not on Muslims but on animistic "tribal" communities found in the southern Philippines, producing a significant study of one such grouping, the Subanen.[54] He devoted particular attention to chronicling "pagan" religious rituals that bore resemblance to Native American "Ghost Dances," describing ceremonies meant to "propitiate . . . the spirits or *diuata*" with "medicine men."[55]

Finley's ethnological investigations, in turn, shaped his racialized conceptions of administration for Moroland, particularly the "tribal ward system" based on past precedent with Native Americans.[56] The officer specifically sought to suppress "nomadic" lifestyles, demarcating "non-Christian territory into wards with boundary lines" and appointing designated "headmen" and "deputy headmen" in each ward. This framework stemmed from Finley's belief that "the 'assimilation of the races' is impossible," and that the tribal ward system would instead facilitate "diverse racial genius, racial morals and racial intellect (the essential racial qualities)."[57] Tribal Wards would thus, in Finley's estimation, contribute to the "progress" of Moros even while reinscribing their racially separate and subordinate status.

Although Finley initially emphasized the "heathen" templates drawn from the American West, he could not ignore the Moro "Mohammedans." Beyond the Tribal Ward system, Finley played a key role organizing a network of colonial marketplaces known as Moro Exchanges, which Michael Hawkins has highlighted as a critical experiment in molding Muslim subjects through capitalist endeavor.[58] Yet, this interest in the Moros extended beyond capitalist transformation to Islam itself. When describing the Subanen peoples, for example, Finley acknowledged that many animists gradually adopted Muslim practices. "The strongest external influence" upon animist Subanen, observed Finley, "has been exerted by the Moros (Mohammedan)," and "once a Mohammedan, always so, is the historical record of this faith."[59] Finley therefore believed Americans would need to directly address Islam.

Specifically, Finley expounded upon an "instrumentality of modern Mohammedanism" that went beyond a mere profession of religious respect; it also involved engaging with Islam itself as a force for progress.[60] The root of Finley's enthusiasm for religion is his belief that Moro resistance to American rule derived not from their devotion to Islam, but rather, their ignorance of it.[61] Finley later recounted in 1915 that "we found that they [Muslim Moros] were not being taught in accordance with the doctrines of their religion . . . in the Koran."[62] Indeed, Finley attributed most of the "Moro Problem," including the dreaded "magsabil or juramentado" attacks precisely to such ignorance. The district governor hoped Americans could "make a campaign against these vicious habits . . . through the application of modern Mohammedanism."[63]

Conceptions of racial hierarchy inflected Finley's desire to cultivate an "instrumentality of modern Mohammedanism" that could serve pacification. The notion that Muslim Filipinos did not understand their own religion had a long, racialized genealogy. For example, after the United States acquired Mindanao and Sulu, the commanding military officer in charge, none other than George Davis who had lamented the legacy of "burned tepees," commissioned a report on his new territory from a Spanish Jesuit Friar named Pio Pi. This prelate emphasized "the religious ignorance of the Moro" and his "poor reading of the Koran."[64] Davis perhaps appended Fr. Pio's findings to his War Department report because this charge of religious illiteracy resonated with people who had served in the American West and engaged with what they perceived as barely converted "heathens."

Yet, religion distinguished Moros from Native Americans or others in a comparable rung of racial hierarchy, according to Finley, allowing for civilizational advancement. In 1915, Finley noted that for most "'Moro' means nothing but the picture of the non-Christian tribes, and to so picture him is to place the Indian and Jew in the same category . . . but he is not a pagan . . . he prays to the God of Abraham, Isaac, and Jacob."[65] As such, the Moro might comprise a "savage," but not a "dirty savage." Colonial tutelage, in Finley's view, could therefore help the Moro rise above the corruptions of their race toward "a better and truer Mohammedan faith."[66] Moreover, Finley believed Arab racial lineage and Islam elevated the Moro's status. For instance, the district governor wrote that "the Moslem religion began its wonderful advance from Arabia," and how once "these Arabs reached . . . the Philippine group, they converted and intermarried with this Hindu aboriginal mixture and formed the progenitors of the present Moro."[67] This genealogy elevated Moros above their Catholic Filipino counterparts, endowing them "with a strong physique and a degree of intelligence, gained from their intercourse with Arabs . . . and from the fact that the Koran had been brought with them."[68] In Finley's view, such origins placed the Muslim Moros on a higher civilizational rung than their non-Muslim neighbors.

Finley Travels to the Ottoman Empire

Given this intertwined framework of race and religion, perhaps it should come as little surprise that Finley turned to Arab and Ottoman Turkish lands in West Asia for support. Here, Americans could find a Muslim adept of "very fine and fair complexion" capable of elevating his Moro coreligionists.[69] Finley believed that Americans might find "a modern Mohammedan from Constantinople" who could be brought back to the Philippines to help in "combatting the vicious habits of the Moros."[70] Indeed, such an interest in the Sublime Porte had started germinating long before 1913. Several years earlier, a Mindanaoan Muslim and a close ally of Major Finley, Haji Abdullah Nuño, had drafted a petition in the local language of Tausug directed to the Ottoman sultan with a request for assistance in Islamic education.[71] Finley forwarded this petition to President William Howard Taft through his mentor, Leonard Wood, explaining the need to recruit a "modern" Mohammedan official.[72]

Finally, in 1913, Finley embarked for distant Istanbul, bearing with him Haji Nuño's petition signed by fifty-eight local leaders.[73] During his visit, the Major received an audience with Sultan Mehmet V and Mehmet Esad Effendi, the *Shaykh al-Islam* and leader of an eponymous Ottoman state bureaucracy responsible for administering the state *'ulama* and issuing fatwas.[74] Through these meetings, Finley negotiated the dispatch of an Ottoman Arab teacher to the Philippines, Sayyid Muhammad Wajih ibn Munib Zayd al-Kilani, or Shaykh Wajih, as he was usually called.[75] A member of a notable family from the Palestinian city of Nablus who excelled in his Islamic studies and moved to Istanbul in 1906 to work for the *Shaykh al-Islam* ministry, Shaykh Wajih was selected in 1913 for this mission to the Philippines.[76] During his journey, he acquired the moniker "Shaykh al-Islam of the Philippines."[77]

The trajectory that brought Finley to the Sublime Porte can be interpreted as part of a long history of Americans conflating different areas of the Islamic world and erroneously believing Filipino Muslims to be under the effective governance of the Ottoman caliph.[78] Indeed, at the outset of their occupation, the US ambassador to Turkey, Oscar S. Straus, sought the intercession of Ottoman rulers with the Moros to ensure their loyalty to the United States.[79] Likewise, Moroland officers such as Leonard Wood traveled to Java, Egypt, and India to gain the advice of European colonial counterparts on managing Muslim populations.[80]

Yet, while Finley drew from long-standing American interest in Ottoman experiences, his enthusiasm for Istanbul reflected a desire to forge an even broader bond of "trans-imperial synchronicity" that could transcend religious distinctions and come together around shared interests in progress, reform, and colonial governance.[81] Although many American officials sought assistance from the Ottoman Empire in combating resistance in the southern Philippines, they usually viewed such assistance as a provisional expedient rooted in dim views of the shared backwardness of Muslim Turks and Moros.[82] Finley, by contrast, appeared to believe that Ottoman intervention could produce genuine civilizational uplift for Muslim Filipinos.[83]

In turn, various factors within Ottoman society bolstered Finley's venture in Istanbul. For example, the Ottoman Empire had extensive experience of sending religious officials to the far-flung Arab provinces of its empire through the *Shaykh al-Islam* ministry.[84] Likewise, the reign of Sultan Abdülhamit II (r. 1876–1908) precipitated an Islamic variant of the "civilizing mission" to reform and control "nomadic" populations—a project with parallels to US efforts against the indigenous peoples of the Americas.[85] Finally, after the "Young Turks" of the Committee of Union and Progress (CUP) ousted Abdülhamit II and assumed power in 1908, they advanced a capacious conception of state authority that was shared by many of its supporters, including the Turkish feminist and erstwhile student of Istanbul's missionary-run American College for Girls, Halide Edip Adivar.[86]

Indeed, a person who is likely Halide Edip interviewed US Major John Finley for *Tanin*, an Istanbul newspaper associated with the CUP.[87] In her interview, Edip and Finley crystallized many of the themes underpinning "trans-imperial synchronicity," emphasizing the commonality of American and Ottoman interests in uplifting various peoples at the margins of empire. Echoing US preoccupations with Native American precedent, Edip asked Finley whether he could bridge the gaps of "race and religion" between himself and the Moro Muslims, and whether these Moros "would live like the American natives . . . as well, once they came into contact with civilization?"[88]

Just a few years later, in fact, Edip looked to the education of Natives Americans in the United States as a model for the Ottoman administration of orphanage schools intended to Islamize and instill loyalty among Armenian Christians in the immediate aftermath of the genocide of 1915.[89] The civilizing missions at the heart of the age of empire thus resonated across boundaries of religion from Washington to Istanbul, from the southern Philippines to Armenia.

Conclusion: Anti-Climax or Lasting Impact?

After years of planning on the part of Finley, Shaykh Wajih finally embarked on his journey to the Philippines in October 1913, leaving Istanbul for Mecca and Egypt before heading east across the Indian Ocean and eventually arriving at the Moroland capital of Zamboanga in late January 1914.[90] Finley traveled separately to greet the Shaykh, and they arrived in Zamboanga to great fanfare. The rapturous welcome for Wajih made a lasting impression on P. D. Rogers, who served in the Moroland administration and recounted his memory of the events.[91] Writing that the "Sheik ul Islam acted like magic on the Moros,"[92] Rogers went on to describe "the first public meeting" held by the Major and the Sheikh ul Islam:

> About ten thousand Moros attended this meeting, including several hundred priests.... Both men and women dressed in their most gaudy raiment.... I have always regarded this as the most beautiful and spectacular congregation I ever saw. No camp meeting in the United States could compare with it.[93]

These enormous crowds reflected the enthusiasm and potentially transformative impact of this visit. Despite Finley's obvious colonial paternalism, Wajih's tour nevertheless seemed to augur expanding Moro connections with the global Islamic community.

Not surprisingly, however, not all of the American military or government establishment approved of this venture; stiff opposition from various quarters quickly scuttled this experiment.[94] Governor Carpenter, for example, regarded Shaykh Wajih as an unacceptable expression of "religious fervor and propaganda" that could undermine colonial authority.[95] The idea that Islam could be folded into American progressivism proved too much for many US officials to countenance. As a result of this, the US colonial government shuttled Wajih out of the Philippines on a military transport within a matter of weeks, never again to return.

Notably, this expulsion from the Philippines did not represent the end of the shaykh's story. In this volume, William Clarence-Smith chronicles Shaykh Wajih's odyssey back to his home region of Palestine and then onward to the United States in 1915, where he sought to petition the president to return to the Philippines. Wajih's visit also elicited significant American media interest around his "liberal" version of Islam, and the aforementioned major Hugh Scott, by now the Army Chief of Staff, even corresponded with Wajih on his prospect of returning to the Philippines. However, ultimately, the shaykh never met President Woodrow Wilson or won permission to go back to the Moro Province, dying of cardiac complications in Richmond in May 1916.[96]

The rapid ejection of Shaykh Wajih from Philippine shores can be interpreted as the triumph of the dominant colonial framework for interpreting Islam over dissonant discourses, the victory of an exclusivist, Christian, and violent version of American progressivism. Yet, the Finley episode also demonstrated the continuity of countervailing pressures on such exclusivist paradigms, from the desire to redeem the atrocities of the American West in the Philippines to the efforts to express "religious respect" to this ill-fated sojourn to the Sublime Porte. These dissonant discourses, however marked by colonial paternalism and racialist thought, perhaps even providing a humanist gloss on genocide, nonetheless provided significant openings to subject communities.

The contradictions of dominant frameworks, for example, caused an advocate of colonial violence like Wood to support Finley and his "modern Mohammedanism." Likewise, the family of the main local Filipino sponsor of Finley's project, Hadji Abdullah Nuño, has continued to play a significant role in Mindanao politics through the twenty-first century, and an organization known as the Sarikatul Islam developed in Zamboanga in the 1920s.[97] The mosque that Shaykh Wajih visited just outside Zamboanga, moreover, survives to the present day and has received prominent gifts from the Gülen movement, a self-described organization of transnational Muslim renewal and service that originated in Turkey.[98]

While such echoes do not supersede the brutal, violent, exclusivist strains of American and colonial progressivism and should not be seen in any ways as exculpation for atrocities like Bud Dajo, they cannot be disregarded either. These dissonant ideas engaged dominant paradigms, provided openings for local agency, and left long-lasting historical imprints. Distress over "the ashes of burned tepees" and the desire to allow Muslims to develop transnational solidarities were themselves enmeshed in colonial power and hegemony. However, such forgotten episodes also suggest such dissonant experiences in the conduct of US empire and relations with Muslims, Native Americans, and others deserve careful historical attention.

Acknowledgment

I would like to thank the editors of this volume, John Ghazvinian and Mitch Fraas, for organizing the 2017 "American and Muslim Worlds" conference at the University of Pennsylvania McNeill Center for Early American Studies and inviting me to contribute to this volume. I would also like to thank my colleagues at Rowan University for their invaluable feedback in the History Department's works in progress series.

11

An Ottoman Notable in America in 1915–16: Sayyid Wajih al-Kilani of Nazareth

William G. Clarence-Smith

Sayyid Wajih al-Kilani's brief residence in the United States helps to illuminate the state of American Islam, as the long nineteenth century was drawing to a close. Arriving in New York on August 12, 1915, Wajih's stay was curtailed by his untimely death on May 5, 1916, in Richmond, Virginia. During less than nine months on American soil, Wajih acted as Ottoman agent, proponent of harmonious Christian-Muslim interaction, propagator of liberal Islam to indigenous Muslims, friend to the "Syrian" immigrant diaspora, and advocate of the Moro Muslims of the Philippines.

Earlier writings on the man have placed little weight on these final months of Wajih's life. Historians of the Middle East have investigated his role as a late Ottoman Muslim notable, participating in the struggle for the future of Palestine.[1] Historians of Southeast Asia, in contrast, have focused on his sojourn among the Muslim Moros of the southern Philippines in early 1914, and on his claim to be their *Shaykh al-Islam*.[2] His contribution to Islamic reform in the wider "Malay World" has also been acknowledged.[3] What is neglected in these accounts is Wajih's place within the unfolding story of America's relations with Islam.

The Genesis of Wajih's Plan to Visit America

Sayyid Muhammad Wajih ibn Munib Zayd al-Kilani was born in Palestine in 1883. The Zayd al-Kilani of Ya'bad near Nablus were a branch of the prestigious al-Kilani clan, which claimed descent from both the Prophet Muhammad and the founder of the Qadiri Sufi order. Wajih went to Istanbul for further studies in 1906, worked as a teacher there, and then became a clerk in the office of the Ottoman Empire's *Shaykh al-Islam*.[4]

As is shown in greater detail in the chapter by Joshua Gedacht, in late May 1913, the Ottoman sultan appointed Wajih as *hoja* ("high teacher") for the Philippines, dramatically reshaping his life. This was in response to a request from John Park Finley, an American military administrator in the southern Philippines, who believed that Muslim Moros would best be "pacified" by being taught correct Islam. Together with a local reformer, Haji Nuño, Finley persuaded a group of Moros to petition the

Ottoman sultan in 1912, asking that he should send them a teacher of their religion.⁵ Enjoying good connections in Washington, Finley overrode the deep objections of many American and Filipino colleagues, brought the Moro petition to Istanbul, and was rewarded by Wajih's appointment.⁶

After some delay, Wajih arrived in the Philippines in late January 1914, but was unable to stay for long. Although he preached obedience to the American authorities, Governor-General Francis Burton Harrison feared disturbances among the Moros. He ordered Wajih to come to Manila, and obliged him to leave the islands in early April.⁷ It was probably as Wajih passed through British Malaya on his return to Istanbul that he assumed the title of *Shaykh al-Islam* of the Philippines, or even of all of Southeast Asia.⁸ He hoped to gain support in Istanbul for his return to the Philippines, but the Ottoman authorities were too preoccupied with the looming war in Europe to pay any attention.⁹

Around November 1914, as the Ottomans entered the war on the side of Germany and Austria, Wajih headed home for Palestine. Some members of his family had already settled in Nazareth, and he claimed that the town's benign climate was beneficial for his fragile health. However, the main attraction was probably the opportunities of meeting influential Americans in this center of Christian pilgrimage. At the same time, Wajih burnished his reputation as a protector of Palestinian Christians, who were endangered by accusations of acting as a fifth column for the Entente powers.¹⁰

The reverend Otis A. Glazebrook, US consul in Jerusalem, became Wajih's main American ally in Palestine, although it remains unclear how the two men came into contact. The consul was a close personal and political friend of President Woodrow Wilson, from their time together in New Jersey. The president had appointed Glazebrook to the Jerusalem post in early 1914, even though he was a retired Episcopalian priest, nearly seventy years old, and lacking in diplomatic experience. In Jerusalem, Glazebrook struck up a good relationship with Ahmet Cemal (Djemal) Pasha, Ottoman governor of Greater Syria.¹¹

Glazebrook then sought to convince the American ambassador in Istanbul, Henry Morgenthau Senior, to make a neutral American warship available to convey Wajih to New York. This was because the "Mufti of the Philippines" needed to return to "the religious instruction of the Moros."¹² In addition, Glazebrook gave Wajih a personal letter of introduction to President Wilson, although this letter is not known to have survived.¹³

To secure permission to leave Palestine, Wajih cultivated good relations with Cemal Pasha, who put further pressure on Morgenthau to secure passage for Wajih on an American warship. In return, Cemal Pasha allowed Jews, Armenians, Entente nationals, and American citizens to be ferried through the Entente blockade to safety in Egypt. Wajih thus left Beirut on June 26, 1915, on the *USS Tennessee*. Heading initially for Alexandria, the ship took him as far as Barcelona, where he boarded a Spanish liner for New York on July 25, 1915.¹⁴

An Ottoman Secret Agent

The political tasks entrusted to Wajih by the Ottoman authorities remain unclear. On returning from an audience with Cemal Pasha in Jerusalem in June 1915, Wajih told friends in Nazareth that he was going to the United States to keep America neutral in the First World War.[15] Palestinian writers have followed this line, also proposing that he was more generally given the task of putting the case of the Central Powers to the American people.[16] In May 1915, Cemal Pasha was allegedly considering making a separate peace with the Entente powers, if they would recognize him as the independent sultan of Greater Syria.[17] However, no commentators mention this project in relation to Wajih's trip to America.

Ismail Enver Pasha, Ottoman minister of war, had more aggressive plans for Wajih. Enver dreamed of fomenting holy wars in the colonies of the Entente Powers, especially in British India, through the workings of his secret special operations unit, the Teşkilat-ı Mahsusa.[18] Around early June 1915, a telegram specified that funds had been allocated to Wajih to spread the news of jihad "in the vicinity of Hindistan."[19] On June 17, Cemal Pasha noted that he had granted Wajih 400 *liras* per day, "to get by until he obtains money," for which he had requested transfers from discretionary funds.[20]

Adding to the cloak and dagger atmosphere, Morgenthau was informed at the last minute that two "attendants" would accompany Wajih on the USS *Tennessee*.[21] One was Tahir, Wajih's fourteen-year old Moro valet, who was personally devoted to Wajih.[22] The other, described as Wajih's "secretary and interpreter," remains a shadowy individual, possibly called Nabu.[23] This "secretary" was no longer mentioned after arrival in New York. Although Finley stated that transport to the Philippines should make provision for the secretary, Wajih himself only mentioned that he wished his "Moro companion" to travel with him to Manila.[24]

Once in America, Wajih continued to receive funds from the Ottoman authorities. After Mehmet Talaat Pasha, interior minister, and Halil Menteşe, foreign minister, had lunched with Morgenthau in Istanbul in January 1916, the latter noted in his diary that they had told him that they were sending funds to "Sheikh Vejihi, who went to the Philippines, but who is ill in Washington."[25] On learning of Wajih's untimely demise, Cemal Pasha's personal secretary wrote that he had been "sent for jihad," and that he had been a "valuable and self-sacrificing individual." In consequence, Cemal Pasha was asking that official funds be allocated to support Wajih's family in Palestine.[26]

There is little sign that Wajih did much to promote Ottoman political goals once he reached America. On his arrival in New York, *The World* claimed that he was the "personal representative of His Imperial Majesty the Sultan."[27] Wajih himself told reporters that he had met with the sultan when the guns of the Entente forces were battering the Gallipoli Peninsula, but that he was not prepared to talk about the war. He was a man of peace, even though the sultan had not specifically sent him on a peace mission.[28]

While Wajih's declarations to the press may have been designed to throw reporters off the scent, his relations with Ottoman diplomats appear to have been surprisingly distant. For example, Wajih did not follow up on several American admonitions that he should seek an audience with President Wilson through the good offices of the highest Ottoman representative in the country.

Abdul Hak Hussein Bey was Chargé d'Affaires in the Ottoman legation in Washington at this time.[29] He had succeeded Ahmet Rüstem Bey, who had resigned in October 1914, having denounced the United States for various alleged evils, including oppressing Filipinos.[30] For Hussein, American intentions concerning possible hostilities against the Ottoman Empire were a burning issue.[31] It therefore seems surprising that he did not make more use of Wajih's pronouncements in favor of peace.

Hussein certainly had contact with Wajih, as he visited him on his deathbed.[32] Indeed, it was Hussein, together with the Ottoman consul-general in New York, who organized Wajih's funeral and burial in Richmond.[33] The consul officially transmitted information of Wajih's demise to Istanbul on July 12, 1916, though there may have been an earlier communication.[34]

American officials appeared unaware that Wajih was receiving Ottoman funds, and that he was charged with stirring up jihad against Christians in Asia. This may be because a dedicated military intelligence service was not set up until America entered the war in April 1917.[35] At most, the *New York Herald* reported that "he was known for awhile [sic] as a man of mystery."[36]

Muslim-Christian Relations in America

Wajih's letters, together with his declarations to the press, indicate that he was not very interested in political matters, but rather that he was keen to present the religion of Islam in a favorable light to the American people. He thus projected an image of himself as an Islamic envoy. That said, he did repeatedly stress that war with Christians was not part of Islamic doctrines.

Glowing press accounts of Wajih's mission contrasted with reports on a similar figure, just a few year years earlier. The Ottoman government had appointed Shaykh Mehmet Ali to be the imam of the embassy mosque in Washington, and then to a similar position in New York in 1910, under the auspices of the Ottoman consul-general.[37] Two years later, the *New York Tribune* vilified Shaykh Mehmet Ali as part of an invasion of the US by "oriental mystics," preying on vulnerable and credulous American ladies. The fact that the *shaykh* spoke no English was highlighted.[38]

The difference between the two cases may reflect Wajih's elevated social status, deep learning, progressive social views, European physical appearance, and tolerable English. Wajih's arrival in New York certainly elicited a blitz of favorable publicity.[39] Reporters were surprised to see that he was "as blond as a Scotchman," with light blue eyes and a pale complexion. He spoke passable English, and dressed partly in Western garb, albeit wearing robes and a white turban. He was scholarly and pious.[40] These details were repeated across wide swathes of the American press, with small variations, such as attributing to him a proclamation that New York skyscrapers would be good places for Muslim prayer.[41]

Press reports constantly emphasized Wajih's high status, noting that he proudly displayed a genealogy that demonstrated his descent from the Prophet Muhammad. The *New York Times* accorded him the titles "Sayid," "Sheikh-ul-Islam," "Imperial Ottoman Religious Commissioner for the Philippines," and "Head of the Mohammedan religion in the Far East."[42] Another newspaper called him "Mohammedan high priest for our far eastern possessions."[43] The Spanish liner's passenger manifest registered his occupation as *patriarca*, above which somebody suggested the translation of "archbishop."[44]

Wajih sustained this initial interest in his arrival by giving public lectures. When in Washington, he addressed the influential National Press Club, and was apparently granted temporary honorary membership of the club.[45] This may have been at the origins of a laudatory article in the *Washington Star* of October 10, 1915.[46]

One of Wajih's main goals in America was to "acquaint Americans with the true principles of Islam," and particularly to improve relations between Muslims and Christians, as Islam was a religion of peace.[47] Writing to the secretary of war, he declared that he was in America partly to propagate his views on Islam, which were "most peaceful and progressive."[48] He further declared that he believed in women's suffrage and monogamy, as well as in liberalism in religion.[49] Wajih told reporters that he was composing a pamphlet or book, to be published prior to his return to the Philippines. Provisionally entitled "What saith Sheik-ul-Islam of the Philippines," the text aimed to clear up American misconceptions about his holy religion. In particular, "Islam wants to be on good terms with other faiths, [and] is anxious to conciliate, to live on friendly terms with Christianity."[50] This text was never published, but it probably corresponds to the manuscript entitled "Truth of the Islamic religion," written in English, which remains in family hands.[51]

Liberal Islam and American Muslims

Muhammad Rashid Rida, the great Syrian Sunni reformer, strongly influenced Wajih's interpretation of Islam. Rida was at this time the editor of the periodical *al-Manar* (the lighthouse), which had been founded by the celebrated Egyptian scholar Muhammad 'Abduh. Published in Cairo, and circulating all around the Islamic world, *al-Manar* was the most influential standard-bearer of modernist Islam.[52]

Wajih's contacts with Rida were both indirect and direct. When in Singapore in late 1913, Wajih had conferred with Sayyid Muhammad b. 'Aqil b. Yahya, one of the leading Hadhrami Arab modernists in Southeast Asia, who was one of Rida's main disciples in the region.[53] Rida himself attended a meeting between the Khedive of Egypt and Wajih, in Cairo in April 1914, when the latter was on his way back from the Philippines. The two scholars established that there was much common ground between their views.[54] Rida's later obituary portrayed Wajih not only as a friend but also as a staunch ally in purifying global Islam.[55]

It is striking, however, that, while in America, Wajih did not denounce the slavery that remained a legal institution in the Ottoman Empire, despite the official abolition of the slave trade.[56] The legitimacy of slavery in Islam had proved a sticking point in Finley's discussions in Istanbul with the Ottoman *Shaykh al-Islam*, who had struck out a draft clause concerning instructing the Moros about the evils of slavery.[57] Such equivocation may have hampered Wajih's outreach to African American Muslims, for whom the issue of slavery was of great importance.[58]

Philadelphia was Wajih's main base for the first months of his stay, although no record of his influence on Muslims in the city has yet been found.[59] While there, he resided at private addresses, 506 Oak Lane Avenue and 629 North 15th Street. He also consulted a doctor who specialized in Bright's Disease, chronic nephritis of the kidneys, from which Wajih had suffered for some time.[60] The city had hosted a small group of Muslims since 1907, influenced by Ahmadi teachings. Converted by an unnamed individual, who had once lived in "Turkey," they had links with Dr. Anthony John Baker, a prominent physician of the city. Probably a secret convert, Baker was Philadelphia's best-known lecturer on Islam by 1913.[61] However, the community's Ahmadi leanings may have been an anathema to an orthodox Sunni Muslim such as Wajih.[62]

Ella May Garber, a white woman originally from rural Indiana, was Wajih's most prominent indigenous American disciple. Garber had become interested in Islam in 1911, after reading Sufi poetry in San Francisco, probably under the influence of Inayat Khan.[63] The latter was an Indian musician, married to an American woman, who toured the United States in 1910–12, preaching a form of Sufism adapted to all religions.[64]

However, Garber seems to have dated her "real" conversion to Islam to her encounter with Wajih in 1915, after which she adopted the Arabic name of Sadiqa ("truthful").[65] Without specifying how she had come into contact with him, she proclaimed him to have been her *shaykh*, "a glorious teacher of light," and her spiritual mentor. Spreading news of his teaching, she stated that she had "lived only for him" for two years after his tragic death.[66] She later became influential in the Ahmadi sect, marrying a Syrian Muslim immigrant from the Damascus region.[67]

Relations with "Syrians" in America

The large and dynamic Arabic-speaking "Syrian" community in America hailed from the whole of Ottoman Syria (al-Sham), which later became Syria, Lebanon, Palestine, and Jordan. The majority of these immigrants were Christians, of various denominations, though there were Muslims among them.[68] For example, a Palestinian Muslim Muhammad Ahmad settled in Philadelphia in 1908, and he and his family prospered there.[69] He was part of a wider group of Muslims from "Turkey," that is the Ottoman Empire, who arrived in the city at around this time.[70]

Wajih had already made valued contacts with diasporic "Syrians" in the Philippines in early 1914.[71] One of them was Dr Najeeb Saleeby, a Protestant Lebanese medical doctor, of a traditionally Greek Orthodox family, who had come to the islands with the US Army in 1901. He had served with distinction in the first American administration of the Moro Province, from 1903 to 1906, and was a renowned ethnographer of the Moros.[72]

After arriving in America, Wajih asked Saleeby informally to sound out the authorities as to whether he could return to the Philippines. He received a welcoming telegram in reply, signed by "Saleeby and Hashim," and he informed the secretary of war that respected leaders of the "Syrian" community were calling for his return.[73] The Hashim who signed the telegram was probably Najib T. Hashim, another Protestant from a Greek Orthodox family from Mount Lebanon, who had become the richest "Syrian" in the islands.[74]

When war broke out in Europe, the expatriate "Syrian" community generally embraced the cause of the Entente Powers. As subjects of the Ottoman sultan, allied to the Central Powers, the community in the United States feared harsh treatment. This was indeed imposed on them as "allies of enemy" after America entered the war on the Entente side, even though Washington never formally declared war on Istanbul.[75] In an attempt to prove their dedication to the Entente cause, quite a few young "Syrians" signed up in the British, Canadian, or French armed forces, much to the displeasure of the Ottoman authorities.[76]

Wajih's good relations with this community may thus have led to friction with Ottoman diplomats. When in New York, he frequented the headquarters of *al-Huda al-'Arabiyya*, the community's leading newspaper in America, and discussed his plans and dreams with its journalists. The newspaper wrote a fulsome obituary and tribute to him after his death, which was reprinted in Cairo's *al-Manar*.[77]

The "Syrian" community of Richmond, where Wajih moved in early February 1916, was involved with him in his last days. The informant for his death certificate was "Mr. Dibb of Richmond."[78] A few years earlier, the "Syrian" Francis Deeb was recorded as a grocer in the town.[79] Furthermore, Khalil al-Dibsi, "a Lebanese merchant residing at Richmond," wrote to Wajih's family in Nazareth announcing his untimely death, although the letter only reached them after the war had ended.[80]

Wajih's relations with this community reflected the fact that he was a man of two Middle Eastern worlds. As a fluent speaker of Ottoman Turkish, and a former religious official in Istanbul, he had significant ties to the empire's ruling elites. However, as a Palestinian, he also had deep social and affective roots in the empire's restive Arab lands.

Seeking a Presidential Audience to Discuss Moro Muslims

One of Wajih's pet themes in his public pronouncements was the need to improve relations between the American authorities and the Muslim Moros in the Philippines. Declaring that the latter "have caused more trouble to the American government than any other race in the Philippines," Wajih attributed this unfortunate situation to a lack of education. He proclaimed that he had come to America in part to raise funds for educating these benighted Muslims, who were good at heart.[81] He expressed his intention to set up an educational association for Moros, with its headquarters in America, and to persuade the Moros not to back the "independence movement" in the Philippines.[82] American newspapers made exaggerated claims about Wajih's influence on the Moros, even stating that he had single-handedly ended a "holy war" between Muslims and Christians.[83]

In addition to his public pronouncements, Wajih strove to secure a presidential audience, banking on his letter of introduction from Consul Glazebrook in Jerusalem. Wajih also wanted to meet with the Secretary of War Lindley M. Garrison, who was ultimately responsible for the Bureau of Insular Affairs, the American equivalent of the colonial ministry. The American consul in Beirut W. Stanley Hollis had communicated Wajih's intention to meet both men, announced prior to his departure.[84]

Although there is no record of Wajih seeking a presidential audience on his first trip to Washington, D.C., he wrote from Philadelphia asking for one on September 2, 1915. He explained that Glazebrook had entrusted him with a letter of introduction. With regard to the Moros, Wajih declared that "my teachings will instill the highest respect and love for the great government which you represent."[85]

Receiving no answer, Wajih wrote to the secretary of war, on September 23. He argued that Finley's mission to Istanbul had implied official American recognition for his mission, and stated that it had been suggested that he would be appointed to an official post in the Philippines. His religious influence would uplift the Moros, and would encourage them to show "proper obedience to the law."[86] He copied this missive to the governor-general of the Philippines, and to the governor of Zamboanga, in the southern Philippines.[87]

American officials did not wish President Wilson to grant Wajih an audience, however, and attitudes in Washington hardened over time. Before Wajih arrived in New York, Garrison had already written to his colleague at the State Department, suggesting that if the president were to receive this Ottoman envoy, news of the event should be kept to a minimum.[88] In a later exchange, the acting secretary of war considered that such an audience would be inadvisable, in view of the determined opposition of Governor-General Francis Burton Harrison of the Philippines. The latter wanted Wajih to be treated merely as a private missionary.[89] The Bureau of Insular Affairs therefore lobbied hard to ensure that Wajih be denied an audience.[90] The State Department eventually wrote to Wajih, explaining that he must act through the "Turkish Chargé d'Affaires" in Washington.[91]

Wajih then approached Major General Hugh Lennox Scott, chief of staff of the US Army, and a former officer and administrator in the southern Philippines. He enclosed his visiting card, which read "Sayid M. Wajih Zeid-ul-Gilani, Sheik-ul-Islam of the Philippines."[92] Wajih asked Scott to contact the president on his behalf, copying Glazebrook's letter of introduction as an annex. He further explained that he had brought a present for the president's fiancée, a "silk-gold clock [cloak?] of Damascus," asking Scott whether this was acceptable according to American norms. He stressed that the Ottoman sultan had appointed him to his post, on the recommendation of Lieutenant Colonel John P. Finley, US Army, and that he was paying the expenses of his mission out of his own pocket.[93]

In a rather embarrassed reply, Scott explained that he had no power to intervene with the president. In the circumstances, Wajih should present his letter through the "Turkish Minister." However, Scott would like to shake Wajih's hand, and would "take pleasure in presenting you to the Secretary of War."[94] Encouraged by Scott's missive, Wajih wrote again to Garrison, on October 23, asking for a meeting mediated by Scott, and repeating his earlier pitch.[95] He apparently received no answer.[96]

Wajih may nevertheless have clung till the last moment to the hope of meeting the president, at least informally. He took up residence in Richmond, Virginia, in early February 1916, allegedly because the climate favored his deteriorating health.[97] He was staying at the expensive and prestigious Jefferson Hotel.[98] It may be no coincidence that President Wilson was known to stay in that very same hotel when he was in Richmond, which was quite a frequent occurrence.[99]

Striving to Return to the Philippines by "Army Transport"

John Finley, showing no interest in Wajih's wider engagement with Islam in America, concentrated on hastening his protégé's return to Manila on an official military vessel. Writing to Hugh Scott, a former colleague in the Philippines, he asked that Wajih be granted a place on an "Army Transport" from San Francisco to Manila in early November 1915.[100] The financial arrangements were unclear, though Wajih undertook to pay for his own expenses.[101]

However, the Bureau of Insular Affairs resolutely set its face against such an option, because Governor-General Harrison of the Philippines opposed the plan.[102] Wajih sought support from Scott, who replied diplomatically that the secretary of war considered that this would be against the rules.[103] Writing privately to Finley, Scott was more open about the matter. Garrison was not prepared to run counter to Harrison's opinion. As a mere missionary, Wajih could have no official accreditation. Moreover, he would be deported if he posed any "menace to the public order." That said, Scott noted that he would personally favor Wajih's return to the Moro zone, as he would be useful "in the pacification of the country."[104]

The Bureau of Insular Affairs wrote on November 15, informing Wajih that he could return to the Philippines, but not by "Army Transport," and not with any kind of governmental accreditation. In a novel but predictable twist, the Bureau argued that official recognition of an Islamic figure would violate the separation of church and state, which was enshrined in the constitution of the United States.[105] Wajih replied that adequate conditions for managing his medical condition, in terms of rest and diet, would not be available on a commercial steamer.[106] The Bureau answered that only American officials and employees had a right to "Army Transport."[107]

Sayyid Wajih's mission was then cut short by his untimely death. His kidney ailment worsened in early 1916, leading to cardiac complications. He passed away in Richmond's Hygeia Hospital, aged only thirty-three, on May 5, 1916.[108] Linley Garrison's successor as secretary of war, Newton Baker, later declared that his officials had only learned of the shaykh's death through press reports.[109]

Conclusion

Death overtook Wajih before any of his projects could come to fruition, and he therefore did not leave much of a historical footprint. Nevertheless, he was involved in crucial aspects of American relations with Islam, however briefly. Further research on this enigmatic and aristocratic Muslim envoy might therefore help to cast more light on these themes.

Historians to date have mainly focused on Wajih's calls for progressive Islam to be taught to the Moros of the Philippines, so as to end endemic violence in the American territory. And yet, he came up against a brick wall in his attempts to gain American recognition of an official religious role for himself. While American administrators did not speak with one voice, they generally opposed an administratively sanctioned status for him in the islands. They eventually justified this in terms of the constitutional separation of church and state, but the surviving correspondence indicates that some officials believed that he might stir up Muslim fanaticism in the Philippines.

As for the high politics of relations between the United States and the Muslim-majority countries, Wajih comes over in the sources as being little interested in intervening in such matters. Despite having gained official support and funds from Enver Pasha for his mission to America, he seems to have completely failed to call the Asian faithful to engage in a jihad against Christian colonialists. Moreover, his own origins, as an Arab Palestinian, facilitated good contacts with Christian "Syrians," who were sympathetic to the Entente Powers in the First World War. This probably greatly displeased Ottoman diplomats in Washington and New York, and may have contributed to the tepid nature of their support for him. While Wajih never formally broke his bridges with Istanbul, he proved to be a sore disappointment to Ottoman politicians and generals.

Wajih concentrated instead on propagating a modernist version of Islam in America. This was ostensibly aimed at reassuring the Christian majority that Islam was a peaceful and progressive religion, and was therefore to some degree related to high politics. However, Wajih's stance also seems to have been intended to support reformist currents within the small American Muslim community of the time. One question that thus needs to be addressed in this context is how far the liberal ideas of Muhammad 'Abduh and his followers in the *al-Manar* movement had penetrated into American Islam.

Another unresolved question that arises from Wajih's experiences concerns the distinction, and possibly the tensions, between "white" and "black" Muslims in the United States, which Patrick Bowen has recently been researching. While Wajih's impact on American Muslims remains to be properly assessed, he conversed essentially with Middle Eastern immigrants and white converts. Indeed, there is no mention in the sources of African American Muslims, and they seem to have conserved no folk memory of the blonde blue-eyed Palestinian *Shaykh al-Islam* who briefly appeared in their midst.

Epilogue: The Global History of American and Muslim Worlds before 1900

Heather J. Sharkey

Rejecting an "Us-and-Them" History

In 1996, the late Bernard Lewis published a slim volume called *Cultures in Conflict: Christians, Muslims, and Jews in the Age of Discovery*. The book, which gathered lectures that Lewis had delivered three years earlier at the University of Wisconsin, offered a "quincentennial" perspective on 1492 as a watershed year in world history.[1] On August 3, 1492, Christopher Columbus sailed with three ships from Palos de la Frontera, in southwestern Spain, heading westward in the Atlantic. Commissioned by Queen Isabella and King Ferdinand to find a new route to India, Columbus and his crew instead found new lands, and new "Indians," inaugurating a series of European explorations and conquests in the Americas.

In fact, Columbus's "discovery" was not the pivot for Lewis's story. More important for *Cultures in Conflict* was an event that had occurred several months earlier, some three hundred kilometers east of the port from which the *Niña*, the *Pinta*, and the *Santa Maria* set out. This other event transpired on January 2, 1492, when the last Muslim emir of Granada, Muhammad XII, surrendered to Isabella and Ferdinand. For these stalwart Catholic monarchs, whose marriage forged Spain from the union of Castile and Aragon, Granada's submission marked the success of a belated crusade. For Muslims, Granada's fall marked the end of more than seven centuries of Islamic imperial rule in Iberia. It closed an age that began in 711, when Tariq ibn Ziyad—by many accounts a Berber Muslim slave—sailed across the Mediterranean from northwest Africa, and landed on the spot that still bears his name: Gibraltar, or in Arabic, *Jabal Tariq* ("Tariq's Mountain"). The fall of Granada proved catastrophic for Iberian Muslims and also Jews, who faced a choice of converting to Christianity or leaving Spain. Some converted but many left, scattering south to the Maghreb or east to refuge in the Ottoman Empire.

Lewis used the events of 1492 to take a binary, us-and-them approach to "cultures in conflict." His narrative posed Muslims against Christians, and an Islamic world (we might now say Middle Eastern world) against Europe. Lewis called it a confrontation between "Europe and Islam," implying that Islam, the religion, was antithetical and inevitably hostile to Europe, the place. He described Islam, further, as a "constant and imminent menace to Christendom"—without citing Christendom as a reciprocal menace to the worlds of Muslims—during the millennium before the Ottoman military withdrew from the outskirts of Vienna in 1683.² If the image he conjured of ineluctable conflict recalls the work of the late Samuel T. Huntington, who in 1993 expounded his post-Cold-War theory about a looming "clash of civilizations" within the journal *Foreign Affairs*, then the similarity is no accident.³ Lewis had evoked a similar notion, with near-identical wording, several years earlier, by advancing a view of modern history caught between a "clash of the two civilizations." This clash pitted a Christian civilization squarely centered in Europe against an Islamic civilization rooted in western Asia and northern Africa.⁴

As Karine Walther shows in her chapter in this volume, the idea of Islamic and Christian civilizations in conflict had a history among US academics that clearly stretched back to the 1820s. In that decade, Greek nationalists fought for independence from the Ottoman Empire, prompting American "Philhellenists" to advocate with the US government on their behalf as fellow Christians. Yet while the concept of civilizational conflict may have had a long pedigree in the United States, Huntington provided the tidy new wording that turned the idea into a mass-media sound bite. And so, when Oxford University Press published *Cultures in Conflict* in 1995, it invoked Huntington's phrase from two years earlier to promote Lewis's book, which it described as showing how 1492, "that climactic year," witnessed "a clash of civilizations—a clash not only of the New World and the Old, but also of Christendom and Islam, of Europe and the rest of the world."⁵

The legacies of 1492 hover over this volume, too, since the onset of European conquest and colonization in the New World forms a critical backdrop to the modern history of "American worlds," and of Muslims as actors within them. The year 1492 represents a starting point for the demographic transformations that shuffled American populations through the decimation of Native Americans (more through "biological expansion"⁶ via the inadvertent spread of disease, than through warfare), the settlement of Europeans, and the transfer of Africans via the trans-Atlantic slave trade. But the fraught history of European religious and sectarian warfare, as exemplified by the fate of Granada, also provides critical context for these American stories. Consider, as Karoline Cook shows in this volume, how the history of the Reconquista in Iberia informed early-sixteenth-century Spanish policy—in theory, if not always in practice—by restricting Muslims (and Jews) as well as baptized Christians of Muslim- (and Jewish-) convert background (*moriscos*) from settling in the Americas.

Here is where the similarities end relative to Lewis's *Cultures in Conflict*. *American and Muslim Worlds* rejects the Manichean vision of world history that pundits like Bernard Lewis and Samuel T. Huntington advanced—a vision that Osama bin Laden, mastermind of the September 11, 2001, attacks and a self-styled jihadist against "Jews and Crusaders"—also embraced.⁷ Likewise, it rejects the reification of "the West" and "the East," or "the West and the rest" in world history, as well as the tendency to reduce religion into a force for stoking primordial hatreds. Instead of advancing hostility, alienation, and discord as grand themes in the history of American and Muslim worlds, this volume focuses on the movement and circulation of people, objects, and ideas. At the same time, it considers the mixed bag of fantasies and attitudes (negative, positive, ambivalent, confused) that have constituted people's imaginings. American and Muslim worlds appear in this book not as separate spheres but as overlapping circles—a narrative version of the shifting sets and colored bubbles that might appear if we were to attempt a Venn-diagram model of history.

Muslim(s) and American(s)

The very title of *American and Muslim Worlds before 1900* signals a few of its arguments. First, American worlds have extended beyond the United States, to encompass the Americas, plural. Second, Muslim worlds, which are plural as well, go beyond the Middle East to include various parts of Asia, Africa, Europe, America, and more—in short, anywhere Muslims have been. Third, American and Muslim worlds have included a plurality of cultures along with peoples of differing outlooks.

The title contains an argument about timing as well. By drawing attention to the period before 1900, the book asserts that connections between American and Muslim worlds run deep. People who moved in these worlds had meaningful encounters before the twentieth century, when the United States became a global superpower, and certainly before the 1960s, when the lowering of racially motivated barriers into the United States and Canada opened the way to new Asian and African immigrants. The latter development enabled the growth of diverse and often highly educated North American Muslim communities, whose members have added in the past half century to the collective tapestry of cultural life.[8]

This book also starts from the premise that Muslims have formed part of the "us" of American peoples. Here, then, is another reason for rejecting an "us-and-them" version of history: it does not make sense in practice. Like Europeans who came to settle, Muslims of African origin who came to the Americas as slaves, starting around 1500, became de facto Americans because they stayed through force of circumstance. Reciprocally, American peoples influenced Muslims abroad through a variety of social encounters occasioned through travel and trade, the circulation of print and visual cultures, and more. William B. Sherman, in this volume, advances this point strongly by illuminating the impact of American Christian missionary writings on both Afghan nationalist and Ahmadiyya Muslim reformist ideas.

Muslims also participated in the off-stage making of American culture, insofar as they interacted with diverse American peoples abroad—merchants, missionaries, soldiers, literati, and others—in ways that reverberated back into American societies.[9] In the realm of the imagination, literary texts associated with Muslims and translated from Arabic, Persian, and other languages—texts like the Qur'an, or anthologies of Sufi poetry—also helped to shape American thinkers. Ideas spread, too, through forms of art, music, and material culture. As an example of material culture, think of something as prosaic and now-ubiquitous as the stuffed armchair, an Ottoman "import" which became a common item of furniture in the United States only after the 1876 World Centennial Exhibition in Philadelphia![10]

The contributors to this volume owe many debts to those who pioneered studies of American Muslim encounters. Some of these trailblazers participated in the conference that inspired this book[11] while a few also contributed articles.[12] This volume seeks to add to the scholarship and to forge new ground by starting conversations across fields of study—for example, connecting scholars from history, religious studies, and literary studies; and specialists in regionally and culturally defined areas, such as African American, Ottoman, and Southeast Asian studies. Together, the stories assembled here range from the local to the global and from microhistory to the grand scale.

Untethering the Muslim World

In their introduction, Mitch Fraas and John Ghazvinian express frustration with "World History" and "Global History" classes as typically taught in US colleges and universities. "There is a lingering tendency among global history textbooks," they lament, "to relegate all discussions of 'Islam' to the earlier chapters that deal with the eastern hemisphere, and more or less forget about the existence of Muslims as history marches steadily and inexorably westward, culminating in the 'American century.'" "In the typical undergraduate history textbook," they continue, "the 'Muslim world' generally seems to disappear sometime after the Mongols and the Ottoman Empire, and does not make another appearance until the last few pages—where it rears its head again in the form of Osama bin Laden."

The studies presented in this volume defy a static or episodic view of the Muslim world in global history. They do so by studying Muslims—and *ideas* about Islam and Muslims—as they moved across empires, nation-states, oceans, and areas across the span of multiple centuries.

Consider some of the characters who appear in the stories told here. In Zeinab McHeimach's chapter, for example, we meet Bilali Muhammad, who was born in Timbo, now Guinea. Captured by slave-raiders, he labored first in the Bahamas, and later in Georgia where he died in 1859. We only know about his life as a Muslim because he left a "diary," containing insights into the daily practice of prayer. With its faded Arabic text, this diary somehow wended its way into a university archive. In William G. Clarence-Smith's study, we meet the charismatic Sayyid Wajih al-Kilani from Nazareth in Ottoman Palestine (now located in Israel). Through diplomats, US military authorities in the Philippines contacted the Ottoman sultan, Mehmet V, seeking a Muslim scholar who could impart modern and progressive Islam to the "primitive" Moro Muslims of the archipelago. Ottoman authorities sent Sayyid Wajih, who traveled to the Philippines, then back to Nazareth, and then to Washington, D.C., where he befriended Syrian Muslim and Christian immigrants and Ahmadi Muslims, as well as the occasional American convert to Islam, before dying an untimely death from kidney disease in 1916. We are likely to call Sayyid Wajih a "traveler" and not an "immigrant" because his time in the United States was brief. Even so, once he came he never left; he found his final resting place in a cemetery in Virginia.

Ira Dworkin presents a figure whose travels were more dizzying in their scope. This was Nicholas Said, veteran of the US Civil War. Born near Lake Chad as Muhammad 'Ali ibn Sa'id, he experienced capture and enslavement before traveling with his owner, a Muslim merchant from what is now Libya, to Mecca. Through an improbable chain of events, he later became a valet to Prince Nicholas of Russia, and was eventually baptized in a Russian Orthodox Church in St. Petersburg, in 1855. Later, he found himself in Massachusetts, where he joined a regiment and fought with the Unionists. Dworkin focuses on the remarkable memoir in English that Nicholas Said published in 1873, and argues that this man's life and literary production were as integral to the African-American experience as his contemporary, Frederick Douglass. The career of Nicholas Said, incidentally, suggests possibilities for plumbing connections not only to US, African, and African American history but also to Russian history—especially given the proximity he gained as a servant to the Russian royal family.

The careers of figures like Nicholas Said, Sayyid Wajih al-Kilani, and Bilali Muhammad can remind us that Muslim worlds have offered flexible spaces for maneuver, not fixed spots; and that the process of coming to the Americas (and perhaps of becoming American) was not a simple, site-to-site transfer, but a journey with many stops. These journeys, moreover, reflected varying degrees of choice and coercion on the one hand, and of intentionality, contingency, and raw luck or misfortune on the other.

Running the Gamut: Islamophobia, Islamophilia, and the Road in Between

Unlike Thomas Jefferson, Benjamin Franklin did not own a Qu'ran. But as Denise Spellberg points out in her chapter, Franklin *did* own many books about Islam and by Muslims. He obviously read them, too, judging from references that pepper his writing. "Franklin's views of Islam ran the gamut," Spellberg observes, "reflecting a broad range of early American views of Islam. He first argued for the theoretical inclusion of Muslims as worshippers [in Philadelphia] in 1739; then derided conversion to Islam as a false faith two years later. In 1763, he reversed position again, holding up the exemplary humanity of the Prophet Muhammad to upbraid violent fellow Christians in Pennsylvania" following a case when a group of Scots-Irish thugs murdered twenty Native Americans in Lancaster county.

I would add to Spellberg's observations by pointing out that interest was reciprocal. After his death, Franklin developed a strong Muslim fan base. As the historian Niyazi Berkes noted in 1964, in a now-classic study of late Ottoman history, Benjamin Franklin's *Poor Richard's Almanac* "suddenly came into vogue in Turkey [*sic*] after 1870; there were at least three translations made of these homilies."[13]

The fact that Franklin's views about Islam and Muslims, again, "ran the gamut" tells us that Islamophobia was not the only position that non-Muslim Americans took toward Islam and Muslims a century ago and more. Islamophilia—admiration for Islam and Muslims—ran through the culture, too. John Ghazvinian and Mitch Fraas offer a vivid example of Islamophilia in their introduction. They cite the case of the Philadelphia merchants who, "in act of revolutionary defiance" against Britain and its navy, rigged up an armed privateer in 1782 and called this ship the *Hyder Ali*. The name signaled their admiration for, and sense of solidarity with, the Muslim ruler of Mysore, who had been struggling against the British East India Company and British imperial encroachment in southern India.

Even more important than Islamophobia and Islamophilia was everything in between: middle-of-the-road views that were neutral, so-so, or simply unsensational. "Middle of the road" is not usually an attribute worth celebrating, but when it comes to the issue of Islam and Muslims in the United States, a lack of sensationalism—the idea that Muslims are or can be "regular folks"—is refreshing in the post-2001 United States amid expressions of xenophobia. Dworkin edged toward this idea in his chapter on Nicholas Said, by noting that one of his goals was to assert the "Americanness" of Islam—perhaps we could say the ordinariness of it—and in so doing to debunk the "rhetoric regarding the permanent foreignness of Muslims." Spellberg's chapter on Franklin achieves a similar aim. Indeed, when Franklin discussed the possibility that Philadelphia, in its religious culture, could accommodate "the Mahometan," or for that matter, "the Hindoo," just as the city was already accommodating Roman Catholics and Jews,[14] Franklin suggested his openness to an everyday kind of religious pluralism that augured well for American futures.

In the literary realm, we can also point to evidence from American writers who engaged in conversations, of sorts, with their Muslim counterparts. Mcheimech mentions Ralph Waldo Emerson, who was fascinated by the "distant Islam" of writers like the tenth-century geographer Ibn Hawkal, even as Emerson remained oblivious to the nearby Islam that some African slaves likely practiced in his midst, especially by engaging in the everyday practice of prayer. We could also cite figures like Emerson's friend and fellow Transcendentalist philosopher, Henry David Thoreau, who in *Walden* rattles off a reference to the thirteenth-century Persian poet, Saadi—a fellow lover of nature, who wrote at the time of the Mongol conquests. Thoreau invokes Saadi with the same familiarity that he used when citing neighbors and potentates from his native Concord, Massachusetts. "Fix not thy heart on that which is transitory"; Thoreau averred, quoting the Persian poet, in one of *Walden*'s many passages extolling frugality, "for the Dijlah, or Tigris, will continue to flow through Bagdad after the race of caliphs is extinct."[15]

Considering the long history of discursive crusaderism—an analogue to the rhetoric of civilizational conflict—few may expect to find that Christian missionaries were favorable witnesses to Islam and Muslim culture. Yet, in her chapter surveying US Protestant writing on the Muslims of India, Susan Ryan suggests that missionaries, who were among the first US citizens to engage substantively with South Asian cultures, adopted a wide range of views. Thus, while some Americans in India echoed contemporary British discourses about fanatical Muslims, especially after the 1857 Mutiny, others wrote positively about Muslims while presenting Islam "as a relatively salutary force in . . . the subcontinent, insofar as its monotheism contrasted starkly with Hinduism's baffling (to [many] westerners) array of gods." At a time when the international Protestant temperance movement was building momentum, other American missionaries wrote favorably about Islamic doctrines that discouraged consumption of alcohol. Ryan concedes that "Americans' impressions of Islamic India were contradictory, even chaotic," but their variability refutes, once again, Manichean visions and versions of history.

Joshua Gedacht, who takes stock of the United States in the Philippines after the Spanish-American War of 1898, also shows how certain Americans—in this case,

US military officials—held a range of views about Islam. Gedacht points out that American officials' positive views toward "progressive" Islam (whatever they thought that would mean) accompanied racist and denigrating views of the Moro Muslims who lived in Mindanao and Sulu. Gedacht examines the efforts of Captain John Park Finley, who in 1913 appealed to the Ottoman state to send a Muslim teacher to impart "modern" Islam—really, he hoped, a quietist Islam—to the Moros as a way of suppressing resistance among them. At this juncture, Gedacht's story intersects with Clarence-Smith's, since the teacher appointed was the urbane Shaykh Wajih of Nazareth. Gedacht also juxtaposes Native American and Southeast Asian history, by pointing out that the US government's experience of "conquering Native Americans at places like Wounded Knee provided a powerful precedent for US military personnel in the Philippines." From the Sioux of South Dakota to the Moros of Mindanao and Sulu, US policies covered long distances.

Writing History as Tragicomedy

General Lew Wallace, a US diplomat to Istanbul in the early 1880s, developed an "unlikely friendship" with the Ottoman sultan, Abdulhamid II: so asserts Bill Hunt, who describes their story as a "tragicomedy." Wallace, a veteran of the US Civil War and its Union army known more for his "military blunders" and "botched campaigns" than his prowess, authored the best-selling US novel of the nineteenth century. This was Ben Hur: an epic set against the context of the Roman Empire in Palestine during the lifetime of Jesus. Abdülhamit II, for his part, was a powerful sultan of the Ottoman Empire who closely directed big policy decisions and the minutiae of administration alike, but he was also a paranoid recluse who had few friends aside from a small circle of faithful advisors.[16] The sultan's reputation for antisocial behavior is enough to make his comradeship with Wallace remarkable. What makes the sultan's camaraderie with this author of a Christian saga even more astonishing is that Abdülhamit II sponsored what historians now call "pan-Islam"—a movement for Muslim solidarity, the assertion of modern Islamic statehood, and resistance against the Christian-inflected forces of Western imperialism. The comic dimension of their story, as Hunt tells it, comes not only from the ridiculous implausibility of their friendship but also from the absurd gift that the sultan bestowed on Wallace as a sign of his esteem. This gift was an oil painting rendered in a style that one could call Orientalist kitsch. Still hanging in Wallace's home-turned-museum in Crawfordsville, Indiana, it features a prepubescent girl posed suggestively on a leopard-skin rug. The tragic dimension of their story is that Wallace remained so loyal to Abdülhamit II that he continued to defend the sultan in the United States during the mid-1890s, even as news broke about the massacres that the sultan's militias had meted out against Armenians in Anatolia.[17] Ultimately, Hunt's story provides a human glimpse of a character, Abdülhamit II, who is otherwise easy to demonize, and adds nuance to the history of US and late Ottoman relations.

Timothy Marr's study of Jamalul Kiram II, the Sultan of Sulu in the southern Philippines, contains elements of tragicomedy, too, but feels more like straight tragedy as it proceeds. US military personnel may have congratulated themselves, and laughed, when they recalled how they terrified the sultan and his followers upon their first meeting by setting off gizmos that the Moros had never seen: electric lights flashed on and off, a phonograph which suddenly blared a ragtime ditty, and so on. Amidst these theatrics, Marr shows the sultan struggling to preserve his dignity and leadership while negotiating with US officials who were bent on asserting control. Eventually, in 1910, Jamalul Kiram II traveled to the United States, by way of Italy (where he "traded in his blackened teeth for gold crowns") and Paris (where he sold his pearls to buy fitted suits), even as US news outlets ridiculed him in reports that followed his journey. The sultan spent less time in the United States than expected, Marr notes. This was because his advisor, a German Jewish merchant named Werble, found himself trying "to fend off Americans" who "were disrespectful, including [some who] wished to put the Sultan on the stage." In other words, some Americans apparently wanted to parade the sultan as keepers had done with Sara Baartman, the South African "Hottentot Venus," a century before, in a kind of human zoo.[18] In the end, US authorities sidelined the Sultan of Sulu, enabling the Filipino state, as it gained autonomy and independence, to sideline him, too.

Expanding the Frame of American Islamicism

Consider part of Karoline Cook's story again: In 1493, Pope Alexander VI issued *Inter Caetara*, a bull in which he granted Isabella and Ferdinand of Spain jurisdiction over newly discovered lands to the west of the Azores and Cape Verde Islands. In return, the pope ordered them to spread Christianity—and only Christianity—in these domains. Heeding this mission, and yet doubting the sincerity of the Christian conversions of Muslims and Jews who had submitted to their regime after the fall of Granada, Isabella and Ferdinand sent orders in 1501 to their governor in Hispaniola—now the Dominican Republic and Haiti—banning settlement by Muslims and Jews, as well as converts from Islam and Judaism. If their decree did not really "stick," it was because Spain was not the only source of Muslim influence. Africa was a source, too. As the Atlantic slave trade intensified, some Muslim men, women, and children found themselves captured and sent as slaves to American lands. Enough of them went to Hispaniola alone that the island witnessed a revolt by Muslim slaves from Senegambia in 1521.

These incidents involving the Spanish territories in the Americas, I would argue, provided early foundations for "American Islamicism," a concept that Timothy Marr advanced in his 2006 book entitled, *The Cultural Roots of American Islamicism*. By "American," Marr was referring in his book only to the United States, and yet his model works well for the Americas broadly. By "American Islamicism," he covered the collection of attitudes, imaginations, and ideologies relating to Islam or Muslim people and culture; these ideas amounted to a "deep and dynamic heritage of Islamic orientalism [*sic*]."[19]

The late Edward Said expounded theories about Orientalism in his now-classic book of the same name. The Orient was a zone of fantasy, he explained, a "place of romance, exotic beings, haunting memories and landscapes, remarkable experiences." Writing in 1978 nearly a quarter century before the US invasion of Iraq in 2003, Said suggested that Orientalism had been more important to Europe than to "Americans" (by which he seemed to mean people of the United States). Being "adjacent to Europe," the Orient for Europeans was "the source of its civilizations and languages, [and] its cultural contestant."[20] Inspired by these ideas, scholars later traced contours of other varieties of Orientalism—American Orientalism, for example, or even late Ottoman Orientalism (during the tenure of Abdülhamit II)—and discussed its relevance to regions beyond the Middle East as well as to fields like postcolonial studies.[21] Still others ventured to discuss "self-Orientalism," meaning the tendency to apply Orientalist ideas to oneself or to promote and reinforce them in others.[22]

If we understand Islamicism and Orientalism in these broader, expanded senses, then we can more fully appreciate William B. Sherman's contribution to this volume. Sherman shows how mythic ideas about Afghans as a lost tribe of Israel arose in the seventeenth century (during a period when beleaguered Afghans were fighting against Mughal expansion), but then acquired new life through the mediation of nineteenth-century American missionaries, including the Presbyterian convert from Judaism, Isidor Loewenthal. The circulation of mythic ideas did not stop, however, with missionaries. Certain Muslims of South Asia embraced the Afghan Lost Tribes narrative, sometimes drawing upon the missionaries' English sources to do so. Notably, followers of the Ahmadiyya movement used these sources to strengthen the "theological grounds upon which [their movement's founder] Ghulam Ahmad claimed his role as Mahdi and messiah." Sherman's chapter rounds out the volume because he ultimately shows how American Orientalist or Islamicist thought flowed "East" to influence the pluralistic Muslim culture of South Asia. The result is a "longer history that cannot be fully claimed as Christian or Muslim, American or Afghan" because it is hybrid and global at once.

Conclusion: Islam Is Not a Country, and Muslim Worlds Are Not a Place

In 2014, Zareena Grewal published a brilliant anthropological study entitled, *Islam Is a Foreign Country: American Muslims and the Global Crisis of Authority*. Grewal studied American Muslims who sought the Muslim worlds of their imagination, often by traveling to study Islam in Middle Eastern cities like Cairo, Amman, and Damascus. Her interlocutors were pursuing a quest to find the "real" Islam that they felt eluded them in their American, and American Muslim, landscapes. Typical was the claim of one young woman in California, the daughter of Bangladeshi immigrants, who told Grewal that her parents' Islam was tainted by Hindu influences. These seekers seemed to cling to the romantic belief that Islam was a religion neatly fused to a place, and that they would be able to find the real capital-M, capital-W "Muslim World"—and presumably the real, "Ur"-Islam, by heading to the Middle East and its source.[23]

The tendency to pin Islam to a fixed place—the Middle East—was, again, one source of frustration that prompted Mitch Fraas and John Ghazvinian to host the conference which led to this book. Equally frustrating was the tendency to treat Islam not just as a religion but also as a place, civilization, collection of people, and so on: all-around, all-encompassing behemoth. Ideas like these inspired some of the thinkers whose work this book has challenged. "Islam has bloody borders," wrote Huntington in his *Foreign Affairs* article on the "clash of civilizations," reifying Islam as a violent place.[24] "Between Europe and the peoples of the Americas" before Columbus and his discoveries, Bernard Lewis wrote, "there was total, perhaps blissful mutual ignorance." And yet, he added, "the history of relations, and therefore of perceptions and attitudes, between Europe and Islam [sic] was very different."[25] Europe and "Islam" (the place-people-religion complex) knew too much about each other, Lewis suggested, recalling Edward Said's observations about Orientalism as a production of intimate enemies.

This book has aimed to question assumptions like these and to leave a picture that provides more detail, not less; more gray shading, not less; between the black and white ends of the spectrum resulting from the overlap of American and Muslim worlds. To be sure, the chapters in this volume recognize that fantasy—like rumor—has a place in history insofar as it can shape peoples' behaviors, imaginations, and attitudes.[26] And yet fantasy must have its limits in shaping historical accounts: we need to have doses of social realism, attending to how people lived and behaved, for the sake of having pasts that are "usable" if not always comfortable.[27]

Islam is not a country—and it is certainly not a foreign country in relation to the Americas. Muslim life and culture, in their variable forms, have long been part of American terrains. American and Muslim worlds likewise have overlapped, on American soil and abroad in the wider world. "The past is never dead," remarked William Faulkner. "It's not even past."[28] *American and Muslim Worlds before 1900* aims to start conversations about long-running histories that have bound Americans and Muslims together and that continue to bind them today, as the twenty-first century unfolds.

Notes

Introduction

1. For more on the *Hyder Ally* see Edgar Maclay, *A History of American Privateers* (London: Sampson Low, 1900), 177–85. On more recent interest in the naming of the vessel see Blake Smith, "Revolutionary Heroes" (Aeon.co) https://aeon.co/essays/why-american-revolutionaries-admired-the-rebels-of-mysore (accessed December 7, 2016).
2. Philip Freneau, "The Sailor's Invitation," in Philip Freneau, *The Poems of Philip Freneau: Written Chiefly During the Late War* (Philadelphia: Francis Bailey, 1786), 270.
3. "Donald Trump declines to correct man who says President Obama is Muslim," *Chicago Tribune*, September 18, 2015. Available online: https://www.chicagotribune.com/news/nationworld/politics/ct-trump-obama-muslim-20150917-story.html (accessed January 2, 2018).
4. For other recent scholarship on Islam and the Americas that takes up this challenge see inter alia Kambiz GhaneaBassiri, *A History of Islam in America: From the New World to the New World Order* (New York: Cambridge University Press, 2010); Edward E. Curtis, IV, "Why Muslims Matter to American Religious History, 1730-1945," in *The Cambridge History of Religions in America : Vol. II, 1790-1945* (Cambridge: Cambridge University Press, 2012) as well as his *Muslims in America* (New York: Oxford University Press, 2009); Alisha Khan ed. *Islam and the Americas* (Gainesville : University Press of Florida, 2015); Michael Gomez, *Black Crescent: The Experience and Legacy of African Muslims in the Americas* (Cambridge: Cambridge University Press, 2005); Robert J. Allison, *The Crescent Obscured: The United States and the Muslim World, 1776-1815* (Chicago : University of Chicago Press, 2000); James H. Johnston, *From Slave Ship to Harvard: Yarrow Mamout and the History of an African American Family* (New York: Fordham University Press, 2012).
5. The literature on the engagement of the contemporary United States with Islam and Muslims world is vast, for a few examples focusing on the antagonism between these categories see among others: Erik Love, *Islamophobia and Racism in America* (New York: NYU Press, 2017); Justin McCarthy, *The Turk in America: Creation of an Enduring Prejudice* (Salt Lake City : University of Utah Press, 2010); Thomas S. Kidd, *American Christians and Islam: Evangelical Culture and Muslims from the Colonial Period to the Age of Terrorism* (Princeton, NJ: Princeton University Press, 2009).
6. For an example, the excellent *Cambridge Companion to American Islam* (Cambridge University Press, 2013) devotes only three of nineteen chapters to the period before the twentieth century.
7. There is a vast literature produced in the last three decades which connects the history of the Atlantic world to that of the United States. For a good overview of this literature and debates on the meaning and importance of the Atlantic world see Alison Games, "Atlantic History: Definitions, Challenges, and Opportunities." *American Historical Review*, 111.3 (2006), 741–57. For a good example of work situating the history of

Muslims within the history of America see Kambiz GhaneaBassiri, *A History of Islam in America: From the New World to the New World Order* (New York : Cambridge University Press, 2010).

Chapter 1

1. Denise A. Spellberg, *Thomas Jefferson's Qur'an: Islam and the Founders* (New York: Knopf, 2013), 81–123.
2. A prior version of this article, without reference to Franklin's evolution from slaveholder to abolitionist, appeared as "Benjamin Franklin and Islam," *Pennsylvania Legacies* 18, no. 1 (2018): 12–19. My thanks to Rachel Moloshok, managing editor and associate manager of scholarly programs at the Historical Society of Pennsylvania, for granting permission to use parts of that earlier article here. Benjamin Franklin, *Autobiography and Other Writings*, ed. Russell B. Nye (Boston: Houghton Mifflin, 1958), 97. Capitalization throughout these eighteenth-century documents, with the exception of two pivotal quotations from Franklin, has been regularized.
3. Ibid.
4. Ibid.
5. Ibid.
6. Thomas Jefferson, *The Papers of Thomas Jefferson*, ed. Julian Boyd, et al., 24 vols. (Princeton: Princeton University Press, 1950–), 1: 548.
7. Thomas Jefferson, "Autobiography," in *Life and Selected Writings of Thomas Jefferson*, eds. Adrienne Koch and William Peden (New York: Modern Library, 1998), 46.
8. George Washington to Tench Tilghman, March 24, 1784, in *The Writings of George Washington from the Original Manuscript Sources, 1745-1799*, ed. John C. Fitzpatrick, 39 vols.(Washington, DC: U.S. Government Printing Office, 1938), 27: 367. (I've corrected Washington's original spelling of "Athiests [sic].")
9. A map designates where there is the plaque today to commemorate at http://philawalk.org/map/ stop #4 (accessed October 13, 2018).
10. H. W. Brands, *The First American: The Life and Times of Benjamin Franklin* (New York: Anchor Books, 2000), 125.
11. Ibid., 130.
12. Ibid.
13. Benjamin Franklin, "Poor Richard," (1741) in *Benjamin Franklin: Writings*, ed. J. A. Leo Lemay (New York: The Library of America, 1987), 1291. Hereafter, *Franklin: Writings*.
14. Ray W. Irwin, *The Diplomatic Relations of the United States with the Barbary Powers, 1776-1816* (Chapel Hill: University of North Carolina Press, 1931), 204; Gary Edward Wilson, "American Prisoners in Barbary Nations, 1784-1816" (PhD diss., North Texas State University, 1979), 321.
15. See the account of the surgeon Jonathan Cowdery, "American Captives in Tripoli," in *White Slaves, African Masters: American Barbary Captivity Narratives*, ed. Paul Baepler (Chicago: University of Chicago Press, 1999), 167, 171, 172, 177, 178, 180.
16. Thomas S. Kidd, "'Is It Worse To Follow Mahomet than the Devil?' Early American Uses of Islam," *Church History* 72, no. 4 (December 2003): 786.
17. Robert J. Allison, *The Crescent Obscured: The United States and the Muslim World, 1776-1815* (Chicago: The University of Chicago Press, 2000), 3–34.

18 Oxford English Dictionary, s.v., "almanac."
19 Franklin quoted in Brands, First American, 122.
20 Franklin, "A Narrative of the Late Massacres in Lancaster County," (1734)," in Franklin: Writings, 540–58.
21 Ibid., 555.
22 Ibid., 549.
23 Ibid.
24 Ibid., 555.
25 Ibid.
26 Ibid., 550. The author of the travel account describes a trek through Daghestan with Czar Peter the Great, and details the distinction between Sunni and Shi'i Muslims.
27 Ibn Hisham, The Life of Muhammad: A Translation of Ishaq's Sirat Rasul Allah, trans. A. Guillaume (Lahore: Oxford University Press, 1967), 561.
28 Ibn Hisham, Kitab Sirat Rasul Allah, ed. Ferdinand Wustenfeld, Das Leben Muhammed's, 2 vols. in three parts (Gottingen, 1859, rptd Frankfurt am Main: Minerva, 1961), 1/2: 834–35.
29 Edwin Wolf 2nd and Kevin J. Hayes, The Library of Benjamin Franklin (Philadelphia: American Philosophical Society, 2006), 175, book number 531.
30 Ibid., 665–66, book number 2826.
31 Wulf and Hayes, Library, 32.
32 Gordon S. Wood, The Americanization of Benjamin Franklin (New York: The Penguin Press, 2004), 56.
33 "Sir William Jones," http://www.notablebiographies.com/supp/Supplement-Fl-Ka/Jones-William.html; all the correspondence of Jones to Franklin, "Founders online," https://founders.archives.gov/search/Correspondent%3A%22Jones%2C%20William%22%20Correspondent%3A%22Franklin%2C%20Benjamin%22 (accessed October 14, 2018).
34 "To Benjamin Franklin from William Jones, 17 September 1781," Founders online, https://founders.archives.gov/?q=Correspondent%3A%22Jones%2C%22William%22%20Correspondent%3A%22Franklin%2C%20Benjamin%22&s=1111311111&r=4 (accessed October 14, 2018).
35 Wulf and Hayes, Library, 85, book number 124.
36 Bernard Cohen, "Anquetil-Duperron, Benjamin Franklin, and Ezra Stiles," Isis 33:1 (March 1941): 20, with the original French letter is in its entirety.
37 Ibid., 21; Wulf and Hayes, Library, 96, no. 182.
38 Franklin, "Sidi Mehmet Ibrahim on the Slave Trade" (1790), in Franklin: Writings, 1157–60. This publication has been defined as both a hoax and a parody. See Gordon Wood, Americanization of Franklin, 228, who defines it as "the literary technique he knew best—a hoax." In contrast, one observer in 1836 refers to this piece as a "parody," see Benjamin Franklin, The Works of Benjamin Franklin; Containing Several Political and Historical Tracts not Included in any Former ed., and Many Letters Official and Private, not Hitherto Published; with Notes and a Life of the Author, ed. Jared Sparks, 10 vols. (Boston: Hillard, Gray, and Company, 1836–40), 2: 517, where in the second volume, dated 1836, a Dr. Stuber opines that this piece is a "parody" so "convincing that it "caused many persons to search the book-stores and libraries for the work from which it was said to be extracted."
39 Wood, Americanization of Benjamin Franklin, 56.
40 Emma J. Lapansky-Werner, "At the End, An Abolitionist?" in Benjamin Franklin in Search of a Better World, ed. Page Talbott (New Haven: Yale University Press, 2005),

277; David Waldstreicher, *Runaway America: Benjamin Franklin, Slavery, and the American Revolution* (New York: Hill and Wang, 2004), xii.
41. Bernard Bailyn, *The Ideological Origins of the American Revolution* (Cambridge: Belknap Press of Harvard University Press, 1967, enlarged edition, 1992), 232.
42. Bailyn, *Ideological Origins*, 233.
43. John Trenchard and Thomas Gordon, *Cato's Letters, or Essays on Liberty, Civil and Religious, and Other Important Subjects* (April 15, 1721) ed. Ronald Hamowy, 2 vols (Indianapolis: Liberty Fund, 1995), 1: 182
44. Bailyn, *Ideological Origins*, 43, n. 27.
45. Trenchard and Gordon, *Cato's Letters* (February 3, 1721) 1:449, where Algiers, Tunis, and Tripoli are mentioned as "free piratical states."
46. Bailyn, *Ideological Origins*, 234.
47. Ibid., 241.
48. Lists of slave names appear throughout this text, intermixed with an accounting of livestock, Thomas Jefferson, *Thomas Jefferson's Farm Book, with Commentary and Relevant Extracts from Other Writings*, ed. Edwin Morris Betts (Princeton: Princeton University Press, 1953), 5–31, 39, 42–43, 49–60, 114, 128–31, 1337–41, 139–40, 142–52, 154–56, 158–62, 164–69, 172, 174–76.
49. Mary V. Thompson, "Mount Vernon," *Encyclopedia of Muslim-American History*, ed. Edward E. Curtis IV, 2 vols. (New York: Facts on File, 2010), 2: 392–93.
50. Jefferson, "Original 'rough draft' of the Declaration of Independence," *Papers*, 1: 423–28, online https://jeffersonpapers.princeton.edu/selected-documents/jefferson%E2%80%99s-%E2%80%9Coriginal-rough-draught%E2%80%9D-declaration-independence (accessed October 30, 2018).
51. Jefferson, "Notes on Virginia," in *Life and Selected Writings of Thomas Jefferson*, eds. Adrienne Koch and William Peden, 239.
52. Jefferson, "Notes on Virginia," 238.
53. Benjamin Franklin, "A Conversation on Slavery," (1770) in *Franklin: Writings*, 649. See also Lapansky-Werner, "At the End, an Abolitionist?" 282.
54. Henry Wiencek, *An Imperfect God: George Washington, His Slaves, and the Creation of America* (New York: Farrar, Straus and Giroux, 2003), 343.
55. Paul Finkelman, *Slavery and the Founders: Race and Liberty in the Age of Jefferson*, 2nd ed. (Armonk NY, M.E. Sharpe, 2001), 153–54, all those freed were Hemingses, part of Jefferson's family.
56. Wiencek, *Imperfect God*, 354.
57. Ibid., 354–55.
58. Ibid., 355.
59. Washington's will quoted in Wiencek, *Imperfect God*, 355–56.
60. Ibid., 358.
61. Benjamin Franklin, "Last Will and Testament, April 28, 1757," *Founders Online*, National Archives, last modified June 13, 2018, http://founders.archives.gov/documents/Franklin/01-07-02-0085 (accessed October 30, 2018).
62. Wood, *Americanization of Benjamin Franklin*, 226, who states that slaves were held by Franklin from 1748 and "for the next thirty years." Waldstreicher, *Runaway America*, xii, suggests Franklin's practice of slavery endured for a longer period, "between about 1735 and 1781," during which time he owned "a series of slaves." In contrast, Lapansky-Werner, 'At the End, An Abolitionist?" 277, asserts that "Franklin employed servants and kept slaves from the 1730s until his death."

63 Lapansky-Werner, "At the End, an Abolitionist?" 294; Waldstreicher, *Runaway America*, xii.
64 Waldstreicher, *Runaway America*, xii.
65 1st Congress, 2nd Session, *Annals of Congress*, A Century of Lawmaking for a New Nation, Library of Congress online, March 8, 1790, p. 1465, http://memory.loc.gov/cgi-bin/ampage?collId=llac&fileName=002/llac002.db&recNum=96 (accessed November 1, 2018).
66 For an approximation of Franklin's negative early views about slaves and their freedom, coupled with doubts about his renunciation of slavery, see Lapansky-Werner, "At the End, an Abolitionist?" 273–96.
67 Wood, *Americanization of Benjamin Franklin*, 227.
68 Ibid.
69 Ibid.
70 Benjamin Franklin, "Plan for Improving the Condition of Free Blacks," in *Franklin: Writings*, 1156–57.
71 Benjamin Franklin, "Petition from the Pennsylvania Society for the Abolition of Slavery," February 3, 1790, http://www.ushistory.org/documents/antislavery.htm (accessed November 1, 2018).
72 Ibid.
73 Quoted in Wiencek, *Imperfect God*, 276–77. Wiencek argues that Washington's observation was a subterfuge necessary for his entire family, who, unlike him, could never countenance the emancipation of their slaves. He does not characterize this comment as an attack, but rather explains that Washington "did not say that the Quakers were wrong, but only that their attempt was ill-timed." The author believes that the Quakers "attempt had confirmed what he [Washington] already suspected, that a legislative plan for an emancipation was a political impossibility."
74 Franklin, "Petition from the Pennsylvania Society for the Abolition of Slavery," February 3, 1790, http://www.ushistory.org/documents/antislavery.htm (accessed November 3, 2018).
75 Lapansky-Werner, "At the End, an Abolitionist?" 295, was the first to point out this very confluence of events.
76 Ibid.
77 Franklin, "Sidi Mehmet Ibrahim on the Slave Trade," in *Franklin: Writings*, 1157.
78 Wilson, "American Prisoners in the Barbary Nations," 320.
79 Richard B. Parker, *Uncle Sam in Barbary* (Gainesville: University of Florida Press, 2004), xxiv.
80 Franklin, "Sidi Mehmet Ibrahim," 1157.
81 1st Congress, 2nd Session, *Annals of Congress*, A Century of Lawmaking for a New Nation, Library of Congress online, March 8, 1790, p. 1466, https://memory.loc.gov/cgi-bin/ampage?collId=llac&fileName=002/llac002.db&recNum=96 (accessed November 3, 2018).
82 Sylviane Diouf, *Servants of Allah* (New York: New York University Press, 1988), 48.
83 Franklin, "Sidi Mehmet Ibrahim," 1158.
84 Ibid., 1159.
85 Ibid., 1160.
86 Ibid.
87 Wood, *Americanization of Benjamin Franklin*, 228.
88 Spellberg, *Thomas Jefferson's Qur'an*, 216.
89 Franklin, "Sidi Mehmet Ibrahim," 1158.

90 Benjamin Franklin, "Petition from the Pennsylvania Society for the Abolition of Slavery," February 3, 1790, http://www.ushistory.org/documents/antislavery.htm (accessed November 3, 2018).

Chapter 2

1. Portions of this chapter taken from *Sacred Interests: The United States and the Islamic World, 1821-1921* by Karine V. Walther. Copyright © 2015 by Karine V. Walther. Published by the University of North Carolina Press. Used by permission of the publisher. www.uncpress.org.
2. Samuel Huntington, "The Clash of Civilizations," *Foreign Affairs* 72, no. 3 (Summer, 1993). Samuel Huntington, *The Clash of Civilizations and the Remaking of World Order* (New York: Touchstone, 1997), 42, 312. For a sampling of scholarly responses to Huntington's theory, see Samuel P. Huntington et al., *The Clash of Civilizations: The Debate* (New York: Foreign Affairs, 1996); Edward Said, "A Clash of Ignorance," *The Nation*, October 21, 2001; Amartya Sen, "What Clash of Civilizations?" *Slate*, March 29, 2006.
3. Michael Dunn, "The 'Clash of Civilizations' and the 'War on Terror,'" *49th Parallel: An Interdisciplinary Journal of North American Studies* 20 (Winter 2006–2007), http://www.49thparallel.bham.ac.uk/back/issue20/Dunn.pdf.
4. See, for example, Albert Weeks, "Do Civilizations Hold?," *Foreign Affairs* 72, no. 4 (1993): 24–25; Robert Marks, "Review: The Clash of Civilizations and the Remaking of Word Order," *Journal of World History* 11, no. 1 (Spring, 2000): 101–04; John M. Hobson, "The Clash of Civilizations 2.0: Race and Eurocentrism, Imperialism, and Anti-Imperialism," in *Re-Imagining the Other*, eds. Mahmoud Eid and Karim H. Karim (New York: Palgrave Macmillan, 2015), 75–97.
5. Historians of the Greek War of Independence have clearly demonstrated that religion was only one facet of the struggle involving wider economic, legal, and political grievances. See Richard Clogg, ed., *The Struggle for Greek Independence: Essays to Mark the 150th Anniversary of the Greek War of Independence* (London: Macmillan, 1973) and Douglas Dakin, *The Greek Struggle for Independence, 1821–1833* (Berkeley: University of California Press, 1973).
6. Michael Hunt, *Ideology and U.S. Foreign Policy*, 2nd ed. (New Haven: Yale University Press, 2009), xi.
7. A long debate exists on this topic. For a broad synthesis, see Bernard Bailyn, *The Ideological Origins of the American Revolution* (Cambridge, MA: Belknap Press, 1965) and Donald Lutz, "The Relative Influence of European Writers on Late Eighteenth-Century American Political Thought," *The American Political Science Review* 78, no. 1 (March, 1984): 189–97.
8. See Asli Cirakman, *From the "Terror of the World" to the "Sick Man of Europe"* (New York: Hill and Wang, 2002), 109, 125; Lutz, "Relative Influence," 190, 192.
9. See Timothy Marr, *The Cultural Roots of American Islamicism* (New York: Cambridge University Press, 2006); Fuad Sha'ban, *Islam and Arabs in Early American Thought: The Roots of Orientalism in America* (Durham, NC: Acorn University Press, 1991).
10. Mark Mazower, *The Balkans* (New York: The Modern Library, 2002), xxxiv.
11. Mary Anne Perkins, *Christendom and European Identity: The Legacy of a Grand Narrative since 1789* (Berlin, Germany: Walter de Gruyter GmbH & Co., 2004), 263.

12 Anthony Anghie, *Imperialism, Sovereignty and the Making of International Law* (Cambridge, MA: Cambridge University Press, 2005), 32–114; Turan Kayaoglu, *Legal Imperialism: Sovereignty and Extraterritoriality in Japan, the Ottoman Empire, and China* (New York: Cambridge University Press, 2010), 106–14.

13 For more on this topic, see Alexander Orakhelashvili, "The Idea of European International Law," *The European Journal of International Law* 17, no. 2, 316–17; Wilhelm H. Grewe, *The Epochs of International Law* (New York: Walter de Gruyter, 2000), 500–40.

14 Emphasis in original. G. F. de Martens, *Summary of the Law of Nations, Founded on the Treaties and Customs of the Modern Nations of Europe: With a List of the Principal Treaties*, trans. William Cobbett (Philadelphia: Thomas Bradford, 1795), 5; Jennifer Pitts, "Empire and Legal Universalism in the Eighteenth Century," *The American Historical Review* 117, no. 1 (February, 2012): 103.

15 For Wheaton's influence on theories of international law both in the United States and in Europe, see Mark W. Janis, "Religion and Literature of International Law," in Mark W. Janis and Carolyn Maree Evans, eds. *Religion and International Law* (Boston: Martinus Nijhoff Publishers, 2004), 141–42, note 53.

16 Henry Wheaton, "An Anniversary Discourse Delivered before the New York Historical Society on Thursday, December 28, 1820," *Collections of the New York Historical Society, for year 1821*, Vol. 3, 293.

17 Ibid., 320.

18 Ibid., 293.

19 See "New York," and "Philadelphia, December 4, 1823," *American Mercury*, December 16, 1823.

20 Henry Wheaton, *Elements of International Law with a Sketch of the History of the Science*, vol. 1 (London: B. Fellowes, 1836), 128–29.

21 Wheaton, *Elements of International Law with a Sketch of the History of the Science*, 93.

22 On the history of American philhellenism, see Myrtle Cline, American Attitude toward the Greek War of Independence, 1821-1828," Ph.D. diss., Columbia University, 1930; Pappas, *The United States and the Greek War for Independence* (Boulder, CO: East European Monographs, 1985); David Roessel, *In Byron's Shadow: Modern Greece in the English and American Imagination* (New York: Oxford University Press, 2002); and Angelo Repousis, *Greek-American Relations from Monroe to Truman* (Kent, OH: Kent State University Press, 2013), chapters 2–3.

23 Athena Leoussi, "Nationalism and Racial Hellenism in Nineteenth Century England and France," *Ethnic and Racial Studies* 20, no. 1 (January, 1997): 42–68.

24 Jeremy Tanner, "Introduction to the New Edition: Race and Representation in Ancient Art: Black Athena and After," in *The Image of the Black in Western Art: From the Pharaohs to the Fall of the Roman Empire*, ed. David Bindman et al. (Cambridge, MA: Harvard University Press, 2010), 7. Although Tanner includes "racial Hellenism" as an American phenomenon, Leoussi's article limits her focus to England and France.

25 William St. Clare, *That Greece Might Still Be Free: The Philhellenes in the War of Independence* (New York: Oxford University Press, 1972), 14.

26 Repousis, *Greek-American Relations from Monroe to Truman*, 49–51.

27 Merle Curti, *American Philanthropy Abroad* (New Brunswick, NJ: Rutgers University Press, 1963), 21, 24.

28 Curti, *American Philanthropy Abroad*, 1–2.

29 St. Clare, *That Greece*, 1. See also E. M. Earle, "American Interest in the Greek Cause, 1821-1827," *American Historical Review* 33, no. 5 (1927): 62. For a more detailed

historical account of the Greek massacres, see David Rodogno, *Against Massacre: Humanitarian Interventions in the Ottoman Empire, 1815–1914: The Emergence of a European Concept and International Practice* (Princeton: Princeton University Press, 2012), 65–66.

30   Rodogno, *Against Massacre*, 67.
31   See, for example, the *Baltimore Patriot and Mercantile Advisor*, May 23, 1821; The Charleston, South Carolina *City Gazette and Daily Advertiser*, May 31, 1821; the *Niles' Register*, May 26, 1821; the *New Hampshire Sentinel*, June 2, 1821; the *Vermont Gazette*, June 5, 1821; the Pennsylvania *Washington Reporter*, June 11, 1821; *St. Louis Enquirer*, June 23, 1821.
32   *Niles' Register*, May 26, 1821.
33   Ibid.
34   Some historians have argued that the appeal was probably authored by a Greek scholar in Paris, perhaps even Korais himself. See Elpida Vogli, "The Greek War of Independence and the Emergence of a Modern Nation-State in Southeastern Europe (1821–1827)," in *Empire and Peninsulas,* ed. Plamen Milev (Piscataway, NJ: Transaction Publishers, 2010), 193–94.
35   To name just a few examples, the appeal was published in the Boston *Repertory*, July 21, 1821; the New Hampshire *Portsmouth Journal of Literature and Politics*, July 21, 1821; the *New York Spectator*, July 24, 1821; the Philadelphia *National Gazette*, July 25, 1821; and the Ithaca, New York, *Republican Chronicle*, August 1, 1821.
36   Pietro Mavromicali, "Manifesto," cited in Philip James Green, Esq., *Sketches of the War in Greece: In a Series of Extracts* (London: Thomas Hurst & Co., 1827), 272–73.
37   "The Greeks and the Turks," *American Mercury* (Hartford, CT) July 31, 1821. Emphasis in original.
38   Ibid. Emphasis in original.
39   Ibid. The editorial was republished in dozens of American newspapers, including *The American Mercury, The Essex Patriot,* The New Hampshire *Gazette*, the *North Star*, the *Farmers' Cabinet*, and the *Washington Gazette*.
40   Some have even called Korais the "Father of modern Greek republicanism." See "An Overview of the Documents in this Edition," in Constantine G. Hatzidimitrious, *"Founded on Freedom and Virtue": Documents Illustrating the Impact in the United States of the Greek War of Independence, 1821–1829* (New York: Carattzas, 2002), xxvii.
41   For Everett's relationship with Korais, see George C. Soulis, "Adamantios Korais and Edward Everett," in *Melanges Offerts a Octave et Melpo Morlier, a l'Occasion du 25e Anniversaire de leur Arrivee en Grece* (Athens: Institute Francais d'Athenes, 1956), 397–407. For Everett's philhellenic background, see Paul Revere Frothingham, *Edward Everett: Orator and Statesman* (Boston and New York: Houghton Mifflin company, 1925), 70–82.
42   Edward Everett, *Mount Vernon Papers* (New York: D. Appelton, 1860), 266.
43   Originally published in the *Boston Daily Advertiser*, October 15, 1821.
44   Ibid.
45   Mayers, *Dissenting Voices*, 60.
46   For analysis of how the Greek Question influenced Adams's foreign policy decisions, see Ernest May, *The Making of the Monroe Doctrine* (Cambridge, MA: Belknap Press of Harvard University Press, 1975), 9–11, 63–64, 185.
47   Carl Schurz, *Life of Henry Clay*, vol. 1 (New York: AMS Press, 1972), 210, cited in Mayers, *Dissenting Voices*, 61.

48 James Monroe, *1822 State of the Union Address*, December 22, 1822.
49 See Harry Ammon, *James Monroe: The Quest for National Identity* (New York: McGraw-Hill, 1971), 484–85.
50 Charles Francis Adams, ed., *Memoirs of John Quincy Adams: Comprising Portions of His Diary from 1795 to 1848*, vol. 6 (Philadelphia, PA: J.B. Lippincott & Co., 1874–1877), 172–73.
51 Adams, *Memoirs*, 173. See also Samuel Flagg Bemis, *John Quincy Adams and the Foundations of American Foreign Policy* (New York: Alfred A. Knopf, 1949), 388–91.
52 Ibid.
53 "Mr. Adams to Mr. Luriottis," August 18, 1823, in *Message from the President of the United States Transmitting A Report of the Secretary of State, Upon the Subject of the Present Condition and Future Prospects of the Greeks*, 18th Congress, 1st Session (Washington: Gales & Seaton, 1824), 17. See also, Paul C. Pappas, "Lafayette and Revolutionary Greece," *Journal of Modern Greek Studies* 2, no. 1 (May 1984): 107.
54 See translation of Peter Mavromichalis's letter in Edward Everett, "The Ethics of Aristotle to Nicomachus," *The North American Review* XVI (October 1823): 415–16.
55 Ibid.
56 Ibid., 413.
57 Thomas Winthrop and Edward Everett, members of the Boston Committee for the Relief of the Greeks, *Address of the Committee Appointed at a Public Meeting held in Boston, December 19, 1823, for the Relief of the Greeks, to their Fellow Citizens* (Boston: Press of the North American Review, 1823).
58 For newspaper articles covering the amount of money raised by Americans in support of the Greek cause, see "Greek Fund," *Newport Mercury*, May 8, 1824; "The Greeks," *Salem Gazette*, May 11, 1824. For the efforts of the Boston committee to pressure government to act, see Thomas Winthrop and Edward Everett, members of the Boston Committee for the Relief of the Greeks, *Address of the Committee Appointed at a Public Meeting Held in Boston, December 19, 1823, for the Relief of the Greeks, to Their Fellow Citizens* (Boston: Press of the North American Review, 1823).
59 Adams, *Memoirs*, 195.
60 James Monroe, *1823 State of the Union Address*, December 2, 1823; Pappas, "Lafayette and Revolutionary Greece," 109.
61 Adams's strong stance on Greece also stemmed from his defense of other American interests. Unbeknownst to the public, an American agent was in the Ottoman Empire during the war trying to negotiate a commercial treaty with the empire. Any American statement on behalf of the Greek cause would endanger this commercial mission. James A. Field, *America and the Mediterranean World, 1776–1882* (Princeton, NJ: Princeton University Press, 1969), 125.
62 For full text of debate, see Webster et al., *Discussion of the Greek Question in the House of Representatives* (Boston: Howard Gazette, 1824). For a sampling of press coverage on Webster's speech, see "The Greeks," *Religious Intelligencer . . . Containing the Principal Transactions of the Various Bible and Missionary Societies, with Particular Accounts of Revivals of Religion* 8, no. 29 (December 20, 1823): 459; "XVIII Congress," *The Christian Register*, January 31, 1824, 31; *The Saturday Evening Post*, January 24, 1824; "Greek Question," *Niles' Weekly Register*, January 31 1821, 342; "Ordinations and Installations," *The Christian Spectator*, February 1, 1824, 111; *Boston Weekly Messenger*, January 17, 1824; *Newport Mercury*, January 17, 1824.
63 "Mr. Webster's Speech, On His Resolution in Favor of the Greeks," *New Hampshire Observer*, February 2, 1824.

64 "Legislative," *National Gazette*, December 13, 1823.
65 Daniel Webster, "The Revolution in Greece: A Speech Delivered in the House of Representatives of the United States, on the 19th of January, 1824," in *The Great Speeches and Orations of Daniel Webster*, ed. Daniel Webster (Boston: Little Brown, 1919), 68.
66 Webster, "The Revolution in Greece," 69.
67 Ibid., 76.
68 Paul A. Varg, *Edward Everett: The Intellectual in the Turmoil of Politics* (Selinsgrove, PA: Susquehanna University Press, 1992), 33.
69 For Poinsett's resolution, see John Randolph, *Speech of Mr. Randolph on the Greek Question* (Washington: Gales and Seaton, 1824), 3.
70 *City Gazette* (Charleston, SC), January 7, 1824, 3.
71 "The Greek Cause!" *Kentucky Gazette*, February 5, 1824.
72 "Greek Slaves," *Essex Register*, April 27, 1826.
73 "Speech of the Hon. Edward Everett, in the House of Representative of the United States, March 9, 1826" (Boston: Dutton and Wentworth, 1826), 15–16.
74 Repousis, *Greek-American Relations*, 44.
75 Ibid., 55.
76 Samuel Gridley Howe, *An Historical Sketch of the Greek Revolution* (New York: White Gallaher & White, 1828), 24. See also, David Roessel, *In Byron's Shadow: Modern Greece in the England and American Imagination* (New York: Oxford University Press, 2002), 285, fn. 3.
77 "Russia," Joseph Blunt, ed., *The American Annual Register for the Years 1827-8-9* (New York: William Jackson & E. G. W. Blunt, 1835), 269.
78 Ibid.
79 Ibid.
80 Ibid.
81 Ibid., 207, 273.
82 Ibid., 274.
83 Ibid., 278.
84 Ibid., 425.
85 Samuel Zwemer, *Mohammed or Christ* (London: Seeley, Service & Co. Limited, 1916), 115, 124.

Chapter 3

1 Susan Goodman, *Republic of Words: The Atlantic Monthly and Its Writers, 1857–1925* (Hanover, NH: University Press of New England, 2011), ix.
2 Quoted in Allan Austin, "Mohammed Ali ben Said: Travels on Five Continents," *Contributions in Black Studies* 12 (1994): 131. In this chapter, I have elected to use the name "Nicholas Said" to refer to the author of "A Native of Bornoo," rather than the author's birth name, which he renders, somewhat idiosyncratically, in the *Atlantic Monthly* as "Mohammed-Ali-Ben-Said." His birth name appears in title case without hyphens in *The Autobiography of Nicholas Said*. See Nicholas Said, "A Native of Bornoo," *Atlantic Monthly* 20 (October 1867): 492; Nicholas Said, *The Autobiography of Nicholas Said: A Native of Bornou, Eastern Soudan, Central Africa* (Memphis: Shotwell & Co., 1873), 145. My work is based on the primacy of Said's authorship and

a belief that he exercised control over the production of his autobiographies, even while he did so under conditions not of his own making. I believe that there are ways to read his autobiographical self-definition—an undertaking I have only begun to do here—as motivated. To be clear, while I have elected to use the name under which he published both of his autobiographies in order to foreground his authorship, I also believe, as discussed herein, that, based on the published text, the author of "A Native of Bornou" was a Muslim whose Christian conversion, and associated name change, were not voluntary.

3 Said, "A Native of Bornoo," 485.
4 Allan Austin, *African Muslims in Antebellum America: Transatlantic Stories and Spiritual Struggles*, revised and updated edn (New York: Routledge, 1997), 174.
5 The *Autobiography of Nicholas Said* was recovered and reprinted by Precious Rasheeda Muhammad in 2000 with an original introduction. See Precious Rasheeda Muhammad, ed. *The Autobiography of Nicholas Said: A Native of Bornou, Eastern Soudan, Central Africa* by Nicholas Said (Cambridge, MA: Journal of Islam in American Press, 2000). The *Autobiography* even more thoroughly omits his Civil War service and is critical of Islam in a way that marks its difference from "A Native of Bornou." See Hussein Rashid and Precious Rasheeda Muhammad, "American Muslim (Un)Exceptionalism: #BlackLivesMatter and #BringBackOurGirls," *Journal of Africana Religions* 3, no. 4 (October 2015): 483. Said traveled, taught, and lectured throughout the South during this period, living for some time in Brownsville, Tennessee. See Paul E. Lovejoy, "Mohammed Ali Nicholas Sa'id: From Enslavement to American Civil War Veteran." *Millars: Espai i Història* 42, no. 1 (2017): 224–25.
6 Henry Louis Gates, Jr. and Valerie Smith, eds., *The Norton Anthology of African American Literature*, third edn (New York: W. W. Norton, 2014), 522–34.
7 Frances Smith Foster, "A Narrative of the Interesting Origins and (Somewhat) Surprising Developments of African-American Print Culture," *American Literary History* 17, no. 4 (December 2005): 715.
8 Ronald A. T. Judy, *(Dis)Forming the American Canon: African-Arabic Slave Narratives and the Vernacular* (Minneapolis: University of Minnesota Press, 1993), 148.
9 Henry Louis Gates, Jr., *Figures in Black: Words, Signs, and the "Racial" Self* (New York: Oxford University Press, 1987), 12.
10 Frederick Douglass, *Narrative of the Life of Frederick Douglass, an American Slave*, 1845, in *Autobiographies*, ed. Henry Louis Gates, Jr. (New York: Library of America, 1994), 6–7. Emphasis in original.
11 On Bingham's misattribution of Daniel O'Connell's "Part of Mr. O'Connor's [sic] Speech in the Irish House of Commons, in Favour of the Bill for Emancipating the Roman Catholics, 1795," see David Blight, *Frederick Douglass: Prophet of Freedom* (New York: Simon and Schuster, 2018), 44.
12 Frederick Douglass, *My Bondage and My Freedom*, 1855, in *Autobiographies*, ed. Henry Louis Gates, Jr. (New York: Library of America, 1994), 169.
13 Foster, "A Narrative of the Interesting Origins," 720, 723–24.
14 Douglass, *My Bondage*, 155.
15 Barbara Jeanne Fields, *Slavery and Freedom on the Middle Ground: Maryland During the Nineteenth Century* (New Haven, CT: Yale University Press, 1985), 39.
16 Douglass, *Narrative*, 16. See also, Douglass, *My Bondage*, 152; Scott Trafton, *Egypt Land: Race and Nineteenth-Century American Egyptomania* (Durham, NC: Duke University Press, 2004), 65. This connection is highlighted by African American Glasgow-educated medical doctor and abolitionist James M'Cune Smith, in his

introduction to *My Bondage and My Freedom*. Douglass, *My Bondage*, 136; Trafton, *Egypt Land*, 68.

17 William S. McFeely, *Frederick Douglass* (New York: Norton, 1991), 5.
18 For a survey of the argument and evidence, see Will Harris, "Phillis Wheatley: A Muslim Connection," *African American Review* 48, nos. 1–2 (Spring/Summer 2015): 1–5.
19 Quoted in Ala Alryyes, "Introduction: 'Arabic Work,' Islam, and American Literature," in *A Muslim American Slave: The Life of Omar ibn Said* by Omar ibn Said, ed. Ala Alryyes (Madison: University of Wisconsin Press, 2011), 18.
20 Alryyes, "Introduction," 19. See, also, Terry Alford, *Prince Among Slaves: The True Story of an African Prince Sold into Slavery in the American South*, 30th anniversary edn (New York: Oxford University Press, 2007), 140, 287n.
21 Douglass, *Narrative*, 36.
22 Douglass, *My Bondage*, 216.
23 Frederick Douglass, "What to the Slave Is the Fourth of July," 1852, in *Narrative of the Life of Frederick Douglass, an American Slave*, ed. Ira Dworkin (New York: Penguin, 2014), 145.
24 Karl Marx, *Grundrisse: Foundations of the Critique of Political Economy*, trans. Martin Nicolaus (New York: Penguin Classics, 1993), 524. Marx may have read Douglass before writing his *Grundrisse*, and by 1852, before delivering his July 4 oration, Douglass may have read *The Communist Manifesto* (1848; English translation 1850), which makes similar arguments.
25 "Fred Douglass Talks," *The Washington Post*, August 22, 1887, 2.
26 Frederick Douglass, *Life and Times of Frederick Douglass*, 1891, in *Autobiographies*, ed. Henry Louis Gates, Jr. (New York: Library of America, 1994), 1007.
27 Trafton, *Egypt Land*, 21.
28 Ibid., 20.
29 Mark G. Emerson, "Scholarly Edition of the Grand Tour Diaries of Frederick Douglass and Helen Pitts Douglass" (MA Thesis, Indiana University-Purdue University Indianapolis, 2003), 89–90.
30 Douglass writes about Haiti in the final chapters of the 1891 edition of *Life and Times*. See Douglass, *Life and Times*, 1023–45. For more on Douglass's term as consul to Haiti, see Robert S. Levine, *Dislocating Race & Nation: Episodes in Nineteenth-Century American Literary Nationalism* (Chapel Hill: University of North Carolina Press, 2008), 228–31; Blight, *Frederick Douglass*, 691–713.
31 Safet Dabovic, "Out of Place: The Travels of Nicholas Said," *Criticism* 54, no. 1 (Winter 2012): 65.
32 Jason Frydman, "Scheherazade in Chains: Arab-Islamic Genealogies of African Diasporic Literature" in *The Global South Atlantic*, edited by Kerry Bystrom and Joseph R. Slaughter (New York: Fordham University Press, 2017), 54.
33 Ousmane Oumar Kane, *Beyond Timbuktu : An Intellectual History of Muslim West Africa* (Cambridge, MA: Harvard University Press, 2016), 5.
34 Said, "A Native of Bornoo," 485.
35 Sylviane A. Diouf, *Servants of Allah: African Muslims Enslaved in the Americas* (New York: New York University Press, 1998), 141–42; cited in Foster, "A Narrative of the Interesting Origins," 725.
36 Douglass, *Narrative*, 15; Said, "A Native of Bornoo," 485. See also, James Olney, "'I Was Born': Slave Narratives, Their Status as Autobiography and as Literature," in *The Slave's*

Narrative, edited by Charles T. Davis and Henry Louis Gates, Jr. (New York: Oxford University Press, 1985), 148–75.
37   Said, "A Native of Bornoo," 485.
38   Ibid., 487. In my prose, I use the common modern spellings and transliterations of proper names such as *Borno*, while preserving earlier variations such as *Bornoo* and *Bornou* as they appear in citations. On the preferred spelling on *Borno*, see J. E. Lavers, "Kanem and Borno to 1808," in *Groundwork of Nigerian History*, edited by Obaro Ikime (Ibadan: Heinemann Educational Books [Nigeria] for the Historical Society of Nigeria, 1980), 187n.
39   Ibid., 485.
40   Austin, "Mohammed Ali ben Said," 134. See also Richard Brent Turner, *Islam in the African American Experience* (Bloomington: Indiana University Press, 1997), 43.
41   Said, "A Native of Bornoo," 488.
42   Ibid.
43   Ibid., 491.
44   Said, "A Native of Bornoo," 486.
45   Ibid., 491–92.
46   Thomas Bluett, *Some Memoirs of the Life of Job, the Son of Solomon the Highest Priest of Boonda in Africa [...]* (London: Richard Ford, 1734), https://docsouth.unc.edu/neh/bluett/bluett.html, 20.
47   James Albert Ukawsaw Gronniosaw, *A Narrative of the Most Remarkable Particulars in the Life of James Albert Ukawsaw Gronniosaw, an African Prince, as Related by Himself* (Bath: Printed by W. Gye, [c. 1772]), https://docsouth.unc.edu/neh/gronniosaw/menu.html, 22–23.
48   Ibid., 486.
49   Ibid.
50   Ibid.
51   Ibid., 494.
52   Ibid.
53   In *Muslim Veterans of American Wars*, Amir N. Muhammad notes that nearly 300 members of the military during the Civil War had Muslim names. Amir N. Muhammad, *Muslim Veterans of American Wars* (Washington: FreeMan Publications, 2007), 17–22; cited in Edward Curtis IV, *Encyclopedia of Muslim-American History* (New York: Facts on File, 2010), 561. Among the 55th Massachusetts Regiment's 980 recruits, "Nearly 500 could read and over 300 could both read and write." Benjamin Quarles, *The Negro in the Civil War* (1953; Boston: Little, Brown, and Company, 1969), 185.
54   Quarles, Negro in the Civil War, 203.
55   Christian G. Samito, "The Intersection between Military Justice and Equal Rights: Mutinies, Courts-Martial, and Black Civil War Soldiers." *Civil War History* 53, no. 2 (June 2007): 180.
56   Noah Andre Trudeau, *Voices of the 55th: Letters from the 55th Massachusetts Volunteers, 1861–1865* (Dayton, OH: Morningside House, 1996), 113n21; Samito, "The Intersection between Military Justice and Equal Rights," 170–71.
57   Christian Samito, ed. *Changes in Law and Society during the Civil War and Reconstruction: A Legal History Documentary Reader* (Carbondale: Southern Illinois University Press, 2009), 123.
58   Trudeau, *Voices of the 55th*, 151; 153–54.

59 See, for example, Frederick Douglass's July 6, 1863, speech at a Philadelphia event "for the Promotion of Colored Enlistments." Samito, *Changes in Law and Society*, 115–19. W. E. B. Du Bois asserted in *Black Reconstruction in America*, "Nothing else made Negro citizenship conceivable, but the record of the Negro soldier as a fighter." W. E. B. Du Bois, *Black Reconstruction in America, 1860–1880* (1935; New York: Free Press, 1998), 104.
60 Barack Obama, "Barack Obama's Cairo Speech," *The Guardian*, June 4, 2009, https://www.theguardian.com/world/2009/jun/04/barack-obama-keynote-speech-egypt.
61 Rashid and Muhammad. "American Muslim (Un)Exceptionalism," 482.
62 The most recent set of data from the Pew Research Center notes that 42 percent of Muslims in the United States are US born, and that the overwhelming majority of Muslims in the United States report being "proud to be American." Pew Research Center, "U.S. Muslims Concerned about Their Place in Society, but Continue to Believe in the American Dream," July 26, 2017 (http://assets.pewresearch.org/wp-content/uploads/sites/11/2017/07/09105631/U.S.-MUSLIMS-FULL-REPORT-with-population-update-v2.pdf), 34, 18.
63 On his death, see Lovejoy, "Mohammed Ali Nicholas Sa'id," 225.

Chapter 4

1 Ibn-Ḥauqal Abu-'l-Qāsim Ibn-ʿAlī, *The Oriental Geography of Ebn Haukal, an Arabian Traveller of the Tenth Century* (London: Oriental Press, by Wilson & Co., 1800), https://archive.org/details/orientalgeograp00agoog. For more on Emerson's engagement with Islam, see Suzan Jameel Fakahani, "Islamic Influences on Emerson's Thought: The Fascination of a Nineteenth Century American Writer," *Journal of Muslim Minority Affairs* 18, no. 2 (1998): 291–303; Jeffrey Einboden, *The Islamic Lineage of American Literary Culture* (New York: Oxford University Press, 2016); *Sufism and American Literary Masters*, ed. Mehdi Aminrazavi (New York: SUNY Press, 2014); and Farhang Jahanpour, "Ralph Waldo Emerson and the Sufis: From Puritanism to Transcendentalism," *Journal of Globalization for the Common Good* (2007): 1–22, https://www.globethics.net/gel/4050599.
2 For a comprehensive history of Islam in America, see Kambiz GhaneaBassiri, *A History of Islam in America from the New World to the New World Order* (New York: Cambridge University Press, 2010), 9–94.
3 Bilali Muhammed, *Ben Ali's Diary. Francis R. Goulding Papers, MS 2807*, Hargrett Rare Book and Manuscript Library, University of Georgia Libraries, 1–13; ʿUmar ibn Sayyid, Letter to John Owen (1819), Beinecke Library, Yale University, JWJ MSS 185.
4 This chapter builds on a growing body of work that is shedding light on Islam in nineteenth-century American literature, most notably Timothy Marr's *The Cultural Roots of American Islamicism* (Cambridge: Cambridge University Press, 2006); Jacob Rama Berman's *American Arabesque: Arabs, Islam, and the 19th-Century Imaginary* (New York: New York University Press, 2012), Einboden's *The Islamic Lineage of American Literary Culture*, and Ronald Judy's *(Dis)forming The American Canon: African-Arabic Slave Narratives and the Vernacular* (Minneapolis: University of Minnesota Press, 1993).
5 Tayler Lewis, "The Koran: African Mohammedanism," in *A Series of Papers on their Character, Condition, and Future Prospects*, eds. E. W. Blyden, Tayler Lewis, Theodore Dwight (New York: Anson D. F. Randolph & CO., 1871), 37.

6 For more on *ta'wīl*, see Seyyed Hossein Nasr, "The Qur'ān and Ḥadīth as Source and Inspiration of Islamic Philosophy," in *History of Islamic Philosophy*, vol. 1, eds. Oliver Leaman and Seyyed Hossein Nasr (New York: Routledge, 1996), 27–39.
7 Stephen Best and Sharon Marcus, "Surface Reading: An Introduction," *Representations* 108, no. 1 (2009): 1–21, doi:10.1525/rep.2009.108.1.1; Heather Love, "Close but Not Deep: Literary Ethics and the Descriptive Turn," *New Literary History* 41, no. 2 (2010): 371–91, doi:10.1353/nlh.2010.0007. For more on the hermeneutics of suspicion, see Paul Ricoeur, *Freud and Philosophy: An Essay on Interpretation* (New Haven: Yale University Press, 1970).
8 Best and Marcus, "Surface Reading," 9.
9 For more on Islamic hermeneutical traditions, see Nasr, "The Qur'ān and Ḥadīth as Source," 27–39.
10 Abu Muhammad ibn Hisham, "Concerning the True Visions with which the Prophethood of Mohammed Began," in *Translations of Eastern Poetry and Prose*, trans. Reynold A. Nicholson (London: Cambridge University Press, 1922), 39.
11 Abdelkebir Khatibi, *Par-dessus l'épaule* (Paris: Editions Aubier, 1988) quoted in Khatibi, "Frontiers: Between Psychoanalysis and Islam," *Third Text* 23, no. 6 (2009): 692.
12 For instance, in the Christian tradition, the central moment or primal scene may be recognized as the annunciation: the moment when the angel Gabriel announces to the Virgin Mary that she will give birth to the Son of God, Jesus.
13 Questions of unreadability connect with a longer American literary tradition that was influenced by the decipherment of Egyptian hieroglyphics in the nineteenth century. As John Irwin argues in his influential *American Hieroglyphics: The Symbol of the Egyptian Hieroglyphics in the American Renaissance* (New Haven: Yale University Press, 1980), for American Renaissance writers, the hieroglyph became a master symbol for language and self-consciousness.
14 Khatibi, *Par-dessus l'épaule*, 692.
15 Einboden, *Islamic Lineage of American Literary Culture*, 124.
16 Quoted in Einboden, 123.
17 Ibid., 124.
18 Ralph Waldo Emerson, *The Journals and Miscellaneous Notebooks of Ralph Waldo Emerson*, vol. 1, 1819–1822, eds. William H. Gilman, Alfred R. Ferguson, George P. Clark, and Merrell R. Davis (Cambridge: Belknap Press of Harvard University Press; Charlottesville: InteLex Corp, 2009), 12; Einboden, 124.
19 Presently, the University of Georgia houses the *Ben Ali Diary* in its collection in the Hargrett Rare Book and Manuscript Library.
20 For more on Bilali, see Allan D. Austin, *African Muslims in Antebellum America: A Sourcebook*, (New York: Garland Press, 1984), 265–307.
21 Efforts at translating this document have been carried out by Joseph H. Greenberg, "The Decipherment of the 'Ben-Ali Diary,' a Preliminary Statement," *The Journal of Negro History* 25, no. 3 (1940): 372–75, doi:10.2307/2714801; Judy, *(Dis)forming the Nation*; Yusuf Progler, "Ben Ali and his Arabic Diary: Encountering an African Muslim in Antebellum America," *Muslim & Arab Perspectives* 11 (2004): 19–60; and Muhammed Abdullah Al-Ahari, *Bilali Muhammad: Muslim Jurisprudist in Antebellum Georgia* (Chicago: Magribine Press, 2010).
22 In 1940, prominent linguist Joseph H. Greenberg offered the first major breakthrough in decoding the script. He concluded that the document consists of excerpts from *al-Risala al-Fiqhiya* (*Treatise on Jurisprudence*), a legal treatise on Islamic ritual

written by the tenth-century Maliki scholar Abdullah ibn Abi Zayd al-Qayrawan of present-day Tunisia (372–75).

23. For more on the role of the American Colonization Society (ACS) in commissioning 'Umar's autobiography and 'Umar's experience of enslavement in the United States, see Ala A. Alryyes, "'Arabic Work', Islam, and American Literature," in *A Muslim American Slave: The Life of Omar ibn Said*, trans. and ed. Ala A. Alryyes (Madison, WI: University of Wisconsin Press, 2011), 3–46.
24. 'Umar ibn Sayyid, *A Muslim American Slave: The Life of Omar Ibn Said*, trans. and ed. Ala A. Alryyes (Madison, WI: University of Wisconsin Press, 2011), 63.
25. See Alryyes, "Arabic Work"; Austin, *African Muslims in Antebellum America* (1984; 1997), and Ghada Osman and Camille F. Forbes, "Representing the West in the Arabic Language: The Slave Narrative of Omar ibn Said," in *A Muslim American Slave: The Life of Omar ibn Said*, ed. Ala A. Alryyes (Madison, WI: University of Wisconsin Press, 2011), 182–94.
26. Nicolas Martinovich as cited in Allan D. Austin's African Muslims in Antebellum America, 1984, p. 306, n. 46.
27. According to Judy, for instance, "The manuscript remains unreadable, a deflecting resistance, whose referential meaning is effectively lost" (224). Similarly, Dabovic "argue[s] that the document reveals novel ways of resisting western codification." *Displacement and the Negotiation of an American Identity in African Muslim Slave Narratives* (Ph.D. Diss., SUNY at Stony Brook, New York, 2009), 107.
28. Judy, *(Dis)forming the American Canon*, 285.
29. Ibid., 240.
30. Ibid., 266.
31. Ibid.
32. Progler, "Ben Ali and his Arabic Diary," 25–26.
33. Michael Sells. "Sound, Spirit, and Gender in Sūrat Al-Qadr," *Journal of the American Oriental Society* 111, no. 2, (1991): 253, doi:10.2307/604017.
34. It is both understandable and important that literary critics gravitate to readings that extract resistive tactics buried deep in slave narratives or aim for restorative or reparative readings. For instance, in his comprehensive work on 'Umar ibn Sayyid's autobiography, Alryyes offers a rich and deep analysis that contends that "the surface of Omar's autobiography [appears] as a 'safe' pro-slavery story . . . [whereas the autobiography] is replete with concealed utterances" (17).
35. See *A Memoir of Ralph Waldo Emerson*, vol. 1, ed. James Elliot Cabot (Cambridge: Riverside Press, 1887), 81.
36. John Hunwick, "'I Wish to be Seen in our Land Called Āfrikā': 'Umar b. Sayyed's Appeal to be Released from Slavery (1819)," *Journal of Arabic and Islamic Studies* 5, no. 3 (2004): 67.
37. Ibid., 73. In a *History of Islam*, GhaneaBassiri also points to the talismanic elements of the manuscript, suggesting that "the manuscript's poor Arabic grammar and orthography is also in line with the Arabic writings commonly found in these amulets in West Africa," 77.
38. For more on 'Umar's borrowings and citations, see Hunwick's "I Wish to be Seen in our Land Called Āfrikā."
39. Ibid., 68.
40. My aim is not to deny or undermine the importance of reading resistive tactics within a slave narrative but to explore other possibilities for reading such narratives by drawing on the rich history of Islamic reading practices and present trends in literary studies.

Chapter 5

1. Archivo General de Indias (AGI), Indiferente 1088, L. 11, 95v. "... la qual es muy buena xptiana y se comulga cada 15 dias y es todo el servicio de la dicha su muger." Item 44 in the *Registro de Peticiones* presented to the Council of the Indies and recorded on April 20, 1583. I would like to thank Adrian Masters for bringing my attention to this reference and several others of enslaved Moriscas cited in this chapter.
2. AGI, Indiferente 1088, L. 11, 95v.
3. AGI, Indiferente 1088, L. 11, 95v.
4. Karen F. Anderson-Córdova, *Surviving Spanish Conquest: Indian Fight, Flight, and Cultural Transformation in Hispaniola and Puerto Rico* (Tuscaloosa: University of Alabama Press, 2017). Anderson-Córdova stresses the multiethnic makeup of the indigenous population of Hispaniola, comprising both people who had been enslaved and transported from other parts of the Americas to the island and the population native to the islands.
5. For a discussion of the legislation prohibiting Muslim and Morisco emigration to Spanish America see Karoline P. Cook, *Forbidden Passages: Muslims and Moriscos in Colonial Spanish America* (Philadelphia: University of Pennsylvania Press, 2016), especially chapter 3.
6. Javier Alvarado Planas, "La polémica de los justos títulos en la iconografía americana," in *Observation and Communication: The Construction of Realities in the Hispanic World*, eds. Johannes-Michael Scholz and Tamar Herzog (Frankfurt: Klostermann, 1997), 219–51.
7. Sylviane Diouf, *Servants of Allah: African Muslims Enslaved in the Americas* (New York, NY: New York University Press, 1998); Michael A. Gomez, "African Identity and Slavery in the Americas," *Radical History Review* 75 (1999): 111–20; Toby Green, *The Rise of the Trans-Atlantic Slave Trade in Western Africa, 1300-1589* (New York: Cambridge University Press, 2012); Jane Landers, "Cimarron and Citizen: African Ethnicity, Corporate Identity, and the Evolution of Free Black Towns in the Spanish Circum-Caribbean," in *Slaves, Subjects and Subversives: Blacks in Colonial Latin America*, eds. Jane G. Landers and Barry M. Robinson (Albuquerque, NM: University of New Mexico Press, 2006), 111–45.
8. AGI, Indiferente 1961, L.2, 223r–v.
9. This was a common practice used by both Christian and Muslim conquerors on the Iberian Peninsula during the medieval period. Although tensions always existed, and the policy could be applied unevenly, religious minority communities were in theory protected. On surrender treaties see Robert I. Burns and Paul E. Chevedden, *Negotiating Cultures: Bilingual Surrender Treaties on the Crusader-Muslim Frontier under James the Conqueror* (Brill, 1999).
10. On the concept of *taqiyya* see Louis Cardaillac, *Moriscos y cristianos: un enfrentamiento polémico (1492-1640)* (Madrid: Fondo de Cultura Económica, 1979), 85–98. Also see Patrick J. O'Banion, "'They will know our hearts': Practicing the Art of Dissimulation on the Islamic Periphery," *Journal of Early Modern History* 20 (2016): 193–217.
11. On Moriscos who petitioned on the eve of the 1609–1614 expulsions to be acknowledged as "good and faithful Christians" and loyal subjects of the Spanish Crown see James B. Tueller, *Good and Faithful Christians: Moriscos and Catholicism in Early Modern Spain* (New Orleans, LA: University Press of the South, 2002).

12 AGI, Indiferente 418, L.1, 39r–42r.
13 AGI, Indiferente 424, L. 22, 240r.
14 AGI, Mexico 1064, L.2, 31v–32r.
15 AGI, Mexico 1089, L. 4, 212r.
16 Solange Alberro, *Inquisition et societé au Mexique, 1571-1700* (Mexico City: Centre d'études mexicaines et centramericaines, 1988); Joan Cameron Bristol, *Christians, Blasphemers, and Witches: Afro-Mexican Ritual Practice in the Seventeenth Century* (Albuquerque: University of New Mexico Press, 2007); Nathan Wachtel, *La Foi du souvenir: Labyrinthes marranes* (Paris: Éditions du Seuil, 2001); Cook, *Forbidden Passages*. Indigenous peoples could still be tried for religious matters but because they were legally viewed as neophytes even after many generations, they remained subject to the authority of ecclesiastical courts, not the Inquisition.
17 *Cedulario Indiano Recopilado por Diego de Encinas*; vol. 1, 47. "por la clemencia y gracia divina nuestros Reynos y señorios han sido alimpiados de todo error, y se ha evitado esta pestilencia y cantagion [sic], y se espera en su divina misericordia que se preservaran de aqui a delante, por evitar y remediar como no passe tan grande offensa de la Fe y religion Christiana a essas partes."
18 See especially Adrian Masters, "A Thousand Invisible Architects: Vassals, the Petition and Response System, and the Creation of Spanish Imperial Caste Legislation," *Hispanic American Historical Review* 98:3 (2018): 377–406; Víctor Tau Anzoátegui, *El poder de la costumbre: estudios sobre el derecho consuetudinario en América hispana hasta la emancipación* (Buenos Aires: Instituto de Investigaciones de Historia del Derecho, 2001); Brian Owensby, *Empire of Law and Indian Justice in Colonial Mexico* (Stanford, CA: Stanford University Press, 2008).
19 For various approaches to analyzing the construction of casta categories see María Elena Martínez, *Genealogical Fictions: Limpieza de Sangre, Religion, and Gender in Colonial Mexico* (Stanford University Press, 2008); Masters, "A Thousand Invisible Architects"; Joanne Rappaport, *The Disappearing Mestizo: Configuring Difference in the Colonial New Kingdom of Granada* (Durham, NC: Duke University Press, 2014); Robert Schwaller, *Géneros de Gente in Early Colonial Mexico: Defining Racial Difference* (Norman: University of Oklahoma Press, 2016); Ben Vinson III, *Before Mestizaje: The Frontiers of Race and Caste in Colonial Mexico* (Cambridge: Cambridge University Press, 2018). On casta paintings see Ilona Katzew, *Casta Painting: Images of Race in Eighteenth-Century Mexico* (New Haven, CT: Yale University Press, 2005).
20 Aurelia Martín Casares, *La esclavitud en la Granada del Siglo XVI: Género, raza y religión* (Universidad de Granada, 2000), 358–59.
21 Martín Casares, *La esclavitud en la Granada del Siglo XVI*, 111–14. Aurelia Martín Casares calculates that 70 percent of the enslaved Granadan moriscos who remained in the city and were not sold elsewhere were women. Of the 10,000 she further estimates that 53 percent or 4,500–5,000 were purchased by residents of the city of Granada while 47 percent were sold to other regions.
22 AGI, Indiferente 1968, L.20, 92v–93r.
23 AGI, Indiferente 2054, N.8; AGI Indiferente, 1968, L.19, 72r–75r.
24 AGI, Indiferente 1968, L.20, 101r.
25 AGI, Indiferente 1968, L.21, 89r.
26 AGI, Mexico 1090, L.8, 173r–174r and 175r–v.
27 AGI, Mexico 1090, L.8, 175r.
28 AGI, Indiferente 1956, L.2, 91r–v.
29 AGI, Patronato 257, N.1, G.6, R.2, 1r.

30 AGI, Patronato 257, N.1, G.6, R.2, 1r.
31 AGI, Indiferente 1087, L. 10, 176r.
32 AGI, Indiferente 1087, L.10, 202r.
33 AGI, Mexico 1091, L. 10, 81r.
34 AGI, Mexico 1091, L. 10, 81v.
35 AGI, Lima 566, L.6, 97r–97v.
36 AGI, Lima 566, L.6, 97v.
37 AGI, Lima 566, L.6, 97v.
38 For examples, see Cook, *Forbidden Passages*. On Moriscas in Spanish America also see Rukhsana Qamber, *Inquisition Proceedings Against Muslims in 16th Century Latin America* (Islamabad: Islamic Research Institute Press, 2007).
39 AGI, Indiferente 1961, L.2, 223r–v. On the uprising in the context of maroon communities in the Spanish Caribbean see Landers, "Cimarrón and Citizen," 117.
40 AGI, Indiferente 1961, L.2, 223v.
41 AGI, Indiferente 1961, L.2, 223v.
42 AGI, Santo Domingo 2280, L.1, 129r. "En lo q me suplicais q los negros gelofes no entren en la ysla por q como sea gente belicosa . . . q sy algund alçami[ent]o de negros se acometiese han de ser movedores dello los desta nacion."
43 Green, *The Rise of the Trans-Atlantic Slave Trade in Western Africa*, 91. However, not all individuals labeled "gelofe" in the documents necessarily practiced Islam, even though Spanish authorities often associated people from the Jolof Empire with Muslims.
44 By contrast, in the Portuguese territories no such religious limitations on emigration were enacted, allowing individuals sentenced by the Inquisition for practicing Judaism or Islam to be deported to Brazil. As a result, the Muslim population of Brazil gained significance by the nineteenth century, especially after the expansion and intensification of the transatlantic slave trade during the eighteenth century, culminating in the well-studied Malê uprising in Bahia in 1835. See João José Reis, *Slave Rebellion in Brazil: The Muslim Uprising of 1835 in Bahia* (Baltimore, MD: The Johns Hopkins University Press, 1993); Manuel Barcia, *West African Warfare in Bahia and Cuba: Soldier Slaves in the Atlantic World, 1807-1844* (New York: Oxford University Press, 2014); Diouf, *Servants of Allah*. Also see John Tofik Karam, "African Rebellion and Refuge on the Edge of Empire," in *Crescent Over Another Horizon: Islam in Latin America, the Caribbean, and Latino USA*, eds. María del Mar Logroño Narbona, Paulo G. Pinto, and John Tofik Karam (Austin: University of Texas Press, 2015). On enslaved Muslims in the early Spanish Caribbean galleys see David Wheat, "Mediterranean Slavery, New World Transformations: Galley Slaves in the Spanish Caribbean, 1578-1635," *Slavery and Abolition* 31, no. 3 (September 2010): 327–44.
45 See the cases of Diego Herrador and other suspected Moriscos in Cook, *Forbidden Passages*, chapter 3.
46 For more on Diego Romero see Karoline P. Cook, "'Moro de linage y nación': Religious Identity, Race, and Status in New Granada," in *Race and Blood in the Iberian World*, eds. Max Hering Torres, María Elena Martínez, and David Nirenberg (Berlin: LIT VERLAG, 2012), 81–97.
47 Cook, *Forbidden Passages*.
48 For a discussion of sources and numbers, see Cook, *Forbidden Passages*.
49 Harry Kelsey, *Sir Francis Drake: The Queen's Pirate* (Yale University Press, 1998). Using archival sources, Kelsey explores the myths surrounding the construction of Sir Francis Drake's image, including contrasting accounts of the freeing of enslaved Africans and galley slaves during the attack on Santo Domingo.

Chapter 6

1. The last sultan to maintain the semblance of sovereignty over Ottoman domains, Abdülhamit II ruled until his deposition in 1909. See Erik Jan Zürcher, *Turkey: A Modern History* (London: I. B. Tauris, 2004), 76–90.
2. Irving McKee, *"Ben-Hur" Wallace: The Life of General Lew Wallace* (Berkeley, CA: University of California Press, 1947), 200–09.
3. "The American Minister at Constantinople," *Boston Daily Advertiser* (Boston, MA), July 7, 1882.
4. "The Numerous Interviews between General Lew. Wallace and the Sultan of Turkey," *Cincinnati Commercial Tribune* (Cincinnati, OH), July 11, 1882.
5. "The Author of 'Ben Hur,'" *Boston Herald* (Boston, MA), July 31, 1892. Regarding the Abdühamit's aversion to self-portraits, see Mary Roberts, "Limits of Circumscription," in *Photography's Orientalism: New Essays on Colonial Representation*, ed. Ali Behdad and Luke Gartlan (Los Angeles, CA: Getty Research Institute, 2013), 53–54.
6. "General Wallace and the Turkish Girl," *Cleveland Herald* (Cleveland, OH), July 10, 1882.
7. Lew Wallace, *Lew Wallace: An Autobiography*, 2 vols. (New York: Harper Brothers, 1906).
8. "Defends the Sultan," *Chicago Inter Ocean* (Chicago, IL), February 22, 1895.
9. "Lew. Wallace as a Turkish General," *Cincinnati Commercial Tribune* (Cincinnati, OH), July 13, 1882.
10. See Henry M. Field, *The Story of the Atlantic Telegraph* (New York: Scribner's Sons, 1893), 306–46.
11. Ibid., and John Steele Gordon, *A Thread Across the Ocean: The Heroic Story of the Transatlantic Cable* (New York: Walker, 2002), 210–11.
12. Jean Baudrillard, *Simulacra and Simulation*, trans. Sheila F. Glaser (Ann Arbor, MI: University of Michigan Press, 1994), 6. For Baudrillard, simulation "masks and denatures a profound reality," and simulacrum "masks the *absence* of a profound reality; it has no relation to any reality whatsoever." Ibid.
13. Walter Benjamin, "The Work of Art in the Age of Mechanical Reproduction," in *Illuminations*, trans. Harry Zohn (New York: Random House, 1968).
14. Susan Elston Wallace, *The Storied Sea* (Cambridge, MA: James Osgood, 1883); *The Repose in Egypt: A Medley* (New York: John Alden, 1888); and *Along the Bosphorus: And Other Sketches* (New York: Rand McNally, 1898).
15. See Harriet Beecher Stowe, *Sunny Memories of Foreign Lands* (Boston, MA: Phillips Sampson, 1854), vol. 2: 340–44.
16. Wallace, *Along the Bosphorus*, 283.
17. See Baudrillard, *Simulacra and Simulation*, 2–5.
18. Lew Wallace, *Autobiography*, vol. 2: 941.
19. Ibid., 938–41; McKee, *"Ben-Hur" Wallace*, 189; and Max Kortepeter, "The Life and Times of General Lew Wallace, Minister Extraordinary to the Ottoman Court, 1881-1885," in *Cultural Horizons: A Festschrift in Honor of Talat S. Halman*, ed. Jayne Warner (Syracuse, NY: Syracuse University Press, 2001), 124. As a result of time spent in the Ottoman, Wallace eventually produced *The Prince of India; or, Why Constantinople Fell* (New York: Harper Brothers, 1893).
20. Public opinion proved enduringly hostile, even in Wallace's home state of Indiana. A January 1896 lampoon from the Indianapolis-based *American Nonconformist* ridicules

Wallace as "the 'hero' of Shiloh," who "has never been regarded as much of a soldier except at long range." "General Lew Wallace neglects to report progress as to that brigade he started to raise for immediate war on England," *American Nonconformist* (Indianapolis, IN), January 2, 1896.

21 Gail Stephens, *Shadow of Shiloh: Major General Lew Wallace in the Civil War* (Indianapolis, IN: Indiana Historical Society, 2013), 210–38.
22 Ibid., 468–84; and Kortepeter, "Life and Times," 119.
23 Ibid., 120–21.
24 Stephens, *Shadow of Shiloh*, 229–39.
25 Quoted in Lew Wallace, *Autobiography*, vol. 2: 940.
26 Ambrose Bierce, "The Devil's Dictionary," *The Wasp* (San Francisco, CA), August 26, 1881.
27 Jeffry Wert, *General James Longstreet: The Confederacy's Most Controversial Soldier* (New York: Simon and Schuster, 1993), 419–20.
28 Quoted in Wert, *James Longstreet*, 410.
29 Ibid., 413–16.
30 Kortepeter, "Life and Times," 124.
31 William Hesseltine and Hazel Wolf, *The Blue and the Gray on the Nile* (Chicago, IL: University of Chicago Press, 1961), 4.
32 Hesseltine and Wolf, *The Blue and the Gray on the Nile*.
33 John Dunn, *Khedive Ismail's Army* (New York: Routledge, 2005), 55–56.
34 Hesseltine and Wolf, *Blue and the Gray*, 78–79, 82–86, 247–60.
35 Elbert E. Farman, *Along the Nile with General Grant* (New York: Grafton, 1904), 26, 32, 300.
36 Lew Wallace, *Autobiography*, vol. 1: 311.
37 Outside of the Muslim world, one notable example of expatriation-via-appointment involves former Confederate colonel John Singleton Mosby, "the Gray Ghost," an ostracized pro-Grant reconciliationist, who served as American consul to Hong Kong from 1878 to 1885. See James Ramage, *Gray Ghost: The Life of Col. John Singleton Mosby* (Lexington, KY: University Press of Kentucky, 2010), 277, 289–99.
38 "The Sultan's Sympathy for the President," *Evening Star* (Washington, DC), September 8, 1881. On this occasion, Wallace vowed to make relations between the United States and the Ottoman, "if possible, more intimate." Ibid.
39 "General Lew Wallace Talks with the Sultan about American Systems," *Boston Herald* (Boston, MA), March 20, 1882.
40 "War Notes," *Boston Herald* (Boston, MA), September 5, 1882.
41 "General Wallace was entertained by the Sultan at his palace at Constantinople," *Denver Republican* (Denver, CO), October 25, 1882.
42 Ibid.
43 American reaction to the friendship was mixed. A July 1882 op-ed complains that "either Gen. Wallace or his dragoman attends the palace almost daily. . . . By what authority does Mr. Wallace so visit?" "What Has the United States to Do with it?" *Baltimore Sun* (Baltimore, MD), July 12, 1882. The *Galveston Weekly News* surmises that "the sultan has designs upon our government, and desires to secure the services of our navy to help him blow those European fleets out of the water." "The Sultan and General Wallace," *Galveston Weekly News* (Galveston, TX), July 13, 1882.
44 "Turkey and America," *New York Herald* (New York, NY), August 16, 1883.
45 Ibid.

46 R.A. Hammond, *A History of the Empire and People of Turkey and the War in the East* (Toronto, ON: A.H. Hovey, 1878), 455. For examples of sketches by Abdülaziz and his collaboration with court painter Stanislaw Chlebowski, see M. Pawlikowski, "Studio Talk," *International Studio* 48, no. 190 (1913), 162–63.

47 See Denise Gill, *Melancholic Modalities: Affect, Islam, and Turkish Classical Musicians* (Oxford, UK: Oxford University Press, 2017), 52.

48 One article insists that Wallace's "intimacy" with the sultan has "occasioned a good deal of jealousy in the diplomatic corps at Constantinople." "Persons and Things," *Wheeling Register* (Wheeling, WV), February 5, 1883. Advocating on behalf of détente, another advises that the Ottoman's "Grand Vizier" would "do well to patch up a peace with Minister Lew Wallace." It cautions that "the present Vizier may escape having his head cut off, but will probably meet his deserts if he doesn't [sic] let Wallace alone. Wallace will put him in a novel." "Will Put Him in a Novel," *Albuquerque Morning Journal* (Albuquerque, NM), March 26, 1884.

49 "General Wallace: The Present the Sultan Made Him," *Indianapolis Sentinel* (Indianapolis, IN), September 18, 1882.

50 Ibid.

51 For an example of Müller's work, see Lou Charnon-Deutsch, *Hold That Pose: Visual Culture in the Late Nineteenth-Century Spanish Periodical* (University Park, PA: Penn State University Press, 2008), 39. Müller's "Charlotte Corday in Prison" (1875) is anthologized in *Famous Paintings of the World*, a collection of photographic reproductions of the paintings exhibited at the 1893 Columbian Exposition in Chicago. Lew Wallace provides an introduction to the volume. See *Famous Paintings of the World: A Collection of Photographic Reproductions of Great Modern Masterpieces*, ed. John Ridpath, Horace Bradly, and Angel Del Nero (New York: Fine Art Publishing Company, 1894), 1–4, 74. May Alcott Nieriker, sister of Louisa May Alcott, is perhaps the most famous of Müller's American pupils. Nieriker heartily endorses Müller in her travel guide for aspiring female painters, *Studying Art Abroad, and How to Do It Cheaply* (Boston, MA: Roberts, 1879), 43, 47.

52 Paris-based Ottoman diplomat Halil Bey/Halil Şerif Pasha represents a possible candidate as the sultan's chief art procurer and cultural interpreter in France. Halil Bey staged a gallery exhibition of his private collection during the year of the exposition. See Thompson Cooper, *Men of the Time: A Dictionary of Contemporaries* (London: Routledge, 1872), 563. Halil, for a time, also owned Ingres' *Le Bain Turc* and gained notoriety for commissioning Courbet's *Le Sommeil* (1866) and *L'Origine du monde* (1866). See Francis Haskell, "A Turk and His Pictures in Nineteenth-Century Paris," *Oxford Art Journal* 5, no. 1 (1982), 40, 44; and Georges Riat, *Gustave Courbet* (New York: Parkstone International, 2012), 179.

53 The gift-exchange that occurred was by no means unilateral. Wallace presented the sultan with an autographed "copy of *Ben-Hur*, handsomely bound" and, in 1885, an English mastiff puppy. Wallace, *Autobiography*, vol. 2: 965, 980. In addition to "The Turkish Princess," Abdülhamit also presented Wallace a diamond-encrusted, gold cigarette case, which survives, and a precursor of the photographic collection later known as *The Yıldız Albums*. Ibid., 987, 978–79. See also Muhammad Isa Waley, "Images of the Ottoman Empire: The Photograph Albums Presented by Sultan Abdülhamid II," *British Library Journal* 17, no. 2 (1991), 111–27.

54 "The American Minister at Constantinople," *Boston Daily Advertiser* (Boston, MA), July 7, 1882.

55 Ibid.

56 "General Wallace and the Turkish Girl," *Cleveland Herald* (Cleveland, OH), July 10, 1882.
57 "Asiatic Civilization," *San Francisco Bulletin* (San Francisco, CA), July 25, 1882.
58 Ibid.
59 Linda Frost, *Never One Nation: Freaks, Savages, and Whiteness in U.S. Popular Culture, 1850-1877* (Minneapolis, MN: University of Minnesota Press, 2005), 57.
60 "An Unwelcome Visitor: How Mrs. Gen. Lew Wallace Received the Sultan's Gift of a Circassian Beauty," *Indianapolis Sentinel* (Indianapolis, IN), September 24, 1882.
61 Ibid.
62 Ibid.
63 Ibid.
64 Ibid. "An Unwelcome Present," *Omaha Daily Bee* (Omaha, NE), August 25, 1882.
65 Ibid.
66 Martin Buinicki and David Owens, "De-Anthologizing Ambrose Bierce: A New Look at 'What I Saw of Shiloh,'" *War, Literature & The Arts* 23, no. 1 (2011): 6.
67 Ibid., 3.
68 "That Present," *The Wasp* (San Francisco, CA), August 5, 1882. In a 2015 blog, Stephen Taylor traces another variation of the narrative, published in the September 1882 *Terre Haute Saturday Evening Mail*, back to *The Wasp* and Bierce. Taylor also recovers a version of "That Present," published in *The New Zealand Herald* in January 1883. Stephen Taylor, "Lew Wallace and the Circassian Girl Hoax," *Hoosier State Chronicles: Indiana's Digital Historic Newspaper Program*, last modified April 30, 2015, http://blog.newspapers.library.in.gov/lew-wallace-and-the-circassian-girl-hoax. Other permutations of the narrative appeared in newspapers throughout the United States. See, for example, "An Unwelcome Present," *Kalamazoo Gazette* (Kalamazoo, MI), August 25, 1882; "An Unwelcome Present," *Daily-Picayune* (New Orleans, LA), September 1, 1882; and "How Mrs. General Lew Wallace Received the Sultan's Gift," *Bennington Banner* (Bennington, VT), September 21, 1882.
69 "Lew. Wallace as a Turkish General," *Cincinnati Commercial Tribune* (Cincinnati, OH), July 13, 1882.
70 See, for example, Orville Stewart, "Summer Vibrations," *Duluth News Tribune* (Duluth, MN), July 12, 1902. In a visit to the Wallace home, Stewart alludes to the uproar of 1882 and toys with the possibility of the painting being readily mistaken as incarnate and real.
71 Benjamin cautions that the mass reproduction of an image forms an opening for the insertion of non-germane politicizations. See Benjamin, "Mechanical Reproduction," 224.
72 Ibid., 223-29.
73 Baudrillard, *Simulation and Simulacra*, 21-23.
74 Wallace, *Autobiography*, vol. 2: 977. Another example of Wallace's authentic personal investment is his attempt at a blank verse epic poem, *The Wooing of Malkatoon*, which romanticizes the founding figure of the Ottoman dynasty. Lew Wallace, *The Wooing of Malkatoon, Commodus* (New York: Harper Brothers, 1898).
75 "Lew Wallace Hissed," *Minneapolis Journal* (Minneapolis, MN), February 22, 1895.
76 "Defends the Sultan," *Chicago Inter Ocean* (Chicago, IL), February 22, 1895. Wallace elsewhere argued that "Abdul Hamid is no more to be blamed for the atrocities committed and the property destroyed by the Khourds than William McKinley would if the Apache Indians should go upon the war path and slay the white settlers." "Sultan is Honest," *Colorado Springs Gazette* (Colorado Springs, CO), April 23, 1900.

77 Edmund Taylor, *The Fall of the Dynasties: The Collapse of the Old Order, 1905-1922* (Garden City, NY: Doubleday, 1963), 99.
78 Lew Wallace, *Ben-Hur: A Tale of the Christ* (New York: Harper Brothers, 1880); *Ben Hur*, directed by Sidney Olcott. (Independent film, 1907); *Ben-Hur: A Tale of the Christ*, directed by Fred Niblo. (Metro-Goldwyn-Mayer, 1925); *Ben-Hur*, directed by William Wyler. (Metro-Goldwyn-Mayer, 1959); and *Ben-Hur*, directed by Timur Bekmambetov. (Metro-Goldwyn-Mayer and Paramount, 2016).

Chapter 7

1 Herman Melville, *Moby Dick* (London: Random House UK, 2008), 6.
2 Following the conventions of my sources, I use the term "Afghan" to refer to communities that we now typically identify as "Pashtun."
3 Revelation 16:12.
4 For a critical assessment of American narratives of the war, consider Robert D. Crews, *Afghan Modern: The History of a Global Nation* (Cambridge, MA: Belknap Press, 2015), 307.
5 Timothy Marr, *The Cultural Roots of American Islamicism* (Cambridge: Cambridge University Press, 2006), 17.
6 Raziuddin Aquil, *Sufism, Culture, and Politics: Afghans and Islam in Medieval North India* (Oxford: Oxford University Press, 2012), 29–31.
7 Abu al-Fadl, *The Akbarnama of Abu-l-Fazl. . .*, edited and translated by Henry Beveridge (Kolkata: Asiatic Society, 1897), 3.733.
8 Niʿmat Allah Harawi, *Tarikh-i-Khan Jahani va Makhzan-i Afghani. . .*, edited by S. M. Imam al-Dīn. Dacca: Asiatic Society of Pakistan, 1960. Reprinted as: *History of the Afghans: Translated from the Persian of Neamet Ullah*. Translated and introduced by Bernhard Dorn. Cambridge: Cambridge University Press, 2013.
9 Nile Green, "Tribe, Diaspora, and Sainthood in Afghan History," *The Journal of Asian Studies* 67 (2008): 171–211; Robert Nichols, *Settling the Frontier: Land, Law and Society in the Peshawar Valley, 1500-1900* (Karachi: Oxford University Press, 2001), 37–40.
10 I have elected to use the common English-language correspondents to the prophetic names included in Harawi's account. Rather than Ibrahim and Sulayman (for example), I have written Abraham and Solomon. Primarily, my intention is to render this chapter more accessible for those unfamiliar with the Arabic/Persian names included in Harawi's narrative, though I readily acknowledge that I risk some imprecision in this regard. "Abraham"—and all the resonances that this name suggests in English—is not quite identical to "Ibrahim" and the meanings that this Arabic name drags it in wake.
11 In many narratives of the Lost Tribes, the descendants of Judah are not considered to be among the "lost." Harawi, *Tarikh-i Khan Jahani va Makhzan-i Afghani*, 10–28.
12 Harawi, *Tarikh-i Khan Jahani va Makhzan-i Afghani*, 29–43; cf. Qurʾan 2:247–251.
13 Harawi, *Tarikh-i Khan Jahani va Makhzan-i Afghani*, 68–72.
14 Ibid., 73–78.
15 Ibid., 110.
16 Ibid., 111. I have consulted Dorn's translation: Harawi, *History of the Afghans*, 37–38.
17 Nichols, *Settling the Frontier*, 25–37.

18 Sana Haroon, *Frontier of Faith: Islam in the Indo-Afghan Borderland* (New York: Columbia University Press, 2007), 9–13 and 25–29.
19 Muhammad Hayat Khan, *Afghanistan and Its Inhabitants*, edited and translated by Henry Priestley (Lahore: Sang-e-Meel Publications, 1981), 50.
20 For consideration of the life of Loewenthal: Matthew Ebenezer, "American Presbyterians and Islam in India, 1855-1923: A Critical Evaluation of the Contributions of Isidor Loewenthal (1826-1864) & Elwood Morris Wherry (1843-1927)" (PhD diss., Westminster Theological Seminary, 1998).
21 Ebenezer, "American Presbyterians and Islam in India," 150–51.
22 "Sons of Israel in Afghanistan," *The Missionary Magazine* (March 1867): 86–88.
23 The report is unattributed, but given its details, it is likely an iteration of Loewenthal's own—and more skeptical—writing on the affair. Loewenthal had previously contributed articles to publication. Elsewhere, he suspected that the Afghan Lost Tribes narrative might be a recent invention. Isidor Loewenthal, "Is the Pushto a Semitic Language?" *Journal of Asiatic Society*, no. IV (Baptist Mission Press, 1860): 323–45.
24 "Sons of Israel in Afghanistan," 86–88.
25 Ibid.
26 Zvi Ben-Dor Benite, *The Ten Lost Tribes: A World History* (Oxford: Oxford University Press, 2009).
27 Benite, *The Ten Lost Tribes*, 24.
28 Richard W. Cogley, "'The Most Vile and Barbaraous Nation of all the World': Giles Fletcher the Elder's *The Tartars Or, Ten Tribes* (ca. 1610)," *Renaissance Quarterly* 58, no. 3 (2005): 785–92.
29 Emily Conroy-Krutz has recently discussed the Anglophilic commitment to Christian civilization that characterizes many American missionaries. Emily Conroy-Krutz, *Christian Imperialism: Converting the World in the Early American Republic* (Cornell: Cornell University Press, 2015), 9 and 13–16.
30 Both Benite and Tudor Parfitt offer an account of the wide range of Lost Tribes identifications made in the early modern period: Benite, *The Ten Lost Tribes*; Tudor Parfitt, *The Lost Tribes of Israel: The History of a Myth* (London: Weidenfeld and Nicolson, 2002).
31 Thomas Patrick Hughes, "Some Account of the Afghans and of the Peshawar Church Mission" (Lahore: Victoria Press, 1877). This article has been transcribed by Wayne Kempton in 2011 and is available online: http://anglicanhistory.org/india/tphughes/account_afghans1877.html
32 Sir William Jones, *The Works of Sir William Jones* (J. Stockdale and J. Walker, 1807), vol. 4, p. 70.
33 Alexander Burnes, *Travels Into Bokhara: Travels into Bokhara* (J. Murray, 1834); James Baillie Fraser, *Historical and Descriptive Account of Persia, from the Earliest Ages to the Present Time . . .*, Harper's Family Library, no. 70 (New York: Harper & brothers, 1834); Joseph Pierre Ferrier, *History of the Afghans* (John Murray, 1858); George Moore, *The Lost Tribes and the Saxons of the East and of the West. . .* (London, Longmans, Green, Longman, and Roberts, 1861); H. G. Raverty, "Some Remarks on the Origin of the Afghan People," *Journal of the Asiatic Society of Bengal* XXIII, no. 6 (Baptist Mission Press, 1855), 550–88; Joseph Wolff, *Researches and Missionary Labours Among the Jews, Mohammedans, and Other Sects* (Published by Mr. J. Nisbet, 1835), 249.

34 For colorful examples of this discourse, consider especially Burnes, *Travels into Bokhara*, 162–64; Rose, *The Afghans*, 19–78.
35 Wherry, "The First American Mission to Afghanistan," 135–36.
36 C. G. Pfander, D.D., *The Mizanu'l Haqq (Balance of Truth): Thoroughly Revised and Enlarged by W. St. Clair Tisdall, M.A.D.D.* (London: The Religious Tract Society, 1910). For more on the career of Pfander, consider: Avril Ann Powell, *Muslims and Missionaries in Pre-Mutiny India*, (London: Routledge, 2014), 132–57.
37 "Mahommedanism Viewed in Relation to Missionary Effort," *The Church Missionary Intelligencer* III, no. 4 99–107 and no. 6 139–144 (1852); "The Aboriginal Races of India," *The Church Missionary Intelligencer* III (1852): 107–14.
38 Ebenezer, *American Presbyterians and Islam in India 1855-1923*, 167–82.
39 Loewenthal, "Is the Pushto a Semitic Language?"
40 Isidor Loewenthal, "Missionary Labor for the Afghans," *The Missionary Magazine* (1862), 50; Ebenezer, *American Presbyterians and Islam in India 1855-1923*, 175.
41 Elizabeth Hughes Clark, "Thomas Patrick Hughes (1838-1911): Missionary to India's 'Northwest Frontier,'" *National Episcopal Historians and Archivists* 62, no. 1 (2004): 2–3.
42 "The Afghan females were taught to read and write, and many of the old manuscripts of Pushto Books have been written by Afghan women." Hughes, "Some Account of the Afghans."
43 The website *Project Canterbury* includes an extensive of Hughes's writings. Some important works for our consideration are the following: Thomas Patrick Hughes, "Twenty Years on the Afghan Frontier," *The Independent* 45 (1893): 455–56, 529–30, 637–38, 845–46, 1075–76;—, "Baptism of an Afghan Family," *The Church Missionary Intelligencer* VI (1881): 247.
44 Hughes, "Some Account of the Afghans."
45 Ibid.
46 Robert Clark, "Opening of the C.M.S. Memorial Mission Church at Peshawar," *The Church Missionary Intelligencer* IX, no. 97 (1884): 177–78.
47 As Hughes writes, "They are a fine manly race of sociable and lively habits, and as such are a striking contrast to the natives of India." Hughes, "Some Account of the Afghans"; Also consider: Burnes, *Travels Into Bokhara*, 162–64.
48 As an article by T. D. Forsyth in *Church Missionary Intelligencer* argued: "Let the wild Pathan tribes ... [through] their mountain-fastness [become] a barrier inaccessible to all enemies from without." "The Pathans," *Church Missionary Intelligencer* vol. 4 (1868): 152.
49 Hughes, "Some Account of the Afghans."
50 Ibid.
51 Thomas Patrick Hughes, *Ruhainah: A Story of Afghan Life* (New York: Cassell, 1886).
52 Elizabeth Hughes Clark, "Thomas Patrick Hughes (1838-1911)," 2–3. Hughes continued to publish, including the 1895 *Dictionary of Islam*—a popular work that was consulted extensively by, among others, James Joyce. J. S. Atherton, "Islam and the Koran in *Finnegans Wake*," *Comparative Literature*, vol. 6, no. 3 (Summer, 1954): 240.
53 Stapled to the first page of Stanford Library's copy of *Ruhainah* is a short news article dated to March 17, 1887, titled "Life in the Mohammedan World." The article describes a lecture by Hughes given in Bleecker Hall on the previous evening in which he mentions the Afghan Lost Tribes.
54 Harawi, *Tarikh-i Khan Jahani va Makhzan-i Afghani*, 14–15.

55 "Sons of Israel in Afghanistan," 86-88; Joseph Towers, *Illustrations of Prophecy. . .* (Printed by T. N. Longman, 1796), vol. 2, esp. pp. 589–603.
56 Examples include John Mason Good, Olinthus Gregory, and Newton Bosworth, *Pantologia. . .* (J. Walker, 1819); *The Bible Cyclopedia* (Parker, 1841). Also see G. H Rose, *The Afghans, the Ten Tribes, and the Kings of the East* (London: Hatchards, 1852); Ethan Smith, *A Dissertation on the Prophecies Relative to Antichrist and the Last Times. . .* (Charlestown, MA: Printed and sold by Samuel T. Armstrong, 1811).
57 Marr, *The Cultural Roots of American Islamicism*, 101.
58 Marr, *The Cultural Roots of American Islamicism*, 112.
59 Consider: Bob van der Linden, *Moral Languages from Colonial Punjab: The Singh Sabha, Arya Samaj and Ahmadiyahs* (New Delhi: Manohar, 2008).
60 Adil Hussain Khan, *From Sufism to Ahmadiyya: A Muslim Minority Movement in South Asia* (Bloomington: Indiana University Press, 2015), 4.
61 Hazrat Mirza Ghulam Ahmad, *Jesus in India: Jesus' Deliverance from the Cross & Journey to India* (Islam International, 2003), 12.
62 Ahmad, *Jesus in India*, 34.
63 Ibid., 13.
64 Cited in Ahmad, *Jesus in India*, 18.
65 Ahmad, *Jesus in India*, 18.
66 Ibid., 62.
67 Ibid., 115–19.
68 While our concern is with Mirza Ghulam's writings of the 1890s, the arguments of *Jesus in India* reverberated in American mosques in the twentieth century. As Richard Brent Turner and Sally Howell have documented, African American Muslims who identified as Ahmadi or as participants in the Nation of Islam presented Jesus as a fully human prophet who experienced a fully human death. Richard Brent Turner, *Islam in the African American Experience* (Bloomington, IN: Indiana University Press), esp. 113–14; Sally Howell, *Old Islam in Detroit: Rediscovering the Muslim American Past* (Oxford: Oxford University Press, 2014), 236–38.
69 A small sample of recent works that contain descriptions of Afghan society as "Biblical": Robert Kaplan, *Soldiers of God: With Islamic Warriors in Afghanistan and Pakistan* (New York: Vintage, 2008), 123; Christina Lamb, *Farewell Kabul: From Afghanistan to a More Dangerous World* (London: HarperCollins UK, 2015), 202; Jake Tapper, *The Outpost: An Untold Story of American Valor* (Boston: Little, Brown and Company, 2012), 158.
70 By way of example, consider the following: Rory McCarthy, "Pashtun Clue to Lost Tribes of Israel," *The Guardian*, January 16, 2010, sec. World news, http://www.theguardian.com/world/2010/jan/17/israel-lost-tribes-pashtun; Dean Nelson, "Taliban May Be Descended from Jews," *The Telegraph*, January 11, 2010, http://www.telegraph.co.uk/news/worldnews/asia/afghanistan/6967224/Taliban-may-be-descended-from-Jews.html.
71 Crews, *Afghan Modern*, 307.
72 Gilles Deleuze, "Nomad Thought," in *New Nietzsche: Contemporary Styles of Interpretation*, ed. David Allison (Cambridge: The MIT Press, 1985), 142–49.
73 Deleuze, "Nomad Thought."

Chapter 8

1. Karine Walther, *Sacred Interests: The United States and the Islamic World, 1821-1921* (Chapel Hill: University of North Carolina Press, 2015), 7.
2. On Islam and American eschatology, see Timothy Marr, *The Cultural Roots of American Islamicism* (Cambridge: Cambridge University Press, 2006), 82–133.
3. See Anupama Arora and Rajender Kaur, eds., *India in the American Imaginary, 1780s-1880s* (London: Palgrave Macmillan, 2017) and Nico Slate, *Lord Cornwallis Is Dead: The Struggle for Democracy in the United States and India* (Cambridge, MA: Harvard University Press, 2019).
4. On the ways in which both India and Hinduism as concepts coalesced in relation to Western (especially British) engagement, see Peter Gottschalk, *Religion, Science, and Empire: Classifying Hinduism and Islam in British India* (Oxford: Oxford University Press, 2013).
5. I refer to the conflict as the Sepoy Rebellion rather than the First War of Independence because the latter name was not applied until the early twentieth century, long after the focus of my study. I have avoided the term "Indian mutiny," common in British accounts of these events, because it presupposes the illegitimacy of the sepoys' actions and suggests a far narrower scope than historical sources support. On the rebellion's consequences for British colonialism broadly, see Jill C. Bender, *The 1857 Indian Uprising and the British Empire* (Cambridge: Cambridge University Press, 2016).
6. Christopher Hanlon rightly emphasizes the importance of US sectional strife to these phenomena (*America's England: Antebellum Literature and Atlantic Sectionalism* [New York: Oxford University Press, 2013]). On American identification with England, see Elisa Tamarkin, *Anglophilia: Deference, Devotion, and Antebellum America* (Chicago: University of Chicago Press, 2007).
7. On American imperialism in nineteenth-century popular culture, see Shelley Streeby, *American Sensations: Class, Empire, and the Production of Popular Culture* (Berkeley: University of California Press, 2002); on notions of expansion into Latin America, see Amy S. Greenbeg, *Manifest Manhood and the Antebellum American Empire* (Cambridge: Cambridge University Press, 2005).
8. On Islam and antebellum temperance reform, see Marr, *Cultural Roots*, 159–84.
9. See, for example, "A Suttee," *Albion* [New York], September 3, 1842, 424.
10. "The Mohammedans," *Forrester's Boys' and Girls' Magazine*, April 1, 1857, 110; Thomas Wentworth Higginson, "The Sympathy of Religions," *The Radical* [Boston], February 1871, 15.
11. "Liquor Legislation. Another Chapter on the Maine Law," *Democrat's Review*, June 1852, 532. Maine's strict law against the sale of alcoholic beverages had passed the previous year. This author refers to Muslims in general—not just those living in India.
12. "Opium-Eating," *New York Evangelist*, February 1, 1855, 18.
13. On Islam's perceived threat to democracy, see Marr, *Cultural Roots*, 20–81 and Malini Johar Schueller, *U.S. Orientalisms: Race, Nation, and Gender in Literature, 1790-1890* (Ann Arbor: University of Michigan Press, 1998), 45–74.
14. Marr, *Cultural Roots*, 217.
15. An article published in the *New Englander*, for example, calls polygamy "that climax of woman's wrongs" ("Liberty of Man, Woman, and Child in Unchristian Lands," *New Englander*, September 1882, 676).

16 "East Indian Poetry—Female Poets," *National Magazine* [New York], December 1855, 547, 549.
17 Reverend T. J. Scott, "Woman in India," *Heathen Woman's Friend*, July 1869, 9.
18 "Condition of Woman in Heathen Countries," *Ladies' Repository*, February 1856, 81.
19 "Suttee, or Widow Burning in India," *Ladies' Repository*, May 1869, 372.
20 "Miseries of Heathenism," *Religious Intelligencer*, October 27, 1827, 351.
21 On early US missionary efforts in India, see Emily Conroy-Krutz, *Christian Imperialism: Converting the World in the Early American Republic* (Ithaca: Cornell Univ. Press, 2015).
22 On nineteenth-century comparisons between Roman Catholicism and Hinduism, see Susan M. Griffin, *Anti-Catholicism and Nineteenth-Century Fiction* (Cambridge: Cambridge University Press, 2004), 137–38, 171.
23 "Address of the Editors," *Methodist Magazine*, January 1, 1823, 4; "Autobiography of Lutfullah, a Mohammedan Gentleman," *Russell's Magazine* [Charleston, SC], December 1858, 288.
24 Bayard Taylor, *A Visit to India, China, and Japan, in the Year 1853* (New York: Putnam, 1855), 109–10.
25 "Abdul Messee, the Convert," *Christian Watchman*, February 16, 1822, 1.
26 A Gentile Christian, "The Missionary Cause in India," *New England Galaxy*, March 18, 1825, 3.
27 "Northern India," *New York Evangelist*, August 8, 1835, 217.
28 "Progress of Christianity in India," *Missionary Herald*, February 1846, 66.
29 "Travels in South Eastern Asia . . .," *Biblical Repertory*, October 1839, 496.
30 "Bombay," *Missionary Herald*, October 1850, 350.
31 Some US commentators on India's Muslims framed them as a relatively privileged or elite group, while others insisted on their marginalization vis-à-vis the Hindu population. These disparities owe, no doubt, to variations in Muslims' status among the subcontinent's many regions, but may also relate to poorly evidenced perceptions.
32 Higginson, "The Sympathy of Religions," 16.
33 "The Present State of India," *Biblical Repertory and Princeton Review*, July 1858, 477.
34 "The People of India," *Ladies' Repository*, September 1871, 194.
35 "Bombay," *Missionary Herald*, October 1850, 349.
36 T. S. Burnell, "Letter from India," *Independent*, February 25, 1858, 8.
37 "The People of India," *Ladies' Repository*, September 1871, 190.
38 "The Present State of India," *Biblical Repertory*, July 1858, 453.
39 See Bender, *1857 Uprising*, 5–9.
40 "The Revolt of the Bengal Army," *Albion*, October 24, 1857, 505.
41 Nikhil Bilwakesh, "'Their faces were like so many of the same sort at home': American Responses to the Indian Rebellion of 1857," *American Periodicals* 21, no. 1 (2011): 1–23; see also Anirudra Thapa, "Cast in Print: The Indian Mutiny, Asiatic Racial Forms, and American Domesticity," in Arora and Kaur, eds., *India in the American Imaginary*, 175–97.
42 On pro- and antislavery responses to the Sepoy Rebellion, see Elizabeth Kelly Gray, "'Whisper to Him the Word "India"': Trans-Atlantic Critics and American Slavery, 1830-1860," *Journal of the Early Republic* 28, no. 3 (Fall 2008): 379–406.
43 Bilwakesh, "'Their Faces,'" 17–18.
44 "Sacrifice of British Ambassadors," *Littell's Living Age*, November 2, 1844, 4. This is one of many references to Russian aggression in Central and South Asia that appeared in US print sources at midcentury.

45. "The Present State of India," *Biblical Repertory*, July 1858, 457; "Scenes, Mutinies, and Executions in India," *Eclectic Magazine of Foreign Literature*, January 1858, 86.
46. "Present State of India," 482.
47. See Ilyse R. Morgenstein Fuerst, *Indian Muslim Minorities and the 1857 Rebellion: Religion, Rebels, and Jihad* (London: I. B. Tauris, 2017), 31–34.
48. On the "cartridge affair," see Bender, *1857 Uprising*, 5–6.
49. "Present State of India," 519–20.
50. "Present State of India," 529.
51. "Present State of India," 456.
52. "Present State of India," 455, 508.
53. On American notions of Islam and sexual license, see Marr, *American Islamicism*, 35–52; Schueller, *U.S. Orientalisms*, 118–19.
54. Jenny Sharpe, *Allegories of Empire: The Figure of Woman in the Colonial Text* (Minneapolis: University of Minnesota Press, 1993), 57–82. Although Sharpe claims that widely circulating narratives of sexual violence during the rebellion were "fictions," she is careful to acknowledge that some English women may have been raped during the conflict.
55. "The Present State of India," 499, 460–61.
56. The *Eclectic Magazine*, which ran from 1844 to 1898, reprinted articles from a range of British and continental sources and served as a key resource for Americans interested in world events.
57. "Scenes, Mutinies, and Executions in India," *Eclectic Magazine of Foreign Literature*, January 1858, 84.
58. "Scenes, Mutinies, and Executions in India," 84. This description resonates with the admiration that many Anglo-American authors expressed for Native Americans' apparent stoicism in the face of pain and death.
59. "Scenes, Mutinies, and Executions in India," 84.
60. "Scenes, Mutinies, and Executions in India," 84.
61. "The Indian Mutiny," *Ballou's Pictorial Drawing-Room Companion*, September 19, 1857, 189.
62. "Mutilations of Women and Children in India: Not One Instance to Be Found," *New York Observer*, June 10, 1858, 181; "India Massacres," *New York Observer*, September 17, 1857, 302. The paper notes that its position on these matters attracted a great deal of criticism.
63. "The Present State of India," *Biblical Repertory and Princeton Review*, July 1858, 452.
64. "The Present State of India," 453.
65. "Scenes, Mutinies, and Executions in India," 86.
66. Marr, *Cultural Roots*, 265.

Chapter 9

1. Karl Irving Faust, *Campaigning in the Philippines* (San Francisco: Hicks-Judd, 1899), 249; reported also in Charles B. Hagadorn, "Our Friend the Sultan of Jolo," *Century Illustrated Magazine* 110 (May 1900): 28.
2. Ríos to William R. Day, November 23, 1898, in US Congress, Senate, *Treaty of Peace Between the United States and Spain*, 55th Congress, 3rd Session, 1898, S. Doc. 62, Part 1, 221.

3   Foreman cited in *Treaty of Peace*, 444, 493, 456.
4   *Making Peace with Spain: The Diary of Whitelaw Reid: September-December 1898*, ed. H. Wayne Morgan (Austin: University of Texas Press, 1965), 265, 27–28, 158.
5   US Congress, Senate, *Treaty with the Sultan of Sulu* [hereafter *TWSS*], 65th Congress, 1st Session, 1900, S. Doc. 136, 55, 65.
6   Hagadorn, "Our Friend," 28.
7   *Report of Major-General E. S. Otis on Military Operations and Civil Affairs in the Philippine Islands* (Washington, DC: GPO, 1899).
8   *TWSS*, July 13, 1899, 2.
9   Otis to Bates, July 11, 1899, *TWSS*, 6, and Memorandum, 13.
10 Agreement, *TWSS*, 28–29.
11 Otis, July 3, 1899, *TWSS*, 4; Bates, August 12, 1899, 48.
12 Bates, July 30, 1899, *TWSS*, 42; Butu, July 19, 1900, 31.
13 August 16, 1899, *TWSS*, 107; Secretary Saleh, August 12, 1899, 52; Inchi Jameela, August 14, 1899, 53; Hadji Usman, July 31, 1899, 100.
14 Bates to Otis, August 9, 1899, *TWSS*, 70–71.
15 Bates, July 24, 1899, *TWSS*, 33.
16 Bates, August 12, 1899, *TWSS*, 47, 49.
17 Hadji Butu, August, 14, 1899, 57; Sultan, *TWSS*, 55.
18 Report of November 14, 1901 by Captain B. F. Hardaway, Bureau of Insular Affairs, War Department, *Fourth Annual Report of the Philippine Commission, 1903*, Part 1 (Washington, DC: GPO, 1904), 506–07.
19 Letter No. 59, Paduka Mahasari Maulana Sultan Hadji Muhammad Jamalul Kiram II to the Governor of Sulu, Major Wallace, in *Surat Sug, Letters of the Sultanate of Sulu*, Vol I. (Manila: National Historical Institute, 2005), 173.
20 John F. Bass, "Jolo & the Moros," *Harper's Weekly* 43 (November 18, 1899): 1159.
21 Richard Henry Little, "Sultan of Sulu and His People," *Chicago Daily Tribune*, October 22, 1899, 49; Frank G. Carpenter, "Butchered by the Moros," *The Atlanta Constitution*, June 10, 1900, A9. "Mexican Dollars and a Phonograph Conquered Sulu," *San Francisco Call*, January 24, 1900, 5; "Astonishing the Natives," *Albury Banner and Wodonga Express* [Australia], March 25, 1905, 8.
22 E. C. Rost, "The Sultan of Moro on the *Charleston*," *The Century Illustrated Monthly Magazine* 85 (November 1, 1912): 958.
23 "Sultan and the Phonograph," *The New York Times*, December 25, 1900, 1.
24 Oscar King Davis, "Sulu and the Sultan," *Ainslee's Magazine* 5 (May 1900): 335.
25 "How the Sulu Islands Became Our Property: Sultan Signed the Treaty When He Heard the Phonograph," *The Pittsburgh Press*, December 26, 1900, 8. Richard Henry Little reported differently that upon hearing the recording, some Moros jumped for side of ship, other drew their barongs, and another lay down and howled. He claims that it was his Javanese secretary, Sheh Saleh, who recorded a speech on the phonograph, not the Sultan. "Sultan of Sulu and His People: See Wonders of Science," *Chicago Daily Tribune*, October 22, 1899, 49.
26 Sultan, August 20, 1899, *TWSS*, 70–80; Theodore Williams Noyes, *Oriental America and its Problems* (Washington: Judd & Detweiler, 1903), 48.
27 Pigman, August 14, 1899, *TWSS*, 61.
28 E. C. Rost, "The Phonograph and How It Figured in the Treaty of Jolo," *Scientific American* 90:4(January 23, 1904), 66.
29 Pigman, August 14, 1899, *TWSS*, 61; August 15, 1899, 65.
30 Bates, August 15, 1899, *TWSS*, 65.

31 One reporter noted: "While the Sultan was signing his name an officer behind him muttered under his breath, 'Esau selling his birthright for a mess of pottage.'" R. H. Little, "Details of the Sulu Compact," *Chicago Daily Tribune*, September 6, 1899, 1.
32 See Michael Salman, *The Embarrassment of Slavery: Controversies over Bondage and Nationalism in the Philippines* (Berkeley: University of California Press, 2003).
33 For a discussion of this issue see Timothy Marr, "Diasporic Intelligence in the American Philippine Empire: The Transnational Career of Dr. Najeeb Mitry Saleeby," *Mashriq & Mahjar* 2:1 (January 2015): 86–87.
34 *TWSS*, 27.
35 *The Kansas Semi-Weekly Capital*, February 28, 1899, 4.
36 *The Mt. Sterling Advocate* [Mt. Sterling, Ky.], October 31, 1899.
37 "The Sultan of the Sulus: 'Twin Relics of Barbarism' to Be Put Under Our Flag," *The Washington Post*, August 23, 1899, 6.
38 "An Italian View of Europe," *North American Review* 173 (October 1901): 571.
39 "The Stupendous Procession," in *Mark Twain's Fables of Man*, ed. John S. Tuckey (Berkeley: University of California Press, 1972), 413.
40 J. T. McCutcheon, "Splendid Picture of Scenes in Sulu," *The State* (Columbia, SC), November 19, 1898, 3.
41 Victor Roman Mendoza, *Metroimperial Intimacies: Fantasy, Racial-Sexual Governance, and the Philippines in U.S. Imperialism, 1899-1913* (Durham: Duke University Press, 2015), 152.
42 Helen Herron Taft, *Recollections of Full Years* (New York: Dodd, Mead & Company, 1914), 169–70.
43 *TWSS*, 48. Quoted in McCutcheon, "Splendid Picture," 3.
44 *TWSS*, 59, 51.
45 Cesar Andres-Miguel Suva, "Nativizing the Imperial: The Local Order and Articulations of Colonial Rule in Sulu, Philippines 1881-1920" (Ph.D. diss., The Australian National University, 2016), 210, 215.
46 Samuel K. Tan, "Resolute But Unsung," *The Journal of History* [Philippines] 45: 1–4 (January to December 1999): 21.
47 For an account of the historical centrality of Sulu in the region, see James Francis Warren, *The Sulu Zone: 1768-1898* (Singapore: National University of Singapore Press, 1981 and 2007).
48 Sweet to Sultan, April 11, 1900, *Annual Reports of the War Department* [hereafter *ARWD*] Part IV (Washington: GPO, 1901), 411.
49 Sultan to MacArthur, November 14, 1900, *ARWD* IV, 374.
50 Sultan to Sweet, August 13, 1900, *ARWD* IV, 381–82.
51 Sultan to Governor-General Luke Wright, May 21, 1905, Letter No. 9 in *Surat Sug: Letters of the Sultanate of Sulu*, Vol 1. (Manila: National Historical Institute, 2005).
52 Sultan to Major General MacArthur, November 15, 1900, *ARWD*, IV, 365.
53 Appended to May 10, 1901 Report of O. J. Sweet, in *Annual Report of General Arthur MacArthur*, Vol 1 (Manila, 1901), 43–44.
54 Appendix 1: "General Davis's Report on Moro Affairs," October 24, 1901, *ARWD*, IX (Washington: GPO, 1902), 514, 517.
55 *Annual Report of Major General George W. Davis* (Manila 1903), 46.
56 "Report of General Wood as to Abrogation Bates Treaty," December 16, 1903, *ARWD*, V, 1903, 489.
57 "So-called" *ARWD*, V, 1903, 489; "The Government of the Moro Province," , 80; Woods to Taft, 5 September, 1903, Leonard Wood Papers, Library of Congress.

58 Woods to Taft, December 20, 1903, Leonard Wood Papers.
59 "Abrogation of the Bates Treaty," *The Independent* 56:28 (March 24, 1904): 636.
60 Translation of letter from Sultan to Governor-General Luke Wright, Hugh Lenox Scott Papers, Library of Congress.
61 Transcription of conversation between Wood the Sultan of Sulu, June 30, 1904, Leonard Wood Papers.
62 *Collier's Self-Indexing Annual, 1905* (New York: P. F. Collier & Son, 1905), 728.
63 Maud Huntley Jenks, *Death Stalks the Philippine Wilds* (Minneapolis, MN: Lund Press, 1951), 189; "The Philippine Native Soldiery," *Los Angeles Times*, July 9, 1904, A3.
64 "Former U.S. Solder is Sultan of Sulu's Right Hand Man," *New York Times*, October 2, 1910, SM9.
65 "The Sultan of Sulu's in Our Midst—Wearing Clothes," *Tacoma Times*, September 30, 1910, 11; "He's Jolly Little Sultan," *New York Tribune*, September 25, 1910, 1, 3.
66 "Will Hadji Kiram Come?" *Kansas City Times*, June 21, 1910, 4.
67 "Sultan of Sulu to Girdle Globe," *The Princeton Union* (Minnesota), July 2, 1910, 2. See Oliver Charbonneau, "Visiting the Metropole: Muslim Colonial Subjects in the United States, 1904-1927," *Diplomatic History* 42:2 (April 2018): 204-27.
68 "Sultan of Sulu Coming," *New York Tribune*, June 21, 1910, 3.
69 "New York's Marvels Awe Sultan of Sulu," *The New York Times*, September 25, 1910, 1.
70 "The Sultan of Sulu," *Outlook* 96:6 (October 8, 1910): 298.
71 "Royal Visitors Invited to Meet," *The Washington Herald*, September 28, 1910, 1.
72 "Our Only Sultan," *New York Times*, July 18, 1910, 6; "Escort for the Sultan Puzzles the Army," July 17, 1910, 7.
73 "Sulu Sultan Here; Taken for a Porter," *Chicago Inter-Ocean*, October 1, 1910, 3.
74 "Sultan Enjoyed Cocoanut Milk," *Hawaiian Gazette*, October 14, 1910, 5.
75 "Sultan Wants a Real House," *Hawaiian Gazette*, October 14, 1910, 4.
76 Journal, November 2, 1910, W. Cameron Forbes additional papers, Houghton Library, Harvard University.
77 "Memorandum Agreement of March 22, 1915, Between the Governor General of the Philippine Islands and the Sultan of Sulu," in *Report of the Philippine Commission to the Secretary of War*, 1915 (Washington: GPO, 1916), 297-98.
78 "That Man Vamenta's a Diplomat," *Graphic* [Philippines], August 18, 1928, 2, 40.
79 Carpenter to the Director of Non-Christian Tribes, May 2, 1920, in Moro Paper No. 63, H. Otley Beyer Collection, National Library of Australia; "Report of the Governor of Mindanao and Sulu," 1919, in *ARWD*, III (1920), 63.
80 See the fifteen pages of attestations in "Frank W. Carpenter," Report No. 873, House of Representatives, 75th Congress, 1st session (May 20, 1937) [Accompanying S. 1699].
81 This March 29 "Letter of the Sultan to All Mohammedans in the Sulu Archipelago" was translated and interpreted in 1935 in a sixteen-page analysis by Dr. Najeeb Saleeby, former member of the member of Executive Council of the Moro Province. Joseph Hayden Papers, Bentley Library, University of Michigan.
82 J. C. Early, Memorandum to Governor-General on "Agama Courts," December 18, 1930, Hayden Papers.
83 Francis L. Link, "The Sultan of Sulu," *Philippine Magazine* 26 (September 1929): 203-04.
84 "Sultan Kiram, in Rich and Colorful Garb, Sworn into Office Today at Senate Hall," August 4, 1932, [newspaper unidentified], Hayden Papers.

85 "Gifts for the Sultan's Wives," *Philippines Free Press* August 1, 1931, 6–7; "'Not Bright, But Very Avaricious'" *Philippines Free Press* July 15, 1931.
86 Tan, "Resolute But Unsung," 21.
87 "Sulu Sultan's Power is Cut," *Bulletin* (May 5, 1934).
88 "Sultan of Sulu, Moro Chief, Dies," *The New York Times*, June 9, 1936, 29.
89 Quezon, "Administration of Affairs in Mindanao," Memorandum to the Secretary of the Interior, September 20, 1937, in *Messages of the President to the President and Congress of the United States* (Manila, 1937).

Chapter 10

1 On the American move to consolidate control over the archipelago, see, for example, Brian Linn, *The Philippine War: 1899-1902* (Lawrence: University of Kansas Press, 2000).
2 Patricio N. Abinales and Donna J. Amoroso, *State and Society in the Philippines* (Lanham: Rowman & Littlefield Publishers, 2005), 109–16.
3 Linn, *The Philippine War*.
4 Karine V. Walther, *Sacred Interests: The United States and the Islamic World, 1821-1921* (Chapel Hill: University of North Carolina Press, 2015), 178.
5 George William Jornacion, "The Time of the Eagles: United States Army Officers and the Pacification of the Philippine Moros 1899-1913" (PhD diss., University of Maine, 1973), 47.
6 Walther, *Sacred Interests*, 157.
7 On Bates Treaty negotiations, see in this volume, Timothy Marr, "Subjugating the Sultan: Imperial Negotiations in the Muslim Philippines," in *American and Muslim Worlds, circa 1500-1900*, eds. Mitch Fraas and John Ghazvinian (New York: Bloomsbury Press, 2019); Bates treaty text quoted in Peter Gowing, *Mandate in Moroland: the American Government of Muslim Filipinos, 1899-1920* (Quezon City: University of the Philippines Press, 1977), 348.
8 While there were arguably no "major military engagements," there were skirmishes and military expeditions in this period, see Gowing, *Mandate in Moroland*, 77–94.
9 For the complex genealogy of the term "Moro," see Vivienne Angeles, "Moros in the Media and Beyond: Representations of Philippine Muslims," *Contemporary Islam* 4, no. 1 (April 2010): 29–30, 32.
10 Gowing, *Mandate in Moroland*, 161; Paul Kramer, *Blood of Government: Race, Empire, the United States and the Philippines* (Chapel Hill: University of North Carolina Press, 2006), 218.
11 Walther, *Sacred Interests*, 167.
12 Kramer, *The Blood of Government*, 19–21.
13 Walther, *Sacred Interests*, 6.
14 Mitch Fraas and John Ghazvinian, "Introduction," in *American and Muslim Worlds, circa 1500-1900*, eds. Mitch Fraas and John Ghazvinian (New York: Bloomsbury, 2019).
15 Ibid., xx–xx.
16 Ibid.
17 In this volume, Timothy Marr describes US engagement in Mindanao and Sulu as a new "transpacific frontier" pushing toward the "wildest west" of Southeast Asia, see Marr, "Subjugating the Sultan," xx.

18 One point of contention in the Bates Treaty was whether religious noninterference extended to Moro practices of slavery; many people considered the provision that people could purchase freedom a tacit recognition of slavery. See Marr, "Subjugating the Sultan"; see Michael Salman, *The Embarrassment of Slavery: Controversies over Bondage and Nationalism in the American Colonial Philippines* (Berkeley: University of California Press, 2003).
19 For example, Joel W. Martin, "Introduction," in *Native Americans, Christianity, and the Reshaping of the American Religious Landscape*, ed. Joel W. Martin (Chapel Hill: University of North Carolina Press, 2010).
20 On Wounded Knee and massacres in the Philippines, see Joshua Gedacht, "'Mohammedan Religion Made it Necessary to Fire': Massacres on the American Imperial Frontier from South Dakota to the Southern Philippines," in *Colonial Crucible: Empire in the Making of the Modern American State*, eds. Alfred W. McCoy and Francisco Scarano (Madison: University of Wisconsin Press, 2009), 398–401.
21 Ibid., 400; "Benjamin Harrison to the Secretary of War, 31 October 1890," quoted in Jeffrey Ostler, *The Plains Sioux and U.S. Colonialism from Lewis and Clark to Wounded Knee* (New York: Cambridge University Press, 2004), 292.
22 Brian Rouleau, "Maritime Destiny as Manifest Destiny: American Commercial Expansionism and the Idea of the Indian," *Journal of the Early Republic* 30 (Fall 2010): 377–411.
23 Peter G. Gowing, "Moros and *Indians*: Commonalities of Purpose, Policy, and Practice in American Government of Two Hostile Subjects," *Philippine Quarterly of Culture and Society* 8, no. 2/3 (June/September 1980), 125–49; Walther, *Sacred Interests*, 11.
24 Gowing, *Mandate in Moroland*, 31–34.
25 Ibid., 41.
26 George W. Davis, "Appendix 9: Notes on the Government of the Country Inhabited by Non-Christians in Mindanao and the Neighboring Islands," U.S. War Department, *Annual Reports of the War Department, 1902*, Vol. IX (Washington: Government Printing Office, 1902), 564.
27 Ibid., 561–562.
28 Ibid., 565.
29 Quoted in Donna Amaroso, "Inheriting the 'Moro Problem': Muslim Authority and Colonial Rule in British Malaya and the Philippines," in *The American Colonial State in the Philippines: Global Perspectives*, eds. Julian Go and Anne L. Foster (Durham: Duke University Press, 2003), 125.
30 Quoted in Walther, *Sacred Interests*, 181.
31 Ibid.
32 Gowing, *Mandate in Moroland*, 100–05, 111–12.
33 Jack McCallum, *Leonard Wood: Rough Rider, Surgeon, and Architect of American Imperialism* (New York: New York University Press, 2006), 160–62, 206–10.
34 Leonard Wood to President Theodore Roosevelt, September 20, 1903, Leonard Wood Papers (hereafter LWP), Library of Congress Manuscript Division, Washington, DC (hereafter LCMD), 8–9; Patricio N. Abinales, "Progressive-Machine Conflict in Early Twentieth Century U.S. Politics and Colonial-State Building in the Philippines," in *The American Colonial State in the Philippines: Global Perspectives*, eds. Julian Go and Anne L. Foster (Durham: Duke University Press, 2003), 163–67; Jack C. Lane, *Armed Progressive: General Leonard Wood* (San Rafael: Presidio Press, 1978).
35 Marr, "Subjugating the Sultan."

36 Wood to Roosevelt, September 20, 1903, 8–9; Leonard Wood to William Howard Taft, December 16, 1903, Box 33, LWP, LCMD; on *juramentado*, see Franklin Ewing, "Juramentado: Institutionalized Suicide among the Moros of the Philippines," *Anthropological Quarterly* 28:4 (October 1955), 148–55.
37 Wood to Taft, December 16, 1903.
38 On Lake Lanao, see Gowing, *Mandate in Moroland*, 88–94; Leonard Wood to Colonel Arthur H. Lee, January 4, 1903, Box 33, LWP, LCMD.
39 Gedacht, "'Mohammedan Religion Made it Necessary to Fire," 403–06.
40 Hugh L. Scott, "Annual Report of the District of Sulu from July 1st, 1905 to June 30, 1906," June 30, 1906, Tasker Bliss Papers, LCMD.
41 Hugh L. Scott to George T. Langhorne, December 5, 1905, Box 37, LWP, LCMD.
42 James R. Reeves, District Secretary and Acting Governor, to The Moro Province Secretary, March 31, 1906, Box 37, Folder 1, LWP, LCMD.
43 Ibid.
44 Ibid.
45 Jornacion, "Time of the Eagles," 173.
46 Omar Bundy to J. W. Duncan, March 12, 1906, Record Group 94, Records of the Adjutant General's Office, NARA.
47 Quoted in Michael C. Hawkins, "Managing a Massacre: Savagery, Civility, and Gender in Moro Province in the Wake of Bud Dajo," in *Philippine Studies* 59, no. 1 (2011): 86.
48 "A Plain Duty Regretfully Performed," *Mindanao Herald*, March 24, 1904, 4.
49 Leonard Wood to Theodore Roosevelt, "Message from the President of the United States Transmitting an Account of the Engagement on Bud Dajo between United States Forces and a Band of Moros," March 15, 1906;' U.S. House of Representatives, RG 350, File 4865, NARA.
50 McCallum, *Leonard Wood*, 160.
51 Record Group 350, File 4865, NARA; John J. Pershing Papers, LC.
52 Joseph G. Galway, "J.P. Finley: The First Severe Storms Forecaster," *Bulletin of the American Meteorological Society* 66, 11 (November 1985): 1389–395.
53 Midori Kawashima, "The 'White Man's Burden' and the Islamic Movement in the Philippines: The Petition of the Zamboanga Muslim Leaders to the Ottoman Empire in 1912," Institute of Asian Cultures, Sophia University, Monograph Series 17 (Tokyo: Institute of Asian Cultures, Sophia University), 6.
54 William Churchill and John P. Finley, *The Subanu: Studies of a Sub-Visayan Mountain Folk of Mindanao* (Washington: Carnegie Institute of Washington, 1913).
55 Finley, *The Subanu*, 33.
56 John P. Finley, "Remarks upon the Tribal Ward System of Government for Moros and other non-Christians," File: Mindanao and Sulu, P.O.—"reports, etc., 1908-1912," volume 7, Dean Worcester Philippine History Collection, University of Michigan Special Collections.
57 Finley, "Remarks upon the Tribal Ward System of Government."
58 Michael Hawkins, *Making Moros: Imperial Historicism and American Military Rule in the Philippines' Muslim South* (DeKalb: Northern Illinois University, 2013), 86–91.
59 Finley, *The Subanu*, 13.
60 John P. Finley, "A Review of the Moro Petition, Its Origin, Scope and Purpose, and How Its Object May Be Realized in Aid of the American System of Control," John P. Finley Papers, Military Historical Institute, Carlisle, PA (hereafter Finley Papers).
61 See Joshua Gedacht, "Holy War, Progress, and 'Modern Mohammedans' in Colonial Southeast Asia," in *The Muslim World* 105, no. 4 (October 2015): 446–71.

62 John Park Finley, "The Mohammedan Problem in the Philippines," *The Journal of Race Development* 5, no. 4 (April 1915): 360.
63 Finley, "A Review of the Moro Petition."
64 Appendix VI, "The Moros of the Philippines," *Annual Report of the War Department for the Fiscal Year ended June 30, 1903* (Washington: Government Printing Office, 1903), III: 365.
65 Finley, "The Mohammedan Problem," 354.
66 Finley, "A Review of the Moro Petition," Finley Papers.
67 Finley, "The Mohammedan Problem," 354.
68 Finley, "The Mohammedan Problem," 355.
69 P. D. Rogers, "Major Finley and the Sheik Ul Islam: A Hitherto Unpublished Chapter of History," *Philippine Magazine* 36, no. 1 (January 1939): 20.
70 Finley, "A Review of the Moro Petition."
71 On these petitions, see Kawashima, "The 'White Man's Burden.'"
72 Finley, "A Review of the Moro Petition."
73 Kawashima, "The White Man's Burden," 1.
74 William G. Clarence-Smith, "Middle Eastern States and the Philippines under Early American Rule, 1898-1919," in *From Anatolia to Aceh: Ottomans, Turks, and Southeast Asia*, eds. Andrew Peacock and Annabel Teh Gallop, Proceedings of the British Academy 200 (Oxford: Oxford University Press, 2015): 202-03.
75 Finley, "A Review of the Moro Petition," Finley Papers; Clarence-Smith, "Middle Eastern States and the Philippines under Early American Rule," 203.
76 For Shaykh Wajih al-Kilani's Nablus background, see William Clarence-Smith, "Wajih al-Kilani, Shaykh al-Islam of the Philippines and Notable of Nazareth, 1913-1916," *Nazareth History & Cultural Heritage: Proceedings of the 2nd International Conference, Nazareth, July 2-5, 2012*, eds. Mahmoud Yazbak et al. (Nazareth: Municipality of Nazareth Academic Publications, 2013), 173-74.
77 Clarence-Smith, "Wajih al-Kilani, Shaykh al-Islam of the Philippines," 176.
78 Walther, *Sacred Interests*, 176-77.
79 Finley, "The Mohammedan Problem," 357.
80 Walther, *Sacred Interests*, 200-02.
81 On US-Ottoman "trans-imperial synchronicity," see Joshua Gedacht, "The 'Shaykh al-Islam of the Philippines' and Coercive Cosmopolitanism in an Age of Global Empire," in *Challenging Cosmopolitanism: Coercion, Mobility, and Displacement in Islamic Asia*, eds. R. Michael Feener and Joshua Gedacht (Edinburgh: Edinburgh University Press, 2018), 183-89.
82 Walther, *Sacred Interests*, 199.
83 Finley did express frustration with Shaykh Wajih over at least one issue, slavery, which was still legal in the Ottoman Empire. See William Clarence-Smith, "A Palestinian Muslim's Mission to America: Sayyid Wajih al-Kilani of Nazareth, 1915-1916," in *American and Muslim Worlds, circa 1500-1900*, eds. Mitch Fraas and John Ghazvinian (New York: Bloomsbury Press, 2019).
84 Jakob Skovgaard-Peterson, "Levantine State Muftis: An Ottoman Legacy?", in *Late Ottoman Society: The Intellectual Legacy*, ed. Elisabeth Özdalaga (New York: RoutledgeCurzon, 2005), 279.
85 See Selim Derengil, "'They Live in a State of Nomadism and Savagery': The Late Ottoman Empire and the Post-Colonial Debate," *Comparative Studies in Society and History* 45, no. 2 (April 2003): 311-42.

86 Feroz Ahmad, *The Young Turks: The Committee of Union and Progress in Turkish Politics, 1908–1914* (New York: Oxford University Press, 1969), 15–18; F. J. Childress, "Creating the 'New Woman' in Early Republican Turkey: The Contributions of the American Collegiate Institute and the American College for Girls," *Middle Eastern Studies* 44, no. 4 (July 2008): 562.

87 The interview with Finley in *Tanin* does not identify Edip, but a translated message from the Shaykh al-Islam ministry mentions the interviewer as "Hallideh Hanoum in the Tanin." Edip also regularly wrote in *Tanin*. See "Message to the Philippine Moslems, Bab-i-Fetva, Department of the Sheikh-Ul-Islmato, Bureau of Correspondence Constantinople," June 1, 1913, C-65.9-050-80, Charles Cameron Papers, Xavier University, Cagayan de Oro, Philippines; on Edip's *Tanin* contributions, see Nader Sohrabi, *Revolution and Constitutionalism in the Ottoman Empire and Iran* (Cambridge: Cambridge University Press, 2011), 141n.

88 All translations from this article are thanks to Ethan Menchinger, "An Appeal to the Seat of the Caliphate concerning Muslim Filipinos," *Tanin*, April 9, 1913.

89 Keith David Watenpaugh, "Introduction," in *Goodbye Antoura: A Memoir of the Armenian Genocide*, ed. Aram Goudsouzian (Stanford: Stanford University Press, 2015), xii–xiii.

90 Clarence-Smith, "Wajih al-Kilani, Shaykh al-Islam," 174.

91 See P. D. Rogers, "Major Finley and the Sheikh Ul Islam: A Hitherto Unpublished Chapter of History," in *Philippine Magazine* 36, no. 1 (January 1939): 19, 28–29.

92 Rogers, "Major Finley and the Sheikh Ul Islam," 28.

93 Ibid., 29.

94 Clarence-Smith, "Middle Eastern States and the Philippines under Early American Rule," 201–04.

95 Carl M. Moore to F.W. Carpenter, June 1, 1918, Zamboanga (Philippines), folder: "Moros: 1918–1920," box 253, Manuel L. Quezon Papers (hereafter MLQ Papers), Philippine National Library, Manila. Philippines.

96 See in this volume, William G. Clarence-Smith, "A Palestinian Muslim's Mission to America," in *American and Muslim Worlds, circa 1500-1900*, eds. Mitch Fraas and John Ghazvinian (New York: Bloomsbury Press, 2019), xx.

97 Teopista Guingona to Manuel Luis Quezon, Jr., January 1, 1924, Box 253 Manobos-Moros, Manuel Luis Quezon Papers, Manila, The Philippines.

98 A Taluksangay mosque chandelier is emblazoned with the words this "is the gift of M. Fethullah Gülen," author visit to Taluksangay, Philippines, October 2010; although controversial for various practices and beliefs, recent scholarship suggests the Gülen movement is rooted in Turkish traditions of Sufi Islam and religious renewal, see Carter Vaughan Findley, "Hizmet among the Most Influential Religious Renewals of Late Ottoman and Modern Turkish History," in *Hizmet Means Service: Perspectives on an Alternative Path within Islam*, ed. Martin E. Marty (Berkeley: University of California Press, 2015), 5–17.

Chapter 11

1 Anon. "Tarikh hayat al-maghfur lahu al-hasib al-nasir sahib al-samahah al-shaykh Muhammad Wajih Zayd al-Kilani" (The History of the Life of the Late and most Noble and Exalted Shaykh Muhammad Wajih Zayd al-Kilani) (undated and

unpublished manuscript, kindly provided to me by Amir Zuʻbi); Ihsan al-Nimr, *Tarikh Jabal Nablus wa al-Balqaʼ* (History of the Jabal Nablus and al-Balqaʼ) (Damascus: Matbaʻat Zaydun, 1938); Asʻad Mansur, *Tarikh al-Nasira, min aqdam ayyamiha ila ayyamina al-hadira* (History of Nazareth, from Ancient Times until the Present) (Cairo: Matbaʻat al-Hilal, 1924); Najib Nassar, *Riwayat Muflih al-Ghassani* (The Tale of Muflih al-Ghassani) (Nazareth: Dar al-Sawt, 1981); Raja Shehadeh, *A Rift in Time: Travels of My Ottoman Uncle* (London: Profile Books, 2010); William G. Clarence-Smith, "Wajih al-Kilani, *shaykh al Islam* of the Philippines and Notable of Nazareth, 1913-1916," in *Nazareth History and Cultural Heritage*, eds. Mahmoud Yazbak and Sharif Sharif (Nazareth: Nazareth Municipality, 2013), 171–92. My thanks are due to Jake Norris and Umar Ryad for translations from Arabic. Wajih's surname was sometimes spelled Jilani or Gilani, and his forename Vejih or Vejihi.

2   Wayne W. Thompson, "Governors of the Moro Province: Wood, Bliss and Pershing in the Southern Philippines, 1903-1913" (PhD diss., University of California at Los Angeles, 1975); Peter G. Gowing, *Mandate in Moroland: The American Government of Muslim Filipinos, 1899-1920* (Quezon City: New Day Publishers, 1983); Midori Kawashima, *The 'White Man's Burden' and the Islamic Movement in the Philippines: The Petition of Zamboanga Muslim Leaders to the Ottoman Empire in 1912* (Tokyo: Institute of Asian Cultures, 2014); Joshua Gedacht, "Holy War, Progress and the 'Modern Mohammedans' in Colonial Southeast Asia," *The Muslim World* 4 (2015): 446–71; William G. Clarence-Smith, "Middle Eastern States and the Philippines under Early American Rule, 1898-1919," in *From Anatolia to Aceh: Ottomans, Turks and Southeast Asia*, ed. A. C. S. Peacock and Annabel Teh Gallop (Oxford: Oxford University Press, 2015), 199–219. See also chapters by Timothy Marr and Joshua Gedacht in this volume.

3   Mohammad Redzuan Othman, "Sayid Muhammad Wajih al-Jilani" (undated and unpublished note, in romanized Malay, kindly sent to me by the author).

4   Anon. "Tarikh"; al-Nimr, *Tarikh*.

5   Kawashima, *The "White Man's Burden"*; chapter by Joshua Gedacht in this volume. A photograph of the petition is held by the Library of Congress, Manuscripts Division (henceforth LC-MD), Francis B. Harrison Papers, Box 38, Finley-1.

6   National Archives and Records Administration (henceforth NARA), I, RG 94, ACP file 1881, 813–924, Box 709, "Special Facts concerning Major John P. Finley."

7   P. D. Rogers, "Major Finley and the Shaik ul Islam: A hitherto Unpublished Chapter of History," *Philippine Magazine* 36, no. 1 (1939): 19, 28–29.

8   Othman, "Sayid Muhammad Wajih al-Jilani," citing the Maly-language journal *Neracha*.

9   NARA-II, RG 350, 1914–1945, Box 1025, 25029, 12, S. M. Wajih to secretary of war, September 23, 1914.

10 Clarence-Smith, "Wajih al-Kilani," 177–1778.

11 University of Illinois Archives, RG 41/93/2, ATO Founders, Box 1, Biographical sketches, Otis T. Glazebrook.

12 NARA-II, RG84, Jerusalem Consulate, Vol. 72, 830, O. T. Glazebrook to H. Morgenthau, June 4, 1915, and O. T. Glazebrook to Djemal Pasha, June 7, 1915.

13 NARA-II, RG 350, 1914–1945, Box 1025, 25029, 19, acting secretary of war to secretary of state, September 20, 1915.

14 Clarence-Smith, "Middle Eastern states," 208–12.

15 Nassar, *Riwayat*, 80–81.

16 Shehadeh, *A Rift in Time*, 100–01; Anon., 'Tarikh', seemingly citing al-Nimr, *Tarikh*.

17 Patricia Goldstone, *Aaronsohn's Maps: The Untold Story of the Man who Might Have Created Peace in the Middle East* (Orlando, FL: Harcourt Inc. 2007), 102, 106, 109–11.
18 Philip H. Stoddard, "The Ottoman Government and the Arabs, 1911 to 1918: A Preliminary Study of the Teshkilat-i Mahsusa" (PhD diss., Princeton University, 1963).
19 Başbakanlık Osmanlı Arşivi, Istanbul (henceforth BOA) DH, ŞFR, 52/82, General Directorate of Police to General Staff 4th Army, Telegram, June (?) 1915. My thanks are due to Ismail Haki Kadi, Hasan Kayali, M. Talha Çiçek, and Benjamin Fortna for translations from Ottoman Turkish.
20 BOA, DH, EUM, KLU, 9/12, Cemal Pasha to Ministry of the Interior, June 17, 1915.
21 NARA-II, RG350, 1914–1945, Box 1025, 25,029, 16, Henry Morgenthau to secretary of state, June 21, 1915.
22 Thompson, "Governors of the Moro Province," 242.
23 *The New York Times*, August 13, 1915; *New York Tribune*, August 13, 1915.
24 NARA-II, RG350, 1914–1945, Box 1025, 25,029, 22, John P. Finley to H. L. Scott, October 2, 1915, and 26, Wajih to Chief of the Bureau of Insular Affairs, November 30, 1915.
25 LC-MD, Morgenthau Papers, Reel 5, Diary, January 15, 1916.
26 BOA, DH. KMS.42/13, personal secretary of Ahmet Cemal Pasha to minister of the interior, November 20, 1916.
27 *The World*, August 13, 1913.
28 *New York Tribune*, August 13, 1915; *Chicago Daily Tribune*, September 5, 1915.
29 *The New York Times*, October 22, 1915.
30 Karine V. Walther, *Sacred Interests: The United States and the Islamic World, 1821-1921* (Chapel Hill: University of North Carolina Press, 2015), 282–84; Laurence Evans, *United States Policy and the Partition of Turkey, 1914-1924* (Baltimore: The Johns Hopkins University Press, 1965), 28.
31 Walther, *Sacred Interests*, ch. 8.
32 *New York Tribune*, May 7, 1916.
33 *Times-Dispatch*, Richmond, VA, May 6, 1916; *New York Herald*, May 6, 1916.
34 BOA, DH. EUM.4.Şb, 8/20, General Director of Administrative Affairs, Foreign Ministry, to Minister of the Interior, November 18, 1916.
35 Military Intelligence files are held in NARA-II, RG 165.
36 *New York Herald*, May 6, 1916.
37 Patrick D. Bowen, "Satti Majid: A Sudanese Founder of American Islam," *Journal of African Religions* 1, no. 2 (2013): 194–209, at 196.
38 *New York Tribune*, August 11, 1912.
39 Some newspaper clippings are scattered through files in NARA-II, RG350, 1914–1945. I thank Patrick D. Bowen for other clippings, and for much assistance on this research.
40 *Courier Journal*, Louisville, September 5, 1913, citing the *New York Sun*.
41 *The Washington Post*, August 17, 1915, copied in many regional newspapers.
42 *The New York Times*, August 13, 1915.
43 *Le Grand Reporter*, Iowa, November 12, 1915.
44 "List or Manifest of Alien Passengers for the United States, SS Manuel Calvo, sailing from Barcelona 25 July 1915," kindly supplied by Patrick D. Bowen.
45 Anon., "Tarikh."
46 LC-MD, Hugh L. Scott Papers, Box 20, John P. Finley to H. L. Scott, October 16, 1915. No clipping remains with the letter.
47 *Courier Journal*, Louisville, September 5, 1913, citing the *New York Sun*.
48 NARA-II, RG350, 1914–1945, Box 1025, 25,029, 23, Wajih, Sheik-ul-Islam for the Philippine Islands to secretary of war, October 23, 1915.

49 *New York Tribune*, May 7, 1916.
50 *New York Tribune*, August 13, 1915.
51 Anon., "Tarikh." I have not seen this text.
52 Charles Kurzman, ed., *Modernist Islam, 1840-1940: A Sourcebook* (Oxford: Oxford University Press, 2002), chapters 3 and 6.
53 Umar Ryad, personal communications, April 7–8, 2013. For Islam in Singapore at the time, see William R. Roff, *The Origins of Malay Nationalism* (New Haven: Yale University Press, 1967), 64.
54 Thomas Eich, *Abu l-Huda as-Sayyadi: eine Studie zur Instrumentalisierung sufischer Netzwerke und genealogischer Kontroversen im spätosmanischen Reich* (Berlin: Klaus Schwartz, 2003), 199, n. 49 (the wrong Wajih al-Kilani is identified here); Thomas Eich, personal communication, January 1, 2011, citing Muhammad Rashid Rida, *Tarikh al-ustadh al-imam al-shaykh Muhammad 'Abduh* [Story of the Teacher, Leader, and Shaykh, Muhammad 'Abduh] (Cairo: al-Manar, 1908–1931), I, 600; Umar Ryad, personal communications, April 7–8, 2013.
55 *al-Manâr*, Cairo 19, no. 2 (July 1916): 124.
56 William G. Clarence-Smith, *Islam and the Abolition of Slavery* (London: Hurst, 2006), 104–10.
57 NARA-I, RG 94, ACP file 1881, 813–924, Box 709, Enclosures 4 and 5 to dispatch no. 451, March 27, 1913, and "Draft encyclical," undated.
58 Patrick D. Bowen, "The African-American Islamic Renaissance and the Rise of the Nation of Islam" (PhD diss., University of Denver, 2013).
59 *al-Huda al-Arabiyya*, cited in *al-Manar*, Cairo 19, no. 5 (October 1916): 317 ff.
60 NARA-II, RG350, 1914–1945, Box 1025, 25,029, 22, J. P. Finley to Major-General Hugh L. Scott, October 2, 1915; LC-MD, Hugh L. Scott Papers, Box 20, Wajih to H. L. Scott, October 11, 1915; *New York Herald*, May 6, 1916.
61 Patrick D. Bowen, *A History of Conversion to Islam in the United States, Volume 1: White American Muslims before 1975* (Leiden: Brill, 2015), 170–72, 177.
62 For Ahmadi Islam at this time, see H. A. Walter, *The Ahmadiya Movement* (Calcutta: Association Press, 1918).
63 Bowen, "The African-American Islamic Renaissance," 255, 307–08; Bowen, *A History of Conversion to Islam*, 184; *The Moslem Sunrise* 1, no. 6 (1922): 147.
64 Edward E. Curtis, IV, *Muslims in America: A Short History* (Oxford: Oxford University Press, 2009), 29–30.
65 Anon., "Tarikh."
66 *The Moslem Sunrise* 1, no. 6 (1922): 147.
67 *The Moslem Sunrise* 1, no. 1 (1921): 13; *The Moslem Sunrise* 1, no. 6 (1922): 147.
68 Gregory Orfalea, *The Arab Americans: A History* (Northampton, MA: Olive Branch Press, 2006); Kathleen Benson and Philip M. Kayal, eds., *A Community of Many Worlds: Arab Americans in New York City* (New York: Museum of the City of New York, 2002); Abdo A. Elkholy, *The Arab Moslems in the United States: Religion and Assimilation* (New Haven, CT: College and University Press, 1966).
69 Patrick D. Bowen, email February 13, 2017.
70 "Muslim Voices of Philadelphia," http://scribe.org/muslim-voices-philadelphia (consulted April 16, 2018).
71 Thompson, "Governors of the Moro Province," 242.
72 Najeeb M. Saleeby, *Studies in Moro History, Law and Religion* (Manila: The Filipiniana Book Guild, 1976), introduction by Cesar A. Majul.
73 NARA-II, RG350, 1914–1945, Box 1025, 25,029, 23, Wajih, Sheik-ul-Islam for the Philippine Islands to secretary of war, October 23, 1915, and appended telegram from

Saleeby and Hashim. The term "Syrian" was used for all people from the Ottoman region of al-Sham, including Syria proper, Lebanon, Palestine, and Jordan.
74 William G. Clarence-Smith, "Middle Eastern Migrants in the Philippines: Entrepreneurs and Cultural Brokers," *Asian Journal of Social Science* 32, no. 3 (2004): 425–57, at 446–48.
75 NARA-II, RG165, 10525–604, "Loyal and disloyal Turkish subjects," October 1918.
76 Stacy D. Fahrenthold, "Former Ottomans in the Ranks: Pro-Entente Military Recruitment among Syrians in the Americas, 1916-18," *Journal of Global History* 11, no. 1 (2016): 88–112.
77 *al-Huda al-Arabiyya*, cited in *al-Manar*, Cairo, 19, no. 5 (October 1916): 317 ff.
78 "Certificate of death, 5 May 1916, Sayid M. Wajih Gilani," kindly sent to me by Dr Nicole Sackley.
79 S. A. Mokarzel and H. F. Otash, *Syrian Business Directory, 1908-1909* (New York: Al-Hoda, 1908): 269.
80 NARA-II, RG350, Personnel, Box 381, Mohamed Majoch, Captain O. M. Tweedy to H. E. the American Diplomatic Agent in Cairo, December 24, 1918. Majoch was a deformation of Wajih.
81 *Courier Journal*, Louisville, September 5, 1913, citing the *New York Sun*.
82 *al-Huda al-Arabiyya*, New York, obituary, cited in *al-Manar*, Cairo 19, no. 5, (October 1916): 317 ff.
83 *Le Grand Reporter*, Iowa, November 12, 1915.
84 NARA-II, RG84, Beirut Consulate, Vol. 187, 833, W. S. Hollis to B. C. Decker, June 21, 1915.
85 NARA-II, RG350, 1914–1945, Box 1025, 25,029, 18A, Wajih, Sheik-ul-Islam of the Philippines to President Wilson, September 2, 1915.
86 NARA-II, RG350, 1914–1945, Box 1025, 25,029, 12, S. M. Wajih to secretary of war, September 23, 1915.
87 NARA-II, RG350, 1914–1945, Box 1025, 25,029, 23, Wajih, Sheik-ul-Islam for the Philippine Islands to secretary of war, October 23, 1915.
88 NARA-II, RG350, 1914–1945, Box 1025, 25,029, 15, secretary of war to secretary of state, June 28, 1915.
89 NARA-II, RG350, 1914–1945, Box 1025, 25,029, 15, acting secretary of war to secretary of state, September 20, 1915.
90 NARA-II, RG350, 1914–1945, Box 1025, 25,029, 22, acting chief of BIA, confidential memorandum for Chief of Staff, October 9, 1915.
91 NARA-II, RG350, 1914–1945, Box 1025, 25,029, 21A, second assistant secretary of state to Wajih Effendi, October 4, 1915.
92 LC-MD, Hugh L. Scott Papers, Box 20, Wajih to H. L. Scott, October 11, 1915.
93 LC-MD, Hugh L. Scott Papers, Box 20, Wajih to Major-General H. L. Scott, October 14, 1915.
94 LC-MD, Hugh L. Scott Papers, Box 20, H. L. Scott to Said Mahammad Wajih Algilano [sic], October 16, 1915.
95 NARA-II, RG350, 1914–1945, Box 1025, 25,029, 23, Wajih, Sheik-ul-Islam for the Philippine Islands to secretary of war, October 23, 1915.
96 The Lindley M. Garrison Papers, held in Princeton University Library, seem to contain no letters to or from Wajih.
97 "Certificate of death"; *New York Herald*, May 6, 1916.
98 *Times-Dispatch*, Richmond, VA, May 6, 1916.

99 "Walking through a Glorious History," http://www.jeffersonhotel.com/experience/history (consulted February 23, 2012).
100 LC-MD, Hugh L. Scott Papers, Box 20, John P. Finley to H. L. Scott, chief-of-staff US Army, September 23, 1915, and October 2, 1915.
101 NARA-II, RG350, 1914–1945, Box 1025, 25,029, 12, S. M. Wajih to secretary of war, September 23, 1915.
102 NARA-II, RG350, 1914–1945, Box 1025, 25,029, 22, acting chief of BIA, confidential memorandum for chief of staff, October 9, 1915.
103 LC-MD, Hugh L. Scott Papers, Box 20, H. L. Scott to Sayid M. Wajih Zeid-ul-Gilani, Sheik-ul-Islam of the Philippines, October 12, 1915.
104 LC-MD, Hugh L. Scott Papers, Box 20, H. L. Scott to Lt. Col. J. P. Finley, October 12, 1915.
105 NARA-II, RG350, 1914–1945, Box 1025, 25,029, 28, Bureau of Insular Affairs to governor-general of the Philippine Islands, February 1, 1916.
106 NARA-II, RG350, 1914–1945, Box 1025, 25,029, 26, Wajih, Sheik-ul-Islam for the Philippine Islands to chief of the Bureau of Insular Affairs, November 30, 1915.
107 NARA-II, RG350, 1914–1945, Box 1025, 25,029, 28, Bureau of Insular Affairs to governor-general of the Philippine Islands, February 1, 1916.
108 "Certificate of death."
109 NARA-II, RG350, Personnel, Box 381, Mohamed Majoch, secretary of war to secretary of state, February 21, 1919.

Epilogue

1 Bernard Lewis, *Cultures in Conflict: Christians, Muslims, and Jews in the Age of Discovery* (Oxford: Oxford University Press, 1995), 5.
2 Lewis, *Cultures in Conflict*, 8–9, 11.
3 Samuel P. Huntington, "The Clash of Civilizations?", *Foreign Affairs* 72, no. 3 (1993): 22–49.
4 Bernard Lewis, *The Jews of Islam* (Princeton: Princeton University Press, 1984), xi.
5 Publisher's description on the back cover of Lewis, *Cultures in Conflict*.
6 Alfred W. Crosby, *Ecological Imperialism: The Biological Expansion of Europe, 900-1900*, second edition (Cambridge: Cambridge University Press, 2004).
7 Osama bin Laden, "Jihad against Jews and Crusaders: World Islamic Front Statement," February 23, 1998, https://fas.org/irp/world/para/docs/980223-fatwa.htm (accessed January 3, 2019).
8 See, for example, Bruce B. Lawrence, *New Faiths, Old Fears: Muslims and Other Asian Immigrants in American Religious Life* (New York: Columbia University Press, 2002); Mae M. Ngai, "The Unlovely Residue of Outworn Prejudices: The Hart-Celler Act and the Politics of Immigration Reform, 1945-1965," in *Americanism: New Perspectives on the History of an Ideal*, eds. Michael Kazin and Joseph A. McCartin (Chapel Hill: University of North Carolina Press, 2006), 108–27; Christian Gabriel, "A Different Road? Canadian Immigration Policy in the 1960s," *Labor: Studies in Working-Class History* 12, no. 3 (2015), 29–33.
9 Heather J. Sharkey, "Innocents Abroad? American Missionaries and the Off-Stage Making of American Culture," paper presented at the Organization of American Historians (OAH), Atlanta, April 10, 2014.

10 Donald Quataert, *The Ottoman Empire, 1700-1922* (Cambridge: Cambridge University Press, 2000), 9–10.
11 For example, Kambiz GhaneaBassiri, *A History of Islam in America* (Cambridge: Cambridge University Press, 2010), and Paul E. Lovejoy, who co-edited the memoir of a Benin-born Muslim slave in Brazil who escaped to New York. See Robin Law and Paul E. Lovejoy, ed., *The Biography of Mahommah Gardo Baquaqua: His Passage from Slavery to Freedom in Africa and America* (Princeton: Markus Wiener Publishers, 2001).
12 Karine V. Walther, *Sacred Interests: The United States and the Islamic World, 1821-1921* (Chapel Hill: The University of North Carolina Press, 2015); Denise A. Spellberg, *Thomas Jefferson's Qur'an: Islam and the Founders* (New York: Alfred A. Knopf, 2013); and Timothy Marr, *The Cultural Roots of American Islamicism* (Cambridge: Cambridge University Press, 2006).
13 Niyazi Berkes, *The Development of Secularism in Turkey* (Montreal: McGill University Press, 1964), 282.
14 Two still-flourishing congregations in Philadelphia from that era, both within walking distance of Independence Hall, are Old St. Joseph's Roman Catholic Church (founded 1733) and Mikveh Israel (whose members gathered in the 1740s and secured a building in the early 1770s).
15 Henry David Thoreau, *Walden, or Life in the Woods* (Chicago: Scott, Foresman, and Company, 1917), 95.
16 François Georgeon, *Abdülhamid II: Le sultan calife (1876-1909)* (Paris: Libraire Arthème Fayard, 2003), 150–52.
17 Heather J. Sharkey, *A History of Muslims, Christians, and Jews in the Middle East* (Cambridge: Cambridge University Press, 2017), 273–74.
18 Pascal Blanchard et al., *Human Zoos: The Invention of the Savage*, Trans. Deke Dusinberre et al. (Arles: Actes Sud, 2011); Clifton Crais and Pamela Scully, *Sara Baartman and the Hottentot Venus* (Princeton: Princeton University Press, 2009).
19 Marr, *The Cultural Roots of American Islamicism*, 5.
20 Edward W. Said, *Orientalism* (New York: Vintage Books, 1979), 1.
21 Douglas Little, *American Orientalism: The United States and the Middle East since 1945* (Chapel Hill: University of North Carolina Press, 2002); Ussama Makdisi, "Ottoman Orientalism," *The American Historical Review* 107, no. 3 (2002), 768–96; Leela Gandhi, *Postcolonial Theory: A Critical Introduction* (New York: Columbia University Press, 1998), 64–80.
22 Arif Dirlik, "Chinese History and the Question of Orientalism," *History and Theory* 35, no. 4 (1998), 96–118.
23 Zareena Grewal, *Islam Is a Foreign Country: American Muslims and the Global Crisis of Authority* (New York: New York University Press, 2014), 69.
24 Huntington, "The Clash of Civilizations?", 35.
25 Lewis, *Cultures in Conflict*, 9.
26 Luise White, *Speaking with Vampires: Rumor and History in Colonial Africa* (Berkeley: University of California Press, 2000).
27 Casey Nelson Blake, "The Usable Past, the Comfortable Past, and the Civic Past: Memory in Contemporary America," *Cultural Anthropology* 14, no. 3 (1999), 423–35.
28 William Faulkner, *Requiem for a Nun* (New York: Random House, 1951).

Bibliography

Introduction

Alisha, Khan, ed. *Islam and the Americas*. Gainesville: University Press of Florida, 2015.
Allison, Robert J. *The Crescent Obscured: The United States and the Muslim World, 1776–1815*. Chicago: University of Chicago Press, 2000.
Curtis, Edward E. IV. *Muslims in America*. New York: Oxford University Press, 2009.
Curtis, Edward E. IV. "Why Muslims Matter to American Religious History, 1730–1945," in *The Cambridge History of Religions in America: Vol. II, 1790–1945*, 393–413. Cambridge: Cambridge University Press, 2012.
"Donald Trump Declines to Correct Man Who Says President Obama Is Muslim," *Chicago Tribune*, September 18, 2015. Available online: https://www.chicagotribune.com/news/nationworld/politics/ct-trump-obama-muslim-20150917-story.html (accessed January 2, 2019).
Freneau, Philip. *The Poems of Philip Freneau: Written Chiefly During the Late War*. Philadelphia: Francis Bailey, 1786.
Games, Alison. "Atlantic History: Definitions, Challenges, and Opportunities." *American Historical Review* 111, no. 3 (2006): 741–57.
GhaneaBassiri, Kambiz. *A History of Islam in America: From the New World to the New World Order*. New York: Cambridge University Press, 2010.
Gomez, Michael. *Black Crescent: The Experience and Legacy of African Muslims in the Americas*. Cambridge: Cambridge University Press, 2005.
Johnston, James H. *From Slave Ship to Harvard: Yarrow Mamout and the History of an African American Family*. New York: Fordham University Press, 2012.
Kidd, Thomas S. *American Christians and Islam: Evangelical Culture and Muslims from the Colonial Period to the Age of Terrorism*. Princeton, NJ: Princeton University Press, 2009.
Love, Erik. *Islamophobia and Racism in America*. New York: New York University Press, 2017.
Maclay, Edgar. *A History of American Privateers*. London: Sampson Low, 1900.
McCarthy, Justin. *The Turk in America: Creation of an Enduring Prejudice*. Salt Lake City: University of Utah Press, 2010.
Smith, Blake. "Revolutionary Heroes" (Aeon.co). https://aeon.co/essays/why-american-revolutionaries-admired-the-rebels-of-mysore (accessed December 7, 2016).

Chapter 2

Abrahamian, Ervand. "The US Media, Huntington and September 11." *Third World Quarterly* 24, no. 3 (2003): 529–44.
Adams, Charles Francis, ed. *Memoirs of John Quincy Adams: Comprising Portions of His Diary from 1795 to 1848*, vol. 6. Philadelphia, PA: J.B. Lippincott & Co., 1874–1877.

Adams, John Quincy. "Mr. Adams to Mr. Luriottis," August 18, 1823. In *Message from the President of the United States Transmitting A Report of the Secretary of State, Upon the Subject of the Present Condition and Future Prospects of the Greeks*, 18th Congress, 1st Session. Washington: Gales & Seaton, 1824.

Adams, John Quincy. "Russia." In *The American Annual Register for the Years 1827-8-9*, edited by Joseph Blunt. New York: William Jackson & E. G. W. Blunt, 1835.

Ammon, Harry. *James Monroe: The Quest for National Identity*. New York: McGraw-Hill, 1971.

Anghie, Anthony. *Imperialism, Sovereignty and the Making of International Law*. Cambridge, MA: Cambridge University Press, 2005.

Armitage, David. "The Declaration of Independence and International Law," *The William and Mary Quarterly* 59, no. 1 (January 2002): 39-64.

Bailyn, Bernard. *The Ideological Origins of the American Revolution*. Cambridge, MA: Belknap Press, 1965.

Bemis, Samuel Flagg. *John Quincy Adams and the Foundations of American Foreign Policy*. New York: Alfred A. Knopf, 1949.

Bernal, Martin. *Black Athena: The Afro-Asiatic Roots of Classical Civilization*, 3 vols. New Brunswick, NJ: Rutgers University Press, 1987.

Çirakman, Asli. *From the "Terror of the World" to the "Sick Man of Europe."* New York: Hill and Wang, 2002.

Cline, Myrtle. "American Attitude toward the Greek War of Independence, 1821-1828." Ph.D. diss., Columbia University, 1930.

Clogg, Richard, ed. *The Struggle for Greek Independence: Essays to Mark the 150th Anniversary of the Greek War of Independence*. London: Macmillan, 1973.

Coit, Margaret L. *John C. Calhoun: American Portrait*. Boston: Houghton Mifflin, 1950.

Curti, Merle. *American Philanthropy Abroad*. New Brunswick, NJ: Rutgers University Press, 1963.

Dakin, Douglas. *The Greek War for Independence, 1821-1833*. Berkeley: University of California Press, 1973.

Dunn, Michael. "The 'Clash of Civilizations' and the 'War on Terror.'" *49th Parallel: An Interdisciplinary Journal of North American Studies* 20 (Winter 2006-2007): 1-20.

Earle, E. M. "American Interest in the Greek Cause, 1821-1827." *American Historical Review* 33, no. 5 (1927): 44-63.

Everett, Edward. "The Ethics of Aristotle to Nicomachus." *The North American Review* XVI (October 1823): 389-424.

Everett, Edward. *Mount Vernon Papers*. New York: D. Appelton, 1860.

Feder, J. Lester. "This is How Steven Bannon Sees the World." *Buzzfeed News*. Retrieved from: https://www.buzzfeed.com/lesterfeder/this-is-how-steve-bannon-sees-the-enti re-world?utm_term=.frWLedk64#.ptXjd4n6o.

Ferguson, Robert A. *The American Enlightenment, 1750-1820*. Cambridge, MA: Harvard University Press, 1997.

Field, James A. *America and the Mediterranean World, 1776-1882*. Princeton, NJ: Princeton University Press, 1969.

Finlay, George. *History of the Greek Revolution and the Reign of King Otto*. Original publication 1861. London: Zeno, 1971.

Foner, Eric. *Free Soil, Free Labor, Free Men: The Ideology of the Republican Party before the Civil War*. Oxford: Oxford University Press, 1995.

Frothingham, Paul Revere. *Edward Everett: Orator and Statesman*. Boston and New York: Houghton Mifflin company, 1925.

Gosset, Thomas. *Race: The History of an Idea in America*. New York: Oxford University Press, 1997.
"The Greek Cause!" *Kentucky Gazette*. February 5, 1824.
"Greek Question." *Niles' Weekly Register*. January 31, 1821.
"Greek Slaves." *Essex Register*. April 27, 1826.
"The Greeks." *Religious Intelligencer . . . Containing the Principal Transactions of the Various Bible and Missionary Societies, with Particular Accounts of Revivals of Religion* 8:29. December 20, 1823.
"The Greeks and the Turks." *American Mercury*. Hartford, CT. July 31, 1821.
Gregory, Derek. *The Colonial Present: Afghanistan, Palestine, and Iraq*. Malden: Blackwell Publishing, 2004. https://fortyninthparalleljournal.files.wordpress.com/2014/07/2-dunn-clash-of-civilisations.pdf.
Grewe, William H. *The Epochs of International Law*. New York: Walter de Gruyter, 2000.
Hatzidimitriou, Constantine G. *"Founded on Freedom and Virtue": Documents Illustrating the Impact in the United States of the Greek War of Independence, 1821–1829*. New York: Carattzas, 2002.
Hobson, John M. "The Clash of Civilizations 2.0: Race and Eurocentrism, Imperialism, and Anti-Imperialism." In *Re-Imagining the Other*, edited by Mahmoud Eid and Karim H. Karim, 75–97. New York: Palgrave Macmillan, 2015.
Howe, Samuel Gridley. *An Historical Sketch of the Greek Revolution*. New York: White Gallaher & White, 1828.
Hunt, Michael. *Ideology and U.S. Foreign Policy*, 2nd ed. New Haven: Yale University Press, 2009.
Huntington, Samuel. "The Clash of Civilizations." *Foreign Affairs* 72, no. 3 (Summer 1993): 22–49.
Huntington, Samuel. *The Clash of Civilizations and the Remaking of World Order*. New York: Simon & Schuster, 2006.
Huntington, Samuel, Fouad Ajami, Kishore Mahbubani, Robert L. Bartley, Liu Binyan, Jeane J. Kirkpatrick, Albert L. Weeks, and Gerard Piel. *The Clash of Civilizations: The Debate*. New York: Foreign Affairs, 1996.
Janis, Mark W. "Religion and Literature in International Law." In *Religion and International Law*, edited by Mark W. Janis and Carolyn Maree Evans, 121–44. Boston and Leiden: Martinus Nijhoff Publishers, 2004.
Kayaoglu, Turan. *Legal Imperialism: Sovereignty and Extraterritoriality in Japan, the Ottoman Empire, and China*. New York: Cambridge University Press, 2010.
"Legislative." *National Gazette*. December 13, 1823.
Leoussi, Athena. "Nationalism and Racial Hellenism in Nineteenth Century England and France." *Ethnic and Racial Studies* 20, no. 1 (January 1997): 42–68.
Lewis, Bernard. *Cultures in Conflict: Christians, Muslims and Jews in the Age of Discovery*. New York: Oxford University Press, 1996.
Lutz, Donald. "The Relative Influence of European Writers on Late Eighteenth-Century American Political Thought." *The American Political Science Review* 78, no. 1 (March 1984): 189–97.
Marks, Robert. "Review: The Clash of Civilizations and the Remaking of World Order." *Journal of World History* 11, no. 1 (Spring, 2000): 101–4.
Marr, Timothy. *The Cultural Roots of American Islamicism*. New York: Cambridge University Press, 2006.
Mavromicali, Pietro. "Manifesto." In Philip James Green, Esq., *Sketches of the War in Greece: In a Series of Extracts*, 272–73. London: Thomas Hurst & Co., 1827.

May, Ernest. *The Making of the Monroe Doctrine*. Cambridge, MA: Belknap Press of Harvard University Press, 1975.

May, Henry. *The Enlightenment in America*. New York: Oxford University Press, 1976.

Mayers, David. *Dissenting Voices in America's Rise to Power*. New York: Cambridge University Press, 2007.

Mazower, Mark. *The Balkans*. New York: The Modern Library, 2002.

Morrison, Larry. "'Nearer to the Brute Creation': The Scientific Defense of Slavery before 1830." *Southern Studies* 19 (1980): 228–42.

"Mr. Webster's Speech, On His Resolution in Favor of the Greeks." *New Hampshire Observer*. February 2, 1824.

"New York," and "Philadelphia, December 4, 1823." *American Mercury*. December 16, 1823.

Noll, Mark A. "The Protestant Enlightenment in America." In *Knowledge and Belief in America: Enlightenment Traditions and Modern Religious Thought*, edited by William M. Shea and Peter A. Huff, 88–124. New York: Cambridge University Press, 1995.

Orakhelashvili, Alexander. "The Idea of European International Law." *The European Journal of International Law* 17, no. 2 (April 2006): 315–47.

"Ordinations and Installations." *The Christian Spectator*. February 1, 1824.

Pappas, Paul C. "Lafayette and Revolutionary Greece." *Journal of Modern Greek Studies* 2, no. 1 (May 1984): 105–16.

Pappas, Paul C. *The United States and the Greek War for Independence, 182–1828*. New York: Columbia University Press, 1978.

Perkins, Mary Anne. *Christendom and European Identity: The Legacy of Grand Narrative since 1789*. Berlin: Walter de Gruyter GmbH & Co., 2004.

Philliou, Christine. *Biography of an Empire: Governing Ottomans in an Age of Revolution*. Berkeley: University of California Press, 2011.

Pitts, Jennifer. "Empire and Legal Universalism in the Eighteenth Century." *The American Historical Review* 117, no. 1 (February 2012): 92–121.

Randolph, John. *Speech of Mr. Randolph on the Greek Question*. Washington: Gales and Seaton, 1824.

Reid-Maroney, Nina. *Philadelphia's Enlightenment, 1740–1800: Kingdom of Christ, Empire of Reason*. Westport, CT: Greenwood Press, 2001.

Repousis, Angelo. *Greek-American Relations from Monroe to Truman*. Kent, OH: Kent State University Press, 2013.

Rodogno, David. *Against Massacre: Humanitarian Interventions in the Ottoman Empire, 1815–1914: The Emergence of a European Concept and International Practice*. Princeton: Princeton University Press, 2012.

Roediger, David. *Wages of Whiteness: Race and the Makings of the American Working Class*. New York: Verso, 1999.

Roessel, David. *In Byron's Shadow: Modern Greece in the English and American Imagination*. New York: Oxford University Press, 2002.

Ryan, David. "'Image, Rhetoric and Nationhood': Framing September 11: Cultural Diplomacy and the Image of America." *49th Parallel: An Interdisciplinary Journal of North American Studies* 10 (Spring, 2003). Retrieved from: http://www.49thparallel.bham.ac.uk/back/issue10/davidryan.htm.

Said, Edward. "A Clash of Ignorance." *Nation*. October 21, 2001.

Said, Edward. *The Myth of the Clash of Civilizations: Professor Said in Lecture*. Northampton, MA: Media Education Foundation, 2002.

Sen, Amartya. "What Clash of Civilizations?" *Slate*. March 29, 2006.

Sha'ban, Fuad. *Islam and Arabs in Early American Thought: The Roots of Orientalism in America*. Durham, NC: Acord University Press, 1991.

St. Clare, William. *That Greece Might Still be Free: The Philhellenes in the War of Independence*. New York: Oxford University Press, 1972.

Soulis, George C. "Adamantios Korais and Edward Everett." In *Melanges Offerts a Octave et Melpo Morlier, a l'Occasion du 25e Anniversaire de leur Arrivee en Grece*, vol. 2, 397–407. Athens: Institute Francais d'Athenes, 1956.

Tanner, Jeremy. "Introduction to the New Edition: Race and Representation in Ancient Art: Black Athena and After." In *The Image of the Black in Western Art: From the Pharaohs to the Fall of the Roman Empire*, edited by David Bindman, Henry Louis Gates, Jr., and Karen C. C. Dalton, 1–39. Cambridge, MA: Harvard University Press, 2010.

Varg, Paul A. *Edward Everett: The Intellectual in the Turmoil of Politics*. Selinsgrove, PA: Susquehanna University Press, 1992.

Vogli, Elpida. "The Greek War of Independence and the Emergence of a Modern Nation-State in Southeastern Europe (1821–1827)." In *Empire and Peninsulas*, edited by Plamen Milev, 191–201. Piscataway, NJ: Transaction Publishers, 2010.

von Martens, Georg Friedrick. *Summary of the Law of Nations, Founded on the Treaties and Customs of the Modern Nations of European: With a List of the Principal Treaties*. Translated by William Cobbett. Philadelphia: Thomas Bradford, 1795.

Walther, Karine. *Sacred Interests: The United States and the Islamic World, 1821–1921*. Chapel Hill: University of North Carolina Press, 2015.

Webster, Daniel, et al. *Discussion of the Greek Question in the House of Representatives*. Boston: Howard Gazette, 1824.

Webster, Daniel. "The Revolution in Greece: A Speech Delivered in the House of Representatives of the United States, on the 19th of January, 1824." In *The Great Speeches and Orations of Daniel Webster*, edited by Edwin P. Whipple, 57–76. Boston: Little Brown, 1919.

Weeks, Albert. "Do Civilizations Hold?" *Foreign Affairs* 72, no. 4 (1993): 24–25.

Wheaton, Henry. "An Anniversary Discourse Delivered Before the New York Historical Society on Thursday, December 28, 1820." In *Collections of the New York Historical Society, for the Year 1821*, vol. 3, 281–320. New York: E.Bliss and E. White, 1821.

Wheaton, Henry. *Elements of International Law with a Sketch of the History of the Science*, vol. 1. London: B. Fellowes, 1826.

Winthrop, Thomas and Edward Everett. *Address of the Committee Appointed at a Public Meeting held in Boston, December 19, 1823, for the Relief of the Greeks, to their Fellow Citizens*. Boston: Press of the North American Review, 1823.

"XVIII Congress." *The Christian Register*. January 31, 1824.

Zwemer, Samuel. *Mohammed or Christ*. London: Seeley, Service & Co. Limited, 1916.

Chapter 3

Alford, Terry. *Prince Among Slaves: The True Story of an African Prince Sold into Slavery in the American South*. 30th anniversary edition. New York: Oxford University Press, 2007.

Alryyes, Ala. "Introduction: 'Arabic Work,' Islam, and American Literature." In *A Muslim American Slave: The Life of Omar ibn Said* by Omar ibn Said, edited by Ala Alryyes, 3–46. Madison: University of Wisconsin Press, 2011.

Austin, Allan. *African Muslims in Antebellum America: Transatlantic Stories and Spiritual Struggles*. Revised and updated edition. New York: Routledge, 1997.

Austin, Allan. "Mohammed Ali ben Said: Travels on Five Continents." *Contributions in Black Studies* 12 (1994): 129–58.

Blight, David. *Frederick Douglass: Prophet of Freedom*. New York: Simon and Schuster, 2018.

Bluett, Thomas. *Some Memoirs of the Life of Job, the Son of Solomon the Highest Priest of Boonda in Africa [. . .]*. London: Richard Ford, 1734. https://docsouth.unc.edu/neh/bluett/bluett.html.

Curtis, Edward IV. *Encyclopedia of Muslim-American History*. New York: Facts on File, 2010.

Dabovic, Safet. "Out of Place: The Travels of Nicholas Said." *Criticism* 54, no. 1 (Winter 2012): 59–83.

Diouf, Sylviane A. *Servants of Allah: African Muslims Enslaved in the Americas*. New York: New York University Press, 1998.

Douglass, Frederick. *Life and Times of Frederick Douglass*. 1891. In *Autobiographies*, edited by Henry Louis Gates, Jr., 453–1048. New York: Library of America, 1994.

Douglass, Frederick. *My Bondage and My Freedom*. 1855. In *Autobiographies*, edited by Henry Louis Gates, Jr., 103–452. New York: Library of America, 1994.

Douglass, Frederick. *Narrative of the Life of Frederick Douglass, an American Slave*. 1845. In *Autobiographies*, edited by Henry Louis Gates, Jr., 1–102. New York: Library of America, 1994.

Douglass, Frederick. "What to the Slave Is the Fourth of July?" 1852. In *Narrative of the Life of Frederick Douglass, an American Slave*, edited by Ira Dworkin, 119–47. New York: Penguin, 2014.

Du Bois, W. E. B. *Black Reconstruction in America, 1860–1880*. 1935. New York: Free Press, 1998.

Emerson, Mark G. "Scholarly Edition of the Grand Tour Diaries of Frederick Douglass and Helen Pitts Douglass." MA Thesis. Indiana University-Purdue University Indianapolis, 2003.

Fields, Barbara Jeanne. *Slavery and Freedom on the Middle Ground: Maryland During the Nineteenth Century*. New Haven: Yale University Press, 1985.

Foster, Frances Smith. "A Narrative of the Interesting Origins and (Somewhat) Surprising Developments of African-American Print Culture." *American Literary History* 17, no. 4 (December 2005): 714–40.

"Fred Douglass Talks." *The Washington Post*. August 22, 1887, 2.

Frydman, Jason. "Scheherazade in Chains: Arab-Islamic Genealogies of African Diasporic Literature." In *The Global South Atlantic*, edited by Kerry Bystrom and Joseph R. Slaughter, 54–65. New York: Fordham University Press, 2017. ProQuest Ebook Central.

Gates, Henry Louis, Jr. *Figures in Black: Words, Signs, and the "Racial" Self*. New York: Oxford University Press, 1987.

Gates, Henry Louis, Jr., and Valerie Smith, eds. *The Norton Anthology of African American Literature*, 3rd ed. New York: W. W. Norton, 2014.

GhaneaBassiri, Kambiz. *A History of Islam in America*. New York: Cambridge University Press, 2010.

Goodman, Susan. *Republic of Words: The Atlantic Monthly and Its Writers, 1857–1925*. Hanover, NH: University Press of New England, 2011.

Gronniosaw, James Albert Ukawsaw. *A Narrative of the Most Remarkable Particulars in the Life of James Albert Ukawsaw Gronniosaw, an African Prince, as Related by Himself*.

Bath: Printed by W. Gye, [c. 1772]. https://docsouth.unc.edu/neh/gronniosaw/menu.html.

Harris, Will. "Phillis Wheatley: A Muslim Connection." *African American Review* 48, nos. 1–2 (Spring/Summer 2015): 1–15.

Judy, Ronald A. T. *(Dis)Forming the American Canon: African-Arabic Slave Narratives and the Vernacular.* Minneapolis: University of Minnesota Press, 1993.

Kane, Ousmane Oumar. *Beyond Timbuktu: An Intellectual History of Muslim West Africa.* Cambridge, MA: Harvard University Press, 2016.

Lavers, J. E. "Kanem and Borno to 1808." In *Groundwork of Nigerian History*, edited by Obaro Ikime, 187–209. Ibadan: Heinemann Educational Books (Nigeria) for the Historical Society of Nigeria, 1980.

Levine, Robert S. *Dislocating Race & Nation: Episodes in Nineteenth-Century American Literary Nationalism.* Chapel Hill: University of North Carolina Press, 2008.

Lovejoy, Paul E. "Mohammed Ali Nicholas Sa'id: From Enslavement to American Civil War Veteran." *Millars: Espai i Història* 42, no. 1 (2017): 219–32.

Marx, Karl. *Grundrisse: Foundations of the Critique of Political Economy.* Translated by Martin Nicolaus. New York: Penguin Classics, 1993.

McFeely, William S. *Frederick Douglass.* New York: Norton, 1991.

Muhammad, Amir N. *Muslim Veterans of American Wars.* Washington: FreeMan Publications, 2007.

Muhammad, Precious Rasheeda, ed. *The Autobiography of Nicholas Said, a Native of Bornou, Eastern Soudan, Central Africa* by Nicholas Said. Cambridge, MA: Journal of Islam in American Press, 2000.

Obama, Barack. "Barack Obama's Cairo Speech," *The Guardian*. June 4, 2009. https://www.theguardian.com/world/2009/jun/04/barack-obama-keynote-speech-egypt.

Olney, James. "'I Was Born': Slave Narratives, Their Status as Autobiography and as Literature." In *The Slave's Narrative*, edited by Charles T. Davis and Henry Louis Gates, Jr., 148–75. New York: Oxford University Press, 1985.

Pew Research Center. "U.S. Muslims Concerned about Their Place in Society, but Continue to Believe in the American Dream." July 26, 2017. http://assets.pewresearch.org/wp-content/uploads/sites/11/2017/07/09105631/U.S.-MUSLIMS-FULL-REPORT-with-population-update-v2.pdf.

Quarles, Benjamin. *The Negro in the Civil War.* 1953. Boston: Little, Brown, and Company, 1969.

Rashid, Hussein, and Precious Rasheeda Muhammad. "American Muslim (Un)Exceptionalism: #BlackLivesMatter and #BringBackOurGirls." *Journal of Africana Religions* 3, no. 4 (October 2015): 478–95.

Said, Nicholas. *The Autobiography of Nicholas Said, a Native of Bornou, Eastern Soudan, Central Africa.* Memphis: Shotwell & Co., 1873.

Said, Nicholas. "A Native of Bornoo." *Atlantic Monthly* 20 (October 1867): 485–95.

Samito, Christian, ed. *Changes in Law and Society during the Civil War and Reconstruction: A Legal History Documentary Reader.* Carbondale: Southern Illinois University Press, 2009.

Samito, Christian, ed. "The Intersection between Military Justice and Equal Rights: Mutinies, Courts-Martial, and Black Civil War Soldiers." *Civil War History* 53, no. 2 (June 2007): 170–202.

Trafton, Scott. *Egypt Land: Race and Nineteenth-Century American Egyptomania.* Durham, NC: Duke University Press, 2004.

Trudeau, Noah Andre. *Voices of the 55th: Letters from the 55th Massachusetts Volunteers, 1861–1865*. Dayton, OH: Morningside House, 1996.
Turner, Richard Brent. *Islam in the African American Experience*. Bloomington: Indiana University Press, 1997.

Chapter 4

al-Ahari, Muhammed Abdullah. *Bilali Muhammad: Muslim Jurisprudist in Antebellum Georgia*. Chicago: Magribine Press, 2010.
Alryyes, Ala A. "'Arabic Work,' Islam, and American Literature." Introduction to *A Muslim American Slave: The Life of Omar ibn Said*, edited by Ala A. Alryyes, 3–46. Madison: University of Wisconsin Press, 2011.
Aminrazavi, Mehdi. *Sufism and American Literary Masters*. New York: SUNY Press, 2014.
Asaad, Fakir Jany Muhammad. *Practical Philosophy of the Muhammadan People: Exhibited in its Professed Connexion with the European, so as to Render either Introduction to the Other: Being a Translation of the Aklak-I Jalay from the Persian of Fakir Jany Muhammad Asaad*. Translated by Muhammad ibn As'ad Dawwānī and W. F. Thompson. Karachi: Karimsons, 1977.
Austin, Allan D. *African Muslims in Antebellum America: A Sourcebook*. New York: Garland Press, 1984.
Austin, Allan D. *African Muslims in Antebellum America: Transatlantic Stories and Spiritual Struggles*. New York: Routledge, 1997.
Berman, Jacob Rama. *American Arabesque: Arabs, Islam, and the 19th-Century Imaginary*. New York: New York University Press, 2012.
Best, Stephen, and Sharon Marcus. "Surface Reading: An Introduction." *Representations* 108, no. 1 (2009): 1–21. doi:10.1525/rep.2009.108.1.1.
Dabovic, Safet. *Displacement and the Negotiation of an American Identity in African Muslim Slave Narratives*. Ph.D Diss., SUNY at Stony Brook, New York, 2009.
Einboden, Jeffrey. *The Islamic Lineage of American Literary Culture: Muslim Sources from the Revolution to Reconstruction*. New York: Oxford University Press, 2016.
Emerson, Ralph Waldo. *Essays and Lectures*. New York: Library of America, 1983.
Emerson, Ralph Waldo. *Journals and Miscellaneous Notebooks of Ralph Waldo Emerson, Volume V: 1835–1838*. Edited by Merton M. Sealts, Jr. Cambridge: Harvard University Press, 1965.
Emerson, Ralph Waldo. *The Journals and Miscellaneous Notebooks of Ralph Waldo Emerson, Volume 1: 1819–1822*. Edited by William H. Gilman, Alfred R. Ferguson, George P. Clark, and Merrell R. Davis. Cambridge: Belknap Press of Harvard University, 1960. Charlottesville: InteLex Corp, 2009. Intelex past masters: full text humanities. http://www.nlx.com/collections/.
Emerson, Ralph Waldo. *A Memoir of Ralph Waldo Emerson*. Edited by James Elliot Cabot. Cambridge: Riverside Press, 1887.
Fakahani, Suzan Jameel. "Islamic Influences on Emerson's Thought: The Fascination of a Nineteenth Century American Writer." *Journal of Muslim Minority Affairs* 18, no. 2 (1998): 291–303. doi:10.1080/13602009808716412.
Felski, Rita. "Suspicious Minds." *Poetics Today* 32, no. 2 (2011): 215–34. doi:10.1215/033353721261208.
GhaneaBassiri, Kambiz. *A History of Islam in America: From the New World to the New World Order*. New York: Cambridge University Press, 2010.

Greenberg, Joseph H. "The Decipherment of the 'Ben-Ali Diary,' a Preliminary Statement." *The Journal of Negro History* 25, no. 3 (1940): 372-75. doi: 10.2307/2714801.

Harris, Joel Chandler. *The Story of Aaron (so Named) the Son of Ben Ali, Told by His Friends and Acquaintances*. Illustrated by Oliver Herford. London: Osgood, McIlvaine, 1896. https://archive.org/details/orientalgeograp00agoog.

Hisham, Abu Muhammad ibn. "Concerning the True Visions with which the Prophethood of Mohammed Began." In *Translations of Eastern Poetry and Prose*, translated by Reynold A. Nicholson, 37-47. London: Cambridge University Press, 1922.

Hunwick, John. "'I Wish to be Seen in our Land Called Āfrikā': ʿUmar b. Sayyid's Appeal to be Released from Slavery (1819)." *Journal of Arabic and Islamic Studies* 5, no. 3 (2004): 62-77.

Ibn-Ḥauqal, Abu-'l-Qāsim Ibn-ʿAlī. *The Oriental Geography of Ebn Haukal, an Arabian Traveller of the Tenth Century*. Translated by Sir William Ouseley. London: Oriental Press, by Wilson & Co., 1800. Internet Archive.

Irwin, John T. *American Hieroglyphics: The Symbol of the Egyptian Hieroglyphics in the American Renaissance*. New Haven: Yale University Press, 1980.

Jahanpour, Farhang. "Ralph Waldo Emerson and the Sufis: From Puritanism to Transcendentalism." *Journal of Globalization for the Common Good* (2007): 1-22. https://www.globethics.net/gel/4050599.

Judy, Ronald A. *(Dis)forming the American Canon: African-Arabic Slave Narratives and the Vernacular*. Minneapolis, MN: University of Minnesota Press, 1993.

Khatibi, Abdelkebir. "Frontiers: Between Psychoanalysis and Islam." *Third Text* 23, no. 6 (2009): 689-96. doi: 10.1080/09528820903371081.

Khatibi, Abdelkebir. *Par-dessus l'épaule*. Paris: Editions Aubier, 1988.

Lewis, Tayler. "The Koran: African Mohammedanism." In *A Series of Papers on their Character, Condition, and Future Prospects*, edited by E.W. Blyden, Tayler Lewis, and Theodore Dwight, 35-43. New York: Anson D. F. Randolph & CO., 1871.

Love, Heather. "Close but Not Deep: Literary Ethics and the Descriptive Turn." *New Literary History* 41, no. 2 (2010): 371-91. doi:10.1353/nlh.2010.0007.

Marr, Timothy. *The Cultural Roots of American Islamicism*. Cambridge: Cambridge University Press, 2006.

Muhammed, Bilali. *Ben Ali's Diary*. Francis R. Goulding Papers, *MS 2807*. Hargrett Rare Book and Manuscript Library, University of Georgia Libraries, 1-13.

Nasr, Seyyed Hossein. "The Qurʾān and Ḥadīth as Source and Inspiration of Islamic Philosophy." In volume 1 of *History of Islamic Philosophy*, edited by Oliver Leaman and Seyyed Hossein Nasr, 27-39. New York: Routledge, 1996.

Osman, Ghada, and Camille F. Forbes. "Representing the West in the Arabic Language: The Slave Narrative of Omar ibn Said." In *A Muslim American Slave: The Life of Omar ibn Said*, edited by Ala A. Alryyes, 182-94. Madison, WI: University of Wisconsin Press, 2011.

Progler, Yusuf. "Ben Ali and his Arabic Diary: Encountering an African Muslim in Antebellum America." *Muslim & Arab Perspectives: International Islamic Magazine* 11 (Fall 2004): 19-60.

Ricoeur, Paul. *Freud and Philosophy: An Essay on Interpretation*. New Haven: Yale University Press, 1970.

Sayyid, ʿUmar ibn. "Letter to John Owen." 1819. Beinecke Library, Yale University, JWJ MSS 185.

Sells, Michael. "Sound, Spirit, and Gender in Sūrat Al-Qadr." *Journal of the American Oriental Society* 111, no. 2 (1991): 239-59. doi:10.2307/604017.

Chapter 7

Abū al-Faḍl ibn Mubārak. *Akbar-Nāmah*. Edited and translated by Wheeler M. Thackston as *The History of Akbar*, 3 vols. Cambridge, MA: Harvard University Press, 2014–2017. Edited and translated by Henry Beveridge as *The Akbarnama of Abu-l-Fazl: The History of the Reign of the Emperor Akbar down to A.D. 1602*. Kolkata: Asiatic Society, 1897. Page references are to Thackston edition unless otherwise noted.

Ahmad, Hazrat Mirza Ghulam. *Jesus in India: Jesus' Deliverance from the Cross & Journey to India*. London: Islam International, 2003.

Aquil, Raziuddin. *Sufism, Culture, and Politics: Afghans and Islam in Medieval North India*. Oxford: Oxford University Press, 2012.

Atherton, J. S. "Islam and the Koran in *Finnegans Wake*." *Comparative Literature* 6, no. 3 (Summer, 1954): 252–55.

Ben-Dor Benite, Zvi. *The Ten Lost Tribes: A World History*. Oxford: Oxford University Press, 2009.

Burnes, Alexander. *Travels into Bokhara: Travels into Bokhara*. J. Murray: 1834.

Clark, Elizabeth Hughes. "Thomas Patrick Hughes (1838–1911): Missionary to India's 'Northwest Frontier.'" *National Episcopal Historians and Archivists* 62, no. 1 (2004): 2–3.

Clark, Robert. "Opening of the C.M.S. Memorial Mission Church at Peshawar." *The Church Missionary Intelligencer* IX, no. 97 (1884): 177–78.

Cogley, Richard. "'The Most Vile and Barbaraous Nation of all the World': Giles Fletcher the Elder's *The Tartars Or, Ten Tribes* (ca. 1610)." *Renaissance Quarterly* 58, no. 3 (2005): 781–814.

Conroy-Krutz, Emily. *Christian Imperialism: Converting the World in the Early American Republic*. Cornell: Cornell University Press, 2015.

Crews, Robert. *Afghan Modern: The History of a Global Nation*. Cambridge, MA: Belknap Press, 2015.

Deleuze, Gilles. "Nomad Thought." In *New Nietzsche: Contemporary Styles of Interpretation*, edited by David Allison, 142–49. Cambridge, MA: The MIT Press, 1985.

Ebenezer, Matthew. "American Presbyterians and Islam in India, 1855–1923: A Critical Evaluation of the Contributions of Isidor Loewenthal (1826–1864) & Elwood Morris Wherry (1843–1927)." PhD diss., Westminster Theological Seminary, 1998.

Ferrier, Joseph Pierre. *History of the Afghans*. John Murray, 1858.

Fraser, James Baillie. *Historical and Descriptive Account of Persia, from the Earliest Ages to the Present Time* ... Harper's Family Library no. 70. New York: Harper & Brothers, 1834.

Good, John Mason, Olinthus Gregory, and Newton Bosworth. *Pantologia*... J. Walker, 1819.

Green, Nile. "Tribe, Diaspora, and Sainthood in Afghan History." *The Journal of Asian Studies* 67 (2008): 171–211.

Haroon, Sana. *Frontier of Faith: Islam in the Indo-Afghan Borderland*. New York: Columbia University Press, 2007.

Howell, Sally. *Old Islam in Detroit: Rediscovering the Muslim American Past*. Oxford: Oxford University Press, 2014.

Hughes, Thomas Patrick. "Baptism of an Afghan Family," *The Church Missionary Intelligencer* VI (1881): 247.

Hughes, Thomas Patrick. *Dictionary of Islam*. WH Allen, 1895.

Hughes, Thomas Patrick. "Some Account of the Afghans and of the Peshawar Church Mission." Lahore: Victoria Press, 1877. This article has been transcribed by Wayne Kempton in 2011 and is available online: http://anglicanhistory.org/india/tphughes/account_afghans1877.html.

Hughes, Thomas Patrick. "Twenty Years on the Afghan Frontier," *The Independent* 45 (1893): 455–56, 529–30, 637–38, 845–46, 1075–76.

Jones, William. *The Works of Sir William Jones*. J. Stockdale and J. Walker, 1807.

Khan, Adil Hussain. *From Sufism to Ahmadiyya: A Muslim Minority Movement in South Asia*. Bloomington: Indiana University Press, 2015.

Kaplan, Robert. *Soldiers of God: With Islamic Warriors in Afghanistan and Pakistan*. New York: Vintage, 2008.

Lamb, Christina. *Farewell Kabul: From Afghanistan to a More Dangerous World*. London: HarperCollins UK, 2015.

Loewenthal, Isidor. "Is the Pushto a Semitic Language?" *Journal of Asiatic Society*, No. IV. Baptist Mission Press (1860): 323–45.

Loewenthal, Isidor. "Mahommedanism Viewed in Relation to Missionary Effort." *The Church Missionary Intelligencer* III, no. 4, 99–107 and no. 6, 139–44 (1852).

Loewenthal, Isidor. "Missionary Labor for the Afghans." *The Missionary Magazine* (1862): 50.

Loewenthal, Isidor. *Ruhainah: A Story of Afghan Life*. New York: Cassell, 1886.

Marr, Timothy. *The Cultural Roots of American Islamicism*. Cambridge: Cambridge University Press, 2006.

McCarthy, Rory. "Pashtun Clue to Lost Tribes of Israel." *The Guardian*. January 16, 2010. http://www.theguardian.com/world/2010/jan/17/israel-lost-tribes-pashtun (accessed July 26, 2018).

Melville, Herman. *Moby Dick*. Reprint edition. London: Random House UK, 2008.

Moore, George. *The Lost Tribes and the Saxons of the East and of the West. . .* London: Longmans, Green, Longman, and Roberts, 1861.

Muḥammad Hayat Khan. *Afghanistan and Its Inhabitants*. Edited and translated by Henry Priestley. Lahore, 1874. Reprinted. Lahore: Sang-e-Meel Publications, 1981. Page references are to 1981 edition.

Nelson, Dean. "Taliban May Be Descended from Jews." *The Telegraph*. January 11, 2010. http://www.telegraph.co.uk/news/worldnews/asia/afghanistan/6967224/Taliban-may-be-descended-from-Jews.html (accessed July 26, 2018)

Nichols, Robert. *Settling the Frontier: Land, Law and Society in the Peshawar Valley, 1500–1900*. Karachi: Oxford University Press, 2001.

Niʿmat Allāh Harawī. *Tarikh-i-Khān Jahānī wa Makhzan-i Afghānī: A Complete History of the Afghans in Indo-Pak Sub-Continent, Edited on the Basis of Its Earliest and Six Other Manuscripts Accompanied with a Critical Introduction in English, Annotations, Geographical and Historical Notes in Persian*. Edited by S. M. Imam al-Dīn. Dacca: Asiatic Society of Pakistan, 1960. Reprinted with Bernhard Dorn's English translation as *History of the Afghans: Translated from the Persian of Neamet Ullah*. Translated and introduced by Bernhard Dorn. Cambridge: Cambridge University Press, 2013. Page references are to 1960 edition unless otherwise noted.

Parfitt, Tudor. *The Lost Tribes of Israel: The History of a Myth*. London: Weidenfeld and Nicolson, 2002.

Powell, Avril Ann. *Muslims and Missionaries in Pre-Mutiny India*. London: Routledge, 2014.

Pfander, C. G. *The Mizanu'l Haqq (Balance of Truth): Thoroughly Revised and Enlarged by W. St. Clair Tisdall, M.A.D.D.* London: The Religious Tract Society, 1910.
Raverty, Henry. "Some Remarks on the Origin of the Afghan People." *Journal of the Asiatic Society of Bengal* XXIII, no. 6 (1855): 550–88.
Rose, G. H. *The Afghans, the Ten Tribes, and the Kings of the East.* London: Hatchards, 1852.
Smith, Ethan. *A Dissertation on the Prophecies Relative to Antichrist and the Last Times. . . .* Charlestown, MA: Printed and sold by Samuel T. Armstrong, 1811. https://books.google.com/books?id=WOliAAAAcAAJ&source=gbs_navlinks_s (accessed August 25, 2019).
"Sons of Israel in Afghanistan," *The Missionary Magazine* (March 1867): 86–88.
Tapper, Jake. *The Outpost: An Untold Story of American Valor.* Boston: Little, Brown and Company, 2012.
"The Aboriginal Races of India." *The Church Missionary Intelligence* III (1852): 107–14.
The Bible Cyclopedia. Parker, 1841.
"The Pathans." *Church Missionary Intelligencer* (1868): 152.
Towers, Joseph. *Illustrations of Prophecy. . . 2 volumes.* Printed by T. N. Longman, 1796.
Turner, Richard Brent. *Islam in the African American Experience.* Bloomington, IN: Indiana University Press, 2003.
Van der Linden, Bob. *Moral Languages from Colonial Punjab: The Singh Sabha, Arya Samaj and Ahmadiyahs.* New Delhi: Manohar, 2008.
Wolff, Joseph. *Researches and Missionary Labours Among the Jews, Mohammedans, and Other Sects.* Published by Mr. J. Nisbet, 1835.

Chapter 10

Abinales, Patricio J. "Progressive-Machine Conflict in Early Twentieth Century U.S. Politics and Colonial-State Building in the Philippines." In *The American Colonial State in the Philippines: Global Perspectives*, edited by Julian Go and Anne L. Foster, 148–81. Durham, NC: Duke University Press, 2003.
Abinales, Patricio J., and Donna J. Amoroso. *State and Society in the Philippines.* Lanham: Rowman and Littlefield Publishers, Inc., 2005.
Amaroso, Donna. "Inheriting the 'Moro Problem': Muslim Authority and Colonial Rule in British Malaya and the Philippines." In *The American Colonial State in the Philippines: Global Perspectives*, edited by Julian Go and Anne L. Foster, 118–47. Durham, NC: Duke University Press, 2003.
Angeles, Vivienne. "Moros in the Media and Beyond: Representations of Philippine Muslims." *Contemporary Islam* 4, no. 1 (April 2010): 29–53.
Bliss, Tasker. Papers. Library of Congress Manuscript Division, Washington DC.
Cameron, Charles. Papers. Xavier University, Cagayan de Oro, Philippines.
Childress, F. J. "Creating the 'New Woman' in Early Republican Turkey: The Contributions of the American Collegiate Institute and the American College for Girls." *Middle Eastern Studies* 44, no. 4 (July 2008): 553–69.
Churchill, William, and John P. Finley. *The Subanu: Studies of a Sub-Visayan Mountain Folk of Mindanao.* Washington: Carnegie Institute of Washington, 1913.
Clarence-Smith, William. "Middle Eastern States and the Philippines under Early American Rule, 1898-1919." In *From Anatolia to Aceh: Ottomans, Turks, and Southeast*

Asia, edited by A. C. S. Peacock and Annabel Teh Gallop, 199–219. Proceedings of the British Academy 200. Oxford: The British Academy by Oxford University Press, 2015.

Clarence-Smith, William. "A Palestinian Muslim's Mission to America: Sayyid Wajih al-Kilani of Nazareth, 1915–1916." In *American and Muslim Worlds, circa 1500–1900*, edited by Mitch Fraas and John Ghazvinian, xx–xx. New York: Bloomsbury Press, 2019.

Clarence-Smith, William. "Wajih al-Kilani, Shaykh al-Islam of the Philippines and Notable of Nazareth, 1913–1916." In *Nazareth History and Cultural Heritage: Proceedings of the 2nd International Conference, Nazareth, July 2–5, 2012*, edited by Mahmoud Yazbak and Sharif Sharif, 171–92. Nazareth Academic Studies Series 2. Nazareth: Municipality of Nazareth Academic Publication, 2013.

Deringil, Selim. "'They Live in a State of Nomadism and Savagery': The Late Ottoman Empire and the Post-Colonial Debate." *Comparative Studies in Society and History* 45, no. 2 (April 2003): 311–42.

Ewing, Franklin. "Juramentado: Institutionalized Suicide among the Moros of the Philippines." *Anthropological Quarterly* 28, no. 4 (October 1955): 148–55.

Findley, Carter Vaughan. "Hizmet among the Most Influential Religious Renewals of Late Ottoman and Modern Turkish History." In *Hizmet Means Service: Perspectives on an Alternative Path within Islam*, edited by Martin E. Marty, 5–17. Berkeley: University of California Press, 2015.

Finley, John P. "The Mohammedan Problem in the Philippines." *The Journal of Race Development* 5, no. 4 (April 2015): 353–63.

Finley, John P. Papers. Military Historical Institute, Carlisle, PA.

Fraas, Mitch, and John Ghazvinian. "Introduction." In *American and Muslim Worlds, circa 1500–1900*, edited by Mitch Fraas and John Ghazvinian. New York: Bloomsbury, 2019.

Galway, Joseph G. "J.P. Finley: The First Severe Storms Forecaster." *Bulletin of the American Meteorological Society* 66, no. 11 (November 1985): 1380–95.

Gedacht, Joshua. "Holy War, Progress, and 'Modern Mohammedans' in Colonial Southeast Asia." *The Muslim World* 105, no. 4 (October 2015): 446–71.

Gedacht, Joshua. "'Mohammedan Religion Made it Necessary to Fire': Massacres on the American Imperial Frontier from South Dakota to the Southern Philippines." In *Colonial Crucible: Empire in the Making of the Modern American State*, edited by Alfred W. McCoy and Francisco Scarano, 397–409. Madison: University of Wisconsin Press, 2009.

Gedacht, Joshua. "The 'Shaykh al-Islam of the Philippines' and Coercive Cosmopolitanism in an Age of Empire." In *Challenging Cosmopolitanism: Coercion, Mobility and Displacement in Islamic Asia*, edited by Joshua Gedacht and R. Michael Feener, 172–202. Edinburgh: Edinburgh University Press, 2018.

Gowing, Peter. *Mandate in Moroland: the American Government of Muslim Filipinos, 1899–1920*. Quezon City: University of the Philippines Press, 1977.

Gowing, Peter. "Moros and Indians: Commonalities of Purpose, Policy, and Practice in American Government of Two Hostile Subjects." *Philippine Quarterly of Culture and Society* 8, no. 2/3 (June/September 1980): 125–49.

Hawkins, Michael C. *Making Moros: Imperial Historicism and American Military Rule in the Philippines' Muslim South*. DeKalb: Northern Illinois University Press, 2013.

Hawkins, Michael C. "Managing a Massacre: Savagery, Civility, and Gender in Moro Province in the Wake of Bud Dajo." *Philippine Studies* 59, no. 1 (2011): 83–105.

Jornacion, George William. "The Time of the Eagles: United States Army and the Pacification of the Philippine Moros." PhD diss., University of Maine, 1973.

Kawashima Midori. "The 'White Man's Burden' and the Islamic Movement in the Philippines: The Petition of the Zamboanga Muslim Leaders to the Ottoman Empire in 1912." Institute of Asian Cultures, Sophia University, Monograph Series 17. Tokyo: Institute of Asian Cultures, Sophia University, 2014.

Kramer, Paul. *The Blood of Government: Race, Empire, the United States & The Philippines.* Chapel Hill: University of North Carolina Press, 2006.

Lane, Jack C. *Armed Progressive: General Leonard Wood.* San Rafael: Presidio Press, 1978.

Linn, Brian. *The Philippine War, 1899–1902.* Lawrence: University of Kansas Press, 2000.

Marr, Timothy. "Subjugating the Sultan: Imperial Negotiations in the Muslim Philippines." In *American and Muslim Worlds, circa 1500–1900*, edited by Mitch Fraas and John Ghazvinian, xx–xx. New York: Bloomsbury Press, 2019.

Martin, Joel W. "Introduction." In *Native Americans, Christianity, and the Reshaping of the American Religious Landscape*, edited by Joel W. Martin and Mark A. Nicholas, 1–20. Chapel Hill: University of North Carolina Press, 2010.

McCallum, Jack. *Leonard Wood: Rough Rider, Surgeon, and Architect of American Imperialism.* New York: New York University Press, 2006.

Ostler, Jeffrey. *The Plains Sioux and U.S. Colonialism from Lewis and Clark to Wounded Knee.* New York: Cambridge University Press, 2004.

Quezon, Manuel L. Papers. National Library of the Philippines, Manila.

Records of the Bureau of Insular Affairs. Record Group 350. National Archives and Records Administration, Washington DC.

Rogers, P. D. "Major Finley and the Sheikh ul Islam: A Hitherto Unpublished Chapter of History." *Philippine Magazine* 36, no. 1 (January 1939): 19, 28–29.

Rouleau, Brian. "Maritime Destiny as Manifest Destiny: American Commercial Expansionism and the Idea of the Indian." *Journal of the Early Republic* 30 (Fall 2010): 377–411.

Salman, Michael. *The Embarrassment of Slavery: Controversies over Bondage and Nationalism in the American Colonial Philippines.* Berkeley: University of California Press, 2003.

Skovgaard-Peterson, Jakob. "Levantine State Muftis: An Ottoman Legacy." In *Late Ottoman Society: The Intellectual Legacy*, edited by Elisabeth Özdalaga, 274–88. New York: RoutledgeCurzon, 2005.

Sohrabi, Nader. *Revolution and Constitutionalism in the Ottoman Empire and Iran.* Cambridge: Cambridge University Press, 2011.

U.S. War Department. *Annual Reports of the War Department, 1902*, vol. IX. Washington: Government Printing Office, 1902.

Walther, Karine. *Sacred Interests: The United States and the Islamic World, 1821–1921.* Chapel Hill: University of North Carolina Press, 2015.

Watenpaugh, Keith David. "Introduction." In *Goodbye Antoura: A Memoir of the Armenian Genocide*, edited by Aram Goudsouzian, ix–xviii. Stanford: Stanford University Press, 2015.

Wood, Leonard. Papers. Library of Congress Manuscript Division, Washington DC.

Worcester, Dean. *Philippine History Collection.* Ann Arbor, MI: University of Michigan Special Collection.

Chapter 11

Anon (n.d.), "Tarikh hayat al-maghfur lahu al-hasib al-nasir sahib al-samahah al-shaykh Muhammad Wajih Zayd al-Kilani" [The History of the Life of the Late and most Noble and Exalted Shaykh Muhammad Wajih Zayd al-Kilani] (undated, and unpublished text, kindly provided by Amir Zuʻbi).

Benson, Kathleen, and Philip M. Kayal, eds. *A Community of Many Worlds: Arab Americans in New York City.* New York: Museum of the City of New York, 2002.
Bowen, Patrick D., "The African-American Islamic Renaissance and the Rise of the Nation of Islam." PhD diss., University of Denver, 2013.
Bowen, Patrick D., *A History of Conversion to Islam in the United States, Volume 1: White American Muslims before 1975.* Leiden: Brill, 2015.
Bowen, Patrick D., "Satti Majid: A Sudanese Founder of American Islam." *Journal of African Religions* 1, no. 2 (2013): 194–209.
Clarence-Smith, William G. *Islam and the Abolition of Slavery.* London: Hurst, 2006.
Clarence-Smith, William G. "Middle Eastern Migrants in the Philippines: Entrepreneurs and Cultural Brokers." *Asian Journal of Social Science* 32, no. 3 (2004): 425–57.
Clarence-Smith, William G. "Middle Eastern States and the Philippines under Early American Rule, 1898-1919." In *From Anatolia to Aceh: Ottomans, Turks and Southeast Asia*, edited by A. C. S. Peacock and Annabel Teh Gallop, 199–219. Oxford: Oxford University Press, 2015.
Clarence-Smith, William G. "Wajih al-Kilani, *shaykh al Islam* of the Philippines and Notable of Nazareth, 1913-1916." In *Nazareth History and Cultural Heritage*, edited by Mahmoud Yazbak and Sharif Sharif, 171–92. Nazareth: Nazareth Municipality, 2013.
Curtis, Edward E., IV. *Muslims in America: A Short History.* Oxford: Oxford University Press, 2009.
Eich, Thomas. *Abu l-Huda as-Sayyadi: eine Studie zur Instrumentalisierung sufischer Netzwerke und genealogischer Kontroversen im spätosmanischen Reich.* Berlin: Klaus Schwartz, 2003.
Elkholy, Abdo A. *The Arab Moslems in the United States: Religion and Assimilation.* New Haven, CT: College and University Press, 1966.
Evans, Laurence. *United States Policy and the Partition of Turkey, 1914-1924.* Baltimore: The Johns Hopkins University Press, 1965.
Fahrenthold, Stacy D. "Former Ottomans in the Ranks: Pro-Entente Military Recruitment among Syrians in the Americas, 1916-18." *Journal of Global History* 11, no. 1 (2016): 88–112.
Gedacht, Joshua. "Holy War, Progress and the "Modern Mohammedans" in Colonial Southeast Asia." *The Muslim World* 4 (2015): 446–71.
Goldstone, Patricia. *Aaronsohn's Maps: The Untold Story of the Man who Might Have Created Peace in the Middle East.* Orlando, FL: Harcourt Inc. 2007.
Gowing, Peter G. *Mandate in Moroland: The American Government of Muslim Filipinos, 1899-1920*, 2nd ed. Quezon City: New Day Publishers, 1983.
Kawashima, Midori. *The "White Man's Burden" and the Islamic Movement in the Philippines: The Petition of Zamboanga Muslim Leaders to the Ottoman Empire in 1912.* Tokyo: Institute of Asian Cultures, 2014.
Kurzman, Charles, ed. *Modernist Islam, 1840-1940: A Sourcebook.* Oxford: Oxford University Press, 2002.
Mansur, As'ad, *Tarikh al-Nasira, min aqdam ayyamiha ila ayyamina al-hadira* [History of Nazareth, from Ancient Times until the Present]. Cairo: Matba'at al-Hilal, 1924.
Mokarzel, S. A., and H. F. Otash. *Syrian Business Directory, 1908–1909.* New York: Al-Hoda, 1908.
"Muslim Voices of Philadelphia." http://scribe.org/muslim-voices-philadelphia (consulted April 16, 2018).
Nassar, Najib. *Riwayat Muflih al-Ghassani* [The Tale of Muflih al-Ghassani]. Nazareth: Dar al-Sawt, 1981.

al-Nimr, Ihsan. *Tarikh Jabal Nablus wa al-Balqa'* [History of the Jabal Nablus and al-Balqa']. Damascus: Matba'at Zaydun, 1938.

Orfalea, Gregory. *The Arab Americans: A History.* Northampton, MA: Olive Branch Press, 2006.

Othman, Mohammad Redzuan. "Sayid Muhammad Wajih al-Jilani" (undated and unpublished note, in romanized Malay, kindly sent to me by the author).

Rida, Muhammad Rashid. *Tarikh al-ustadh al-imam al-shaykh Muhammad "Abduh* [Story of the Teacher, Leader, and Shaykh, Muhammad "Abduh]. Cairo: al-Manar, 1908–1931.

Roff, William R. *The Origins of Malay Nationalism.* New Haven: Yale University Press, 1967.

Rogers, P. D. "Major Finley and the Shaik ul Islam: A hitherto Unpublished Chapter of History." *Philippine Magazine* 36, no. 1 (1939): 19, 28–29.

Saleeby, Najeeb M. *Studies in Moro History, Law and Religion.* Manila: The Filipiniana Book Guild, 1976 (introduction by Cesar A. Majul).

Shehadeh, Raja. *A Rift in Time: Travels of my Ottoman Uncle.* London: Profile Books, 2010.

Stoddard, Philip H. "The Ottoman Government and the Arabs, 1911 to 1918: A Preliminary Study of the Teshkilat-i Mahsusa." PhD diss., Princeton University, 1963.

Thompson, Wayne W. "Governors of the Moro Province: Wood, Bliss and Pershing in the Southern Philippines, 1903–1913." PhD diss., University of California at Los Angeles, 1975.

"Walking through a Glorious History." http://www.jeffersonhotel.com/experience/history (consulted February 23, 2012).

Walter, H. A. *The Ahmadiya Movement.* Calcutta: Association Press, 1918.

Walther, Karine V. *Sacred Interests: The United States and the Islamic World, 1821–1921.* Chapel Hill: University of North Carolina Press, 2015.

Contributors

William G. Clarence-Smith is Professor of the Economic History of Asia and Africa at SOAS University of London. He has published two earlier book chapters on Sayyid Wajih al-Kilani, and is preparing books on "Syrian" migrants to the colonial Philippines, and on Nazareth in the First World War. He is the author of *Islam and the Abolition of Slavery* (2006).

Karoline P. Cook is Lecturer in the history of the Atlantic world at Royal Holloway, University of London. She is the author of *Forbidden Passages: Muslims and Moriscos in Colonial Spanish America* (2016).

Ira Dworkin is Assistant Professor of English at Texas A&M University, where he specializes in African American and African diaspora literature, as well as Islamic diasporas and transatlantic studies. He is the author of *Congo Love Song: African Americans Confront the Colonial State* (2017).

Arthur Mitch Fraas is Senior Curator of Special Collections at the Kislak Center for Special Collections, Rare Books and Manuscripts at the University of Pennsylvania Libraries. He holds a doctorate in history from Duke University, and is a specialist in the legal culture of British India in the seventeenth and eighteenth centuries.

Joshua Gedacht received his PhD in history from the University of Wisconsin-Madison in 2013, and is currently an honorary fellow at the Center for Southeast Asian Studies, University of Wisconsin-Madison. His current book project, *Islam, Colonial Warfare and Coercive Cosmopolitanism in Island Southeast Asia*, considers the ways in which conquest engendered paradoxical dynamics of exclusion and inclusion, disconnection and reconnection.

John Ghazvinian is Associate Director of the Middle East Center at the University of Pennsylvania. He is the author of *Iran and America: A History* (forthcoming). He holds a doctorate in history from Oxford University, and specializes in early modern east-west encounters, as well as modern Middle East history.

Bill Hunt is Assistant Professor of English at Barton College. He earned his doctorate at Duke University, with concentrations in American literature and Middle East Studies. He specializes in American feminist orientalist literature of the late nineteenth and early twentieth centuries.

Timothy Marr is Bowman and Gordon Gray Distinguished Professor of American Studies at the University of North Carolina. A specialist in the life and writings of Herman Melville and American engagements with Muslims, he is the author of *The Cultural Roots of American Islamicism* (2006).

Zeinab Mcheimech recently earned her PhD in English at Western University. Her project, *Low Mutterings at High Tide: Enslaved African Muslims in American Literature*, introduces "Allahgraphy" as a methodology for reading traces of Islam in American writings. She specializes in literary and cultural representations of Islam in America, nineteenth- and twentieth-century American literature, and diaspora studies.

Susan Ryan is Associate Professor of English at the University of Louisville, where she teaches nineteenth-century American literature and culture. She is the author of *The Grammar of Good Intentions: Race and the Antebellum Culture of Benevolence* (2003) and *The Moral Economies of American Authorship: Reputation, Scandal and the Nineteenth-Century Marketplace* (2016). Her current book project addresses how India—and South Asia generally—figured into nineteenth-century American reform discourse.

Heather J. Sharkey is Professor in the Department of Near Eastern Languages and Civilizations at the University of Pennsylvania. She is the author of numerous books on the history of American and British missionaries in the Middle East and North Africa, including *American Evangelicals in Egypt: Missionary Encounters in an Age of Empire* (2008). Her most recent book is *A History of Muslims, Christians and Jews in the Middle East* (2017).

William E. B. Sherman is Assistant Professor of religious studies at UNC Charlotte. He earned his doctorate at Stanford University in religious studies, with a concentration in Islamic studies. He specializes in late medieval and early modern Afghanistan, Sufism, Islamic eschatology and the history of Islam in America.

Denise A. Spellberg is Professor of history at the University of Texas at Austin, where she specializes in intellectual, religious, and gender history of the medieval Islamic world, from Iran to North Africa, as well as Islam and Muslims in early modern and contemporary Europe and the United States. She is the author of *Thomas Jefferson's Qur'an: Islam and the Founders* (2013).

Karine Walther is Associate Professor of history at the Georgetown University School of Foreign Service in Qatar. She holds a PhD from Columbia University and a Maîtrise and Licence in sociology from University of Paris VIII. She is the author of *Sacred Interests: The United States and the Islamic World, 1821-1921* (2015).

Index

Abd-el-Kader 40
'Abduh, Muhammad 143
Abdülhamit II, Sultan of Ottoman
    Empire 71–84, 136
abolition of slavery 9, 14–16
Act 1259 123
Adams, John Quincy 25–7, 29–30
Ade, George 118
The Advertiser 79
Afghans
    Ahmad's narrative 93–6
    Christian missionaries 89–93
    as a lost tribe 85–96, 157
    Mughal Empire and 87–9, 157
Afghan Treasure Chest (Harawi) 87–9,
    90, 93, 95
African American narrative 33–44
    Douglass 34–8
    literacy 35–6
    Said (*see* Said, Nicholas)
African Muslim slave narratives
    45–56
    Bilali 3, 45–6, 47, 48, 49–53
    Emerson's synthesis 49
    surface reading of 47–8
    Umar ibn Sayyid 3, 45–6, 47, 48, 49,
        50, 54–6
African slaves 3
"Age of Revolution" 19
Ahmad, Mirza Ghulam 85, 93–6
Ahmad, Muhammad 144
Ahmadiyya Movement 85
Alexander VI, Pope 156
al-Habashi, Bilal 36
al-Harir, Abu Muhammad 55
Ali, Haidar 1, 129, 153
Ali, Muhammad 43
Ali, Shaykh Mehmet 142
Aliaga, Martin de 63
'Ali al-Rahbi, Muhammad ibn 12
al-Kanemi, Mohammed 41, 42

al-Kilani, Sayyid Muhammad Wajih ibn
    Munib Zayd (Shaykh Wajih) 136,
    137–8
    American mission 139–47
    Bright's Disease 143–4
    Bureau of Insular Affairs 145, 146,
        147
    Muslim-Christian relations 142–3
    political tasks 140–2
    return to the Philippines 147
    seeking presidential audience 145–6
    Syrian community and 144–5
al-Kilani clan 139
All Saints' Memorial Church 92
almanac 11
"*al-manakh*" 11
al-Mulk 36
"*al-munakh*" 11
al-Rahbi, Muhammad ibn 'Ali 12
Alryyes, Ala 36, 51
al-Walid, Khalid ibn 11, 12
"American and Muslim Worlds, circa
    1500–1900" 2
American Annual Register 29
"The American Dreyfus" 76
American Islamicism 156–7
American missionaries 4
American Muslims 3
American Revolution 13
ancient Greece 21
Andrada, Alonso Bazo de 62–3
Andrada, Pedro Fernandez de 63
Anglo-American Christians 20
Anquetil-Duperron, Abraham
    Hyacinthe 12
*Appeal in Four Articles; Together with a
    Preamble, to the Coloured Citizens
    of the World* (Walker) 36
Arabian Nights 2
Army Appropriations Act 43
Army Transport 147

Index

Asaad, Fakir Jany Muhammad 45
Atlantic Monthly 33, 34
Atlantic Telegraph Cable 74
Austin, Allan 33, 51
Autobiography (Franklin) 9

Bailey, Harriet 35–6
Bailyn, Bernard 13
Baker, Anthony John 144
Baker, Wallace 43
The Balance of Truth (Pfander) 91
Ballou's Pictorial 108
Banu Jadhima tribe 12
"Barbary States" 10
Barnum, P. T. 80
Bates, John C. 115–18
Bates Agreement/Treaty 114–23, 125, 128, 129, 130, 131, 132
Battle of Ball's Bluff 76
Battle of Liberty Place 76
Battle of Navarino 29
Battle of San Juan Hill 131
Battle of Shiloh 76
Battle of Wounded Knee, in South Dakota 130
Baudrillard, Jean 75
The Bee 81
Ben Ali Diary (Muhammad) 45, 49–53
Benezet, Alexander 14
Ben-Hur: A Tale of the Christ (Wallace) 71
Best, Stephen 46, 47
Bey, Abdul Hak Hussein 141–2
Bey, Ahmet Rüstem 141–2
The Bible Cyclopedia 93
Biblical Repertory 103, 106, 109
Bilwakesh, Nikhil 105
Bingham, Caleb 35
bin Laden, Osama 2, 150, 152
bismillah 16
Blackwood's/Eclectic Magazine 108–9
Blaine, James G. 38
The Boston Herald 77
Brands, H. W. 10
Bright's Disease 143–4
British Empire 4, 13, 88, 90, 91, 92, 94, 98–9, 141
  Haidar Ali and 1, 129, 153

Philadelphians' fight against 1
Sepoy Rebellion (1857–58) 99, 105–10
British Whigs 13
Bryant, William Cullen 22
Bud Dajo 132–3
Bureau of Insular Affairs 145, 146, 147
Butu, Hadji 115–16, 122, 126

Calhoun, John C. 25
Cardona, Pedro Aznar 61
Carpenter, Frank 125
Carpenter-Kiram Agreement 115, 125–6
Casares, Aurelia Martin 62
Cato's Letters 13
Charles V 60
"Christian Family of Nations" 18
Christianity 156
Christians, non-Christians vs. 20–1
Christian Watchman 102
The Church Missionary Intelligencer 91
Church Missionary Society 91
The Cincinnati Commercial Tribune 71
Cisneros, Francisco Jimenez de 59
Clarence-Smith, William Gervase 122, 137
Clark, Robert 92
Clay, Henry 27
Cleveland Herald 79
Cogley, Richard 90
The Columbian Orator (Bingham) 35
Columbus, Christopher 149
Committee of Union and Progress (CUP) 136
Conde de Coruna 63–4
Conestoga Native Americans 11
Constitutional Convention of 1787 14
Cook, Karoline 4, 150
Count de Capomanes 12
Cultures in Conflict: Christians, Muslims, and Jews in the Age of Discovery (Lewis) 149–50
Curtis, Edward, IV 44

Dabovic, Safet 38
Daoud, Hadji 41
Davis, Dwight 126
Davis, George W. 122, 130–1
Day, William 114

Delaware Bay   1
Democratic Press   23
Democrat's Review   100
Denver Republican   77
Diallo, Ayyub ibn Suleiman   34
Diouf, Sylviane   44
Douglass, Frederick   34–8
  globalization   38
  Life and Times of Frederick Douglass   37–8
  My Bondage and My Freedom   35–7
  Narrative of the Life   34–5, 36, 37
  political appointments   38
Dunbar, Joshua   43
Dunbar, Paul Laurence   43
Dworkin, Ira   4

Einboden, Jeffrey   49
Elements of International Law (Wheaton)   20
Emerson, Ralph Waldo   45, 46, 49
Enlightenment   19–20
  American interpretations of   19
  Christianity and   19
  Islamic despotism   20
Enriquez, Martin   63
Equiano, Olaudah   41
Everett, David   35
Everett, Edward   22, 24, 25–6, 28

Fakahani, Suzan Jameel   49
Felski, Rita   46, 47
Ferdinand, King of Spain   58, 59, 60, 149
Fields, Barbara J.   35–6
Finley, John Park   133–7, 147
  mission to Istanbul   135–7, 138, 139–40, 141, 143
  modern Mohammedanism   134–5
  US Army Signal Service   133–4
First World War   30
Foreign Affairs   18
Foreman, John   114
Foster, Frances Smith   34
Fraas, Mitch   157–8
Franklin, Benjamin   3, 9–17
  almanac   10, 11
  Autobiography   9
  Islamic texts   12
  on Prophet   11–12
  reference to "Mahometanism"   10
  slavery and   13, 14–17
  Spanish-Latin-Arabic dictionary   12
Freneau, Philip   1
Frydman, Jason   38

Gallatin, Albert   24
Garber, Ella May   144
Garfield, James   75–6
Garrison, Lindley M.   145, 146, 147
Garrison, William Lloyd   34–5
Gates, Henry Louis, Jr.   34
Gedacht, Joshua   4
GhaneaBassiri, Kambiz   44
Ghazvinian, John   157–8
Ghost Dance   130
Global War on Terror   18
Gomez, Michael   44
Goodman, Susan   33
Granada   149
  Moriscos   59–60
  Muslims   59
  Nasrid Emirate of   59
Grant, Ulysses   76–7
Greek War of Independence   19
  Christian nationalism   19
  ideological framing of   19
  newspapers and journals   22–6
  public supporters of   22
  relief movement   21
  relief organizations and   28–9
  revolutionaries   23–4
  US support to   19
  Wheaton and   21
Grewal, Zareena   157
Grundrisse (Marx)   37

Ḥāfiẓ, Muḥammad Shamsuddīn   49
Hallowell, Norwood P.   33
Hamidian Massacres   82–3
Harawi, Niʿmat Allah   87–9, 90, 93, 95
Harrison, Francis Burton   146
Hashim, Najib T.   144
Hawkins, Michael   134
Hayes, Kevin   12
hayrah   48
Heathen Woman's Friend   101
Hemings, Sally   14
hermeneutics of suspicion   46

Higginson, Thomas Wentworth   103
Hinduism   98–9, 102, 104, 105
Hisham, Abu Muhammad ibn   12, 47
Hollis, W. Stanley   145
Holy Alliance   25
Howe, Samuel Gridley   26
Howells, William Dean   118
Hughes, Thomas Patrick   91–3
Hunt, Bill   4–5
Huntington, Samuel
   "The Clash of Civilizations?"   18
   "clash of civilizations" theory   18, 19, 30, 150
Hyder Ally   1, 2

Iberian Muslims   149
Ibn-Ḥauqal, Abu-'l-Qāsim Ibn-'Alī   45
Illustration of Prophecy (Towers)   93
The Indianapolis Sentinel   78–9, 80
Indian Muslims   98–110
   Hinduism   98–9, 102, 104, 105
   overview   98–100
   polygamy   101
   Sepoy Rebellion (1857–58) and   99, 105–10
   US print media and   100–10
   women   101–2
Indian Wars   129, 130
Inter Caetara   156
Interesting Narrative (Equiano)   41
international law   20–1
Isabella, Queen of Spain   58, 59, 60, 149
Islam. *See also* Muslims
   colonial massacres   132–3
   as a false faith   11, 17
   Franklin's views on   9–17
   Lewis on   149–50
   Orientalist depictions of   20
   as a place   157–8
   as political threat   11
   polygamy   101
Islam Is a Foreign Country: American Muslims and the Global Crisis of Authority (Grewal)   157

Jabal Tariq   149
Jefferson, Thomas   3, 9, 24
   Hemings and   14
   on slavery   13–14

Jesus in India (Ahmad)   94, 95–6
Jews   149
Jolof   58, 64–5
Jones, William   12, 90
Judy, Ronald A. T.   34, 52

Kane, Ousmane Oumar   38
katam (concealment/preservation)   48, 53
Key, Francis Scott   51
Khan, Adil Hussain   94
Khan, Inayat   144
Khatibi, Abdelkebir   12, 47, 48
Khuwaylid, Khadija bint   47–8
Kidd, Thomas   11
King, Charles   22
Kiram, Amirul   114
Kiram, Jamalul   126–7
Kiram, Jamalul, II   114, 121–2, 127
Kobbe, William   131
Korais, Adamantios   24

Ladies' Repository   102
Lakota Sioux   130
Lapansky-Werner, Emma J.   14
Legislation orientale (Anquetil-Duperron)   12
Leoussi, Athena   21
Letter to John Owen (Sayyid)   45, 50, 54–6
Lewis, Bernard   149–50
Life and Times of Frederick Douglass (Douglass)   37–8
Lincoln, A.   43
Locke, John   9
Loewenthal, Isidor   91
Longstreet, James   76
Louisiana Purchase Exposition   123
Love, Heather   46, 47
Lowrie, John C.   103
Luriottis, Andreas   25

The Mahomedan Law of Succession to the Property of Intestates (Jones)   12
Mahomet (English spelling of the Prophet's name)   9, 10
Mahometan   9–10, 11, 154
Mahometanism   9, 10, 16, 28
Marcus, Sharon   46, 47

Marr, Timothy 4, 93, 101, 109, 132, 155-6
Marx, Karl 37
Mazower, Mark 20
McCutcheon, John 118
McFeely, William S. 36
McHeimech, Zeinab 3
Mendoza, Lorenzo Suarez de 60-1
Mendoza, Victor Roman 119
Methodism 9
Middle East, Islam in 157-8
missionaries, Afghans and 89-93
The Missionary Magazine 89-91, 93
modern Mohammedanism. *See* Mohammedanism
Mohammed (Prophet) 29, 100, 102, 103
"Mohammed-Ali-Ben-Said." *See* Said, Nicholas
Mohammedanism 45, 98, 133-5, 138
Monroe, James 25, 26
Monroe Doctrine 26-7, 30
Monroy, Cristobal de 66
Moriscos, in Spanish America 4, 57-67
  as baptized Christians 59-60
  early expeditions 65-6
  enslavement 62-5
  prosecution 61-2
  vigilance over 61
  voluntary emigration 65-7
  women 63-4
Mormonism 101
Moro Province 128
Moros. *See* Philippines
Mufti of Constantinople 9
Muhammad, Bilali 3, 45-6, 47, 48, 49-53
  Ben Ali Diary 45, 49-53
  Qur'anic citations 52-3
Muhammad, Precious Rasheeda 44
Muhammad, Prophet 11-12, 17, 20, 47-8
Muhammad XII 149
Müller, Charles Louis Lucien 79
Muslim African-Americans 3
Muslims. *See also* Islam
  African American narrative (*see* African American narrative)
  African slave narratives 45-56
  American politicians on 3

Indian 98-110
  orientalist fantasies 2
  Sepoy Rebellion (1857-58) 99, 105-10
  Spanish America 57-67
  televised images of 2
  Trump on 1-2
  Washington's worldview of American citizens and 9-10
Muslim world 3-4
My Bondage and My Freedom (Douglass) 35-7

A Narrative of the Late Massacres, in Lancaster County (Franklin) 11
Narrative of the Life of Frederick Douglass, an American Slave (Douglass) 34
Nasrid Emirate of Granada 59
National Gazette 27
Native Americans 11, 129-31
"A Native of Bornoo" (Said) 33, 34, 38-41, 44
The Natural History of Man (Pritchard) 36
natural law, theories of 20
New York American 22
New-York Commercial Advertiser 22
New York Evangelist 100
New-York Evening Post 22
The New York Herald 78
New-York Historical Society 20
New York Observer 108
Niles, Hezekiah 22
Niles Weekly Register 22
North American Review 22, 26
Norton Anthology of African American Literature 34

Obama, Barack 1, 43-4
O'Connell, Daniel 34-5
Oglethorpe, James 34
oil painting 72
The Omaha Daily Bee 81
The Oriental Geography of Ebn Haukal (Ibn-Ḥauqal) 45
Orientalism 156-7
Otis, Elwell 114
Ottoman Empire 3, 129, 133-7, 149
  Abdülhamit II 71-84, 136

despotism in 13
Finley's mission 135-7, 138, 139-40, 141, 143
modern Mohammedanism 133-5
Shaykh al-Islam 139
Shaykh Wajih 136, 137-8, 139-47
Ovalle, Cristobal de 57, 62, 67
Ovando, Nicolas de 60
Owen, John 45, 50, 54-6

Pasha, Cemal 140-1
Pasha, Ismail Enver 141
Pasha, Mehmet Talaat 141
Paxton Boys 11
Pennsylvania Society for the Abolition of Slavery 14-15
"Petition from the Pennsylvania Society for the Abolition of Slavery" 15
Pfander, Carl G. 91
philhellenism 21, 22
Philip II 60, 61
Philip III 60
Philippine Free Press 126
Philippines
  Act 1259 123
  Bates Agreement of 1899 114-15
  colonial massacres 132-3
  modern Mohammedanism 133-5
  religious intolerance 131-2
  Sultan of Sulu 113-27
  tribal ward system 134
  US colonial project in 5, 6, 128-38
Phillips, Wendell 34
Pigman, George 117
Poinsett, Joel 27
polygamy 101
Pontiac's War 11
Poor Richard 10, 11
Practical Philosophy of the Muhammadan People (Asaad) 45
Pritchard, James Cowles 36
Protestant Christians 11

Quesada, Gonzalo Jimenez de 66
Qur'an 9, 16, 46, 52-3, 87, 94, 96, 102, 151, 153

Ramadan 40
Rashid, Hussein 44

Religious Intelligencer 102
religious intolerance 131-2
Richmond Enquirer 22
Rida, Muhammad Rashid 143
Ríos, Eugenio Montero 114
Ritchie, Thomas 22
Roberts, Brigham H. 118
Rogers, P. D. 137
Romero, Diego 66
Ruhainah 92
Ryan, Susan 4

Sacred Interests (Walther) 129
Said, Edward 156-7
Said, Nicholas 4, 33-4
  American exceptionalism and 41-4
  autobiographical accounts 33-4
  Civil War and 33, 42-3
  European travels 42
  as a hospital medic 43
  racial harassment 41
  reading 34-8
Saleeby, Najeeb 144
Samito, Christian G. 43
The San Francisco Bulletin 79-80
The San Francisco Wasp 81
Sayyid, Umar ibn 3, 36, 45-6, 47, 48, 49, 50, 54-6
  Letter to John Owen (Sayyid) 45, 50, 54-6
Scott, Hugh Lenox 124, 132, 137, 146, 147
Seacole, Mary 41
Seal of Solomon 54
Second Great Awakening 22
self-Orientalism 157
Sells, Michael 53
The Sentinel 81
Sepoy Rebellion (1857-58) 99, 105-10
September 11, 2001, terrorist attacks of 150
Sharkey, Heather 5
Shaykh al-Islam 139
Sherman, William B. 5, 157
Shirazi, Saadi 49
Sidi Mehmet Ibrahim (fictional Muslim name) 15-16, 17
Simulacra and Simulation (Baudrillard) 75

simulation   75
"Slaves in Barbary, A Drama in Two Acts" (play by Everett)   35
Spanish America   57–67. *See also* Moriscos, in Spanish America
Spanish-Latin-Arabic dictionary   12
Spellberg, Denise   3
"The Star-Spangled Banner" (Key)   51
Stone, Charles Pomeroy   76, 77
Stone, William L.   22
Sufi mysticism   49
Sultan of Sulu   113–27
   Bates Agreement/Treaty   114–23, 125
   Carpenter-Kiram Agreement   115, 125–6
   journey to the United States   123–4
The Sultan of Sulu: An Original Satire in Two Acts (Ade)   118
Surat Al-Baqarah (The Cow)   48
Surat al-Mulk   36
Suva, Cesar   120
Sweet, O. J.   121
Syrians   144–5

Taft, Helen   119
Taft, William Howard   119, 132
Tan, Samuel   120–1, 126–7
Tanin   136
Tarikh-i Khan Jahani va Makhzan-i Afghani. *See Afghan Treasure Chest* (Harawi)
Taylor, Bayard   102
Towers, Joseph   93
Transcendentalism   45, 49
Treaty of Paris   115
Treaty of Tripoli   43
tribal ward system   134
Trotter, James Monroe   43
Trotter, William Monroe   43
Trump, Donald   1–2
"Turkey and the Turks, With Glimpses of the Harem"   83
"The Turkish Princess"   72–4
   media on   79–81
   simulacral narratives   81–2

University of Pennsylvania   2
us-and-them approach to "cultures in conflict"   149–51
US Army Signal Service   133–4

Vamenta, Isidro   125–6
Velasco, Luis de   61
Virginia Statute for Religious Freedom   9
von Martens, G. F.   20

Waldstreicher, David   14
Walker, David   36
Wallace, Lew   71–84
   Battle of Liberty Place   76
   Battle of Monocacy   76
   Battle of Shiloh   76
   Hamidian Massacres   82–3
   "Turkey and the Turks, With Glimpses of the Harem"   83
Walther, Karine   3, 98, 150
Washington, George   9–10
   on slavery   13, 14
   worldview of American citizens   9–10
Washington Post   37
The Wasp   81
Webster, Daniel   27
Werble, Charles J.   123, 124
Wheatley, Phillis   36
Wheaton, Henry   20–1
Whitefield, George   9
Wiencek, Henry   14
Wilson, Woodrow   125
Wonderful Adventures (Seacole)   41
Wood, Leonard   122, 131–2
Wright, Luke   122

Ypsilanti, Alexander   23

zāhir (literal meanings)   46–7
Zāhirism   46
Zarathustra   12
The Zend-Avesta   12
Zoroastrianism   12
Zwemer, Samuel   30

www.ingramcontent.com/pod-product-compliance
Lightning Source LLC
Chambersburg PA
CBHW052037300426
44117CB00012B/1865